RIDERS IN THE STORM

The Triumphs and Tragedies of a
Black Cavalry Regiment in the Civil War

JOHN D. WARNER JR.

STACKPOLE
BOOKS

Guilford, Connecticut
Blue Ridge Summit, Pennsylvania

STACKPOLE BOOKS

An imprint of Globe Pequot, the trade division of
The Rowman & Littlefield Publishing Group, Inc.
4501 Forbes Blvd., Ste. 200
Lanham, MD 20706
www.rowman.com

Distributed by NATIONAL BOOK NETWORK

British Library Cataloguing in Publication Information available

Library of Congress Cataloging-in-Publication Data

Names: Warner, John D., Jr., 1961– author.
Title: Riders in the storm : the triumphs and tragedies of a Black cavalry
  regiment in the Civil War / John D. Warner Jr.
Other titles: Triumphs and tragedies of a Black cavalry regiment in the
  Civil War
Description: Guilford, Connecticut : Stackpole Books, [2022] | Includes
  bibliographical references and index. | Summary: "This book tells the
  story of the African American cavalrymen of the 5th Massachusetts during
  the Civil War—a story of resilience in the face of adversity, one that
  will resonate not just during the present moment of reckoning with race
  in the United States but in the annals of American history for all
  time"— Provided by publisher.
Identifiers: LCCN 2021038811 (print) | LCCN 2021038812 (ebook) | ISBN
  9780811770859 (hardback) | ISBN 9780811770866 (epub)
Subjects: LCSH: United States. Army. Massachusetts Cavalry Regiment, 5th
  (1864–1865) | United States—History—Civil War, 1861–1865—Regimental
  histories. | Massachusetts—History—Civil War, 1861–1865—Regimental
  histories. | United States—History—Civil War,
  1861–1865—Participation, African American. | African American
  soldiers—History—19th century.
Classification: LCC E513.6 5th .W37 2022 (print) | LCC E513.6 5th (ebook)
  | DDC 973.7/415—dc23
LC record available at https://lccn.loc.gov/2021038811
LC ebook record available at https://lccn.loc.gov/2021038812

This work is dedicated, with gratitude and respect,
To the Officers and Troopers
Of the 5th Massachusetts Volunteer Cavalry Regiment
And to three ancestors who wore The Blue:
My great-great grandfather, Private Irwin Elroy Warner,
Who, at sixteen, ran away from home and joined the
2nd Connecticut Volunteer Heavy Artillery Regiment.
This regiment, armed as infantry, lost during its service
12 officers and 242 enlisted men killed or mortally wounded
And 2 officers and 171 enlisted men to disease;
Private Stephen Graves Warner, Company H,
37th Massachusetts Volunteer Infantry Regiment,
Killed in action at Fredericksburg, Virginia, 13 December 1862, and
Private Sumner Warner, Company H,
37th Massachusetts Volunteer Infantry Regiment,
Killed in action at The Wilderness, 5 May 1864.
Their sacrifice ensured the continued existence of this Republic.

Contents

Maps from Atlas to Accompany the Official Records of the Union and Confederate Armies

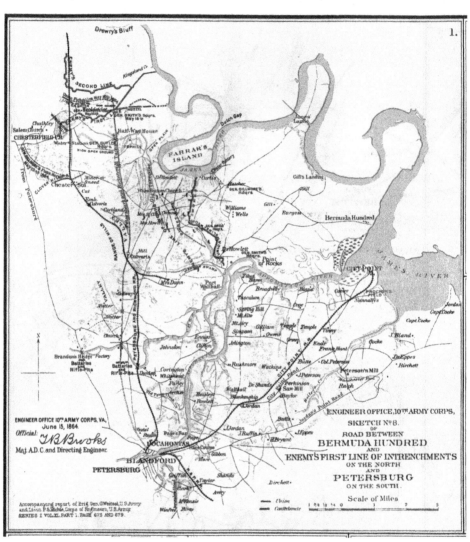

CREDIT: AOR

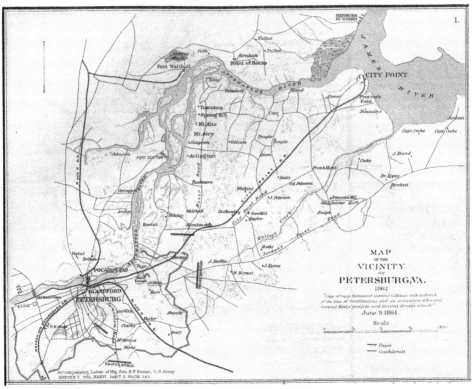

MAP
OF THE
VICINITY
OF
PETERSBURG, VA.
1862

"Copy of map furnished General Gillmore with a sketch
of the line of fortifications and an indication of his and
General Hinks' position and General Kautz's attack."

June 9, 1864.

Scale

— — Union
——— Confederate

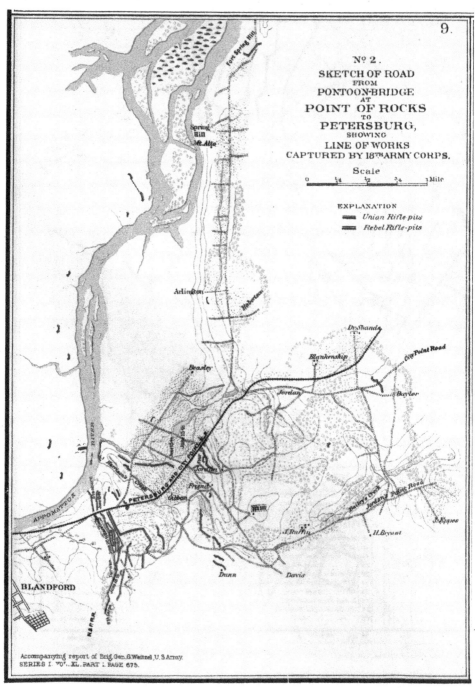

Nº 2.

SKETCH OF ROAD
FROM
PONTOON-BRIDGE
AT
POINT OF ROCKS
TO
PETERSBURG,
SHOWING
LINE OF WORKS
CAPTURED BY 18TH ARMY CORPS.

Scale

0   ¼   ½   ¾   1 Mile

EXPLANATION
Union Rifle-pits
Rebel Rifle-pits

Accompanying report of Brig. Gen. G. Weitzel, U. S. Army.
SERIES I. VOL. XL. PART I. PAGE 675.

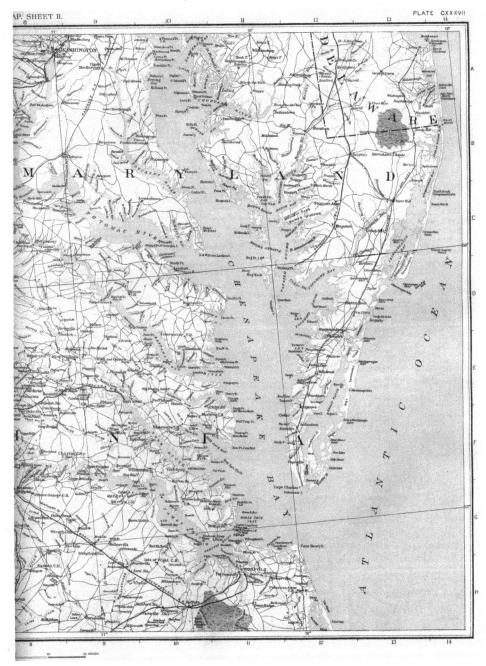

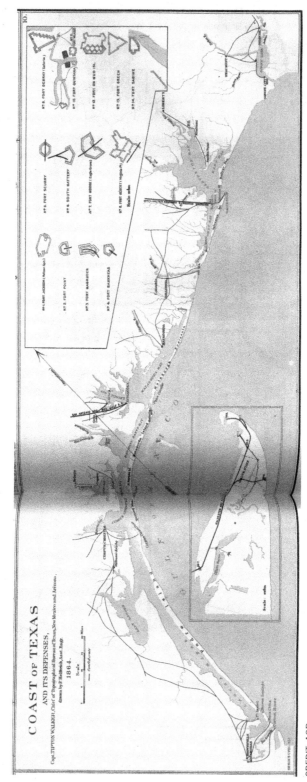

PREFACE

UNTIL NOW, THE VALOR OF COLONEL ROBERT GOULD SHAW's 54TH Massachusetts Infantry Regiment, the first black regiment raised in the North, has overshadowed the service of the 5th Massachusetts Cavalry. The 54th's charge across an open beach against a fortified enemy was instrumental in bringing about acceptance of African Americans as soldiers. Interestingly, the 5th Massachusetts did make an assault across open ground against rebel works, in Petersburg, Virginia. Perhaps from a historical viewpoint, the regiment was "unlucky" in suffering only a few casualties. A grateful citizenry usually erects monuments for dead heroes, not those who survive combat.

With the exception of the African American Civil War Memorial in Washington, DC, there is no monument for the officers and men of the third black regiment raised in Massachusetts, the 5th Massachusetts Volunteer Cavalry. Only stark gravestones in Virginia, Maryland, and Texas stand to mark the regiment's passing. A history of the 5th Massachusetts has never been written. *Riders in the Storm: The Triumphs and Tragedies of a Black Cavalry Regiment in the Civil War* is about the only African American regiment of cavalry raised in the Northern states during the Civil War. This black cavalry regiment was officered by some of the scions of the first families of Massachusetts. The story of this alliance between black enlisted men and white officers, along with their recruitment, training, and combat, deserves to be told after more than one hundred years of silence.

This book is about one of only four African American regiments to retain its state designation. That state designation was important to Massachusetts governor John A. Andrew because he did not want his black cavalry regiment to be "United States Colored Troops." Andrew wanted the state that had made history with African American infantry regiments (the 54th and 55th Massachusetts Infantry Volunteers) to carry the social experiment further: black men in uniform on horseback. When Governor Andrew wrote to Secretary of War Edwin Stanton proposing the 5th Massachusetts Cavalry, he referred to the 54th and 55th Infantry Regiments: "They are known on our books and rolls and orders only by their numbers and their arm of service, and not by their color."

In fact, the designation of the regiment is only partially accurate; most of the men were not from the Bay State, and when the regiment reached the "seat of war" (as the area of operations was called then), through no fault of its own, its horses were taken away. The regiment fought dismounted in the spring of 1864, taking part in the fighting leading up to the siege of Petersburg. At one point the 5th Massachusetts was part of the XXV Army Corps. Composed of black soldiers from twenty-two regiments separated into two divisions of seven brigades, the XXV Army Corps numbered some twenty thousand men, had a major general in command, along with its own artillery and cavalry units; corps, division, and headquarters flags; and a unit patch. After participating in the early part of the siege of Petersburg, the regiment was assigned to the prison camp at Point Lookout, Maryland. Confederate prisoners guarded by the 5th Massachusetts kept several diaries. The Confederates' reactions, as recorded in these diaries, range from rage that blacks could be soldiers, let alone cavalrymen (which was seen as an elite branch of the service), to disbelief and the unfounded hope that somehow these black soldiers were still loyal and respectful to their old "masters."

During the last weeks of the war, the regiment, mounted at last, took the field in the campaign leading up to the Confederate surrender at Appomattox. The 5th Massachusetts was one of the first units to enter Richmond when that city fell to Union forces on 3 April 1865. Retreating Confederates had set fire to supplies to deny them to the enemy; the resulting fire spread and destroyed a great deal of the city. Amid the devastated capital of the defeated South, the 5th Massachusetts and other African American troops of the XXV Army Corps were greeted as saviors and avenging angels by members of their newly freed race.

After the war, instead of the grand review and rapid demobilization that was accorded white units, the 5th Massachusetts Cavalry, as part of the Cavalry Brigade of the XXV Army Corps, was sent to Texas to encourage French troops occupying Mexico to leave that country and to prevent any Confederate units from escaping over the border and "coming back to fight another day." While in Texas, morale deteriorated because the men felt they were being subjected to excessive fatigue duty and unhealthy living conditions. Several of the officers resigned, apparently feeling that they had done their part. This option was not available to the enlisted men. Toward the end of their sojourn in Texas, Brevet Brigadier General Samuel E. Chamberlain, formerly of the 1st Massachusetts Cavalry, took command of the regiment and helped restore its pride and discipline. The 5th Massachusetts finally took ship for Boston at the end of October 1865 and was paid off and mustered out some seven months after the end of the war.

What happened to the officers and men after the regiment was mustered out? Some of the former members of the 5th Massachusetts Cavalry became famous, like Lieutenant Daniel Chamberlain, who was elected Republican ("carpetbag") governor of South Carolina in 1874, and Charles Francis Adams Jr., who had been colonel of the regiment, who wrote history. Others quietly got on with their lives. They joined the segregated Grand Army of the Republic; they remembered fallen comrades and marched on Memorial Day. They were justifiably proud of having participated in one of the great chapters in American history. These men persevered; they proved themselves. They showed great courage and resolution, and then they were largely forgotten.

We think of the Civil War as a great opportunity for study because so many of the participants were literate; censorship did not exist, and much paper was saved. People knew they were living through momentous times, making history. The ones who lived sought to make sense of what they had lived through; those who were left behind kept letters and diaries as talismans of memory, for "The Fallen."

The 5th Massachusetts Volunteer Cavalry was dramatically different from other regiments raised in the small towns of the Bay State, regiments filled with men related to each other by marriage or blood, who had grown up together and known each other all their lives. This book seeks to understand what these men, black and white, previously unknown to each other, went through together.

We know that Massachusetts outsourced its troop quotas by sending recruiters out of state and even out of the country. In 1863 and 1864, state recruiting agents were sent to the Midwest, the Mid-Atlantic states, and the occupied South to specifically recruit African Americans for the Union army. High bounties (signing bonuses) were promised. We know that most of these soldiers were illiterate. Of the thousand or so troopers who entrained for Virginia in 1864, more than eight hundred of them had to "make their mark" rather than sign their name.

We do have some letters from troopers in the regiment: from Frederick Douglass's son, First Sergeant Charles Douglass; from Trooper Charles Beman; and from an anonymous trooper writing to the *Weekly Anglo-African* who used the pen name "Africano." We also have a fair number of carefully preserved letters written by white officers from the Bay State. There are newspaper accounts and official records. But we do not have the caches of letters and diaries associated with other regiments—the layers of eyewitness accounts that make the Civil War such a rich field to explore. Instead, we use the sources available to us as a guide to imagine the men's hopes and dreams and motivations, and, yes, their courage and commitment.

If, through some magic, we could interview the troopers and officers of the 5th Massachusetts Cavalry, I believe the most important question we could ask these men, now long dead, is: Why did they serve? Why did they join the United States Army in the midst of "the Rebellion," as Northerners called it? What did they think of their experiences? The natural follow-up question would be "Was it worth it?" True, the answers might vary as much as the individuals who gave them. But the war in 1863 was brutally different from the one that broke out in April 1861. This was a fight to the finish, an existential contest far removed from the days of ninety-day regiments in clean uniforms. These men were all volunteers. Did they know what they were getting into? A few of the white officers did. Colonel Henry Sturgis Russell had been in it from the beginning and seen heavy fighting. In some, no doubt, the fires of patriotism burned bright. They were filled with idealism and felt a mystic connection to the concepts of freedom and democracy, liberty and union. These men agreed with Abraham Lincoln that the United States was the last best hope for man on earth and worth dying for. That patriotism is even more commendable given that it existed after years of murderous blunders, corruption, and waste.

There were abolitionists who served—usually as well-educated, affluent officers. For them, serving with African Americans was an opportunity to right a terrible wrong done to fellow human beings, to blot out the national sin. Radical abolitionists all had a millenarian streak, to some degree. Some believed with John Brown that the "crimes of this guilty land will never be purged away but with Blood." These men recognized the images from the Book of Revelation in the "Battle Hymn of the Republic" and concurred with Julia Ward Howe that a fiery sword would bring God's redemptive grace.

There were economic incentives for both officers and enlisted. "A dollar a day is a white man's pay" (a common saying in the 1860s) gives an idea of how little white laborers earned. How enormous a bounty of several hundred dollars must have seemed! If you are poor enough, you will take another man's money to risk your life for his. If you are poor enough, regular meals, a pair of shoes, and a government-provided suit of clothes might seem like a good bargain for that risk. Prior enlisted white soldiers had a chance to become officers and gentlemen. Some of the officers were new to America. If you are a recent immigrant, putting on a uniform may be a way of being accepted by the earlier immigrants. One immigrant group, despised by the earlier arrivals who viewed them as dirty, violent, dangerously fecund illiterates under the sway of a foreign power (the pope), formed whole regiments that received extreme unction as they went forward to the slaughter. Those who survived had indisputably earned a place at the table. There may have been a social stigma attached to serving in a black regiment, but the chance to go from corporal to captain might make up for that drawback. And besides, the 5th Massachusetts was a cavalry regiment, one of the elite units of the day. Cavalrymen were the fighter pilots of the nineteenth century: expected to show initiative; to be scouts, the "eyes of the army"; to make destructive raids into enemy territory; to make earth-pounding, saber-wielding charges with great élan. A sponsoring government needed a massive commitment in time and resources to mount, equip, and train the twelve hundred men who made up a regiment of cavalry.

We can understand how the motivations mentioned above would lead a young man to volunteer for the 5th Massachusetts. However, there is one more set of circumstances that must always be remembered when we try to get into the heads and hearts of the African American troopers.

Consider: In 1861, a black man, born in the United States, with few exceptions, was deprived of the right to marry; to rear a family; to own property; to give or receive gifts; to earn a living, learn a trade, or receive an education; to purchase his own freedom or that of his family. He was further forbidden to enter into contracts, to use the courts, to assemble, to speak freely, to worship, to vote, to bear arms, to travel without hindrance or harassment, or to simply ensure the physical inviolability of his person or that of his family. The Supreme Court had ruled that despite being an American, he would never be a citizen.

Yet, by the winter of 1863, when Governor Andrew won authorization for the 5th Massachusetts Volunteer Cavalry and began recruiting, life for African Americans had changed. A previously ostracized, marginalized, barely tolerated race, whether north or south of the Mason-Dixon Line, had proven themselves as combat troops. Black men were being accosted, sidled up to, invited to meetings, and addressed with courtesy. "How would you like an expenses-paid trip to Philadelphia, to Washington, DC, to Boston, Massachusetts? Would several hundred dollars in bounty interest you? Rest assured, your families will be taken care of." In return, black men had the opportunity to free their race, to fight their oppressors, to fight for liberty. In so doing, they also embarked on a journey as much of self-discovery as it was of serving their country.

Certainly, African Americans knew that there was expediency in the promises that the government made—some promises would be kept, and some would not. Racial prejudice was not going to disappear overnight because the Republic desperately needed the contributions of African Americans. For instance, the Union army (indeed, American society) was willing to allow African Americans to become soldiers but would not consider—could not even conceive of—taking orders from a black officer. This was why the handful of African Americans who became officers in the Civil War were chaplains, recruiting officers, or in black units. A black man with authority over whites was unthinkable. This mindset was part of the subconscious, pervasive, corrosive nature of racism in the United States. But other promises were kept: To wear the uniform of the United States and to be treated with dignity as soldiers, to receive equal pay, to participate in combat rather than serving as labor or support troops, to serve as cavalry troopers. That is the story of the 5th Massachusetts Cavalry—a thousand men, more or less, white and black, enlisted and officer, Boston Brahmin and former slave, who made their way from all over the country to Camp Meigs, Readville, Massachusetts, in the winter of 1863.

Introduction

Riders in the Storm is divided into eight chapters. There are also two appendices; one is a "Report from the Joint Standing Committee on Military Claims of the Massachusetts House and Senate," dated 30 April 1866, about recruiting troopers for the 5th Massachusetts Cavalry. The report describes a particular, documented instance of recruiting for a specific Black regiment, but more general conclusions may be drawn from it. The other appendix is a reprint of Paul Dunbar's "The Colored Soldiers." Dunbar's father, Joshua Dunbar, mustered out as a sergeant in Company F of the 5th Massachusetts Cavalry, so Paul Dunbar had personal knowledge of what it was like to serve as an African American soldier during the war and then to have that service ignored.

The eight chapters of the book proceed in a linear and chronological way. Each chapter has a phrase or theme introducing it; often the phrase used is a direct quote from a primary source. Chapter 1, "Black Men in Blue Uniforms," introduces the reader to the use of African American troops by going back to their enlistment during the American Revolution and the War of 1812. Sources such as Dudley Cornish's *The Sable Arm: Black Troops in the Union Army*, Benjamin Quarles' *Lincoln and the Negro* and Mary Berry's *Military Necessity and Civil Rights Policy* are cited to give a general overview of the first two years of the Civil War and the tentative steps toward recruitment. Ray Basler's edited *Works of Lincoln* as well as a biography of Edwin Stanton and Gideon Welles's published diary give quotes from the president and his cabinet. Chapter 1 sees the first of hundreds of quotes from *The War of the Rebellion: A Compilation of the Official Records of the Union and Confederate Armies*, the records published over the twenty-eight years from 1880 to 1901 in 128 volumes. The chapter shifts to Massachusetts from the national scene once the Emancipation Proclamation is promulgated. Central figures in raising three black regiments from Massachusetts include Governor John A. Andrew, Adjutant General William Schouler, and businessman and philanthropist John Murray Forbes, each of whom left a voluminous written record of their activities. Raising those African American regiments was a challenging, almost impossible task. Public opinion in Massachusetts at the time was almost exclusively expressed in newspapers, all of which had a specific editorial slant. This overview of public opinion is framed by Edith Ware's book, *Political Opinion in Massachusetts during the Civil War and Reconstruction.* Ware's work, supplemented by research in newspapers on microfilm at the Boston Public Library, gives an accurate picture of the Bay State during the Civil War. The chapter then moves on to the winter of 1863, when Governor Andrew decided to continue the experiment that Massachusetts had begun with the two infantry regiments of African American soldiers.

There are two series of records at the Massachusetts Archives that were extensively used which make their first appearance in this narrative. In the files of Governor John Andrew, there is "Letters Official." These are several hundred letterpress volumes arranged chronologically. A letterpress volume is a blank, leather-bound book of onion-skin pages. Official stationery was placed under the onion skin and the letter written through the onion skin, thus making a copy of all outgoing correspondence. The other record series, filed by subject matter and by date, is known as the "Executive Files." Incoming correspondence to Governor Andrew's office was separated by subject and pasted into scrapbooks with marbled covers. Stamps were created for the spines of these scrapbooks covering dozens of subjects the governor and his staff dealt with, including an Executive Department file for every regiment raised in Massachusetts. The Letters Official and the Executive Files thus consist of that rare find in historical records: a conversation. The remainder of chapter 1 examines the efforts to gain official federal authorization to raise a state-sponsored regiment of cavalry. The Bureau of United States Colored Troops had been created in May 1863 as a subdivision of the War Department. Governor Andrew needed federal approval of a state regiment of African American troopers because he needed those men to count toward Massachusetts's quota of required recruits. Equally important, and for more altruistic reasons, Andrew wanted to continue to show that black men could be just as good as white in the specialized branch that was the cavalry. Also, Andrew wanted to be able to ensure that success by having the authority to pick the white officers.

Chapter 2's theme is drawn from a newspaper advertisement for the regiment: "That Dashing and Brilliant Arm of the Service." Proceeding chronologically, the chapter opens in December 1863 with several newspaper articles about the regiment and official notice from the Massachusetts governor and adjutant general. This chapter introduces the reader to the recruitment of African American men for the Union army at the end of 1863 and beginning of 1864. Drawing on records from the Massachusetts Archives, the *Official Records*, and published primary sources, the network of recruiters, both black and white, for the 5th Massachusetts is presented. The system of offering bounties and defraying transportation costs for African American recruits is examined, as well as the challenges facing those recruits—specifically, the issue of unequal pay, threat of murder or enslavement if captured, and the unwillingness of state or federal authorities to commission black men as officers. Chapter 2 closes at the end of January 1864, with a full battalion, organized into companies, recruited and sworn into federal service, and a description of the camp of instruction (Camp Meigs) in Readeville, Massachusetts.

Chapter 3, titled "'Officers of the Best Character and Experience,'" looks at the commissioning of officers into the 5th Massachusetts Cavalry. This chapter begins with an examination of the difference between volunteer and regular army officers. There are examples of the close interconnectedness of the nineteenth century in that personal relationships played a much larger role in the commissioning of officers than credential or bureaucratic process. Sources for this chapter include an article in the *Atlantic Monthly* by Colonel Thomas Wentworth Higginson and a paper by Colonel Norwood P. Hallowell that was published in the *Papers of the Military Historical Society of Massachusetts*. Governor Andrew's papers at the Massachusetts Archives continue to serve as a rich source, as are John Murray Forbes's published letters. Two nineteenth-century accounts of Massachusetts regiments: James Bowen's *Massachusetts in the War* and the two-volume *Massachusetts in the Army and Navy*, edited by Thomas W. Higginson, provide background on the prior service of several officers. The Massachusetts Historical Society has a plethora of wartime letters written by participants. The letters of Henry Sturgis Russell and Charles Pickering Bowditch give an accounting of events as they happened to these two men. In the 1930s, after almost forty years of work, the Massachusetts Adjutant General's Office published the regimental muster rolls in six indexed volumes as *Massachusetts Soldiers, Sailors and Marines in the Civil War.* The best way to describe this invaluable source of records about the regiment is to quote it directly. From the preface to volume 1 of *Massachusetts Soldiers, Sailors and Marines*:

> *The movement to provide for the compilation and publication of a revised record of the Massachusetts soldiers, sailors and marines in the military and naval service of the United States in the Civil War was inaugurated about the time of the Spanish-American War and found embodiment in Chap. 475 of the Acts of 1899. . . . Some idea of the magnitude of the work accomplished may be gained from the following details. Over 1, 000, 000 original records have been examined and copied, in most cases each on a separate slip, records found on original enlistment papers, muster-in rolls, descriptive rolls, town reports, casualty lists, monthly reports, hospital records, muster-out rolls, and miscellaneous papers. All the cards or slips relating to men who served in Massachusetts units were then sorted and allocated by companies and regiments. First the slips belonging to each individual soldier had to be selected out and arranged in order in little packs by themselves. Then the packs had to be arranged alphabetically under their proper company heads. Finally the assembled records of the companies were arranged in order under their respective regimental designations.*

Massachusetts Soldiers, Sailors and Marines is used extensively throughout this book beginning in chapters 2 and 3, which take place in Massachusetts and are about the recruitment and formation of the regiment.

Continuing with the linear and chronological style of the narrative, chapter 4, "'Trained to the Sabre,'" takes the reader from January/February 1864 until the end of April 1864. With the exception of, most notably, a lieutenant colonel and a few enlisted men short of the maximum allowed for each company, the 5th Massachusetts Cavalry was complete, and training as cavalry troopers was progressing. That training is documented in the regimental order books, held by the National Archives, as the regimental documents were turned over to the War Department in 1865. Additionally, there is information in this chapter about the procurement of weapons and horses for the regiment, numbering in April 1864 over 950 officers and men. The rescinding of the promise to pay a $325 bounty to the African American men who traveled to Massachusetts to enlist in the regiment is examined, as is the impact that decision had on recruiting and desertion. Chapter 4 ends in dramatic fashion, with the regiment ordered to the front in Virginia and Governor Andrew insisting that the 5th Massachusetts be accepted as a regiment of African American cavalry.

Chapter 5, "Actuated by Patriotism,'" is somewhat longer than previous chapters because the six weeks covered in the narrative, May to mid-June 1864, include a discussion of the regiment's deployment to Virginia as part of the Union army. The chapter begins with the train trip south, recounting events as told in the letters of Captain Charles Bowditch and First Sergeant Charles Douglass. Regimental records and the governor's records at the Massachusetts Archives are consulted. When the four battalions of the regiment joined together outside of Washington, DC, the *Official Records* describe what occurred next. *Battles and Leaders of the Civil War* and Stephen Starr's *Union Cavalry in the Civil War* describe the use of cavalry and the formation of Army Corps in May 1864. Overall strategy for the Union attacks against the Confederacy that month are outlined in Grant's *Memoirs*, Hattaway and Jones's *How the North Won*, and the masterful account by a contemporary general officer, Andrew Humphreys's *The Virginia Campaign of '64 and '65: The Army of the Potomac and the Army of the James*. The memoirs of other participants, including Benjamin Butler (*Butler's Book*) and William Farrar Smith (*From Chattanooga to Petersburg under Generals Grant and Butler*), are also consulted. The overall theme of this chapter is going from the "big picture" strategy down to the enlisted trooper. The best modern study of the campaign the 5th Massachusetts participated in is William Glenn Robertson's *Back Door to Richmond: The Bermuda Hundred Campaign, April–June 1864*. One additional voice, added to official reports and contemporary letter and newspaper accounts, is that of Thomas L. Livermore, a captain on the staff of Brigadier General Edward Hincks, the 5th Massachusetts's division commander. Livermore's *Days and Events* was an indispensable source for an eyewitness account from a veteran officer. Chapter 5 ends with the regiment going into battle, with accounts provided by trooper Charles Beman and Captain Charles Bowditch.

Chapter 6, "Cavalry in Fact as Well as Name," traces events in the regiment's history from 15 June 1864 until the end of September 1864. The reports issued by Generals Hincks and Smith of XVIII Army Corps are examined, as well as Major General Butler's reaction and that of the Union army high command. The failure to capture the city of Petersburg, Virginia, is examined in the writings of several participants. Regimental events are related in Captain Bowditch's letters as well as "soldier letters" published in the pages of the black-owned *Weekly Anglo-African* newspaper. Toward the end of June 1864, the 5th Massachusetts Cavalry (dismounted) was taken out of its assigned infantry brigade and sent to Point Lookout, Maryland, to guard Confederate prisoners of war. A description of the camp is given, along with reactions to being guarded by African American troopers, found in letters from Confederate prisoners as well as the writing of Sidney Lanier, who was prisoner in the camp and wrote about his experiences in his novel *Tiger Lilies*. A petition to Governor Andrew from forty-three noncommissioned officers and three privates requesting that he make good on his promise that the regiment would be cavalry (found in the Massachusetts Archives) is discussed. Also drawn from records in the Massachusetts Archives, there is an extensive discussion about securing a lieutenant colonel for the regiment, critical for the leadership of the regiment after Colonel Russell and Major Zabdiel Adams were wounded in battle on 15 June. The promotion of Captain Charles Francis Adams Jr. of the 1st Massachusetts Cavalry to serve as lieutenant colonel of the 5th Massachusetts Cavalry and his efforts to procure horses for the regiment is discussed, largely drawn from his letters and the Adams Family papers held by the Massachusetts Historical Society. September 1864 found the regiment still guarding prisoners of war in Maryland but now also training as cavalry.

Chapter 7 covers the fourteen months or so from August/September 1864 until the regiment returned to Boston in November 1865 and was paid off and the men returned to civilian life. The chapter begins with the regiment at Point Lookout, guarding Confederate prisoners of war. The discharge and departure of Captain Charles Bowditch and First Sergeant Charles Douglass due to illness in August and September is noted, as well as activity in the regiment as described in the letters Lieutenant Colonel Charles Adams Jr. wrote to his family. October 1864 saw the arrival of Second Lieutenant Edward J. Bartlett from Concord, Massachusetts. Bartlett was a keen observer and a faithful correspondent. His description of guard duty and cavalry training are invaluable. There is an in-depth discussion of military justice and the court-martial process during the Civil War, as shown by events in the regiment garnered from records in the National Archives. In late March 1865, Colonel Charles Adams, who acceded to command of the 5th Massachusetts Cavalry after the resignation of Colonel Russell in February, had the regiment returned to service in the field. The regiment, as part of the XXV Army Corps, was one of the first units (and the only African American cavalry regiment) to march into Richmond, Virginia, on April 3, 1865, mere hours after the Confederate army and government had abandoned the city. Vivid descriptions of a burning Richmond are provided by trooper Charles Beman, whose letter to his father was published by the *Weekly Anglo-African*, as well as letters by Adams and Bartlett and an account by Colonel George A. Bruce, who was present with a detachment of the 4th Massachusetts Cavalry, writing for the Military Historical Society of Massachusetts. Eyewitness civilian accounts are found in Burke Davis's *To Appomattox: Nine April Days*. Regimental records and letters from participants show what the regiment was doing after the two main Confederate armies had surrendered, bringing the narrative to May and June 1865. Sources concerning the situation in Mexico during the 1860s are found in the *Cambridge History of Latin America*, James Callahan's *American Foreign Policy in Mexican Relations*, and William Richter's *The Army in Texas During Reconstruction*. The National Archives again provided orders and reports that give a good picture of the Union army's deployment of the XXV Army Corps to Texas in 1865. Chapter 7's introductory phrase, "He had No Effects," refers to a report from the Corps D'Afrique Hospital in New Orleans, Louisiana, reporting on the death by dysentery of trooper Morris Herman in August of 1865.

Chapter 8 is titled "Losing the Peace," and it describes the postwar activities of some of the troopers and officers. Manuscripts in the Library of Congress were consulted for the papers of Frederick Douglass as well as a letter from Sergeant Major Christian Fleetwood of the 4th United States Colored Infantry Regiment. The poetry of Paul Dunbar, son of Sergeant Joshua Dunbar, is examined, as well as articles in the *Dictionary of American Biography* on brothers Charles and Henry Bowditch. Charles Adams Jr.'s posthumously published autobiography features the author's reflections on his service with the 5th Massachusetts Cavalry. A "biographical sketch" of Colonel Harry Russell was found in a John Morse's *Sons of the Puritans*, published in 1908. The career of Lieutenant Daniel Chamberlain, who became attorney general and governor of South Carolina after the war, is examined in the larger context of Reconstruction. For Reconstruction, Eric Foner's masterful *Reconstruction: America's Unfinished Revolution* is consulted, along with other primary and secondary sources. The records of the Robert A. Bell Post of the Grand Army of the Republic, which had several members of the 5th Massachusetts Cavalry as members, were also useful. The chapter ends with reflections given in two speeches by Frederick Douglass in 1880, highlighting how far African Americans had come since the war and how far they had to go.

CHAPTER ONE

Black Men in Blue Uniforms

We cannot conform to the prejudices of heathenism. We must raise and organize the Colored Volunteers just as we do white ones, our cavalry if raised at all must be the [5th] Mass. Cavalry Vols. They must be state troops. Volunteers according to the law and not U.S. Colored. The precedents of the 54th and 55th were rightly set. They are known on our books and rolls and orders by their numbers and arm of the service, and not by their color.

—MASSACHUSETTS GOVERNOR JOHN A. ANDREW
TO JOHN MURRAY FORBES, 30 NOVEMBER 1863

DOES IT SOUND STRANGE THAT THE 5TH MASSACHUSETTS CAVALRY WAS the brainchild of a Harvard Law School professor? Perhaps, but no stranger than the assertion that "Lewis Hayden, the colored janitor at the state house, always claimed the credit of having suggested to Governor Andrew to organize a colored regiment of Massachusetts volunteers." It would be more accurate to say that John Albion Andrew, Republican governor and abolitionist, and John Murray Forbes, Republican businessman and philanthropist, provided the impetus behind the regiment. Theophilus Parsons, "noted juridical scholar" at Harvard, had sent a letter to Andrew that did "put a bee in his bonnet"; however, before delving into the start of this unique regiment in November 1863, some historical background offers perspective.

President Lincoln's attitudes toward slavery, race, and the use of black troops in the field have long swirled in historical controversy, but we know that no policy existed for the use of black troops at the time of Lincoln's inauguration in March 1861.

Fifteen states had significant slave populations when Lincoln was elected in 1860. One, South Carolina, seceded from the Union in late December. Trying to forestall more states from leaving the Union, the Crittenden Plan was proposed in Congress. This plan called for two constitutional amendments, the first guaranteeing slavery forever in the states where it already existed, the second dividing the territories between slavery and freedom. Lincoln had no objection to the first, but he was unalterably opposed to the second, which would have negated the free-soil plank of the Republican Party. A territorial division, Lincoln wrote, would only encourage planter expansion and thus "put us again on the highroad to a slave empire," and on this point "I am inflexible."

Five more Southern states saw the failure of the Crittenden Plan as their cue and seceded in January 1861: Alabama, Florida, Georgia, Louisiana, and Mississippi. Texas followed on 1 February. Seven states were gone as Lincoln prepared his inaugural address on 4 March. The stakes were enormous: eight slave states, all in the strategically significant upper South, still remained in the Union. If war began, their allegiance would be invaluable; the inaugural address could help achieve that. Moreover, the address should reach out to the North and express the unifying goals of the new president and his party. Lincoln's first inaugural address is a model of compromise and common sense. There is no sign of the rabid abolitionist or "Black Republican" of Southern fear and fantasy. Lincoln tried to reassure Southerners about his intentions: "There needs be no bloodshed or violence, and there shall be none unless it be forced upon the national authority. . . . There will be no invasion, no using of force against or among the people anywhere." Nowhere in this speech is there threat or bluster. Slavery is mentioned only in regard to the effect secession would have on the "peculiar institution": "One section of our country believes slavery is right and ought to be extended, while the other believes it is wrong and ought not to be extended. This is the only substantial dispute. . . . This I think cannot be perfectly cured, and it would be worse in both cases after the separation of the sections than before."

Lincoln argued that secession was anarchy, despotism, and physically impossible since "we cannot remove our respective sections from each other nor build an impassible wall between them." And then Lincoln asked a rhetorical question of the secessionists, a question that would reverberate through the next four years: "Suppose you go to war, you cannot fight always;

and after much loss on both sides and no gain on either, you cease fighting, the identical old questions, as to terms of intercourse, are again upon you."

And war came. When Fort Sumter was fired at on 12 April 1861, the total strength of the U.S. Army was only 16,402 troops, clearly inadequate for putting down the rebellion. Three days after the firing on Fort Sumter, President Lincoln called for seventy-five thousand volunteers for three months. The response was an outpouring of patriotic feeling, and the quota was quickly met and surpassed.

The surprising defeat of the Union forces at the First Battle of Bull Run (21 July 1861), however, made it clear that the war would last longer than the three months most people expected when it began. "The effect of Bull Run at the North, as its meaning sank in," wrote Alan Nevins, "was as stimulating as a whiplash. It blew away illusions like rags of fog in a northwest gale."

From the beginning of hostilities, black leaders and abolitionists had urged the use of black troops. Frederick Douglass, the great African American orator, made his famous assertion that "once they let the black man get upon his person the brass letters U.S.; let him get an eagle on his button and a musket on his shoulder and bullets in his pocket, and there is no power on earth which can deny that he has earned the right to citizenship in the United States."

But Douglass in the spring of 1861 was almost two years ahead of his time. The prevalent feeling in the North was that the war was to restore the Union and defend the Constitution, not to destroy slavery. Northerners feared that enlisting blacks would cause a flood of ex-slaves to come north, competing with whites for jobs and creating racial tension.

There was also the important issue of the border states—Delaware, Maryland, Kentucky, and Missouri—states with substantial slave populations but which had remained loyal to the Union. Arming black men would excite the fear of servile insurrection in these states, driving them to secede. Lincoln had to consider this issue in the early stages of the war, when the tide ran so heavily against the Union.

There were, however, precedents for the use of black troops. Eighty-five years earlier, blacks, both freed and slave, had fought at Lexington, Concord, and Bunker Hill. At Bunker Hill, Peter Salem, one of several freed slaves present, shot British major Pitcairn, who had ordered the Lexington "rebels" to disperse. Salem was considered "undoubtedly one of the chief heroes of that ever memorable battle" and was given a purse and presented to General Washington. There were a few blacks in most New England militia companies in the early months of the Revolutionary War.

The opportunity for blacks to fight for freedom was soon curtailed, however. When the Continental Army was formed in June 1775, Southerners urged the exclusion of black soldiers. On 10 July 1775, Adjutant General Horatio Gates, acting on Washington's orders, instructed recruiting officers that they should not enlist "any deserter from the Ministerial army, nor any stroller, negro, or vagabond."

Blacks already in the army were permitted to stay, at least for the time being. In September, Edward Rutledge, delegate to the Continental Congress from South Carolina, moved that Washington discharge all blacks in the American army, slave or free. He was strongly supported by Southern members, but delegates from the Mid-Atlantic and New England states voted down the measure, perhaps conscious of how shabby it would look to turn out men who had performed bravely.

Washington and his staff considered what to do when current black enlistments ran out. Slaves were unanimously rejected for further service; freed blacks were allowed to reenlist only after General Washington had laid the matter before the Continental Congress. Slaves were excluded for three primary reasons: fear that arming slaves would lead to insurrection, reluctance to interfere with a slave owner's "property," and that allowing a slave to fight for the rhetoric and ideal of liberty might well entitle him to the physical fact of freedom.

Despite this negative congressional decision, the patriot army soon found it necessary to enlist slaves. There was a critical shortage of men for the army brought on by short enlistments (usually three months) and the reluctance of white farmers to fight any distance from their homes. Congress had no authority to force men to enlist, depending on the states to furnish the men Congress begged for. When men did enlist, Congress couldn't pay them.

By 1777, Congress had reversed its stand on excluding slaves: slaves could serve as substitutes for their masters. Other advantages of using slaves as soldiers included the belief that, with fewer ties to the land, they would be less likely to want to go home, and the fact that they were strongly motivated by the shining promise of freedom at the end of their enlistments.

Perhaps the most famous example of African American soldiers in the Revolution is the black battalion of Rhode Island. First mustered in July 1778, the battalion consisted of four companies totaling 19 commissioned officers and 144 enlisted men. Later, another company was added, bringing the aggregate to 226 officers and men. The officers were white; the colonel, Christopher Greene, was a Quaker who had been "read out of meeting" for taking up the sword. All the enlisted men were former slaves freed when they signed on. The battalion was the suggestion of Rhode Island general James Varnum, who saw recruitment of freedmen as a military necessity. The patriot cause in Rhode Island was in dire straits in 1778: the British had occupied most of the state, including the capital, in 1777; her commerce had been destroyed and her treasury was empty. Rhode Island governor Nicholas Cooke wrote Washington that it was "impossible to recruit our battalions in any other way" than by accepting slaves.

Another black American unit of note in the Revolution was composed of French-speaking blacks and mulattoes from the island of Saint-Domingue, now Haiti. Designated as "volunteer chasseurs," some six hundred freemen were part of the French force under Count D'Estaing that tried regaining Savannah, Georgia, captured by the British in 1778.

Blacks in the Revolution fought side-by-side with whites in mixed units. They also served as cooks, laborers, and teamsters and helped man the Continental navy, the states' navies and privateers. But with the exception of Maryland, no Southern state allowed the enlistment of blacks, slave or free.

When the War for Independence ended, some five thousand black soldiers had fought on the Continental side. The regions that had the fewest blacks enlisted the largest number, and only when forced to by the "times that tried men's souls." The states with the largest black populations were too afraid of the idea of the armed black man to enlist him, even if that enlistment might mean victory. The few black soldiers set free by their military service were from the North and thus offered no threat to the institution of slavery.

During the War of 1812, black men served America with distinction in such varying locations as the Great Lakes and New Orleans. Black sailors were a common sight in the American navy, as the following letter written by Usher Parsons, a naval surgeon, attests, "In 1814, our fleet sailed to the Upper Lakes to co-operate with Colonel Croghan at Mackinac. About one in ten or twelve of the crews were black. In 1816, I was surgeon of the *Java*, under Commodore Perry. The white and colored seamen messed together. About one in six or eight were colored. . . . There seemed to be an entire absence of prejudice against the blacks as messmates among the crew."

At New Orleans, General Andrew Jackson led his outnumbered troops against the flower of the British army, veterans of the Napoleonic Wars commanded by General Edward Pakenham, Wellington's brother-in-law. On 21 September 1814, General Jackson had issued a proclamation, "To the Free Colored Inhabitants of Louisiana," in which he appealed to the patriotism of those he called "sons of freedom." General Jackson proclaimed that the country now looked to her "adopted children" to "rally round the standard of the Eagle" as a return for the "advantages enjoyed under her mild and equitable government." Jackson promised that the freemen who enlisted would receive the same bounty as white soldiers and "be entitled to the same monthly pay, and daily rations, and clothes, furnished to any American soldier." Although the general appointed white officers, the men could choose their own noncommissioned officers. As a further incentive, Jackson proposed to eliminate prejudice: "You will not, by being associated with white men in the same corps, be exposed to improper comparisons or unjust sarcasm."

Some 430 free black troops, organized into two battalions, saw action at the Battle of New Orleans in 1815. After the victory, their courage and loyalty was praised by the state legislature, by General Jackson, and in the local press.

Despite historical precedent and the contemporary urging of abolitionists, however, the policy of the Lincoln administration was made clear in the early months of the Civil War: nothing must be done to disturb the loyalty of the border states. There would be no black soldiers in the Union army, and fugitive slaves would be returned to their masters.

Union officers seemed willing to comply with this policy. In late April 1861, Brigadier General Benjamin F. Butler, commanding Massachusetts troops in Maryland, offered his command to that state's governor, Thomas H. Hicks, to help suppress a rumored slave uprising. A month later, when General George B. McClellan began his campaign in the mountains of what is now West Virginia, he made his attitude toward slavery clear to the members of his command: "See that the rights and property of the people are respected, and repress all attempts at negro insurrection." General Robert Patterson, then commanding the Department of Pennsylvania, reiterated this "hands-off" policy in an address to troops in early June 1861: "You must bear in mind you are going for the good of the whole country, and that while it is your duty to punish sedition, you must protect the loyal, and should occasion offer, at once suppress servile insurrections."

Although slaves were anxious enough for freedom and ran away from slavery whenever they could, flocking into the Union lines, there was no insurrection during the war. But in the beginning of the war, slaveholders—in active rebellion against the government—came into Union camps under truce flags and retrieved their runaway slaves.

They were first refused on 26 May 1861 by General Benjamin F. Butler, who changed his tune little more than a month after assuring Maryland slaveholders he would support them against a slave outbreak. Butler had his headquarters at Fort Monroe, Virginia. Three slaves belonging to a Colonel Mallory, commander of Confederate forces near Hampton, Virginia, came inside Butler's lines that day saying they had run away because they were about to be sent south. Colonel Mallory sent a flag of truce to claim their return under the Fugitive Slave Law. Butler replied that as slaves could be made very useful to the enemy in working on fortifications and other labor, he considered them contraband of war, like lead or powder or other war matériel, and they therefore would not be handed over. Butler offered to return the three if Colonel Mallory would come to his headquarters and take an oath of loyalty to the United States. This was the first direct blow at slavery and brought forth a new term for fugitive slaves: "contraband."

The next step was when Congress passed what became known as the First Confiscation Act. The law said that property, including slaves, actually employed in the service of the rebellion with the knowledge and consent of the owner, should be seized by federal troops wherever found. But it cautiously provided that slaves thus confiscated were not free at once, but to be held subject to some future action by Congress or the courts.

In 1856, General John C. Fremont had been the first Republican presidential candidate. In 1861 he was made major general and given command of the Western Department, headquartered in St. Louis. In August 1861, Fremont issued a proclamation placing the whole state under martial law, confiscating the property of all those who had taken up arms against the

United States or had aided by burning bridges, cutting telegraph wires, or destroying railway tracks. Fremont added that the slaves of rebellious Missourians, "if any they have, are hereby declared free men."

This was too radical a step for President Lincoln: even as a military measure, it went too far. Drumhead courts-martial would invite resistance and reprisals, and Fremont, to make matters worse, had not bothered to telegraph the War Department of his intentions before acting. Lincoln wrote to Fremont outlining his objections. He forbade Fremont to shoot any Confederates without presidential approval and called the general's attention to the fact that the clause relating to slaves was not in conformity with the Confiscation Act, which sanctioned the seizure of property only when actually used in the rebel cause. President Lincoln asked Fremont to modify his proclamation to conform to the act. Fremont's pride and sense of conviction were hurt, so he refused. He requested Lincoln direct the modification by open order, which Lincoln did in a courteous letter. Taking the power out of Fremont's proclamation, Lincoln knew that he had to retain the loyalty of Republicans and Democrats, conservatives and radicals, and that he must keep the border states at least neutral. "He believed in evolution, not revolution; he wished to shorten the conflict, not lengthen it," wrote Alan Nevins. "He wished to maintain conditions favorable to the fraternal reunion of North and South after the war."

Perceptions were changing: although Lincoln insisted that the war was for the restoration of the Union, for the idea of one great nation, others now saw it as a war for a great humanitarian ideal.

The first time Lincoln himself acted against slavery came on 6 March 1862, when he sent Congress a special message on gradual, compensated emancipation in the border states. This proposal was so legalistic and conservative in content, according to Lawanda Cox in her book *Lincoln and Black Freedom*, "as to obscure the audacity of the executive initiative and its radical contemporary significance." In contrast to the Confiscation Act of August 1861, which affected only slaves used for strictly military purposes, and the geographically limited bill to abolish slavery in the District of Columbia (then not yet passed by either the House or the Senate), Lincoln's message was the first mentioning emancipation as a specific war aim.

In his proposal, Lincoln argued that compensated emancipation was "one of the most efficient means of self-preservation" for the federal government, because the Confederacy was hoping for the eventual support of the border states. "To deprive them of this hope substantially ends the rebellion and the initiation of emancipation completely deprives them of it." To Lincoln, the logic of this proposal was that the people of each state would decide the issue for themselves without federal interference. Even the approval of one border state would "make it certain to the more Southern that in no event would the former join the latter in their proposed confederacy." Lincoln furthermore made a veiled threat or promise, depending on one's view, of a more general emancipation. Referring to his annual message of 1861 in which he stated that all indispensible means would be employed to preserve the Union, the president wrote, "Such as may seem indispensable, or may obviously promise great efficiency towards ending the struggle, must and will come."

Before Lincoln had decided that the federal government was ready to move against slavery, however, he had to deal with another general who decided to make federal policy on his own. David Hunter succeeded John C. Fremont in command of the Department of the West in the fall of 1861. When transferred to the Department of the South on 31 March 1862, Hunter followed Pathfinder Fremont's trail of unilateral emancipation. The Department of the South was based at Hilton Head, South Carolina, and included the Sea Islands and various other bits of sand and mud along the southern Atlantic coast. The region had come under Union control after a combined army-navy assault in November 1861.

The Union general in command of the Department of the South in November had been Thomas W. Sherman. This "other" Sherman had been authorized to use contraband in whatever way he deemed helpful. Sherman did not arm the fugitive slaves but put them to work under the direction of the Treasury Department growing cotton on abandoned plantations. When General Hunter succeeded Sherman in March, he quickly assessed the white troops at his command as too few and decided to make soldiers of the local black men.

On 16 April 1862, Hunter issued a proclamation declaring that all slaves of rebel owners were confiscated and freed. Hunter based this order on the provisions of the First Confiscation Act of August 1861. In May, General Hunter went even further. He declared that the states of Florida, Georgia, and South Carolina were under martial law. The general reasoned that since slavery was incompatible with advancing the war effort under martial law, all slaves in those states were declared free.

When President Lincoln found out about Hunter's order, he issued a proclamation of his own, declaring that "neither General Hunter nor any other commander or person has been authorized by the Government of the United States to make proclamations declaring the slaves of any state free; and that the supposed proclamation now in question, whether genuine or false is altogether void, so far as respects such declaration."

Despite being stymied in his proclamation of freedom, General Hunter moved forward with his plan for arming African Americans. His idealism was commendable, but his methods were not. On the same day he issued his "emancipation proclamation," he requested that the district officers under his command (brigadier generals) "order the commanding officers in your district to send immediately to these headquarters, under guard, all the able-bodied negroes capable of bearing arms within the limits of their several commands."

Removal by force was not a tactic designed to win the support of either the black people in his department or his superiors in Washington. Edward L. Pierce, a Boston lawyer with abolitionist sympathies, had gone to work for the Treasury Department as supervisor over abandoned plantations in the Department of the South. He sent a report about the effects of General Hunter's order to Secretary Salmon P. Chase that included this eyewitness account: "As those on this plantation were called in from the field, the soldiers, under orders and while on the steps of my headquarters, loaded their guns, so that the negroes might see what would take place in case they attempted to get away. . . . Wives and children embraced the husband and father thus taken away, they knew not where, and whom, as they said, they should never see again." This did not seem to Northerners, like Pierce, to be recruiting but impressment, conscription by force.

Such practices raised a firestorm in the Northern press. Not only was conscription denounced as being contrary to the principles of free volunteers, but questions were also raised about whether blacks would be made officers and whether whites would serve alongside blacks. Hunter's experiment with an African American regiment failed because the War Department refused to authorize such action, and the Treasury Department refused to pay the men of the "First South Carolina Colored Regiment" because they had not been mustered into federal service.

Hunter's actions did have positive results, however unsavory the methods. As Dudley Cornish wrote, "He had forced the issue into the open, and from the middle of May on through the rest of 1862 the question of arming the Negro, slave or free, occupied column after column of newspaper space and stirred the expression of every kind of opinion, conviction and reaction."

The summer of 1862 was one of death and mutilation. McClellan's Peninsula Campaign had failed in the Seven Days' Battles, which raged from 25 June to 1 July, and he was forced to withdraw the Army of the Potomac back to the defenses around Washington by the middle of July. Lincoln made one last appeal for cooperation on compensated emancipation from the border states. He called their members in Congress to the White House on 12 July and told them that if they had voted for the graduated, compensated emancipation bill of March, "the war would be substantially ended." He pressed home the fact that slavery was doomed, even though "you prefer that the constitutional relation of the states to the nation shall be practically restored, without disturbance of the institution." The war itself, "by mere friction and abrasion," would end slavery, he argued, so why not be paid for "that which is sure to be wholly lost in any other event?"

Lincoln reiterated his promise to colonize blacks outside the United States, in South America where land was cheap and abundant. The president also mentioned the negative response to his annulment of General Hunter's emancipation order. "Yet in repudiating it, I gave dissatisfaction, if not offence, to many whose support the country can not afford to lose. And this is not the end of it. The pressure, in this direction, is still upon me, and is increasing." President Lincoln appealed to the border state congressmen as "patriots and statesmen" to approve gradual, compensated emancipation; "at least, commend it to the consideration of your states and people."

Lincoln's appeal fell on deaf ears. On 14 July a majority of the border state congressmen, twenty representatives and senators, rejected Lincoln's proposal on the grounds that compensated emancipation was too expensive, would only strengthen secessionists' resistance, and would not reduce the likelihood of "unconstitutional" emancipation by proclamation.

Lincoln knew that morale in the country and the army was low after McClellan's humiliating defeat on the peninsula. Liberal opinion in Europe could not understand why he was taking so long to strike at slavery. By making emancipation a war measure, a military necessity, the president hoped to retain control of federal policy toward slavery, both during the war and after it.

On 22 July 1862, Lincoln met with his cabinet and presented the first draft of his Emancipation Proclamation. The last sentence read, "And as a fit and necessary military measure for effecting this object, I, as Commander-in-Chief of the Army and Navy of the United States, do order and declare that on the first day of January in the year of Our Lord one thousand, eight-hundred and sixty-three, all persons held as slaves within any state or states, wherein the constitutional authority of the United States shall not then be practically recognized, submitted to, and maintained, shall then, thenceforward, and forever, be free."

Postmaster General Montgomery Blair was opposed to the proclamation, feeling that it would cost the Republican Party the fall elections and "put the power in the House of Representatives in the hands of those opposed to the war." Secretary of State William H. Seward was in favor of the measure but suggested that the president wait until military victory ensured that the administration did not appear to be acting out of desperation. Treasury Secretary Chase suggested that compensated emancipation be abandoned and that military commanders be allowed to arm the slaves within their districts. Lincoln disagreed with Chase, was willing to risk the fall elections, and concurred with Seward on the importance of timing.

Lincoln might not have been ready to arm African Americans, but there were plenty in Congress who agreed with Secretary Chase. On 17 July 1862, two important pieces of legislation became law, the Second Confiscation Act and the Militia Act. The Second Confiscation Act went further than the First in that it charged the president with seizure of property of rebels and made "all other persons who abetted the rebellion, sixty days after he gave public warning, equally liable to loss of their estates."

The real importance of the bill, however, was its attack on slavery. Provisions were made for declaring the slaves of those in rebellion forever free, for the president to employ such African Americans in whatever tasks he saw fit, and for the colonization of freed slaves outside the United States.

Lincoln was greatly troubled by this bill because he felt it too vindictive. It also took slavery, which the president felt was at the heart of postwar reconstruction, out of his hands. The president threatened a veto and refused to sign the bill until some portions of it had been removed. After the changes were made, Lincoln included a draft of his veto message when he sent the signed bill back to Congress. One of his objections ran, "It is also provided, that the slaves of persons convicted under the sections shall be free. . . . It is startling to say that Congress can free a slave within a state; and yet if it were said the ownership of the slave had first been transferred to the nation, and that congress had then liberated him, the difficulty would at once vanish." The president was thus questioning Congress's authority to act against slavery without the support of the executive branch.

The Militia Act authorized the president "to receive into the service of the United States for the purpose of constructing entrenchments, or performing camp duty, or any other labor, or any military or naval service for which they were found competent, persons of African descent, and provided that such persons should be enrolled and organized, under such regulations, not inconsistent with the Constitution and laws, as the president might prescribe." Section 15 of the law set pay rates: "That persons of African descent, who under this law shall be employed, shall receive ten dollars per month and one ration, three dollars of which monthly pay may be in clothing." White soldiers at the time received thirteen dollars a month of which three dollars might be in clothing. This disparity, this discrimination, became a problem when blacks were enlisted as soldiers, one that lasted for two years until the government decided to amend the act.

Besides the pay issue, the vague language of the bill presented other problems. Were black men to be actual soldiers, or only service personnel used for "camp duty"? If soldiers, would they be allowed to become officers? Other than this flawed act, for almost a year there were no further regulations dealing with African American troops.

The war was not going well for the Union in late summer 1862. Union recruiting was at a standstill. Many wondered why the Confederacy was not being attacked through the institution of slavery. At the end of August, General Pope, who had replaced McClellan, was defeated at the Second Battle of Bull Run. Earlier in the month, Horace Greeley's "Prayer of Twenty Millions," an open letter to President Lincoln, was printed in his newspaper, the *New York Tribune*. Greeley's letter was impassioned and powerful; a single passage will show its tone:

On the face of this wide earth, Mr. President, there is not one disinterested, determined, intelligent champion of the Union cause who does not feel that all attempts to put down the rebellion, and at the same uphold its exciting cause, are preposterous and futile; that the rebellion, if crushed out tomorrow, would be renewed within a year if slavery were left in full vigor; that army officers who remain to this day devoted to slavery can at best be but half-way loyal to the Union; and that every hour of deference to slavery is an hour of added and deepened peril to the Union.

Anyone with less wit and common sense than Lincoln would have been hard put to answer Greeley at all, and his answer was not really a refutation of Greeley's points. Instead, Lincoln took the opportunity to air his own views:

If there be perceptible in it [the Prayer] an impatient and dictatorial tone, I waive it in deference to an old friend whose heart I have always supposed to be right. . . . As to the policy I "seem to be pursuing" as you say, I have not meant to leave anyone in doubt. . . . My paramount object is to save the Union, and not either to save or destroy slavery. If I could save the Union without freeing any slave, I would do it; if I could save it by freeing all the slaves, I would do it; and if I could do it by freeing some and leaving others alone, I would also do that. I have here stated my purpose according to my views of official duty; and I intend no modification of my oft-expressed personal wish that all men everywhere could be free.

In truth, the president was already contemplating emancipation as a war measure, and about that time had prepared his preliminary proclamation; but he did not wish to issue it until it could follow a Union victory.

On 17 September 1862, the Battle of Antietam was fought near the Maryland creek that bears that name. The battle raged for some fourteen hours, and thousands were killed and wounded. The battle was not a clear-cut victory for either side, but afterward Lee turned his army southward, so it was all the victory Lincoln needed. On 22 September, Lincoln issued his Preliminary Emancipation Proclamation, announcing that on the first day of January 1863, "all persons held as slaves within any State or designated part of any State, the people whereof shall then be in rebellion against the United States, should be then, thenceforward, and forever free."

But that Preliminary Emancipation Proclamation did not specifically mention arming blacks. It was only in the proclamation of 1 January 1863 that recruiting African Americans was mentioned: "And I further declare and make known, that such persons of African descent, of suitable condition, will be received into the armed service of the United States to garrison forts, positions, stations, and other places, and to man vessels of all sorts in said service."

On 8 January 1863, Lincoln wrote to Major General John A. McClernand, a "political general" from Illinois, to explain his thinking about emancipation and military service for African Americans: "After the commencement of hostilities I struggled for nearly a year and a half to get along without touching the 'institution;' and when I finally conditionally determined to touch it, I gave a hundred days fair notice of my purpose, to all the states and people, within which time they could have turned it wholly aside, by simply again becoming good citizens of the United States. They chose to disregard it, and I made the preemptory proclamation on what appeared to me to be a military necessity."

In September 1862, Governor John Andrew of Massachusetts had been on his way to Altoona, Pennsylvania, for a conference of Northern governors when he read about the Preliminary Emancipation Proclamation. "The Proclamation of Emancipation is out," he wrote to his friend and military secretary, Albert Browne. "It is a poor document but a mighty act; slow, somewhat halting, wrong in its delay until January, but grand and sublime after all. 'Prophets and kings have waited for this day, but died without the sight.'" Among other things, Lincoln's proclamation provided Andrew with the opportunity for launching a project he had long contemplated: bringing the black man into the war as a soldier.

John Albion Andrew had not always had the support of the Massachusetts majority when it came to questions about the African American. Andrew had raised money for John Brown's legal defense after the Harper's Ferry raid and had praised "Captain" Brown in public: "I sympathize with the man, I sympathize with the idea, because I sympathize with and believe in the eternal right."

Many saw this as defending a dangerous madman. Even members of his own party criticized Andrew's actions as too radical. In 1860, Samuel

Bowles, editor of the *Springfield Republican*, gave this reaction to Andrew's nomination for governor: "His John Brown sympathies and speeches, his Garrisonian affiliations, his negro-training predilections and all that sort of extreme anti-slaveryism, with which his record abounds, will be trumpeted far and wide in the state to injure him, [and] out of it to harm Lincoln."

Andrew toned down his abolitionism during the election and adopted a more conciliatory tone during the "secession winter" of 1860–1861. After winning election in 1860, Andrew realized that unity within the Republican Party was perhaps more important than inflammatory abolitionist rhetoric, and as Henry Pearson, Andrew's biographer, put it, "he for once in his life checked his tongue on the subject of slavery."

After Fort Sumter, the wisdom of continuing silence on the slavery issue was repeated to the governor. In May 1861, Andrew was in Washington conferring with Lincoln administration officials in preparation for a special session of the Massachusetts legislature. When Andrew asked Postmaster General Montgomery Blair what tone he should take in his speech, the Maryland-born Blair bluntly told him to "drop the nigger." When he addressed the legislature on 14 May, Andrew stated, "This is no war of sections, no war of North and South. It is the struggle of the People to vindicate their own rights, to retain and invigorate the institutions of their fathers ... and therefore while I do not forget, I will not name today that subtle poison which has lurked always in our national system."

As John Murray Forbes wrote in his *Letters and Recollections*, "many Northern people had no clear conception of the evils of slavery, nor were all aware that this inherited curse was at the bottom of the strife, but all understood an attack on the Union." Indeed, such newspapers as the *Boston Daily Advertiser* and the *Springfield Republican*, aligned with the policies of the Lincoln administration, made it clear that abolition was not a war aim.

On 17 September 1861, the *Advertiser* carried an editorial in response to "a party among us—not large we believe, but earnest and active," who believed that the government "dallies, that it coolly measures out its harmless severity towards those who are striking at its life." To those who argued that striking at slavery would give a "new definition of the objects of the war," the editor replied that emancipation would "raise up more earnest opponents than friends of the war." Furthermore, the paper pointed out that the Lincoln administration "must accept those relations which the Constitution enjoins upon it," particularly those relations "in regard to the status of slavery in the States." The editorial ended by reminding "zealous extremists" that weapons which "in a military view might appear most effective, must be laid aside, if they embarrass the civil ends which the war is meant to secure."

The editor of the *Springfield Republican* had written along the same lines that June: "Of course, the general government can contemplate no such thing as the abolition of slavery. Abolition has not been, and will never be, except under the absolute exigencies of war, the policy of this administration." A month later, the *Republican* ran this editorial: "The American people have fully decided that the Union and Constitution are worth fighting for. . . . To demonstrate to the world that a republic is a real government, not to be overthrown by a violent faction . . . is preferable to peace bought by submission to traitors. . . . The Constitution gives the slaveholders all the guaranties they need for their peculiar institution."

Newspapers opposed to the Republican administration made their mistrust of abolitionism even clearer. The organ of Boston Irish Catholics, loyal Democrats to a man, was *The Pilot*, which under the headline "Abolition License" had this to say:

> *The civil war by which the Republic is now on the verge of dissolution is the effect of two causes: the disappointed political ambition of the South and the abolition doctrine of the North frantically used for the overthrow of the chief Southern interests. . . . Abolitionism, which has been the principal cause of Southern disloyalty springing to action, has never been so violent, so extreme, so wicked, so fanatical as at this very instant [January 1862]. Its clergymen, its editors, and its "wretched spouters"—both men and women—are now in bold enjoyment of the utmost license of action. . . . The pillars of the abolition churches are made to vibrate every day and evening with emancipation sermons of the most turbulent kind. . . . For the abolitionist journalists no excess is too wild for advocacy, and the speakers of the tribe are utterly unbridled in their speech.*

Perhaps with more of a voice of reason, William Schouler, in his *History of Massachusetts in the Civil War*, described the abolitionist "party" as "small in number" but "powerful in eloquence, moral character, and cultivated intellect." The abolitionists, as remembered by Schouler, possessed zeal and a "martyr spirit" that "made no compromises, sought no office, asked no favor and gave no quarter." It should be remembered that up until December

1861, the motto of *The Liberator*, William Lloyd Garrison's newspaper, was "The Constitution is a Covenant with Death and an Agreement with Hell." Edith Ware, in her work *Political Opinion in Massachusetts during the Civil War and Reconstruction*, agreed that in 1861, "abolitionists continued to be an isolated group unapproved by regular Republicans and attacked by Democrats and Conservatives." Yet the purpose of the war would not remain static. General Butler's "contraband" policy and General Fremont's unauthorized confiscation policy unavoidably brought the African American to the fore of public debate.

Although applauded by some as a first step on the road to general emancipation and vilified by others as a usurpation of the Constitution, the majority in the state agreed with President Lincoln that Fremont had gone beyond the law. And, as the *Springfield Republican* reminded its readers, "we are fighting for the maintenance of the Union, the Constitution, and the laws. We have a recent law of Congress [the First Confiscation Act], made to treat this particular emergency . . . and to this law we must bow, if we would hope to establish law." Three days later, however, the *Republican* had some tough words for the administration: "The people ask, with much doubt and mistrust, why property in men is to be treated in this exceptional and considerate way, while all other property belonging to rebels may be confiscated under martial law." The paper praised General Fremont's patriotism in acquiescing "in the will of the chief magistrate" despite the modification of the policy that "seemed to meet so admirably the exigency of the case."

An astute political observer like John Murray Forbes could thus write in the summer of 1861, "We must wait until the military necessity demands more positive action. When that necessity comes, the North will be reasonably united—now we are divided." Forbes had been a delegate to the "Peace Congress" of 1860, the final attempt of Northern conservatives to stave off secession. After the war broke out, Forbes worked tirelessly for the Union cause. W. S. Robinson, who wrote for the *Springfield Republican*, the *Boston Atlas and Bee*, and the *Boston Weekly Commonwealth* under the pen name "Warrington," made a "pen portrait" of Forbes during the war: "John M. Forbes" is "a man of headlong energy, long time an abolitionist, and more than any other man the confidential adviser of Governor Andrew. He attends to everything; writes letters, raises money (liberally contributing himself), sends messages to Washington to direct and organize congressional opinion, makes or persuades editors to write leading articles to enforce his views."

From across the ocean, American minister to Great Britain Charles Francis Adams wrote to Forbes that first August of the war, "The slave question must be settled this time once for all. It is surprising to see the efforts made here to create the belief that our struggle has nothing to do with slavery. . . . Of course the measure of emancipation is a most grave one. . . . But there is no alternative in my mind between taking it up and absolute submission."

Some in Massachusetts saw the controversy surrounding Fremont's confiscation proclamation as evidence that the people were beginning to think about emancipation as a war measure. Amos A. Lawrence, one of the leading industrialists in the state, who had been a Constitutional Unionist in the election of 1860, wrote to the *Boston Courier*: "The present opinion is that there should be no more compromise to sustain the Union by sustaining slavery. But, on the contrary, I believe in the propriety of the policy of confiscating the property and freeing the slaves of all active rebels wherever it can be done. And now that we must bear the hardships of war, I believe in securing the benefits of it for the advancement of freedom for the blacks and the elevating of our national character."

As 1861 drew to a close, the people were presented with specific approaches to the problem of slavery: colonization, compensated emancipation, and the Second Confiscation Act were all discussed in public and in private. It was the actions of General Hunter that drew the sharpest reactions from both sides.

John Murray Forbes wrote to Hunter, whom he had met while visiting his son, an officer in the 1st Massachusetts Cavalry stationed in Beaufort, South Carolina: "We have then got to the point that we must either draft men and force them into the war, or resort to some measures for sapping the strength of the enemy, which now lies in what ought to be, and has always been supposed to be, their weakness—their slaves. If we could only at all points of contact set them traveling toward our lines, to do our drudgery, it would help us to weaken the enemy."

Forbes had just returned from South Carolina when he wrote to Senator Sumner on 16 May 1862, "I do hope the President will not make another Fremont blunder or rather Missouri blunder by disavowing Hunter's act.

Whatever may be the case elsewhere, it is time the Kidglove and Rosewater mode of carrying on the war should be exploded in South Carolina."

Lincoln's decision not to sustain General Hunter prompted Governor Andrew to break his silence on the issue of emancipation and the arming of the slave. In a rather extraordinary series of events, Andrew took the opportunity of airing his views in an exchange of letters with Secretary of War Stanton.

On 3 April 1862, in a move described as a "colossal blunder" by his biographer, a move undertaken with the mistaken notion that McClellan's Peninsula Campaign was about to win the war, Stanton closed the government recruiting offices in the Northern states and instructed the officers and men who had been detailed to that service to return to their regiments. Recruiting for state regiments had already been suspended on 1 January. Consequently, when McClellan's campaign suffered losses and bogged down in May, Stanton was in a real fix when bombarded with requests for more men by the "Young Napoleon." On 17 May, the secretary of war telegraphed the Northern governors inquiring as to how soon they could raise regiments, the number for each state varying from one to six and totaling fifty-one in all. Governor Andrew was asked how soon he could "raise and organize three or four infantry regiments." These regiments were not to go into camps of instruction; instead they were to be sent directly to Washington and equipped there.

The governor wrote back that "if our people feel that they are going into the South to help fight rebels, who will kill and destroy them by all means known to savages, as well as civilized man . . . [who] will use their negro slaves against them, both as laborers and as fighting men, while they themselves must 'never fire at an enemy's magazine,' I think that they will feel that the draft is heavy on their patriotism." Andrew wrote that if President Lincoln sustained General Hunter and "recognize[d] all men, even black men, as legally capable of that loyalty the blacks are waiting to manifest," then "the roads will swarm if need be with multitudes whom New England would pour out to obey your call."

Andrew sent that message on 19 May, by coincidence the same day that President Lincoln canceled General Hunter's order. By presuming to make patriotism "conditional," Governor Andrew had overreached himself, as editorials in the *Boston Post* and *Springfield Republican* show. The *Post* quoted an unnamed army officer as saying that the army would not fight for the "emancipation, education and improvement" of the slaves, and that such a policy would "break up the Army in twenty-four hours."

On 30 May, the *Republican* had some strong words for the governor. Andrew "had gone off at half cock" and had "unwisely chose[n] a bad time to do a little private pushing of his opinions on the subject of slavery. Still more unwisely, he undertook to do it in the name of Massachusetts. . . . And now we say to Governor Andrew, as he does not appear to be acquainted with the truth . . . that the soldiers who have enlisted in Massachusetts have not enlisted with a thought of slavery in their minds. Its destruction, however desirable . . . has never entered their minds as an object of the war." Interestingly, however, the paper noted that "the time may come when such a policy will be necessary, and this is strongly hinted at by the president himself, who, with all the rest of us, hates slavery in all its aspects."

Andrew had apparently considered Stanton's request for troops as more of an opportunity to support General Hunter and express his opinion on emancipation than as a genuine military emergency. So he offered the only troops he had readily available, not even a regiment but a battalion of six hundred men. The situation changed, however, when it was believed that Stonewall Jackson was advancing down the Shenandoah Valley to attack Washington, denuded of troops by McClellan.

Stanton panicked and sent requests to the governors of Massachusetts, New York, and Pennsylvania to send troops to save the Capitol immediately. Receiving the request on a quiet May Sunday (the 25th), Governor Andrew set aside all abolitionist concerns and issued a dramatic and alarming proclamation calling for troops. He had four thousand militia ready to go by the 27th. The governor (not to mention Stanton) found himself in something of a political tempest when the threat to Washington did not materialize and the militia were told to stand down. Andrew had issued a proclamation on 25 May filled with patriotic rhetoric excoriating the "wily barbarous horde of traitors to the people" and calling for the militia to "march to relieve and avenge their brethren and friends." When this proclamation was printed side-by-side with Andrew's previous epistle to Stanton, finding the "draft heavy on their patriotism," people in Massachusetts weren't sure what to think.

But Governor Andrew stood firm and weathered the storm, placing his faith in himself and the common sense of the people. Not long after this incident, Andrew expressed his thoughts about that faith to Senator Sumner: "Most public men despise the people, think they are foolish and knowing their own personal limitations, believe the people not to be honest. . . . In the long run he will always dupe himself who doubts the people. An honest and brave man who looks into his own heart will find public opinion just there. He need not look at the clouds nor the church steeple, watching the wind for evidence."

Governor Andrew needed such faith as the truth of the defeat and losses from the Peninsula Campaign came to be known in the Bay State. Day after day the newspapers printed lists of the killed and wounded, culminating in the terrible losses from the Seven Days' Battles and McClellan's decision to retreat. At about the same time that those casualty lists were being printed, in the first week of July, President Lincoln issued a call for three hundred thousand volunteers to serve for three years or to the end of the war. For fifteen months Northerners had heard the cry of "On to Richmond!" and read admonitions in the press not to interfere with slavery, that the war was being fought for the Constitution and the Union "as it was." Northerners had heard the arguments that the war would be over quickly, that it was important to keep the border states on the side of the government, and that it was unconstitutional to interfere with slavery. But with millions of dollars and thousands of lives spent, many began to question the wisdom of leaving slavery alone, especially since it appeared in the summer of 1862 that thousands more would have to die before the war was brought to a successful conclusion.

John Murray Forbes wrote Parke Godwin, editor of the *New York Evening Post*, on 23 June: "I believe today that the old Union Democrats, and even the true men of the border states, are ahead of Lincoln upon the question of hitting the rebels hard—with the negro or any other club. It is strange that when a rattlesnake is attacking us that we should be so delicate about the stick we hit him with." On 21 June, Forbes had written to Senator Charles Sumner, "I used to think emancipation only another name for murder, fire and rape, but mature reflection and considerable personal observation have since convinced me that emancipation may, at any time, be declared without disorder. . . . I am no philanthropist, but I do want to see the promptest and hardest blows struck. I only ask that the weakest point of the enemy shall be assailed before throwing away more valuable lives."

Even the conservative *Boston Daily Advertiser*, prompted to editorialize by Greeley's "Prayer of Twenty Millions," wrote, "The great phenomenon of the year, as it seems to us, is the terrible intensity which this resolution [emancipation] has acquired. A year ago men might have faltered at the thought of proceeding to this extremity in any event. The majority do not now seek it, but we say advisedly, they are in great measure prepared for it."

There were those, however, who did not concur with the staid editors of the *Advertiser*, those whose minds had always been made up on the subject of African American freedom. In February 1862, *The Pilot* ran an editorial on the subject of the recognition of Liberia by the U.S. government: "We are not Abolitionists; but it should not therefore be presumed that we abominate the Negro race. Adherence to the constitution of the country does not imply utter hatred to an unfortunate branch of the human family." However, after noting that Liberia was the second independent black republic, the first being Haiti, the paper went on to doubt the capacity of the Liberians for "continued national life." The reason given was that nature had given blacks "the worst color in its possession; the great majority of them have forbidding, facial ugliness; their bodily conformation is seldom symmetrical; deformity, lameness, blindness and deafness and the want of speech, mark them in a frightful number of cases; as a race, they must be allowed to have nothing near a decent measure of intellect; and to crown the catalogue, an intolerable effluvia exudes from their persons." This is not the writing of an editor willing to entertain thoughts of emancipation.

In October 1862, *The Pilot* replied to President Lincoln's Emancipation Proclamation of September. Once again the paper purported to judge the capacity of blacks. "Will they accept emancipation? Nineteen out of twenty of them will not, because they love their masters as dogs do, and servile plantation life is the life nature intended for them. It would be against the laws of nature for the happy slaves of the South to run into certain distress. No matter what emancipation decree may be published, the Southern slaves will either disobey them at once, or, if they accept them, they will, in a little time, regret their temerity, and slink back to their natural protectorate as suspended bodies oscillate to their center of gravity." According to *The Pilot*, the only hope for the salvation of the country lay in the Democratic Party: "Give it power, and everything will soon be reversed."

These two examples give an idea of the depth and virulence of opposition to emancipation among a segment of the population in the Northern states. Men such as Patrick Donahoe, editor of *The Pilot*, and others like him needed to be shown that African Americans would not "slink back" to slavery and that the black man would make a loyal, disciplined, and courageous soldier.

In January 1863, after the Emancipation Proclamation had been promulgated, Governor Andrew's and the abolitionists' wish to arm black men became a reality. Secretary of War Stanton authorized Governor Andrew to raise "such corps of infantry for the volunteer service as he may find convenient, such volunteers to be enlisted for three years or until sooner discharged, and may include persons of African descent, organized into separate corps."

Four days later, Andrew wrote to Francis G. Shaw in New York proposing that the command of a newly forming black regiment, the 54th Massachusetts Infantry Volunteers, go to his son, then serving as a captain with the 2nd Massachusetts Infantry. Andrew felt that young Shaw, then only twenty-five, had the proper qualifications to lead what he hoped would be "a model for all future colored regiments."

"I am desirous to have for its officers—particularly for its field officers—young men of military experience, of firm antislavery principles, ambitious, superior to a vulgar contempt for color, and having faith in the capacity of colored men for military service," wrote Andrew. "Such officers must necessarily be gentlemen of the highest tone and honor; and I shall look for them in those circles of educated antislavery society which, next to the colored race itself, have the greatest interest in this experiment." Robert Gould Shaw accepted the commission and arrived in Boston on 15 February.

In the 54th, "line-officers were commissioned . . . by commanders of regiments in the field, [after nomination] by tried friends of the movement, by the field-officers, and [from] those Governor Andrew personally desired to appoint," wrote Luis Emilio, the regimental historian and a captain in the unit. It was important to have men who were "tried friends of the movement" because the duty they faced was even more dangerous than usual active service. Besides the prejudice and scorn within the Union army, officers of African American regiments had to deal with a law passed by the Confederate Congress on 11 May 1863 threatening to execute or punish "every white person being a commissioned officer, or acting as such, who, during the present war shall command negroes or mulattoes in arms against the Confederate States." White officers of black units were considered "as inciting servile insurrection," a most heinous crime in the South. The black enlisted men faced the same sentence, with the alternative threat of being sold into slavery.

The selection of the officers for the 54th might have been easy, but there was greater difficulty procuring the enlisted men. On paper, an infantry regiment consisted of ten companies of one hundred men each. Boston supplied one company, New Bedford another, and the western part of the state a third, but because there were too few blacks of military age in Massachusetts, it became obvious to Governor Andrew that he would have to look outside the boundaries of Massachusetts for the remaining men. Secretary of War Stanton was not helpful; in the spring of 1863, when the 54th was being raised, no machinery existed in the War Department for dealing with black regiments. Stanton had no specific power in the first few months of 1863 to recruit the men, pay them bounties, select officers, or commission them. John Andrew, however, did have these powers.

When Andrew found that the federal government was not forthcoming in helping to recruit his African American regiment, he enlisted the aid of several prominent citizens to raise money and travel outside the state recruiting. George L. Stearns, a wealthy manufacturer and supporter of abolitionist John Brown, became chairman of a committee composed of such distinguished Massachusetts Republicans as John Murray Forbes, Amos A. Lawrence, William I. Bowditch, and Dr. LeBaron Russell, while Francis G. Shaw raised money for the regiment in New York City.

On a recruiting trip to Buffalo, Stearns stopped first in Rochester and enlisted Charles and Lewis Douglass, two of Frederick Douglass's sons. These were the first recruits in New York for the regiment, of which Douglass was extremely proud. Lewis Douglass became the regiment's first sergeant major, while Charles subsequently transferred to the 5th Massachusetts Cavalry and became first sergeant of Company I.

Governor Andrew's committee for recruiting black soldiers was made up of private citizens; therefore there could be no legal claim that Massachusetts was sending agents to other states and luring their men away. As Captain Luis Emilio wrote, "the delicacy of the situation, as well as its absurdity, lay in the fact that these other governors, though themselves refusing to enlist the negro, still claimed him, as soon as he manifested his intention to enlist elsewhere, as potentially part of their quota. Technically speaking, Andrew sent no Massachusetts recruiting officers outside the state; practically, Stearns' agents went everywhere through the Middle States and even penetrated beyond the Mississippi."

On 18 May 1863, in a ceremony of great solemnity and moment, the completed 54th paraded through Boston, received its battle flags and the National Color with appropriate remarks, and embarked for Hilton Head and the seat of war. Of the subsequent service of the 54th, not much need be said here. The regiment made a charge against Fort Wagner, near Charleston Harbor, that was poorly supported and poorly timed and was probably doomed from the start. Yet that gallant charge lives on in our imagination as a supreme example of courage and self-sacrifice.

A few days after the 54th had marched through the streets of Boston in May, the Adjutant General's Office of the War Department published General Order No. 143 establishing a bureau "for the record of all matters relating to the organization of colored troops." General Order No. 143 also established boards to "examine applicants for commissions to command colored troops" and set forth specifications for recruiting. No one was allowed to recruit unless passed by an examining board and authorized by the War Department. Even when passed by a board and allowed to recruit, commissions would be issued only "when the prescribed number of men is ready for muster into service."

The War Department also wanted to tighten up the recruiting of African Americans by state recruiters—in fact, to end that practice. Black soldiers would be accepted as companies until battalions and regiments were filled up, and then the regiments would be "numbered seriatim, in the order in which they are raised, the numbers to be determined by the Adjutant General. They will be designated '_____ Regiment of U.S. Colored Troops.'"

Major Charles W. Foster, assistant adjutant general, was appointed head of the Bureau of U.S. Colored Troops, headquartered in Washington. As Dudley Cornish wrote, "with the publication of this order, the whole movement to arm the Negro moved off its original amateurish, haphazard, and volunteer basis to a new footing of professional, organized, regularized activity under central control from Washington." After the establishment of the Bureau of Colored Troops, supposedly all black soldiers were mustered directly into federal service and led by officers who were commissioned volunteers, approved by the bureau in Washington. But there are always a few exceptions to any rule. The 5th Massachusetts Volunteer Cavalry is one.

In the first week of September 1863, Governor Andrew received a letter from Theophilus Parsons, professor of law, Dane School of Law, later renamed Harvard Law School. After reminding Andrew of his interest in the enlistment of black soldiers, Parsons wrote that he was "quite sure, on good grounds, that many influential persons would be glad to see a Massachusetts cavalry regiment of colored men." The professor went on to give his reasons for thinking that blacks would make good cavalrymen: "The negro is particularly suited for this service. . . . He loves horses and horses love him. And it is a generally recognized fact that he is bold, fierce and obstinate in all contests with the steed, while he has the common apprehension of lead and gunpowder; though he seems to be rapidly getting over this. And for scouting, obtaining intelligence and getting assistance from his brothers, and exerting a wholesome influence among them he would have an obvious and important advantage."

Professor Parsons did anticipate two closely linked problems with trying to raise a black cavalry regiment in Massachusetts. There were not enough African Americans in the state to fill up a regiment, "But you could easily bring them here from abroad. This would cost you money, but we think you would be willing to expend it and we are sure you would be sustained by your constituents." It is not clear what Professor Parsons meant by "abroad," although it seems unlikely that he was suggesting recruiting for the regiment in Africa or Europe. Probably Parsons was hoping that men could be brought from Canada or other states, wherever there was a substantial black minority. The related question was whether Massachusetts would receive credit on her quota (the number of troops to be raised per state as computed by the War Department) for the soldiers brought into the state by her bounty money.

On 5 September, Governor Andrew forwarded Parsons's letter to Secretary of War Stanton for his consideration. Andrew stated that he had stopped recruiting blacks "because the order of the War Department [General Order No. 143] seemed to afford an opportunity for colored men in other free states to volunteer for the defence of their country," and

Massachusetts had no the right to take soldiers from other states, "nor had I the right by our laws to pay bounties to these men unless they came here and enlisted here, in our regiments and were entitled to be credited as our soldiers." Andrew wrote that he believed he could raise a regiment of black cavalry if he was allowed to pay the men bounties, and be credited them on his state quota, and with the understanding "that we open no offices, and recruitment agencies in any other state but with the consent of the governor thereof." The governor also asked permission to appoint his own officers from Massachusetts regiments already in the field, so to obtain "brave, devoted and noble fellows, like who were selected for the 54th and 55th (infantry) volunteers."

On 10 September, Secretary Stanton wrote back that he was "entirely in favor of the measure." Stanton praised Andrew for having "settled the question of the colored man's fitness for infantry service" and expressed confidence that the Massachusetts governor would be equal to the task of showing that blacks would make good cavalrymen, "which is the only point of dispute remaining unsettled." Stanton was in agreement with Professor Parsons and Governor Andrew that the main recruiting difficulty lay in finding black men outside of Massachusetts, but he did not see this issue as "insurmountable." Stanton ended his letter by writing that he needed some time to think about the problem but would get back to Andrew "speedily."

The matter hung fire until the third week of November, when Governor Andrew wrote John Murray Forbes, then staying in Washington. Andrew had met with a "Dr. Ross of Canada" who was confident that he could raise five hundred black men in Canada. The governor responded that he could take about 250 to fill up the vacancies in the 54th and 55th but could accept no more men because no new organizations were authorized under the new quota. Andrew went on to suggest that Forbes approach Stanton on the subject of raising a regiment of African American cavalry, even a battalion: "Try him [Stanton] and see if he does not think it worthwhile to have this experiment tried of Colored Cavalry enough to accept four companies to be mustered in at the minimum one by one." Andrew urged Forbes to "press him hard . . . always remembering that all events we must muster in by companies . . . to be credited generally to this state, as an addition to this present [1863] quota of 15,120 men." Andrew thus hoped that by presenting Stanton with the fait accompli of having raised the men in Canada, or at least the strong assurance of having the men, Stanton would let him commission the regiment, pay the men bounties, and receive credit for some of Massachusetts's quota.

Forbes replied on 23 November 1863: "I came straight to Stanton, assumed official airs with the help of your envelope—and got admission! Mr. Stanton was very kind and fresh from his Sunday's visit and at once agreed to let you raise a battalion to grow into a regiment of cavalry. Col. Foster [of the Bureau of Colored Troops] was directed in my presence to put it into shape & I to help him."

In the same letter, Forbes suggested his son, William Hathaway Forbes, then a major in the 2nd Massachusetts Cavalry, and his son-in-law, Henry Sturgis Russell, lieutenant colonel of the same regiment (and a first cousin of Robert Gould Shaw), as possible officers in the new regiment. Forbes's letter ended on a note alarming to Governor Andrew: "N.B. I have seen Major Foster [Forbes had earlier referred to him as Colonel Foster] who is writing the order & has got the minimums all right—the officers to be nominated by you without the usual examination [there was an 'entrance exam' for men who desired to become officers of U.S. Colored Troops] but commissioned by the President!" Thus Andrew would not be able to claim this regiment as Massachusetts troops and would not receive credit on Massachusetts's quota.

The official order from the War Department was sent the same day as Forbes's letter, 23 November. Major C. W. Foster wrote that Andrew was "authorized to raise a battalion or regiment of cavalry to be composed of colored men and to be mustered into the service of the United States for three years or during the war." As Forbes's letter had said, "the prescribed number of commissioned officers will be appointed on your recommendation by the President of the United States." This was not what Andrew had asked for. What really galled him was the phrase, "To these troops no bounties will be paid."

Governor Andrew wasted no time in dispatching Brigadier General Richard A. Peirce, commander of the commonwealth's training camp, Camp Meigs, to carry his case to Secretary Stanton and the Adjutant General's Office. He also wrote Forbes, "It becomes absolutely necessary here that any colored men we get should contract towards our contingent under the present call, of which there must be no misunderstanding between the War Department and ourselves. . . . As I interpret the order it would make our proposed black cavalry only another regiment of U.S. Colored Troops. This we must never submit to."

Andrew chastised the government for not paying black soldiers the same as white but described it as a mistake of law. But to refuse to designate as state troops men raised by the state, paid bounties and transportation by the state, and officered by men from the state seemed to him "pure cussedness."

"We must raise and organize the colored volunteers just as we do white ones. . . . They must be state troops, volunteers according to the law and not U.S. Colored." The governor pointed to the precedent set by the 54th and 55th Infantry Regiments: "They are known on our books and rolls and orders only by their numbers and their arm of the service, and not by their color."

On 25 November, the governor sent a rather preemptory note to Secretary of War Stanton. Of "absolute importance" to Andrew was the fact that he could pay state bounties only to state troops, and "Major Foster sends me an order which is in effect to raise U.S. colored troops, but I can only pay Massachusetts Volunteers." The governor wanted the same kind of authorization that enabled him to raise the two black infantry regiments. "Please give me similar order to former one."

On 2 December 1863, the governor got his way, after a fashion. C. W. Foster sent the following order: "In consequence of your dispatch to the effect that the laws of Massachusetts will not permit the payment of bounties to volunteers unless their officers are commissioned by the Governor of the State, I am directed by the Secretary of War to say that so much of Department letter of the 23d ultimo as states that the officers of the colored cavalry regiment which you were therein authorized to raise would be appointed by the President is annulled, and the officers of said regiment may be appointed by you." This order did not explicitly state that the regiment would be designated state troops, but it did not need to. Governor Andrew had all the authorization he needed to start the 5th Massachusetts Cavalry Volunteers. Now all he had to do was find the men.

CHAPTER TWO

"That Dashing and Brilliant Arm of the Service"

Those qualities in the colored man which particularly fit him for a dragoon will be called out and disciplined, and we doubt not he will write his certificate of capacity with his sabre on the body of his former tyrant, the Virginia cavalier.
—BOSTON COMMONWEALTH, 18 DECEMBER 1863

ON 3 DECEMBER 1863, AN EDITORIAL APPEARED IN THE *BOSTON JOURNAL* newspaper. Under the title "The Elevation of a Race," the editor took stock of the situation for African Americans after almost three years of war. "The war has now burst the bonds of a portion of this race, and will yet complete the emancipation of all," the editor wrote. After noting that "this wonderful dispensation to a whole people" was accompanied by "many failures and much suffering," the *Journal* praised the "military opportunity" for blacks to serve their country. African Americans had proven themselves in battle at Port Hudson, Louisiana, and at Fort Wagner, South Carolina, and there was now a general willingness to enlist "the strongest force possible." The editor also estimated that since the promulgation of the Emancipation Proclamation, there were some fifty thousand "effective colored troops" already in the Union army and expressed the hope that one hundred thousand black troops would be enlisted by the time of the spring campaign of 1864. "The inestimable importance of such a force, not only insuring the extinction of the rebellion, but in vindicating and commending their own race in the eyes of the whole world, is apparent at a glance."

Two days later, on 5 December, a small article appeared on the front page of the *Boston Journal*, headlined "A Regiment of Colored Cavalry in Massachusetts." The article consisted of only two sentences: "Gov. Andrew received yesterday forenoon a telegram from the Secretary of War authorizing the recruitment of a regiment of colored cavalry in this state. This gives an opportunity for the enlistment of such troops by the towns and cities, and their incorporation into the quotas of those places." This brief item was carried in other Northern newspapers, notably the *New York Tribune*, which had one of the highest circulations in the country. The response to these small notices is a remarkable testimony to the importance of newspapers as a source of information in the nineteenth century. On 6 December, George W. Johnson of Utica, New York, wrote to "Sir[:] Oliver Warner," secretary of the Commonwealth of Massachusetts: "I see in the *Tribune* dated December the 5th that the Governor is authorized by the Secretary of War to recruit Colored Cavalry in Massachusetts. I wish to join the cavalry or the 54th regiment and will you inform me if you furnish Transportation Fee to me and others that wish to enlist as you did when that regiment was formed."

A. R. De Blair wrote to Governor Andrew from Detroit, Michigan, on 7 December: "I see by newspapers that you have been authorized by the Government to raise a regiment of colored cavalry, and Sir, I should like a recruiting Sergeant's Commission. I think that I can raise quite a number of men in this area and other western states for instance, they are raising a regiment of colored men in this state (Michigan) and they have agents in Kentucky, Virginia and Missouri." De Blair mentioned the "liberal bounties" being offered by cities and counties in Michigan: "By such means they [the regiments] are filling up fast." If authorized by the governor, De Blair promised to go to the states he had mentioned and also to Canada. He wrote that he had already recruited "some fifty men" for a Rhode Island regiment and assured Andrew that he would "go far on myself if you will send transportation."

Black men were not the only ones to see opportunity in the 5th Massachusetts Cavalry. The governor received a letter from a Captain C. H. Wayne of Green Castle, Indiana, dated 7 December 1863. "I see by the Eastern Papers that a Colored Regiment is to be raised in Massachusetts, for Cavalry," Wayne wrote. "Will you accept of a company from this state? If so I can raise one at the shortest notice, providing I have the selection of my lieutenants, as there are horsemen here, who have seen service and would make excellent officers." Wayne wrote that he had resigned his commission the previous May "on account of wounds received in action" but that he was recovered and fit for duty. Captain Wayne suggested that Governor Andrew consult, "for character and military qualifications," Colonel L. B. Stoughton and Lieutenant Colonel Albert Heath of the 100th Regiment, Indiana Volunteers (no address given); Colonel H. B. Read at Fort Wayne, Indiana; or "General Hurlburt's report of the Battle of Shiloh, Tenn. Also the files of recommendation for promotion at the Adjutant General's Office, Indianapolis. Ind." Governor Andrew was apparently not impressed by Captain Wayne's offer. Scrawled on the back of this letter, in John Andrew's hand, is the comment "I wd. [would] have nothing to do with this man. But it wd. be well for some col'd man to reconnoitre in his vicinity."

Other letters came to the Executive Rooms at the State House that first week of December, like the one from John Jones of Chicago offering to help recruit the men: "In connection with some able and influential colored men I am perfecting arrangements for recruiting our people which will doubtless be more successful than any yet adopted." Jones exerted subtle pressure by writing, "We believe that under existing circumstances this work can be effectually done only through colored men," and he noted that he had had the "honor of rendering some assistance" in raising the 54th and 55th Massachusetts Infantry Regiments. There is no paper trail indicating that the governor ever employed his services, although a few men from Illinois did serve in the regiment.

Besides offers to enlist or recruit, inquiries were sent about transportation and bounties. A Doctor G. H. Atwood wrote from Woodbury, Connecticut: "A colored man, a resident of this town aged about 30, having a wife and 2 children says he will enlist if he could join the cavalry. He desired to know what bounties he would receive and if his expenses from here to the rendezvous would be defrayed and by whom." The doctor was full of questions and full of patriotism. He, too, had learned from the papers that the governor was authorized to raise a regiment of African American cavalry. "Being desirous of encouraging all suitable colored persons to assist in putting down this Southern rebellion," Atwood wrote, "I most respectfully write you relative to the bounty each colored man who is accepted will receive, also where the candidate should present himself and when, and also if his necessary expenses would be paid and when and by whom and where and any other information pertinent to the matter in question." Doctor Atwood explained that such information would oblige "me and my friends who are anxious to secure the military aid of all colored citizens in conducting our war to a successful issue." The endorsement on the back of Governor Andrew's letter to Atwood reads, "The colored cavalry recruits at Camp Meigs, Readville (Depot at Dedham) on the Bost. & Prov. R.R. near Boston. Each volunteer receives $325 bounty or $50 bounty down and $20 per month, (from the state) as he may prefer." Regimental records show that of the three men who said they were from Connecticut, none were from Woodbury and all were in their twenties, so we do not know what happened to Dr. Atwood's prospective recruit.

As late as 23 December, when men had already started to enlist in the regiment, letters were written to the governor soliciting information or authority to recruit. One of the latter was received from Peter W. Downing, who wrote from Providence. "Please pardon me the liberty which your humble servant takes in addressing you the following," he wrote. "I ask for a letter of introduction to the Hon. E. M. Stanton, so as to secure me a pass as I propose to go South after contrabands for your cavalry." Peter Downing was the brother of George T. Downing, a prominent and affluent black patriot who owned a hotel in Newport. George Downing had helped in raising the 54th and 55th Massachusetts Infantry Regiments.

Another letter dated 23 December was from M. M. Cass of Watkins, New York, who signed himself "Chairman of Union County Committee." Cass introduced and recommended the bearer, "John D. Berry, a colored Gentleman." Cass wrote that he had known Berry for the last ten years and had always found him to be an "upright, honest man, a good citizen, a firm and devoted friend of the Administration and Country and a most intelligent advocate and champion of his unfortunate race." Cass wrote disparagingly of the leadership of New York's Democratic governor, Horatio Seymour. John Berry was "so well justified in refusing our Executive, he goes to your state to seek service. . . . It is quite unfortunate for the people of our state that such men have to leave it, in order to get respectfully into the service of their country." Mr. Cass described Berry as "of great personal strength and activity and as courageous as a Lyon" and expressed confidence

that with one hundred such men the Southern Confederacy would be anni-
hilated. Cass finished his letter with a last burst of patrio-religious fervor:
"May God and Governor Andrew speed all men, white and black who love
their race, their country, its institutions and laws well enough to be willing
to fight and if need be to die for them."

There was a John D. Berry in the regiment, a forty-two-year-old barber
who enlisted in Company C on New Year's Day, 1864, giving his residence
as Somerville, Massachusetts, not Watkins, New York. We cannot be sure
it was the same man, but it seems reasonable. John Berry must have been
motivated to say he was from Somerville by the lure of a town bounty. Men
were credited to towns (or to wards in cities like Boston). Newspapers were
full of advertisements for town bounties. Massachusetts adjutant general
William Schouler, in his *History of Massachusetts during the Civil War*, noted
the competition engendered by town bounties: "The offer of large bounties by the cities and towns brought to the surface a class of men known
as recruiting agents, who offered for a given sum to fill the quotas of the
cities and towns who employed them." Schouler also wrote of some of the
amounts paid by towns: "The bounties paid by the towns varied in amount,
ranging all the way from fifty dollars to five hundred, very few, however, were
paid more than two hundred dollars each."

It seems likely that men such as John D. Berry would have run across
recruiting agents who could have prevailed upon them to apply for a town
bounty. Ten of the regiment's twelve companies, more than eight hundred
men, gave their residence as Massachusetts; the 54th and 55th Infantry
Regiments had been hard-pressed to enlist two hundred men each from
the Bay State. Either African Americans in Massachusetts had suddenly
decided to go into the army en masse or some thousand men misstated
their place of residence. The records of the 5th Massachusetts Volunteer
Cavalry are thus complicated by the fact that only in two companies of
twelve (A and C) are the true hometowns of the men given and recorded
in the muster rolls.

Not to get too far ahead of our narrative chronologically, it would be
useful to note the frenzy of recruiting in the winter of 1863–1864, particularly for African Americans. A couple of examples from a newspaper published in New York, the *Weekly Anglo-African*, should illustrate this point.

From the front page of the 9 January 1864 edition:

Important to Colored Men!

GREAT INDUCEMENTS
TO VOLUNTEER!

Connecticut Pays Larger Bounties than any other State.

5000 MEN WANTED!

ENLIST IN CONN. REGTS AND
KEEP OUT OF THE DRAFT.

$300 Bounty, Cash in Hand
$30   "   Paid Yearly.

$13 PER MONTH AND
CLOTHING FURNISHED!

For further Information
address JAMES R. W. LEONARD, 25 Sullivan Street,

Or Dr. GEO. W. JOHNSON, 12 Sullivan Street, New York.

From the 16 January 1864 edition:

TO COLORED RECUITING OFFICERS AND AGENTS

I will give immediate employment to fifty smart, active men to obtain colored recruits in every State,

For both

INFANTRY AND CAVALRY REGIMENTS,

Giving the highest bounties.

To those, especially,

NOW HAVING SQUADS,

Or knowing where to get them, I will pay from

THREE TO FIVE DOLLARS MORE PER MAN

Than they are getting or can get elsewhere—

ALL CASH DOWN.

Transportation money advanced. Address or bring your men to Lieut. J. HIGHWARDEN, 163 West Washington Street, Indianapolis, Ind., or to Headquarters, 64 Sullivan Street, New York City, and get the cash.

A. J. Works

General Recruiting Officer for Conn't and Massach's.

Such advertisements also appeared in newspapers with national circulation, such as Horace Greeley's *New York Tribune*.

During the second week of December, Governor Andrew and Adjutant General Schouler sought to answer questions about the 5th Massachusetts Cavalry by putting a notice in the newspapers. This notice appeared in the *Boston Journal*, the *Boston Commonwealth*, *The Liberator*, and other papers beginning on 16 December. Under the headline "Commonwealth of Massachusetts" and the state seal appeared "General Order Number 44," which explained that "a regiment of Cavalry Volunteers, to be composed of men of color" was being recruited. "It is known as the Fifth Regiment of Massachusetts Cavalry Volunteers." Lieutenant Colonel Henry S. Russell of the 2nd Massachusetts Cavalry was designated the new regiment's colonel. State leaders could not be accused of misleading potential recruits in regards to federal inducements to enlist. The third paragraph of the notice read, "The U.S. pays no bounty to the recruit for this regiment under existing regulations, nor wages exceeding $10 dollars per month, including $3 for clothing." General Order No. 44 countered the federal government's racist economy with a bold statement: "But this Commonwealth offers precisely the same bounty offered to all other volunteers," $325 bounty paid in Massachusetts on mustering in or $50 down and $20 dollars monthly, "in addition to the pay hereafter received from the United States." The notice gave 21 School Street, Boston, as Colonel Russell's headquarters for recruiting and designated Camp Meigs, Readville, as the regimental rendezvous.

The advertisement also held a table of organization for a cavalry regiment in the volunteer army of the United States. Field-grade officers of the regiment consisted of a colonel, a lieutenant colonel, and three majors. Staff officers were the surgeon, his two assistants, the chaplain, and the regimental adjutant, regimental quartermaster, and regimental commissary of subsistence, the last three being extra lieutenants. Noncommissioned staff comprised a veterinary surgeon, a sergeant major, a regimental quartermaster sergeant, a regimental commissary sergeant, two hospital stewards, a saddler sergeant, and a chief bugler. A cavalry company (also known as a troop) had a captain, a first lieutenant, and a second lieutenant as officers. Noncommissioned staff on the company level consisted of a first sergeant, a quartermaster sergeant, a commissary sergeant, five sergeants, six corporals, two buglers, three farriers or blacksmiths, a saddler, and a wagoner. The minimum number of privates in a troop was sixty, the maximum seventy-eight. A cavalry regiment consisted of twelve companies lettered A through M, excluding the letter J. Two companies formed a squadron, two squadrons (four troops) a battalion, commanded by a major. Besides their bounty, as an incentive to enlist black men were offered the opportunity of becoming noncommissioned officers in a regiment of cavalry, a branch of service considered more prestigious than infantry.

General Order No. 44 also contained an appeal to patriotism in addition to the offer of bounty and the opportunity for advancement. The last paragraph of the notice is worth quoting entire, as it gives an accurate picture of the reasons for raising the 5th Massachusetts:

The governor regards with great satisfaction the progress made since the inauguration of the 54th Massachusetts Infantry Volunteers. And he confidently contemplates the accession from this Commonwealth to the National Army of a Cavalry Regiment of Colored Americans, which will illustrate their capacity for that dashing and brilliant arm of the military service. In this hour of hope for our common country and for themselves; at a time when they hold the destiny of their race in their own grasp; and when its certain emancipation from prejudice, as well as slavery, is in the hands of those now invited to unite in the final blow which will annihilate the rebel power, let no brave and strong man hesitate. One cannot exaggerate the call sounding in the ears of all men in whose veins flows the blood of Africa, and whose color the badge of slavery. It offers the opportunity of years crowded into an hour. It bids them come and be numbered with the peoples of every race, who by their own arms, have vindicated their right to all the blessings and all the powers of Liberty.

By order of His Excellency John A. Andrew, Governor and Commander-in-Chief. William Schouler, Adjutant General

Governor Andrew had long been hammering this last point home to all who would listen. In late November 1863, he had written to Lewis Hayden, then in Philadelphia recruiting for the 54th and 55th Infantry Regiments, that he did not want to profit from the blood and courage of black men, but that he did "rejoice in having been instrumental in giving them a chance to vindicate their manhood, and to strike a telling blow for their own race." Andrew noted that "every race" had fought for its liberty, and if the Confederacy fell without the aid of African Americans, "the result would leave the colored man a mere helot: the freedmen a poor, despised, subordinated body of human beings, neither strangers or citizens, but 'contrabands,' who had lost their masters but not found a country." In contrast, Andrew wrote, the day the African American donned Union blue "made him a power in the land. . . . No one can ever deny the rights of citizenship in a country to those who have helped create it or to save it."

Professor Theophilus Parsons also found opportunity to air his views about blacks in the military and the importance of that service. On 14

December, Parsons wrote to advise the governor that Captain Henry Bowditch of the 1st Massachusetts Cavalry, at home recovering from a wound, "would accept a Majority in the coloured cavalry." Parsons went on to assert that he had the enlistment of black troops "nearest at heart," but for reasons other than the obvious ones "which now exert much influence upon public opinion and have made this measure rather popular." We can infer the motivations that made black soldiers "popular": battlefield proof that African Americans were willing to fight and die for the republic, and, equally important, the knowledge that a black man would be credited to the quota of the town where he enlisted, thus allowing a white man who actually resided in the town to (possibly) escape the meat grinder.

Parsons wrote that he hoped blacks would be "lawfully retained in the army, after peace." Keeping African Americans in the army would have two benefits, according to Parsons: "It will help to discharge the duty of finding employment and subsistence for as many as we can of them" after their former "means of subsistence" was eliminated. Second, military service for African Americans would be "a most excellent method of counteracting by education the influence of the oppression which has made them, for ages, things and not men, without place, rights or law." Parsons recognized that there would be bitter opposition to retaining blacks in the military because of the "contempt and dislike of the negro common in the free states." The professor believed that such racism would be mitigated if a commission in the African American regiments "become[s] acceptable, if not sought, by men who were thorough gentlemen in character, position and connections. . . . The enlisted men would become better soldiers" because they would "respect and obey such men as they would not others," and the officers and gentlemen (gentlemen officers?) would give the regiments prestige. In Parsons's words, they would "raise their regiments in the common estimation towards their own level."

Henry Sturgis Russell certainly fit Theophilus Parsons's description of a man of position and connections. Indeed, when appointed colonel of the 5th Massachusetts Cavalry, Russell listed "gentleman" as his occupation. Governor Andrew probably concurred with Parsons as to the necessity of finding the right officers, particularly those of field grade.

"Now," Andrew wrote to Stanton on 22 August 1863, "my experience of two years and a half in raising regiments has taught me to begin a regiment with its Colonel. If I can get a good Col. and begin with him, I can always have a good regiment."

There was a flurry of letters in late November that passed between John Murray Forbes, who was in Washington, and Governor Andrew. Forbes first suggested Russell as an officer in the 5th Massachusetts Cavalry at that time: "If my son in law Lt. Col. Russell and my son [Major William H. Forbes] can be of any use in taking office in the new regiment I am sure you may call upon them. The 2nd [Massachusetts Cavalry] has more than its share of good officers and you will hear no grumbling from [Col. Charles Russell] Lowell if you use his officers to improve new regiments." Governor Andrew replied that he would prefer to separate "two young men [both were under thirty] so nearly related" so that they would not be "involved in the fortunes of the same regiment." The governor wrote that he had similarly separated the Hallowell brothers, Edward and Norwood, sending one to the 54th Massachusetts Infantry and the other to the 55th. Andrew agreed with Forbes that Russell would be the best man to command the regiment.

The press also approved the appointment of Henry S. Russell as colonel of the 5th Massachusetts Cavalry. The *Boston Commonwealth* carried an article titled "The Colored Cavalry Regiment" on 18 December 1863. After mentioning General Order No. 44 and paraphrasing its last paragraph, the paper noted that the regiment would be commanded by "Henry L. [*sic*] Russell, a near kinsman of Col. [Robert Gould] Shaw, [Russell and Shaw were first cousins] and an officer of much experience. Under his command those qualities in the colored man which particularly fit him for a dragoon will be called out and disciplined, and we doubt not he will write his certificate of capacity with his sabre on the body of his former tyrant, the Virginia cavalier."

As 1863 gave way to 1864, the 5th Massachusetts Cavalry was off to a good start. The regiment was widely advertised. Recruiting agents were active in the places where blacks fleeing slavery congregated. It had a prestigious and well-known officer in command. African Americans were offered cash bounties along with the possibility of advancement and increased responsibility. They also had the opportunity to prove their courage and refute prejudice, not to mention to wear a handsome uniform and swing a saber from the back of a galloping horse.

Although African Americans were welcomed into the Union army, once mustered in, a black man faced risks and challenges unique to his race: the prisoner of war problem and the issue of equal pay. In November 1863, Governor Andrew had written to Henry A. J. Williams, a black resident of the town of Oxford in Worcester County, Massachusetts. Andrew queried Williams as to how many men might be available for the then-proposed 5th Massachusetts Cavalry. On 7 December, Williams wrote back: "I would say to you that I have consulted with a number [of men] but they have not much desire to enlist in a cavalry reg't. as there being no other cavalry reg't. in service and there would be a great danger if it should happen to be there [*sic*] lot to be taken prisoners they would suffer the penalty of death and if they could go into infantry or artillery they would stand a better sight not to be taken." Williams went on to mention seven men who were willing to enlist and had been examined by a "Dr. Brown of Webster [Mass.] and one is going in the 57th Mass. Vols. Regt." All but one of the seven, according to Williams, were "mulattos or mixed." Williams promised the governor to do his best "to encourage the boys to enlist" but noted that "there are one or two more in town that think they would rather wait and see if the Gov't is not going to take some measures to protect the colored man if he got taken prisoner. You see it is a little discouraging for a colored man to enlist."

This concern was not without foundation. When Southerners saw an African American with a weapon, they saw an apocalyptic nightmare. As Dudley Cornish wrote in *The Sable Arm*, "for many Southerners it was psychologically impossible to see a black man bearing arms as anything but an incipient slave uprising complete with arson, murder, pillage and rapine." The Confederacy had reacted to the efforts of Union general David Hunter to recruit blacks in the middle months of 1862 with Confederate War Department General Order No. 60, dated 21 August 1862. The order declared that since Hunter had "organized and armed negro slaves for military service against their masters, citizens of this Confederacy," the Confederacy would adopt "such measures of retaliation as shall serve to prevent their repetition." Consequently, General Hunter was to be treated as an "outlaw," as was "any other commissioned officer employed in drilling, organizing or instructing slaves, with a view to their armed service in this war." The punishment for such a crime was contained in General Order No. 60. An outlawed officer was not to "be regarded as a prisoner of war, but held in close confinement for execution as a felon at such time and place as the President shall order."

The Confederate administration again threatened harsh reprisals against black troops and their officers after publication of the Emancipation Proclamation on 1 January 1863. Confederate president Jefferson Davis declared that officers captured commanding black troops would be turned over to the "several State authorities . . . that they may be dealt with in accordance with the laws of those States providing for the punishment of criminals engaged in exciting servile insurrection." In what was perhaps a show of faith in the Southern belief that African Americans were "peaceful and contented laborers in their sphere," Davis recommended that black enlisted men themselves be treated as "unwilling instruments in the commissions of these crimes," and he advised "their discharge and return to their homes on the proper and usual parole."

The Confederate Congress, however, was not inclined to let black prisoners be paroled. In joint session on 1 May 1863, that body passed a law charging President Davis "to cause full and ample retaliation to be made" for perceived breaches in the rules of civilized warfare. The fourth section of this act threatened commissioned officers who "command negroes or mulattoes in arms against the Confederate States, or who shall voluntarily aid negroes or mulattoes in any military enterprise, attack or conflict in such service, [they] shall be deemed as inciting servile insurrection and shall, if captured, be put to death." African American soldiers, if captured, were to "be delivered to the authorities of the State or States in which they shall be captured to be dealt with according to the present or future law of such State or States."

President Lincoln responded to these threats with his own proclamation dated 30 July 1863, stating that the duty of every government was to protect its citizens regardless of "class, color or condition" and that "to sell or enslave any captured person on account of his color, and no offense against the laws of war, is a relapse into barbarism and a crime against the civilization of the age." Lincoln pledged equal protection for all Union soldiers and stated, "If the enemy shall sell or enslave any one because of his color, the offence shall be punished by retaliation upon the enemy's prisoners in our hands."

Specifically, "for every soldier of the United States killed in violation of the laws of war, a Rebel soldier shall be executed, and for every one enslaved by the enemy or sold into slavery, a Rebel soldier shall be placed at hard labor on the public works, and continue at such labor until the other shall be released and receive the treatment due a prisoner of war."

There was one well-publicized instance of retaliation on prisoners of war. Confederates placed captured Union officers in the path of shells fired into Charleston, South Carolina, in 1864, although none of the prisoners of war was reportedly hurt. In retaliation, Major General Benjamin Butler put captured Confederate officers into a stockade under fire near his Dutch Gap Canal on the James River. Both sides soon desisted, for they recognized how dangerous retaliation could become.

Confederate authorities decided, as 1863 wore on, not to report black prisoners taken, thus avoiding having to exchange them for "superior" white men. Union officials were not fooled by this ploy and refused to exchange any prisoners until the Confederates agreed to exchange officer for officer and man for man, regardless of color. Eventually, after his promotion to lieutenant general and accession to overall command of all Union armies, Ulysses S. Grant decided not to exchange prisoners of war at all; he viewed the practice as helping the Confederate war effort.

The Union army had been accepting black units for almost a year in December 1863, when the 5th Massachusetts Cavalry was getting started. The officers and troopers of the regiment knew that they would probably be murdered if they fell into rebel hands. The prospect of being stripped of all possessions and condemned without exchange to the living hell of the prisoner of war camp at Andersonville, Georgia, was not much better. Confederate extremism had the effect of making black regiments fight harder. Knowing that they would not be treated as prisoners of war had a tendency to concentrate the minds of black soldiers, to motivate them. Black regiments seldom took prisoners; instead, they treated their Confederate opponents with a brutal equality. During the Union assault on the Petersburg works on 15 June 1864, for example, white soldiers noted in their diaries and letters home that they had observed (and intervened in some cases) instances of African American soldiers murdering Confederates after they had surrendered and "finishing off" wounded rebels.

Another issue that might have given pause to a potential recruit for the 5th Massachusetts Cavalry was that of equal pay. On 16 December 1863, the *Boston Evening Journal* printed a letter under the headline "The Pay of

Colored Soldiers." The writer, Theodore Tilton, who closed his letter "Yours for fair play," stated that he had received a letter from "a Massachusetts soldier in the 54th on Morris Island, South Carolina" noting that "a strange apprehension exists as to the matter of pay; and it pains us deeply."

Tilton pointed out that Governor Andrew had told the men of the 54th twice that they would be "subsisted, clothed, paid, and treated in all respects the same as other Massachusetts soldiers": the first time on their enlistment and the second time at the presentation of flags to the regiment prior to its departure from the state. Black soldiers in the Union army had been promised the thirteen dollars a month paid to white troops but had been actually offered only ten. The soldier of the 54th continued: "Three times have we been mustered in for pay. Twice have we swallowed the insult offered us by the United States paymaster, contenting ourselves with a simple refusal to acknowledge ourselves, in this matter, different from other Massachusetts soldiers. Once, in the face of insult and intimidation, such as no body of men and soldiers were subjected to before, we quietly refused, and continued to do our duty."

Now, upon learning that Governor Andrew had proposed a bill to the state legislature to have Massachusetts make up the deficit, Tilton wished to point out that "it is not enough that Massachusetts call them men; the Federal Government must call them so too." This feeling was echoed by Tilton's correspondent in the 54th: "Our men have concluded, if Congress does not recognize us as men on an equality with white soldiers, that they would scorn to take from your noble State the remaining three dollars that the Government does not pay them."

The controversy over equal pay for African American soldiers arose out of Secretary of War Stanton's query to the solicitor of the War Department, William Whiting, for a decision as to what pay "persons of African descent" should receive for military service. Whiting wrote that the only legal precedent that existed for paying blacks was the Militia Act of 17 July 1862. This act, as noted in chapter 1, limited pay (and precluded bounty) to African Americans on the basis of their being laborers. When blacks were mustered into the service as fighting men, Solicitor Whiting and Secretary of War Stanton concluded that those wages still held despite any notions of humanity, justice, or common sense to the contrary. Secretary Stanton replied in June 1863 to an inquiry by Governor Tod of Ohio about the pay issue by stating that "For additional pay or bounty colored troops must trust to state contributions and the justice of Congress at the next session."

In September 1863, Governor Andrew went to Washington for talks with President Lincoln and Secretaries Stanton, Seward, and Chase specifically about the issue of equal pay. Although it meant delay in redressing the wrong done to the 54th and 55th Massachusetts Infantry Regiments, the governor suggested that Lincoln require a ruling on the matter from the attorney general. To Stanton, Andrew suggested that the secretary urge Congress to take up the issue. His meetings in Washington initially encouraged Governor Andrew, but weeks wore on without action on the part of the government. Consequently, Andrew summoned the Massachusetts legislature to an extra session in November in which he proposed to make up the black soldiers' pay. The black Massachusetts regiments' continued refusal to accept unequal pay created an impasse, however. Secretary of War Stanton did request that Congress pass legislation equalizing pay in his annual message of 1863. "There seems to be inequality and injustice in this distinction," Stanton wrote, "and an amendment authorizing the pay and bounty as white troops receive, is recommended."

During the entire time the 5th Massachusetts Volunteer Cavalry was forming and training, African American troops were receiving pay as laborers. When the regiment left Massachusetts for Virginia in May 1864, the pay situation remained the same. It was not until 15 June 1864 that Congress passed legislation equalizing the pay of soldiers in the Union army. The very day the law went onto the books, the 5th Massachusetts Cavalry was earning that pay, going into action with the XVIII Army Corps assaulting the rebel works at Petersburg.

Still another issue that applied to all black units in the Civil War was commissioning officers of color. Governor Andrew had asked the secretary of war for permission to grant commissions to blacks as line officers, assistant surgeons, and chaplains. Andrew wrote that "power would not be used, except, possibly, for a few cases of plainly competent persons, recommended by the field officers, who shall be gentlemen and soldiers of the highest merit and influence." Stanton was extremely reluctant to have blacks commissioned, and no black men in the 5th Massachusetts Volunteer Cavalry became officers. The *Boston Traveller* had a couple of editorial comments on these matters on 18 January 1864: "Our colored soldiers in the 54th and 55th will not accept the additional pay offered them by Massachusetts. They say, and they say correctly, that they are soldiers of the United States, and claim to be treated like other members of an honorable service." The editor continued, in what we hope was an ironic vein, "Officers are wanted for colored regiments. Why not give commissions in those regiments to colored men? There are intelligent, educated, capable colored men enough in the United States to officer every regiment of the kind in the federal service. Conquer your prejudices, and the conquest of the enemy will be effected all the sooner, and with much less of cost to us poor whites who have to pay the taxes. Why object to the colored race being killed a little for the benefit of our pockets?"

Despite the possibility of getting "killed a little" and other drawbacks, men were enlisting in the new regiment even before Governor Andrew had received the final authorization from Secretary of War Stanton. The first volunteer to the 5th Massachusetts Cavalry was twenty-one-year old Horace M. Powers of Ludlow, Massachusetts, who enlisted on 28 November 1863. Powers would never rise above the rank of private, but he would serve with the regiment until it mustered out in November 1865.

All through December and into the new year, men joined Company A. Lieutenant Colonel Russell and the state authorities were not satisfied with recruiting the minimum (sixty men) for each company. Instead, eighty men or more were enlisted before a company could be paraded and sworn in before the U.S. Army mustering officer in order to gain the maximum credit for Massachusetts's federal quota and to give the regiment a better chance in the field.

All of the field-grade officers and many line officers of the regiment were veterans. They had seen what campaigning did to a regiment, whittling it down not only in battle but also by daily attrition to disease, detached duty, and desertion. A regiment was always shrinking. Even before it embarked for the "seat of war," before it heard a shot fired in anger, a regiment might well be reduced by dozens of men.

The men of Company A were from all points of the compass. The state that contributed the largest number of men was not Massachusetts, nor was it a state in the North. Eighteen men said they were from Maryland, followed by sixteen who said they came from Virginia. Massachusetts was third with thirteen. Eleven men each came from Pennsylvania and New

York. Five men were from Delaware, and three each came from Connecticut and Louisiana. Two men each came from Indiana, Kentucky, New Jersey, North Carolina, Ohio, and Tennessee. Men came to the 5th Massachusetts Cavalry from the North, like George W. Gool, twenty-eight, a blacksmith in St. Albans, Vermont, or William Gardner, thirty-seven, a seaman from St. Andrews, New Brunswick. Men came from the South, such as Samuel Laws and John E. Mezzeck. Mezzeck was a tailor in Charleston, South Carolina, before the war. He would desert the regiment on 30 April 1864, a week before the 5th Massachusetts Cavalry entrained for Virginia. Samuel Laws was thirty-eight years old, a laborer from Claiborne County, Mississippi. Laws would muster out as one of the two buglers in Company A.

Recruits also came from overseas. Henry L. Brison was a twenty-year-old sailor who gave Havre, France, as his residence. Brison died of disease on 25 March 1864 at the Camp Meigs Hospital, Readville, Massachusetts. John Doughty was twenty-seven, a seaman who gave Mexico as his residence. He also died of disease at Readville on 4 April 1864. Charles Stuart, twenty-nine, gave his residence as "Valparaiso, Chili." Perhaps the possibility of sudden and violent death increased Stuart's homesickness to an intolerable level, for he deserted on 15 June 1864, the day the regiment went into battle. John Frank gave the exotic Sandwich [Hawaiian] Islands as his home. Like Stuart, Doughty, and Brison, he was a sailor. Frank wore the chevrons of a corporal when he mustered out. There were several other men in Company A who gave "sailor" or "seaman" as their occupation, like Lewis F. Mills, eighteen, from Nantucket, or Aaron J. Moore from Baltimore, who had prior service in the U.S. Navy. Moore would make sergeant before dying of disease in the Corps D'Afrique Hospital, New Orleans, Louisiana, on 19 September 1865.

But by far the two occupations most mentioned were "laborer," which thirty-six recruits replied when asked what they did for a living, and "farmer," with fifteen out of eighty-three men. It should be noted that America in 1863 was still a predominantly agrarian nation. James McPherson in his *Battle Cry of Freedom* calculated that 47.8 percent of all white soldiers had left the plow to go into the army. "Laborer" can also be taken to mean "slave," since it is highly unlikely that having escaped slavery a person would give forced servitude as an occupation. Other occupations listed by recruits in Company A further reveal the economic status of black people in

American society at the time. Five of the men had been hostlers; presumably they would have found a home in the cavalry. Three of the men said they were waiters, one was a porter, two were teamsters (useful in the army), and three were blacksmiths, extremely useful in the cavalry, although none is listed as company farrier. Two men said they were coachmen before joining the 5th Massachusetts. There were two boatmen in Company A. There were two painters, two masons, and two bricklayers in the company. The men of the company could be sure of having their hair and beards well taken care of: there were six barbers listed.

Barbers were important in the black community; running a shop gave a person the independence and status of a proprietor, a businessman. Barbershops were more than just a place to get a haircut and a shave—they were clearinghouses of information and centers of political discussion. Not surprisingly, therefore, two positions of responsibility came to barbers in Company A. Samuel Carey, twenty-six, from Putnam, Ohio, became commissary sergeant, in charge of requisitioning, transportation, and preparation of food for the company. James W. Collins, a twenty-four-year-old from Ithaca, New York, was company quartermaster. As senior noncommissioned officer responsible for logistics, Collins had charge of everything in the company that was not meant to be eaten or used to harm the enemy (ordnance), including clothing, bedding, tents, accoutrements, horse furniture, and horses—everything from horseshoes to pen nibs. The first sergeant of Company A was not a barber, however: Irenas J. Ralmer was a twenty-two-year-old laborer from Hinsdale, New York.

As one can imagine, the recruitment of the men of the 5th Massachusetts Volunteer Cavalry occurred in various ways. Frank P. Stearns, the son of George Luther Stearns, Massachusetts manufacturer and abolitionist, wrote a book about his father that contains an interesting anecdote. In January and February 1863, Governor Andrew was attempting to recruit men for the 54th Massachusetts Infantry. By the end of February, "less than two companies had been recruited," Stearns wrote, "and the prospects of the Massachusetts Fifty-fourth did not look hopeful." George L. Stearns went to the governor and reportedly said, "If you will obtain funds from the Legislature for their transportation, I will recruit you a regiment among the black men of Ohio and the Canadian West." With Andrew's blessing, Stearns went to Buffalo, New York, where he straightaway "went to a colored barber to have his hair cut. He disclosed the object of his mission, and the barber promised to bring some of his friends together to discuss the matter that evening." The next night, Stearns was able to call a meeting "of the colored residents of Buffalo." Stearns spoke at the gathering, "urging the importance of the occasion, and the advantage it would be to their brethren in slavery and to the future of the negro race, if they were to become well drilled and practiced soldiers. 'When you have rifles in your hands,' he said, 'your freedom will be secure.'"

Another contact Stearns made in Buffalo was Samuel Wilkerson. According to Frank Stearns, Wilkerson came up to his father and said, "I hear you are recruiting colored regiments for Governor Andrew. Now I am a black Republican myself, and I wish you all success. I know everybody in Buffalo, and if I can be of any service to you at any time please inform me." Wilkerson was a valuable ally, instrumental in recruiting African Americans in Upstate New York for Massachusetts's two black infantry regiments. In early December 1863, Stearns turned to him again, telegraphing to Wilkerson, "Governor Andrew wants to raise a colored cavalry regiment. Will you aid him? He will pay fifty dollars bounty in hand and twenty dollars a month wages extra or three hundred twenty-five dollars bounty at the volunteer's election. [Signed] George L. Stearns, Major and A.A.G. [assistant adjutant general]." There were a number of men from upper New York State in the regiment, and we can assume that Wilkerson aided and encouraged their enlistment.

George Luther Stearns had long been a leader in recruiting African Americans, but he was not alone. Lewis Hayden, Charles Lenox Remond, and George and Peter Downing were prominent black patriots who were part of Massachusetts's unofficial recruiting agency. The competition for black recruits was keen in the winter of 1863. Hayden wrote Governor Andrew from Philadelphia, where he had met Robert Corson, (federal) "agent for the recruiting of colored regiments" in that city. Corson told Hayden that he was "anxious to do all he [could] to assist Mass. without officially committing himself" and that it would be best to "have men mustered in the regiments at Philad. PA and accredited to the state of Mass." Hayden continued, writing that Corson "further says that the regiments here are U.S. Colored Troops; that men can be mustered in these regts and credited to any County or District in Mass., stating on the Muster Roll, the Town or Ward from which they came, a copy of which can be forwarded to you to show to the Adjutant General of the state." Hayden was in favor of this plan, writing that transportation expenses would be saved and recruiting aided because "the men much prefer to go into Regiments here." Besides removing the "difficulties in regard to the taking of men out of the state," Hayden added weight to his proposal by writing that Corson had told him "that the same thing is done in New Jersey and one other state" and that he could make "immediate arrangements with a Gentleman here recommended to me by Mr. Corson [of course] to act as our Recruiting Agent."

Governor Andrew was not pleased with Lewis Hayden's proposal, and he outlined his objections in a letter written the next day. For those who question the efficiency of the U.S. Mail, note that in 1863 Hayden's letter to Governor Andrew traveled from Philadelphia to Boston in time for Andrew to send a reply the following day. The governor stated that there were "insurmountable objections to your suggestions in your letter of yesterday's date." This letter is interesting because it was dictated to a secretary, thus showing the governor's train of thought. Andrew had six specific problems with Hayden's plan. The placements of the objections show how they occurred to him. The governor noted first that a War Department order only allowed the states of Pennsylvania, Delaware, and New Jersey to receive credit for recruits raised in Philadelphia. Andrew wrote that he was "present when the Secretary ordered the inclusion of Delaware and New Jersey, with directions to enlist each Congressional District of those three states with recruits sent respectively to camp Wm. Penn," the training camp for black soldiers outside of Philadelphia.

Second, Andrew was concerned that Massachusetts's quota could not be credited conclusively. "Questions of fact would inevitably occur, even after we had paid bounties," and a "controversy would grow up between Governor Curtin [of Pennsylvania] and myself." As a third point, the governor wrote, "I have authority to raise a regiment of Colored Cavalry in Massachusetts. This affords an ample field for all colored men who wish to enlist under the banner of the Commonwealth." Andrew's fourth point is rather muddled. It seems to be an objection on moral grounds (unlike his practical and legalistic first and second points) to the idea of Massachusetts receiving credit for federal troops: "I do not wish [to] get other people's men away from them. To recruit men for a U.S. Colored regiment at Camp Wm. Penn would be doing so." In strong language, Andrew stated that such a policy "would be not only an error, but would have no possible chance for success if attempted."

The fifth paragraph or point has the ring of oft-repeated phrasing: "If any man desires to move to Massachusetts from Canada, or the South or Elsewhere, he has a right to come. If he offers himself as a volunteer fit for military service there is yet room, and he will be cordially received."

In his sixth and final point, the governor perhaps organized his argument better than in paragraph four. He wrote that he doubted much good could be done in Philadelphia. "They are recruiting colored men for the quota of that state; Pennsylvania wants her own inhabitants, I presume, and has a right to them." Perhaps in an attempt to soften his rejection of Hayden's plan, the governor added a postscript: "Do you wish to be considered a candidate for the sutlership of the Cavalry Regiment[?]—If so I would be glad to recommend you to the Colonel."

On 7 December 1863, Andrew wrote to Frank E. Howe, head of an organization known as the New England Soldiers' Relief Association, at 194 Broadway in New York City. This organization was run for the relief of soldiers from the New England states that passed through New York. Commonly known as the New England Rooms, a soldier could get a meal and a bed there, free medical care if wounded or ill, and money for transportation if needed. Governor Andrew wrote to Howe in his official capacity, however, as military agent for the state of Massachusetts in New York. "Lieut. Col. Howe as A.QM Gen'l [assistant quartermaster general] of Massachusetts," the letter read, "is authorized and requested to secure transportation to Camp Meigs at Readville Mass. for all recruits for Mass. Regiments who being in New York require Transportation thither to join their Regiments." Colonel Howe was ordered to give vouchers with the recruits' names and dates of departure "to the Rail Roads or boats furnishing the Transportation." Those vouchers were turned over to the officer in command of Camp Meigs, Brigadier General R. A. Peirce, for payment on a weekly basis. Andrew ordered Howe to "send any recruits whom he may personally know to be such and also any who may be presented by Fr's G. [Francis Gould] Shaw, Esq." This was the late Colonel Robert Gould Shaw's father, who had lent his time and money to recruiting African Americans for his son's regiment and the 55th Massachusetts Infantry. Now he had come to the aid of the commonwealth again.

The governor also wrote to Colonel Norwood Penrose Hallowell, who had been colonel of the 55th Massachusetts Infantry. Hallowell had resigned command of that regiment in November 1863 because of disability from a wound received at Antietam. He was now back home in Philadelphia. The governor's letter asked whether Hallowell was "at liberty, and could you do anything towards recruiting for a colored cavalry regiment, either in Canada, upon the Ohio or elsewhere?" Andrew assured the colonel that he would make "such arrangements as will be satisfactory to us both." There is no record of Hallowell's reply to Governor Andrew, but it is possible that he sent word to Boston with a friend or saw the governor himself. In any case, there is no record of him ever going to Canada or the Ohio River Valley to recruit blacks for the Bay State.

Hallowell had used his good offices already in Philadelphia for Massachusetts, as Lewis Hayden's answer to Governor Andrew's letter of 3 December shows. Hayden wrote on 12 December that he had not forgotten "the particulars certain which you gave me prior to leaving your office" but that upon arriving in Philadelphia, he "was introduced to Mr. Corson by Col. N. P. Hallowell who I suppose had made him acquainted with my mission." Hayden maintained that his work in Philadelphia had been successful, "for by going, and remaining there a few days we have been enabled to secure some of the best recruiting agents to be found, who are now in different parts of the country, earnestly at work." Hayden also gave Governor Andrew some interesting news that "a large number of freedmen are constantly coming into this state." Some of those freedmen claimed to "have been in the Rebel service both infantry and cavalry who claim to be well drilled . . . and anxious to join your cavalry."

It seems extremely unlikely that this last point was true. As it was impossible to check the stories of the freedmen, perhaps some of them "embroidered the truth" a little to enhance their candidacy. Hayden further reassured the governor that there would be "no conflict with state claims; as we have not received any but those who will immediately settle their families in Massachusetts" or those who had recently escaped from slavery and had "neither gained nor fixed upon a residence in this state." On the whole, Hayden was optimistic, believing that when the freedmen "do begin to go into the state of Massachusetts that the current will set in strongly." This despite the fact that "Rhode Island & Conn. are making exertions everywhere. . . . No state is permitted to escape them where the presence of an agent will be tolerated." Hayden noted in his letter that Connecticut, recruiting for its 29th Infantry Regiment, and Rhode Island, enlisting men for its Heavy Artillery Battery, "had secured the leading men of Canada in advance of us, by paying liberally for their services." Hayden wrote, "The Cavalry will offset their Battery finely." After telling the governor that he was still considering the sutlership of the regiment, Hayden concluded by writing that he was off to Cincinnati, Ohio, to continue the work.

Massachusetts received some unexpected help in raising the regiment from the U.S. government. The Provost Marshal's Department was responsible for registering men available for the draft throughout the Northern states. On 17 December, C. W. Foster, assistant adjutant general, U.S. Army, telegraphed the Massachusetts governor: "Do you desire to have colored recruits enlisted in the New England states by officers of Provost Marshal's Department sent to your cavalry reg't. at Readville?" There is some question about the legality of taking drafted men from other states to fill another state's quota of volunteers, but we can be assured that Governor Andrew would have accepted any men made available.

Adding his name to the list of recruiters for the regiment that included George L. Stearns, Lewis Hayden, Francis G. Shaw, N. P. Hallowell, and the Downing brothers was the prominent African American abolitionist Charles Lenox Remond. Remond wrote Governor Andrew from Salem, Massachusetts, on 18 December 1863: "Expecting to leave immediately in the purpose of recruiting for the 'Fifth Masstts Cavalry Regiment.' I have the honor to ask the favor of a letter from your Honor which will serve me as introduction or authority in prosecuting my mission. And by me to be used with such persons and on such occasions as I may deem prudent or of usefulness." Remond received his letter and was soon on his way to Washington, DC, to join George and Peter Downing.

By the third week of December 1863, Company A was nearing repletion, with over fifty recruits in camp. Frank Howe sent a note to the governor on 21 December illustrating how one of those recruits made his way to Readville: "The bearer, Richard Allen, is one of a squad of recruits from Pennsylvania for the cavalry regiment raising in Mass. He got separated from the rest and came to our rooms on Saturday night. He has been cared for by me—and I now send him to you, as per your instructions."

Howe noted in a postscript that he had heard that "Work's friend [Lewis Hayden] went that night to Ohio—this is well, for it will test the matter without committing you."

It is important to remember that competition for men in late 1863 and early 1864 had reached desperate levels, and the practice of recruiting men within one state to serve on the quota of another was common. It was also sharp practice and was frowned upon as illegal. Massachusetts's recruiters got in trouble particularly when they tried to enlist men in Washington, DC; Maryland; and Union-occupied Virginia. Henry Pearson has an anecdote about this in his biography of John A. Andrew. Interestingly, the public did not know the story until it was printed in the *Boston Herald* in 1878. According to Pearson, Secretary of War Stanton ordered "that every negro in the District of Columbia should be either in the commissary or the quartermaster's department, or else enlisted to help fill the quota of the District itself." When a Massachusetts recruiter tried to bring some blacks out of the city "to chop wood," the provost marshals turned them back. In January 1864, Charles Lenox Remond and George T. Downing sent a strong letter to *The Liberator* protesting the restrictions not only on their personal movements but also on the movements of freedmen "who find that Washington and all its connections with other points are closely watched by officers, whose unenviable business it is, to arrest all negroes not liable for draft here, who are willing, and on their way, to volunteer and fight in New England regiments."

Thomas Drew, another recruiter for the Bay State, wrote Governor Andrew from Alexandria, Virginia, across the Potomac from Washington, that there were "a large number of 'contrabands' in this city or vicinity, who would be glad to enlist in our 5th Regt. (Colored) Cavalry volunteers." But "the most rigid restrictions" kept them from doing so, as all the while "agents of Connecticut are permitted to recruit here *ad libitum* and not only this but to have the men actually mustered into the service here as Ct. volunteers by officers of the United States, and forwarded both by land and water to that state."

A "Capt. Herman of Ct." further informed Drew that "he had his authority direct from the Secretary of War," and without such authority the "New York and Southern line of steamers in this city" would not transport volunteers for Massachusetts. Apparently someone from the commonwealth had gotten on the nerves of the always touchy secretary of war, for Drew reported that Stanton "has repeatedly refused his sanction to Massachusetts citizens who have applied to him for similar authority." Why is it, Drew wrote to Governor Andrew, "that such discrimination should be made against our own state which was the first to enter upon the work of strengthening the Union armies with the strong arms of patriotic black men who were willing to do and die in the service of their country?"

This situation prompted Governor Andrew to appeal directly to President Lincoln. Andrew wrote in a tone of hurt surprise at the slight done to the Bay State. "I am at a loss to understand by what color of pretended authority people not charged with crime, and not being engaged in the military service, and being in the peace of the law are thus subjected to hardship and wrong," he wrote. Seeking to fool no one, Andrew appealed, "in behalf of the Commonwealth of Massachusetts, whose right to receive immigrants from all parts of the Union choosing to come here is thus unlawfully interfered with."

The governor asked rhetorically that Lincoln "suppose the passage of Germans or Irishmen seeking to buy land and make their homes in the great land states of the West was denied. . . . How long would such an embargo on population be endured by Illinois, and her neighboring states?" Andrew went on to remind the president that Massachusetts, "in addition to furnishing her quota of soldiers," made great economic contributions to the war. "How long then can we continue to furnish soldiers, help clothe the army, fabricate ships, machinery and munitions of war, subscribe to the National Loans, and furnish internal revenue if persons desiring to make their way hither are forbidden to come?"

This letter was delivered to the president by Mr. Oliver C. Gibbs, postmaster (a patronage position then) of Wareham, Massachusetts, whom Andrew employed as a messenger to Washington and also as an occasional recruiter of African American troops. In 1878, Gibbs told the *Boston Herald* that he had informed President Lincoln at the time that there were "hundreds of negroes anxious to go to Massachusetts" from Virginia. According to Gibbs, Lincoln was understandingly skeptical about the status of these freedmen as "immigrants," so he told Gibbs that written permission was needed from Francis H. Pierpoint, the governor of Union-controlled Virginia, before the men could be sent north. When this permission was obtained, Lincoln endorsed the letter on the back: "I understand from the within that there are a hundred colored men in Alexandria who desire to go to Massachusetts; with their own consent and the consent of Governor Pierpoint—Let Them Go." The president's order effectively removed any further hindrance to Massachusetts's recruiters in and around Washington, DC.

As 1863 gave way to 1864, men were coming into the 5th Massachusetts Cavalry at a steady pace. Their life was not perfect at Readville, however, as the following missive from John Murray Forbes attests. It was typical of Forbes that he would go directly to the top, suggesting the governor telegraph the secretary of war. Dated "Milton, Jan'y 2, '64," Forbes wrote to Andrew that "the weather is awful[,] a gale of wind and low thermo—& I am told from Russell that notwithstanding repeated applications he has only 40 overcoats for over 100 men." Forbes's son-in-law further reported that other outfits were in the same fix, "probably 1000 men are suffering at Readville—I renew to suggest for your consideration a telegram something like the following—Wishing you a happy new year." Under this note Forbes centered the word "Telegram" and then "E. M. Stanton—Secretary of War—Washington—Thermometer near zero with gale blowing—large numbers recruits suffering—Requisitions for overcoats unfilled a month—Some Quartermaster should be kept out of doors until remedy is provided." This situation was corrected in due time, without, it is believed, the intervention of the secretary of war being necessary.

The weather was perhaps a determining factor as well in the petition Henry S. Russell passed on to the governor on 6 January 1864. A group of 54th and 55th Infantry Regiment recruits wanted transfer to the 5th Massachusetts Cavalry. Certainly these men wished to prove themselves in the cavalry, but they were also stuck in the "Camp for Drafted Men" on Long Island in Boston Harbor in the middle of winter. By January, Russell had had stationery printed up with "Headquarters, Fifth Reg't. Mass. Cavalry, No. 21 School Street, (up stairs)," but he still signed himself "Lt. Col. 2nd Mass. Cavalry." The lieutenant colonel wrote that he would be glad to have the men, "especially as the 54th wants no more men." The petition read, "The undersigned volunteers having enlisted in the Glorious Fifty-Fourth and now in camp on Long Island without the knowledge of their formation of a cavalry regiment feel to regret it and do humbly pray" to be transferred to the 5th Massachusetts Cavalry.

The writer, a Joseph T. Wilson, noted, "The Fifty-Fourth has won for itself, state and race a name second to none as an Infantry regiment & we feel anxious to prove to the world that Massachusetts can send on the field of battle a colored regiment of cavalry second to none."

Twenty-eight signatures appear on the back of this petition. Unfortunately, none of the names is contained in any of the company records, and Governor Andrew's response has not been found. If these men soldiered for Massachusetts, it was not in the 5th Cavalry. It seems likely that the recruiting officers for the two infantry regiments would not let the men go.

Despite having to turn men away, the efforts of commonwealth recruiters were paying off. Company A was formally mustered into the service of the United States on 9 January 1864. Companies B, C, and D followed on the 29th of that month, so that by the end of January 1864 the 1st Battalion, 5th Massachusetts Volunteer Cavalry, had been enlisted. Professor Theophilus Parsons wrote to Governor Andrew on 20 January, telling him that he had visited his son, First Lieutenant Charles Chauncy Parsons, formerly of the 1st Massachusetts Cavalry, at Camp Meigs: "This morning Chauncy (acting commissary of recruits) told me that four companies of his regiment would be full tonight & that the colored recruits are now coming rapidly in. . . . Chauncy is delighted with the men and is firm in the faith that the 5th Cavalry will be your crack regiment."

When a recruit arrived at the Camp Meigs depot in Readville, Massachusetts, he was about nine miles south of Boston's heart on the main north–south railroad into the city and not far from the Boston–Providence road, one of the main highways into Boston. The camp was a level plain consisting of about 125 acres laid out along the Neponset River, which was used for drinking water for men and animals, including Sprague Pond, used for bathing and washing clothes. Camp soil was spongy and thus much given to mud most of the winter and spring. The camp center, bisected by the railroad, was the parade ground. Barracks were built at the east and west ends, about fifty buildings, each housing one hundred men, or a company. Behind each barrack stood the company cookhouse. Behind that was company headquarters, where the company's commissioned officers lived and where they had offices. In addition to each company's barracks, headquarters, and cookhouse, Camp Meigs had a hospital, a pesthouse for quarantining those with infectious diseases like smallpox, a mortuary or dead house, stables for a thousand horses, a prison, a chapel, guardhouses, storehouses, an armory, various sutlers' stores, and the post commandant's quarters. In all there were an estimated two hundred structures spread out over the landscape; Camp Meigs was a busy place. Adjutant General William Schouler reported that on 1 January 1864, 2,270 men were at the camp.

The raw recruit would have been led away from the depot into the human anthill that was the camp. The first order of business was a visit to the regimental barber for a military haircut, known as a "fighting cut" in the Civil War army. Then the recruit would bathe (or not, if it was winter) and receive his uniform items, including that famous belt buckle with "U.S." stamped on it. The recruit's civilian clothes were packed into a barrel and stored (or burned if they were in poor shape). Once in uniform, the new man was assigned to a squad and subjected to the tender mercies of a corporal or sergeant. The recruit would (one hoped) quickly learn that there was a correct way to stand, to turn, and to get from one place to another and that at practically every waking moment of his day someone would have something for him to do. Those who had joined the cavalry thinking they would be riding instead of walking, and thus have an easy time, were quickly disabused of that notion. The "school of the soldier" began first, with lesson one being the position of attention, followed by lesson two, how to march.

CHAPTER THREE

"Officers of the Highest Character and Best Experience"

I went before some U.S. officer and was probably mustered out and in again for
I left the regiment there and started North. On some accounts I regretted leaving
the Fifty-Fifth, but I was not in a condition to do marching and the opportunity
to have a horse and to be with Henry was too good a one to be lost.
—NOTE OF CAPTAIN CHARLES P. BOWDITCH IN
"WAR LETTERS OF CHARLES P. BOWDITCH," *PROCEEDINGS*
OF THE MASSACHUSETTS HISTORICAL SOCIETY 57 (1923–1924)

GOVERNOR ANDREW WANTED HIS BLACK CAVALRY TO BE A "CRACK" REGI-
ment to prove that the African American was suited to the most elite branch
of the service. Andrew had fought for and won the right to pay the black
troopers bounties and to enlist them as Massachusetts volunteers, not U.S.
Colored Troops. The governor had also held out for the right to appoint his
own officers. John Andrew was conscious of the opportunity the regiment
presented. The 5th Massachusetts Volunteer Cavalry was Andrew's reaf-
firmation, in the name of the Bay State, of the high ideals of the Radical
Republicans during the Civil War: commitment to the abolition of slavery,
to the advancement of black Americans, and to a new birth of freedom. The
5th Massachusetts Cavalry also represented commitment to the ideal of the
citizen soldier and the patriotic volunteer, willing not only to answer his
country's call but also—without draft, bounty, or coercion of any kind—to
make the ultimate sacrifice to preserve the Union.

The selection of regimental officers was possibly the most difficult aspect of Governor Andrew's job, particularly when it came to picking officers for Massachusetts's three black regiments. Thomas Wentworth Higginson, author, Unitarian minister, abolitionist, and commander of African American troops, had this comment on the task facing the governor: "No one now can appreciate how difficult it was, after a prolonged period of peace, to look around upon the community and say of this man or that 'He would make a good military officer.'" No man could feel humbler about this process of selection than Governor Andrew. Higginson continued, quoting Andrew, "He said once, 'It seems very absurd that I, who am a man of peace and always hated soldiering, should be the man to choose these officers; but Providence has put this duty upon me, and I shall do it as best I can.'" Andrew paid particular attention, in the selection of officers for the 5th Massachusetts Cavalry, to choose men who represented the ideals of courage, equality, and justice; who understood and lived the code of duty, honor, and loyalty; and who, furthermore, had been tried in battle. The governor reached out to men of education, experience, and background, to men of the oldest and most distinguished families in the Old Bay State. These were men whose ancestors had been part of the Great Migration of the 1630s, whose forebears had stood on the Lexington Green on that April morning, who had waited for the command to fire while the lines of British regulars marched up Breed's Hill. In the War of the Rebellion, these were men who had put aside a life of comfort and privilege and volunteered to serve their country. Such a man was Henry Sturgis Russell. Known from childhood as "Harry," Russell was from the best and oldest families of New England on both sides.

Harry Russell's acceptance of the colonelcy of the 5th Massachusetts Volunteer Cavalry must have gratified Governor Andrew. Russell epitomized the Civil War volunteer officer. He had responded with alacrity to his country's call, giving up home, family, and career to enter the service. He was appointed second lieutenant in April 1861 and had marched in review with the 2nd Massachusetts Infantry up State Street in Boston on the Fourth of July 1861, with band playing and flags and hopes held high. Colonel Russell had learned, like other volunteers who enlisted during the first flush of enthusiasm for the war, that there was more to army life than high ideals and handsome uniforms. Some of those patriotic volunteers had been killed or maimed; some had died of disease or had resigned. Some had "skedaddled," while others had taken refuge in the amber glow of liquid courage. Russell had not run away, nor had he taken to drink. Harry Russell had lived and learned; he had endured. Through all weathers, captivity, battle, the monotony of drill and winter quarters, and the criminal wastefulness of general officers, he had not given up. He had endured the loss of men he had known since boyhood: classmates, fellow officers, friends, and relatives. In surviving, Russell had proven himself a good soldier: competent, respected, earnest, loyal, and tenacious, with a self-deprecating humor that carried him through the most difficult experiences. As 1863 drew to a close, Harry Russell had few illusions about the glory of war. Yet he continued to serve.

Harry Russell had paid his dues on the drill field. He had begun with the 2nd Massachusetts Infantry Volunteers, the "Gordon Regiment," named after its first colonel, U.S. Military Academy graduate and Mexican War veteran George Henry Gordon. The 2nd Massachusetts Infantry was considered one of the best-trained volunteer regiments in the Union army. Russell had then transferred, as lieutenant colonel, to the 2nd Massachusetts Cavalry. While true that he had never led cavalry in the field, the recruiting, organizing, and drilling of a regiment of cavalry gave Russell invaluable experience. In almost two years as an infantry lieutenant and then captain commanding an infantry company, Russell had learned leadership, one of the most difficult tasks of the volunteer officer: to give and take orders, to inspire respect without undue familiarity, to discipline without threats or screaming. What's more, in the crucible that was Civil War combat, Harry Russell had learned to lead by example and to never show fear. The men called it "coolness under fire" and would not follow an officer who did not have it. Russell had earned the respect of his men and had become competent through the hard school of experience.

Harry Russell had learned the habit of command and the mechanics of leadership: how to move men, how to set up camp, how to post guards, and how to behave under fire. He had also learned how to account for everything and how to fill out the forms necessary to get his men paid, clothed, and armed, or to get a pension to their family if they died in the service of their country. Courage in battle was a necessary part of every officer's makeup. As important as individual gallantry, however, was taking care of one's men, paying attention to the myriad details that kept a regiment functioning smoothly.

The premise, rather commonplace today, that good order and discipline are essential to combat effectiveness had to be learned and relearned by Civil War volunteers. Colonel Thomas W. Higginson put this more poetically in an article in the 1864 *Atlantic Monthly* titled "Regular and Volunteer Officers": "It is hard to appreciate, without the actual experience, how much of military life is a matter of mere detail. The maiden at home fancies her lover charging at the head of his company, when in reality he is at that precise moment endeavoring to convince his company cooks that salt-junk needs five hours' boiling or is anxiously deciding which pair of worn-out trousers shall be ejected from a drummer-boy's knapsack." As far as courage was concerned, Higginson wrote that "men are naturally brave, and when the crisis comes, almost all men will fight well if well commanded." Further on in the same piece, Higginson was more emphatic. "Courage is cheap," he wrote. "The main duty of an officer is to take good care of his men, so that every one of them shall be ready, at a moment's notice, for any reasonable demand. A soldier's life usually implies weeks and months of waiting, and then one glorious hour; and if the interval of leisure has been wasted, there is nothing but a wasted heroism at the end, and perhaps not even that." Besides being an experienced and patriotic volunteer officer Colonel Russell was also of the proper social background and education to lend prestige to a regiment of African American cavalry. A Harvard graduate from one of the first families of the Old Bay State, Russell was a gentleman "of the highest tone and honor," to quote Governor Andrew. Russell may not have been active politically or even thought that much about politics, but he was certainly a Republican, if only by association. His parents; his parents' friends and acquaintances; his father-in-law, John Murray Forbes; and his classmates and fellow officers all believed that the Republican Party would—must—save the Union.

A Republican by association, Russell was also antislavery: again, at least by association. In *Sons of the Puritans*, John T. Morse Jr. drew the distinction between abolitionist and antislavery principles rather neatly. "The Shaw family had long been ultra-Abolitionist," Morse wrote. Harry's father, while "more moderate, was yet decidedly antislavery. Colonel Russell shared his father's views, insisting always that the war was for the Union, but welcoming the disappearance of slavery as a happy result."

Does this mean that Harry Russell was less than committed to the social revolutions of emancipation and to African Americans serving in the army, that perhaps Russell sought to satisfy his ego with the silver eagles of a full colonel? On the contrary, Harry Russell was not a conceited or self-centered man. In 1862, Russell had passed up the offer of a more glamorous (and safer) staff job against the express wishes of his father, choosing instead to stay with his infantry company. At the Battle of Cedar Mountain, he was captured while giving medical attention to a wounded friend—not the actions of a man interested only in himself. There were certainly plenty of opportunities for promotion given the formation of new regiments and the vacancies that came from active campaigning. Russell might have remained with the 2nd Massachusetts Cavalry. Morse, in *Sons of the Puritans*, confirms this situation, describing Lieutenant Colonel Russell's decision to accept command of the 5th Massachusetts Cavalry: "He was loath to leave his comrades in the Second Cavalry; the advancement in rank was inconsiderable; the command of colored troops was then little desired. The inducement, however, was characteristic. Between Russell and his cousin, Robert G. Shaw [Harvard], '60, there had existed since childhood a close, even romantic friendship. Shaw's death at the head of his colored troops at Fort Wagner had then lately occurred; and now Russell, taking the offered colonelcy, quietly said, 'Bob would have liked me to do it,' and thus simply settled the matter."

Morse's anecdote is revealing, although he does not tell us to whom Russell made his rather poignant statement. Russell did not mention his late cousin when he wrote Governor Andrew about the colonelcy of the regiment. Though Shaw's name appeared in almost every letter of his that survives from 1861 and 1862, Russell apparently never recorded his thoughts about his cousin and friend.

Instead, we must turn to another colonel of an African American regiment, Norwood P. Hallowell, to try and understand how Shaw's death affected Russell. Hallowell paid a particularly moving tribute to Colonel Shaw in a paper read to the Military Historical Society of Massachusetts in 1892. "I have always thought that in the great war with the slave power the figure that stands out in boldest relief is that of Colonel Shaw," Hallowell wrote. "There were many others as brave and devoted as he,—the humblest private who sleeps in yonder cemetery or fills an unknown grave in the South is as much entitled to our gratitude,—but to no others was given an equal opportunity. By the earnestness of his convictions, the unselfishness of his character, his championship of an enslaved race, and the manner of his death, all the conditions are given to make Shaw the best historical exponent of the underlying cause, the real meaning of the war." Hallowell saw Shaw as "the fair type of all that was brave, generous, beautiful, and all that was best worth fighting for in the war of the Slaveholders' Rebellion."

We can only guess what Harry Russell's thoughts were when he set out to train a regiment of black cavalry in the winter and spring of 1863–1864. This was Russell's third spring at Readville, drilling recruits in the mud, sleet, and raw wind of New England. We can only wonder whether Harry recalled other days, other men's voices and faces, as the troopers of the 5th Cavalry slogged through the dismounted drill while noncoms and junior officers shouted commands.

Colonel Henry Sturgis Russell, then, was the complete officer: he had the qualities that the other officers of the regiment sought to emulate. He was a patriotic volunteer officer with cavalry experience. He had been tried in battle. His education and breeding were of the best. He was a Republican with antislavery principles willing to lead black troops. Keep in mind that the 5th Massachusetts Cavalry was a state regiment, and as such the governor had appointive power. Governor Andrew, as a committed abolitionist, had an obvious desire to appoint "tried friends of the movement," as he had written to Francis G. Shaw. Colonel Russell, by contrast, felt that military experience, preferably cavalry experience, should take precedence over a declared warmth and sympathy for a downtrodden race. The result, inevitably, was compromise. If an officer candidate lacked cavalry experience, did he have any military experience at all? If never in uniform, was the prospective officer a committed abolitionist or connected in some way to the Republican Party? Was he a gentleman; had he gone to Harvard? If the candidate was no particular friend of the black race, was he an efficient and tested soldier—a veteran? One final, perhaps deciding factor was availability. In the case of Lieutenant Colonel Russell of the 2nd Cavalry, he did not have to be sent for from Virginia or from out west, begged from his commanding officer, or requested through the War Department. This mattered a great deal, for a regiment had to begin with its colonel. If the 5th Massachusetts

Volunteer Cavalry was to be recruited, organized, and trained in time for the 1864 spring offensive, there was not a moment to be lost. Russell's energy and leadership, coupled with his presence in Boston, got the regiment off the ground. It was Russell who requested the detachment of promising noncommissioned and junior officers from other regiments. It was Russell who interviewed the men sent to him by Governor Andrew, as well as the men who climbed the stairs to his office on School Street in Boston or later appeared at Camp Meigs, south of the city.

Factors like availability, experience, and social class were important in choosing officers for the regiment. We also gain a clearer understanding of the remarkable connectedness of the nineteenth century. The people you knew well enough to sponsor or recommend you were as important as, and sometimes more important than, your experience, education, or merit. In the twentieth century we became used to military organizations without regional identity filled with draftees from all over the country. This arrangement has been seized upon as a sign of strength: "E pluribus unum" in practice as well as rhetoric. Indeed, diversity has become a film cliché of the Second World War: all units had to have a hillbilly, a shy intellectual, a steady older man, an immigrant, and a tough city kid. Somebody always had to be from Brooklyn. The 5th Massachusetts Cavalry was certainly diverse, a mixture of black and white, social backgrounds, and professions, from illiterate freedman to Boston Brahmin. But the nineteenth-century world was a much smaller place than the United States today in that personal relationships had greater value. Insulating layers of bureaucracy did not exist, nor was there an overzealous media to hound those in public life, seeing malfeasance and influence peddling in every public act. One's family and education were important, but so was the basic reciprocal relationship between petitioners and petitioned. People wrote directly to a governor, the secretary of war, or the president of the United States, and they did not receive a form letter signed by a secretary in reply. People stopped in to see the state's chief executive, expecting and usually gaining admission by uttering a name, brandishing a letter, or sending in one's card. This was how John Murray Forbes had gotten in to see Secretary of War Stanton and secured authorization for the regiment in the first place. All of the patriotic African American recruiters for Massachusetts—Lewis Hayden, Peter and George Downing, John Rock, Charles Lenox Remond—were authorized by and corresponded directly with Governor Andrew. Their work was too important and too risky to be trusted to a committee or a faceless bureaucracy.

Consider also how Harry Russell became colonel of the 5th Massachusetts Cavalry. Russell had heard about the regiment from his father-in-law, John M. Forbes, who had written Russell from Washington, DC. Russell wrote Governor Andrew on 27 November 1863 informing Andrew that Forbes had suggested Russell as "possibly" willing "to have the colored cavalry." Russell felt no need to be reminded to the governor or to present his credentials. He also did not bother to ask whether Andrew had received final authorization for the regiment from the War Department, since Forbes undoubtedly had told him it was a "done deal." Russell "took the liberty of saying to [Andrew] that I should consider it an honor to have the command offered to me, which I should accept with pleasure."

Three days later, on 30 November, Colonel Charles R. Lowell Jr., Russell's commanding officer, wrote to Governor Andrew's military secretary, Albert Browne. Lowell was well acquainted with affairs in Massachusetts, despite the 2nd Massachusetts Cavalry being stationed in Vienna, Virginia.

Colonel Lowell supposed "that the Governor's Black Cavalry Regiment has now gone so far that he is beginning to look about for a Colonel." Lowell wrote to recommend "officers who would, I believe accept the command if offered—and would, I am sure, fill it well if accepted." Colonel Lowell was apparently so desirous of success for the African American regiment that he did not mind losing some of his best officers. Lowell mentioned three individuals. Harry Russell was recommended first: "I do not speak of Lt. Col. Russell for he is well known to the Governor; and if he would make the change, is naturally the first officer for the Governor to select and for me to recommend but you know my opinion of him."

Lowell's next recommendations are interesting because he gave his opinion on some of the qualities that made a good officer. John Murray Forbes's son, William Hathaway Forbes, was the 2nd Massachusetts Cavalry's junior major. Forbes had begun his military service as a second lieutenant in the 1st Massachusetts Cavalry, appointed in December 1861. Like the 2nd and 20th Massachusetts Infantry Regiments, the 1st Massachusetts Cavalry was largely officered by young Bay State gentlemen. Indeed, several of Harry Russell's fellow officers in the 2nd Massachusetts Infantry, Henry Lee Higginson and Caspar Crowninshield, for example, had transferred with promotion to the 1st Cavalry. Lowell considered Forbes "in every way qualified for the colonelcy of your Regiment." Forbes was more than "sufficiently familiar with the professional duties," Lowell wrote; he also possessed "the tact, the judgment and the strength of character, which in such an undertaking are more important." Colonel Lowell was not one to bemoan the vicissitudes of army life and saw the same quality in Forbes: "He is a hard worker, not merely when work is evidently telling, but also when work may or may not be of use. I never know him to grumble over wasted work—this is very important in organizing a crack regiment." The third officer Lowell recommended was Captain Francis Washburn. His colonel felt "sure that the Governor would like him." According to Lowell, Washburn was a "very good officer . . . cautious in affairs, apparently cold in temperament but really with a deep enthusiasm in his character which would tell in anything he took hold of heartily. He has for some time taken much interest in the Black Movement." Unfortunately for the 5th Cavalry, neither Forbes nor Washburn served with the regiment. W. H. Forbes, it will be recalled, was not commissioned into the regiment because of the governor's concern for the fortunes of two officers "so nearly related" as brothers-in-law Forbes and Russell were. Forbes served out the war with the 2nd Massachusetts Cavalry, rising to lieutenant colonel. Captain Washburn transferred, as lieutenant colonel, to the 4th Massachusetts Cavalry, which was organized around the same time as the 5th Massachusetts. He was promoted to colonel of the regiment in February 1865. Francis Washburn was mortally wounded and brevetted brigadier general of volunteers for gallantry in action at the Battle of High Bridge, Virginia, 6 April 1865.

It was Governor Andrew who chose the first man commissioned into the regiment after Harry Russell. Instead of a man of war, Andrew chose to appoint a man of God. From 5 to 10 December 1863, Andrew received five recommendations for the Reverend George Bourne Farnsworth, Harvard, 1847. Under the printed heading "Assessor's Office, United States Internal Revenue, Third District, Mass.," James Ritchie wrote the governor that "this will be handed you by Mr. Geo. B. Farnsworth of Roxbury a gentleman of property & character who feels like offering his services to the country in the capacity of Captain of Cavalry in the new colored regiment, for raising which you have just received authority from the War Department." Ritchie, who was related to Harrison Ritchie on the governor's staff, believed Farnsworth "well fitted to be an aid in this new effort" because of his "well known energy and enterprise." Ritchie vowed to "esteem it a favor if you will give [Farnsworth] a hearing and accept his services." Further down on the same page, dated "Roxbury, Dec. 5, 1863," is another message to Governor Andrew explaining that the bearer, Mr. Farnsworth, "desires to obtain a Commission in the new Regiment about to be raised in this commonwealth." The writer, a J. M. Gastin, in less than specific praise noted that he had "been acquainted with Mr. Farnsworth for some time and regard[ed] him as a gentleman of energy and ability and I feel confident that he would faithfully devote all his energy to the discharge of the duties of any office to which he may [be] appointed."

These recommendations show Farnsworth with a reputation for being a "gentleman" and in possession of a certain amount of "energy." He also knew two fairly powerful (tax assessors make bad enemies) political appointees. We assume that Gastin was associated with Ritchie because his note appears under the latter's.

Farnsworth had other, bigger guns in his arsenal, however. Theodore Otis, from one of the oldest and most distinguished families in Massachusetts, "took great pleasure in writing" Governor Andrew on 5 December. Otis bore "testimony to the excellent character and unqualified earnestness and loyalty of the bearer Mr. Geo. B. Farnsworth, who is a gentleman, thoroughly educated, of high principle & patriotic in the fullest sense." Farnsworth, wrote Otis, was "desirous of serving the country in some capacity suited to his position in society and his abilities" and therefore thought a captain's bars not beneath him. Otis thought Farnsworth suitable because he was "deeply interested for this class of our countrymen [African-Americans], has good capacity and abundant means."

On 7 December, Wendell Phillips, one of the most famous abolitionists of the nineteenth century, wrote to the governor's military secretary: "Dear Browne: my friend Geo. B. Farnsworth who sends you this, has noticed the report of the papers that the Governor is about to raise a colored Regiment of Cavalry—he wishes to inquire as to its truth & whence commissions for it are issued." Phillips felt that Farnsworth, "by hereditary right as well as personal feeling," was a person "to be reckoned with [in] such a movement & his presence in any regiment would give it strength and secure the trust of those who have long known him."

Dr. Henry Ingersoll Bowditch, long a friend of the abolition movement, also believed in Farnsworth's fitness as a prospective officer. Dr. Bowditch was the uncle of Captain Charles P. and Major Henry P. Bowditch, brothers who served in the regiment. The Bowditches were a "first family" of Massachusetts, settling originally in Essex County in the 1630s. Dr. Bowditch wrote Governor Andrew on 10 December 1863, "Rev. Mr. G. B. Farnsworth desires a letter of introduction from me to you. He would like to have a commission in the African Cavalry Regiment. I have known him five years. He is an educated honourable man, one who was early taught by example to claim justice for the black man." On the back of these letters, which were bundled together and pasted into a file book, appears Governor Andrew's endorsement, "Respectfully referred to Col. Russell for a report."

The governor must have known that Russell would be less than enthusiastic about accepting a man who had no time in uniform at all, a man who thought that a captaincy might be about right. A captain of cavalry commanded at least a company of enlisted men plus a first and second lieutenant; some cavalry captains commanded squadrons of two companies. But Russell was presented with a fait accompli. Farnsworth was a gentleman with pronounced abolitionist sympathies, at least acquainted with the likes of Otis, Phillips, and Bowditch. Russell, in his terse endorsement, noted that "Mr. Farnsworth, never having been in service, should start out as a good lieutenant before assuming a captaincy." George Farnsworth, a thirty-six-year-old minister from Roxbury, Massachusetts, became the first second lieutenant commissioned into the regiment.

The next officer candidate accepted in the 5th Massachusetts Cavalry also had no military experience. On 7 December 1863, a Mr. N. G. Chapin, a principal in the merchant firm of Fisher and Chapin, Boston, sent Governor Andrew a letter. After obliquely mentioning plans and individuals concerned with the recruitment of African Americans, Chapin recommended to the governor "Davenport Fisher, whom you may recollect." Chapin reported that Fisher had "just come from Illinois, on purpose to do something for his country," and wanted "to start from good old Massachusetts. He cannot restrain himself any longer." Davenport Fisher may not have had any time in service, but he had certainly been well educated and well traveled. "His late history is this," Chapin wrote, "After graduating at the Boston Latin School, he went through the scientific school at Cambridge [later renamed the Massachusetts Institute of Technology] then graduated at Heidelburg in '55 after studying three years there, making chemistry a speciality." Fisher, accompanied by N. G. Chapin, had then traveled in Europe for nine months, "after which, he spent another year in a laboratory in Paris."

Despite all his training and study, Fisher "became rather disgusted" on returning to America "with the want of encouragement extended practically" to chemistry in this country. Chapin and the young man's father persuaded him to give up chemistry and move to Illinois to supervise their business there. Fisher had "importuned his Father" to take part in the war from its beginning, "until he finally prevailed." Chapin reported that Fisher had "been studying military tactics for the last year, and his constant riding all about the country on horseback, had given him some qualifications and taste for cavalry service." Chapin finished in straightforward praise of a man he knew well but would not idealize to Governor Andrew. Using an extinct nineteenth-century word, Chapin wrote that Fisher's "principles and habits are unexceptionable." He described Davenport Fisher as "conscientious and modest to a fault, he will not shrink from danger or discomfort if duty calls." Chapin felt that Fisher was reliable, would be "glad of a commission in the new colored regt. of cavalry," and "would prefer to start" as a second lieutenant. At thirty-one, J. Davenport Fisher was "physically deficient only in being rather near sighted." Governor Andrew's scrawl appears on the back of Chapin's letter: "Ref'd to Col. H. S. Russell with especial reference to Davenport Fisher. He used to be a bright boy when I knew him. The stock is good. I wd not fail to take him. But you had best see him. Send for him to call." J. Davenport Fisher, former chemist, of Boston by way of Illinois, Paris, and Heidelberg, was commissioned second lieutenant in the 5th Massachusetts Volunteer Cavalry.

Perhaps it should come as no surprise that the first two officers commissioned into the regiment had no military experience. Harry Russell was still lieutenant colonel of the 2nd Cavalry in December 1863, in charge of recruiting for that regiment. Russell had to make a transition as colonel of his own regiment. In fact, he did not get around to asking (in writing) to be relieved of recruiting for the 2nd Cavalry until 16 January 1864. Russell remembered to ask for a formal order commissioning him colonel only on 2 March 1864. Colonel Russell had thrown himself into the work of the 5th Massachusetts Cavalry by the beginning of the second week of December, however. He sent his own first recommendations for commissions to the governor on 9 December. Russell did not delineate the particular qualities of each individual to Andrew; he knew the governor trusted his judgment. There were six names on Russell's first list, all soldiers—three officers and three enlisted. Two of the men served briefly or not at all with the 5th Cavalry. Lieutenant Charles Eliot Perkins of the 2nd Massachusetts Cavalry was in Boston, "never having been mustered into U.S. Service," wrote Colonel Russell. Perkins was commissioned into the 5th on 17 December but resigned on New Year's Day 1864. Perhaps he had second thoughts, or maybe his parents were fearful of losing their son. Another man, Sergeant William N. Percy of the 2nd Massachusetts Cavalry, was selected and then dropped for a commission. His name appears only once, without amplifying information.

The first name on Russell's list was that of Captain Zabdiel Boylston Adams, then commanding Company L of the 2nd Massachusetts Cavalry. The moniker seems original, but there were actually two officers in Massachusetts regiments named Zabdiel Boylston Adams. An explanation lies in the fact that Zabdiel Boylston was a renowned and respected doctor in the Bay Colony, credited with saving the population of Boston by introducing vaccination during a smallpox epidemic in 1727. The Adams name was common enough. The Zabdiel B. Adams we are concerned with was born and grew up in Fitchburg, Massachusetts. He traveled overland to California as a young man. When the war began, a group of Californians, transplanted New Englanders mostly, wanted to come east to fight for the Union. J. Sewall Reed, who was from Massachusetts, was living in San Francisco in 1861. Reed corresponded with Governor Andrew, seeking to recruit a company of one hundred cavalrymen in California to be offered to the Bay State. Authorization finally came in October 1862, and recruiting for the "California Hundred" began in San Francisco.

In three weeks, over five hundred men volunteered. Reed was thus able to pick the men he wanted. Samuel W. Backus, "Late Co. 'L,' 2d Massachusetts Cavalry and Late 2d Lieutenant 2d California Cavalry, Ex Adjutant-General State of California," read a paper before the California Commandery of the Military Order of the Loyal Legion of the United States in December 1889 titled "Californians in the Field: Historical Sketch of the Organization and Services of the California 'Hundred' and 'Battalion,' 2d Massachusetts

Cavalry." Backus noted that "the one hundred men that comprised the company were chosen with great care; every member was young and an expert equestrian, as were nearly all Californians in those days."

The "California Hundred" was mustered into federal service on 10 December 1862. The company was reviewed by the mayor of San Francisco and attended services at the church of the noted evangelist Reverend Starr King before departing San Francisco by steamer for the northeast via Panama. The "Hundred" arrived at Camp Meigs, Readville, Massachusetts, on 4 January 1863 and was assigned to the nascent 2nd Massachusetts Cavalry. Comrade Backus continued in his paper: "As was evidenced by the large number of men who applied to be enrolled in the California Hundred when it was being recruited, the raising of this one company gave but little opportunity to the patriotic citizens of this state, who desired to take an active part in the nation's struggle for the preservation of its liberties."

Californian DeWitt C. Thompson requested authorization to raise another four companies of cavalry for Massachusetts; he proposed himself as major of this battalion. Negotiation and discussion with Governor Andrew and the War Department kept the telegraph lines humming until permission was granted on 15 January 1863. Men came from all over the state to San Francisco to join the "California Battalion." The companies were designated A, B, C, D (later E and F), L, and M of the 2nd Massachusetts Cavalry and "commanded respectively," wrote Backus, "by Captains Charles S. Eigenbrodt, killed in battle August 26, 1864, in Shenandoah Valley; Z. B. Adams, promoted to Major, 5th Mass. Cavalry, severely wounded before Petersburg, June 15, 1864, now [1889] a member of this Commandery; Geo. A. Manning, taken prisoner February 22, 1864, exchanged April 1865; D. A. DeMerritt discharged 1864, by reason of disability incurred in the line of duty."

The service of these four men can sum up all the hazards of the Civil War. One could be killed in action, wounded, or captured and sent to the living hell of a prisoner of war camp, or one could have one's health shattered by bad food, polluted water, or disease. The California Battalion, after much oration and a splendid dinner provided by the patriotic ladies of San Francisco, and "amid the firing of cannons and the huzzas of the people," wrote Backus, "took its departure for the East on the steamer *Constitution*, March 21, 1863." The battalion arrived in Massachusetts on 15 April and was assigned to Colonel Lowell. Less than three weeks later, the 2nd Massachusetts Cavalry was ordered to Virginia.

The fact that Massachusetts accepted five hundred men from California shows how desperate recruiting had become in the North by 1863; their urgent dispatch to the front shows the real need for cavalry in the Army of the Potomac in the summer of that year. The presence of the California Hundred and Battalion explains why several officers of the 5th Massachusetts Cavalry put down "San Francisco, Calif." as their residence. Besides Major Zabdiel B. Adams, Captain Horace B. Welch and Lieutenants John Anderson, George F. Wilson, and Robert M. Parker were all from the Golden State, by way of Panama and the 2nd Massachusetts Cavalry.

Adams had attracted the attention of his commanding officer early on. Colonel Lowell had in turn contacted John Murray Forbes, who strongly supported the policy of enlisting African Americans, as long as white men commanded them. Forbes wrote major general and former Massachusetts governor Nathaniel P. Banks on 8 October 1863. Banks had transferred his efforts from the Shenandoah Valley to the Department of the Gulf in Louisiana. Forbes "was delighted to hear" of Banks's progress "with the black regiments, as in that direction, it seems to me, lies the solution of more problems than one. We are now all agreed on this mode of putting down the rebellion, and of ending slavery so far as this will do it, and upon no other mode are we agreed among ourselves." Forbes went on to write that he had tried to have the 2nd Massachusetts Cavalry sent to Banks. He even wrote to Secretary of War Stanton, unfortunately with negative results. Forbes supposed, "They are pestered to death there by the many understandings and promises with which men are induced to enlist, and I don't mean to complain of their disregarding my letter; only I don't like to be rebuffed twice." Forbes then wrote, in response to a previous letter from Banks, "I should think the blacks would make first-rate cavalry! This reminds me that some time since Lowell wrote me suggesting the names of two of his officers for promotion into black regiments. One of them I remember well, Capt. Adams of the Californians—a wiry, smart fellow, whom Lowell valued among his best Captains."

The second name on Russell's list of 9 December was that of Lieutenant Albert R. Howe, who had served with the 44th Regiment, Massachusetts Volunteer Militia. This was a nine months' regiment that had its nucleus in the 4th Battalion of Massachusetts Rifles, a militia unit that had been formed back in April 1861. The 44th was raised in the fall of 1862 and saw service in North Carolina, using New Bern as a base to operate against the enemy. As James Bowen noted in *Massachusetts in the War*, "the warfare in North Carolina at that time largely consisted of expeditions from either side to feel the position of the enemy and occupy strategic points, and on one of these the Forty-fourth were soon engaged." The regiment was on active service in North Carolina until June 1863 and saw action at Rawls's Mill, on the expedition to Goldsboro, and at Washington near the confluence of the Tar and Pamlico Rivers.

The 44th Massachusetts returned to the Bay State and was mustered out of U.S. service on 16 June 1863. But this was not the complete end of the 44th's service. Bowen wrote, "Owing to the danger of a draft riot . . . the state authorities on the 14th of July called on the Forty-fourth, with other militia organizations. They reported promptly and remained on duty for a week."

Albert Howe, who was twenty-four, gave "clerk" as his occupation and Boston as his home. He did well in the 5th Massachusetts Cavalry. Howe was captain of Company A in May 1864. He was promoted to major in February 1865, which put him over several officers with more cavalry experience than he.

Two of Howe's comrades from the 44th also joined the 5th Cavalry. James S. Newell, twenty-two, was a bookkeeper from Boston who wrote with a beautiful hand. It's a pleasure to read his copperplate script. He had been a lieutenant in the 4th Battalion and then the 44th Massachusetts Volunteer Militia. Newell became first lieutenant and regimental adjutant on 29 December 1863. Lieutenant Newell was promoted to captain and took over Company A in February 1865, when Captain Howe made major.

Curtis H. Whittemore was also a clerk from Boston. Unlike Howe and Newell, he had not served in the 4th Battalion, nor had he been an officer. But Private Whittemore of the 44th Regiment was available and willing. Whittemore was commissioned a second lieutenant on 7 January 1864.

The two remaining names on Russell's first list of officer candidates were those of Abner F. Mallory and James L. Wheat. Mallory, thirty-two, had been a farmer in Roxbury, Massachusetts, before the war. Wheat was also from Roxbury. He was nine years younger than Mallory, but he gave no occupation. Both men were sergeants in the 2nd Massachusetts Cavalry.

When the 5th Cavalry went off to war, James Wheat was captain of Company L; Abner Mallory was F Company's first lieutenant.

The same day that Colonel Russell sent his first recommendations to the governor, Professor Theophilus Parsons of the Cambridge Law School also put pen to paper to Governor Andrew. Previously, Parsons had expressed his opinions on the natural aptitude of African Americans for cavalry service and their place in American society. Now he wrote on behalf of his son, First Lieutenant Charles Chauncy Parsons of the 1st Massachusetts Volunteer Cavalry. The "Major Chamberlin" referred to was Major Samuel E. Chamberlain of the 1st Massachusetts Cavalry. Parsons was then waging a campaign to have Chamberlain named lieutenant colonel of the regiment. "When I spoke to you of Major Chamberlin," Parsons wrote, "I had not the slightest thought of my son. But when he learnt that his friend and classmate Russell would command the Coloured Regiment, and that Major Chamberlin would probably join it, he expressed some desire to join it." Parsons continued in the humble tones of the petitioner: "He calls now, not to make any,—even the slightest request, but to put himself at your disposal." Governor Andrew endorsed the letter that he "wd. be pleased to have Lt. Parsons in our Movement."

Professor Parsons had also written that Captain Henry Pickering Bowditch of the 1st Massachusetts Cavalry would accept a major's commission in the African American cavalry. The governor and Colonel Russell had already acted on this, however. On 11 December, Russell had written to the governor that he would "see Captain Bowditch as soon as possible." Henry Bowditch was graduated from Harvard in 1861 and joined the 1st Massachusetts in November of that year as a second lieutenant. Bowditch served with that regiment in South Carolina and Virginia. He was promoted to captain on 13 May 1863. He had been offered a majority in one of Massachusetts's African American infantry regiments but had chosen to remain with the cavalry. Captain Bowditch was wounded on 27 November 1863 during the Mine Run or Rappahannock Campaign.

Henry Pickering Bowditch became the 5th Massachusetts Cavalry's third major. He was young, just twenty-three, but he had experience and came from a prominent Bay State family. Bowditch was not fit enough to take his place with the regiment until spring. Chronologically, although his name was mentioned early in the records and we know he met with Russell in December, he was not commissioned as major until 22 March 1864.

It also took time to pry some of these white officers loose from their various commands. Captain Z. B. Adams was not appointed major until 2 March. Instead, Lieutenant Horace N. Weld of the 1st Massachusetts Cavalry became the 5th Massachusetts Cavalry's first major on 22 January 1864. Weld had been in Readville already, training recruits for a new battalion for the 1st Massachusetts Cavalry. Major Henry Lee Higginson of the First Massachusetts was at home recovering from wounds (two pistol balls and a saber cut) received that summer. Major Higginson wrote on 14 December 1863 to Brigadier General R. A. Peirce, "Commander of Military Camps of Rendezvous, Mass.," to try and remedy a potentially awkward situation in regard to promotions within the 1st Massachusetts Cavalry.

Higginson's letter to Brigadier General Peirce contained three numbered points. Point two was the recommendation "that Messrs. Leavitt and Stone be sent to the Camp at Readville as Cadets, there to show their ability or inability as officers: without commissions until report of them has come to you." The third issue Major Higginson wished to address was "the consequences of commissioning new officers in this Battalion to places above a 2nd Lieutenancy." There were men in the regiment, Higginson noted, "who have served faithfully and most intelligently their country for two years and more as Lieutenants." These men "must necessarily feel disheartened, when new men, quite ignorant of any real duties or hardships are put over them." The veteran officers knew their business. They were "fit and ready for an emergency day or night (it must be remembered that a Cavalry Subaltern has continually a separate command quite unlike an infantry subaltern as in picket, reconnaissance, &c., while a new officer cannot, for a time at least, be more than ready to obey orders under the immediate eye of a superior)." Higginson requested that he should be put in charge of recruiting the new battalion so that "their Battalion shall be filled up and be made ready for the field more quickly than by leaving it as it is and by advancing new officers to high places: for a Captain is a very important man in the service." Higginson wrote that he submitted his letter most respectfully, begging the general's pardon if he had "exceeded [his] proper limits," but that his "only wish in the matter" was to "serve my State to the best advantage."

Major Henry Lee Higginson's first point, the matter that had perhaps prompted him to write, was the promotion of Lieutenant Horace N. Weld to captain. Higginson wanted Weld commissioned captain in the new battalion "to antedate the Commissions of all officers in that Battalion." According to Higginson, Lieutenant Weld "was in the First Massachusetts Cavalry from the very start (having previously served five years in the regular cavalry and then in a three months battery) was promoted for marked merit by Colonel Williams, was rated as a most thorough, efficient reliable officer, versed in all the duties of his position in the camp and in the field." The records of the 1st Massachusetts Cavalry note that Weld was promoted to captain on 7 February 1862 but was not confirmed as such. He then resigned from the regiment on 16 March 1863. Higginson noted to General Peirce that Weld "was forced to leave the service a year [ago] on account of ill health much against the wishes of his superior and inferior officers." Higginson and fellow 1st Cavalry officer Lieutenant Colonel Greely S. Curtis, who was also home on sick leave, convinced Weld to rejoin the regiment as a second lieutenant to train the new recruits, presumably in the autumn of 1863. Weld had "worked faithfully and to a good purpose" and "has earned reward, which his great modesty and his love of his country will never persuade him to ask for." Besides the endorsement of Lieutenant Colonel Curtis, Higginson wrote that the 1st Cavalry's "Colonel Sergeant prizes Lieutenant Weld highly as an officer."

Brigadier General Peirce thought it politic to forward Major Higginson's letter to the governor but commented only on his first point, noting that "Lieutenant Weld, within referred to is an experienced officer—the best I have seen in the Cavalry Battalion for First Regiment men being organized at Camp Meigs. I feel that I cannot recommend him too highly." Governor Andrew, however, chose to respond to the latter points of Higginson's letter, with some asperity. Andrew "sought the services of Major Higginson in superintending the recruitment of the battalion, but that his health did not permit. I may add that while I have the benefit of much criticism no officer of the First Cavalry save Captain Tewksbury has been in a condition to render me & the battalion any service."

Governor Andrew had missed the forest for the trees, concerning himself more with Major Higginson's criticism and lack of support than with promotion for a deserving officer (Horace Weld). Due to a promotion practice that was in general unfair to the officers who were serving with the 1st Massachusetts in the field, Horace N. Weld was not promoted to captain in the 1st Cavalry; he sought opportunity elsewhere.

Weld represents a group of officers, experienced cavalrymen, who were not gentlemen but good soldiers. These were men who became officers in the 5th Cavalry after serving what might be called an apprentice period of leadership as noncommissioned or junior officers. These men had been recognized for their skills in warfare. We can infer that they saw the war and the army as an opportunity to advance their status in American society.

If Horace Weld expressed his feelings about commanding African American troopers, a record of those thoughts has not been found. The reports and forms that bear his signature deal solely with the regiment and army business. At forty-three, Weld was one of the oldest men in the regiment. He had been a mason in Belmont, Massachusetts, before the war. In April 1861, he enlisted in Cook's Battery, sometimes referred to as the 1st Massachusetts Light Artillery, a ninety-day militia unit. His rank was chief of piece (sergeant). Weld had been a militiaman in the Boston Light Artillery before the war. Since all field artillery was horsed, it can be inferred that Weld had a great deal of experience with horses. We do not know whether age and experience had given Weld wisdom or what he thought about politics or religion. We can say that Weld was a loyal and tenacious man. When the 5th Massachusetts Volunteer Cavalry arrived in Boston for muster out on 30 November 1865 and Lieutenant Colonel Horace N. Weld walked down the gangway of the troopship, he had served with the regiment continuously, without furlough or sick leave, for twenty-two months and nine days.

On 18 December, at Harry Russell's suggestion, Governor Andrew wrote Assistant Adjutant General Thomas M. Vincent to request that Lieutenants Horace B. Welch and Cyrus C. Emery and Sergeant Abner F. Mallory of the 2nd Massachusetts Cavalry be ordered to report to the governor "for duty in organizing the Fifth Cavalry (colored)" in which he proposed to "commission and promote them." This was not as easy as it sounds, however. Men had to be discharged from federal service, which required War Department paperwork, before they were free to enter another regiment. The governor knew this and anticipated Vincent's response: "I hope you will not reply in answer to this that the rules of the Department will not permit officers and men to be thus detailed—as their immediate presence is necessary for the instruction and discipline of the Regt. in camp." Besides necessity, Governor Andrew mentioned an arrangement, an "understanding between the War Department and myself, through General Peirce," that Andrew "should have the assistance of such officers as wanted in raising our quota, instead of having details from the regiments, under the general rule, whenever they could be spared." Once again, we see the governor of Massachusetts bending the rules a bit for the Bay State. As in the fiction that the African Americans who enlisted in the regiment were residents of the towns that enrolled them, which allowed those towns (and the state) to receive credit for them against their federal quota, the governor was asking Major Vincent to subscribe to the fiction that the requested white soldiers were to be sent immediately to Massachusetts to be recruiters, not officers commanding and training troops. Assistant Adjutant General Vincent let the governor have his way, although it usurped War Department authority. Doubtless Secretary Stanton was aware of the situation.

On the same day that Governor Andrew sent his request to the Adjutant General's Office, a potentially graver situation arose with the reception of a letter from a Colonel S. M. Bowman, U.S. Army. It was Colonel Bowman's understanding, he wrote to Andrew, "that the officers of the Cavalry Regt. of colored troops which you are authorized to raise will have to pass an examination before the Board of which Major General Casey is President." This was the examining board for men who wished to receive commissions in the federal African American regiments, the U.S. Colored Troops. The Bureau of Colored Troops, a subsection of the Adjutant General's Office, administered the U.S. Colored Troops. In May 1863, when the Bureau of Colored Troops had been set up, an examining board for officer candidates had also been started. Major General Silas Casey had written the infantry tactical manual then in use. "I believe," Colonel Bowman continued, that "I am the only officer on that board at all schooled in the cavalry branch of the service—and unless some addition is made to the board, a large share of the work and responsibility will fall upon me." Colonel Bowman was willing to help Governor Andrew's officer candidates by providing "the heads of subjects to be mastered by the candidates—such as are regarded as fundamental, so that the parties interested may have a fair chance to prepare for examination." Bowman also offered to travel to Boston to meet "the officers themselves and explain in detail what they must know before they can hope to pass. No doubt, the War Department would grant me leave for such purpose especially during the holidays." Bowman wanted the governor's nominees well prepared, for although the board did not want to disappoint good men, "we can only pass such as show themselves qualified for the special duty designated." According to the colonel, qualifications came through assiduous book learning: "No man, whatever his attainments, is capable without previous study, to take command of cavalry. He requires educating, in tactics, in arms, in the care discipline and management of troops, in the care use and training of the horse, and I recommend that you put it into the hearts of the officers to study diligently until they can come before the Board duly prepared to pass a good examination."

Colonel Bowman's letter presented a number of potential problems. In the first place, it must have been disturbing to the governor to have an officer in the Adjutant General's Office assume that the regiment was a federal one. Added to this was the assumption that officer nominees would have to pass a rigorous written and oral examination in Washington, DC. Governor Andrew wrote to Bowman on 22 December 1863 thanking the colonel for his suggestions and expressed willingness to see him in Boston and listen to any suggestions he might make. His excellency quickly set Bowman straight, however, about the 5th Regiment of Massachusetts Cavalry Volunteers: "In regard to the regiment of colored cavalry, which I was authorized to raise, however, it will not be necessary that they be examined before the board at Washington, because they will be commissioned here by me, the same as officers of other Massachusetts regiments, and before being commissioned, will be carefully examined by a skillful and experienced cavalry officer." We assume that the officer the governor meant was Colonel Russell. Governor Andrew and the regimental officers had avoided a potentially complicated, if not disheartening, situation. Colonel Russell would certainly have preferred to commission only competent veteran cavalry officers, but he had to take what he could get. We are left to wonder which officers of the 5th Massachusetts Cavalry would have passed Colonel Bowman's examination.

On 21 December, Governor Andrew took the opportunity to informally report the regiment's progress to Secretary of War Stanton. Colonel Russell had written the governor the day previously to request that five noncommissioned officers of the 2nd Massachusetts Cavalry "be discharged, that they may receive commissions in the Fifth Massachusetts Cavalry." The men were Sergeant Major George F. Wilson and Sergeants Edgar M. Blanche, James L. Wheat, John Anderson, and Charles E. Allan. Andrew duly wrote to Edwin Stanton requesting that the men be discharged "with the consent of Colonel Lowell . . . in order to receive commissions as Second Lieutenants in the Fifth Reg't. of Mass. Vol. Cavalry now raising in this state." As a postscript, Andrew wrote, "The colored men are coming into camp now; & competent officers of experience to govern this kind of recruits are needed daily. As fast as companies are lead to be mustered, these officers will be mustered." Andrew's comment as to the need to "govern this kind of recruits" shows how even in abolitionist, Republican Massachusetts in the winter of 1863, African American soldiers were still seen as a dangerous "other." We also see that recruitment for the regiment was progressing well. Like several other officers, however, the five noncoms mentioned in Andrew's letter came to the regiment at different times. James L. Wheat, who had also been mentioned on 9 December, was commissioned a second lieutenant in the regiment on 13 January 1864. John Anderson was a miner from San Francisco, a member of the California Battalion. Charles E. Allan, a year older than Anderson at thirty-four, gave no occupation but listed Louisville, Kentucky, as his residence. Both Sergeants Anderson and Allan were commissioned on 18 January. Sergeant Edgar M. Blanche, who had been a wagon maker in Pennsylvania before the war, joined the regiment on 8 February. Colonel Russell had to request Sergeant Major George F. Wilson's detachment from the 2nd Massachusetts Cavalry twice more before he was sent to the regiment in March. Interestingly, Wilson appears to have lobbied personally for a commission, not necessarily with a black regiment, beginning in October 1863.

There are three recommendations in the 5th Massachusetts Cavalry file for the Sergeant Major. The first was from an Alex A. Rice, who wrote from Boston on 16 October 1863: "I have personal assurances from gentlemen whose judgment I know to [be] discriminative and whose testimony is reliable; respecting the character and qualifications of Sergeant Major G. F. Wilson; and I cheerfully write in a request that he may receive a commission in some Cavalry Regt. of this State, believing he will, if appointed, serve the country with zeal and ability." The second recommendation was from George H. Quincy, recruiting agent for the 2nd Massachusetts Cavalry, who knew Wilson better than Rice did. Quincy wrote that he had known the sergeant major since he had joined the regiment. "Knowing him as I do," Quincy wrote, "to be faithful to his duties as a soldier, and perfectly competent to fill the position of a commissioned officer, I would cheerfully recommend him for a commission in a Massachusetts Regiment." From Vienna, Virginia, Headquarters of the 2nd Cavalry, came the 24 October response to a letter Wilson sent on the 21st. Colonel Lowell wrote that he was glad to hear of Wilson's prospect for immediate promotion; "if you had remained with us, I should have expected to see you a Lieutenant in time." Lowell took pleasure in recommending Wilson "unqualifiably; during the three months that you were acting as Sergeant Major of my regiment. I of course, had constant opportunity of observing you—I found you always diligent and faithful, intelligent and anxious to learn; I believe you to be sufficiently familiar with the duties to be fit for a 2nd Lieutenancy."

We can infer from these recommendations that Wilson was on recruiting duty in Boston in October but returned to his regiment later that fall. Wilson was another San Franciscan who had come east to put down the rebellion. At twenty-two, he was relatively young to be a senior noncommissioned officer, but he had obviously impressed Colonel Lowell. He would be promoted to first lieutenant of Company H before leaving the regiment in September 1864.

Although Colonel Russell usually sought experience, preferably cavalry experience, Governor Andrew was willing to accept men without experience if he thought it might oblige a friend or powerful person. Henry R. Hinckley was a twenty-four-year-old accountant from Northampton, Massachusetts. Governor Andrew wrote to William Lloyd Garrison, publisher of *The Liberator* newspaper, two days before Christmas. Andrew suggested that "Mr. Hinckley, of whose presence in the City I am just apprised by your note, oblige me by calling on Colonel Henry S. Russell at No 21 School Street." Andrew wanted Hinckley to use the governor's letter to gain a hearing from Colonel Russell. "Let this letter be evidence of Colonel Russell's strong satisfaction with Mr. Hinckley as an honorable man, a devoted and faithful citizen, energetic & upright & and a friend of the colored people & to true to their rights," Andrew continued. In addition to Garrison, the governor noted that Hinckley's "standing at home is well vouched besides, by Major Day (late ___th Mass. Inf. Vols.) [Andrew could not remember the number of the regiment] Judge of Probate for Barnstable County," and by "the chairman of the selectmen," although Andrew did not mention the name of the town. Governor Andrew reminded Garrison that "Mr. Hinckley is not wholly a stranger to myself, having successfully and triumphantly aided in securing the arrest of certain persons charged with kidnapping a man of color, in which I was concerned in the task of bringing the offenders to justice."

The governor had been asked to appoint Hinckley to a specific position, that of regimental commissary of subsistence, the first lieutenant in charge of everything edible for the regiment. Governor Andrew did not want to usurp Colonel Russell's authority, so he sent Mr. Hinckley to Russell so that the latter "might have a chance to make up an opinion of his adaptation and special fitness for such an officer." Andrew explained to Garrison that he depended on Russell's "experience, an apparently active and extended one, [to] enable him now as is better to judge than I, how far a man's training and qualities and his general capacities adapt him to duties so much more familiar in their detail to the Colonel than to myself." Although promising Garrison that he would see Hinckley the next day, Andrew emphasized again his confidence in "Col. R. as a good man, as well as a good soldier, I invoke his help & confer with him as regards in making up the roster of the Regt." The next day, Harry Russell wrote the governor, as usual coming right to the point: "Governor, I have seen and talked with Mr. Hinckley; and, as you want my opinion, I will say that I think his experience fits him better for [accounting, although] keeping accurate accounts is certainly necessary." The page is torn; the words in brackets are the most likely.

This was not the end of the matter, however. Henry R. Hinckley did not let the matter drop in December, and eventually persistence and strong abolitionist credentials secured him a second lieutenancy in March. Perhaps it would have been better for all concerned if Hinckley had been given a staff position, for he proved a poor line officer.

By the end of December, the officer corps of the regiment was beginning to take shape. On 29 December, Russell requested commissions for Abram O. Swain of Boston, Francis L. Gilman of New Bedford, George A. Fisher of Milton, and Jacob B. Cook of Charlestown. The latter was the only one of the four who had prior military experience, having served as a private in the 5th Regiment, Massachusetts Volunteer Militia, a ninety-day regiment. All four were in their twenties, but we know little else about them since none of the men put down an occupation when they were commissioned. George Fisher left Harvard to join the army; he would have been class of 1865. As a Milton resident, Fisher was probably acquainted with

Russell's Forbes in-laws. A lack of amplifying information means their stories are briefly told: Jacob Cook was promoted to first lieutenant on 18 January 1864; he resigned because of disability in September 1864. George Fisher was promoted in July 1864. He chose not to accompany the regiment to Texas, resigning on 24 June 1865. Abram Swain and Francis Gilman both mustered out with the 5th Massachusetts Cavalry on 31 October 1865. Gilman was captain of Company L; Swain was G Company's first lieutenant.

Colonel Russell sent for officers and noncommissioned officers from the 2nd Massachusetts Cavalry; he sought out available soldiers in Massachusetts and carefully interviewed men who felt compelled to leave civilian life to follow the fortunes of an African American cavalry regiment. Russell and the governor did not accept everyone who applied, however.

The pages of the 5th Massachusetts Cavalry file at the Massachusetts Archives contain several instances of men who applied for commissions but were turned down. Page 1 of the "Fifth Mass. Cav. (colored)" file is a letter dated 29 September 1863, sent to "Governor Andrews" from Springfield, Massachusetts. The writer, Homer F. Fox, had "been contemplating writing you for some time to see if you would grant me a commission in one of our colored regiments if any vacancies there are." Fox was a private in the 34th Massachusetts Infantry on recruiting duty in Springfield. He felt he could "obtain a good recommend from the Captain and approved by our Colonel G. L. Wells a recommend for good conduct as a soldier and am called as good a soldier as there is in the Company." Fox had been on special details for six months and was tired of the monotonous life in the 34th; he wanted "to enter the field where I can do more for our cause, or where I think I can." Unfortunately for Fox, he wrote that "outsides of our Regt. I cannot say as I have any influential friends to assist me what I do I must do by myself but I can procure recommends for character &c. from a [few] good men as there are in Springfield and Westfield as I am known in both places." Fox asked that the governor please address him "if this is worth your attention .. . and you can do anything for me," but he closed his letter by writing "yours fraternally, H." Fox's note was endorsed by Albert G. Browne, the governor's military secretary, thus: "The 'yours fraternaly' [sic] signed with the initial of the writer's Christian name, is a cock-eye expression."

The reasons for Homer Fox's rejection seem obvious. Less obvious was the rejection of Private William H. McNeill, Company A, 2nd Massachusetts Cavalry, unless it was the brevity of his application and recommendations. McNeill wrote to Governor Andrew on 3 December 1863 upon "hearing that you were about to raise a Negro Regiment of Cavalry . . . to apply for a commission as second lieutenant in that regiment." McNeill noted that he had "served a year in an infantry company in California" and had "been a year now a member of the 2nd Massachusetts Cavalry." After mentioning that letters of recommendation from Captains Reed and Washburn were enclosed, McNeill closed respectfully. J. Sewall Reed wrote, "Private McNeill was enlisted by me in the 'Cal. 100' and during one year's service has proved himself a good soldier and would in my opinion make a good officer." Captain Francis Washburn "cordially rejoin[ed] in the recommendation of Private McNeill for the position he asks." Perhaps the governor was expecting more than a sentence from each man, for private McNeill remained with the 2nd Cavalry.

Like McNeill, perhaps W. M. Walton of Ware, Massachusetts, was hurt by a lack of specificity. Walton wrote the governor on 21 December 1863 that he "would like a commission in the regiment with authority to recruit a company or part of a company for the same." Walton had never been in uniform but had "qualifications to recommend [him] for the position sought." Walton was willing to travel to Boston to "present testimonials from any of the citizens of this place whom you may choose to mention." The writer asked for an early reply, which was forthcoming. The last thing Governor Andrew wanted was an unknown without experience interfering with his recruiting operation.

The above applicants were turned down for lack of influence or less than fulsome recommendations. In the case of Jonathan Walker, Governor Andrew was presented with a legitimate hero of abolitionism, but one who was perhaps too idealistic, too old, and too eccentric to be a help to the 5th Massachusetts Cavalry. Jonathan Walker wrote to the governor from Crimea, Muskegon County, Michigan, on 4 January 1864: "Is there any part that I can act, or position that I can occupy beneficially in connection with the fifth Regt. Mass. Cavalry volunteers?" Walker explained that he was "not a colored, or a military man, nor [did he] wish to shed the blood of any human being, had much rather save life than destroy it, would far sooner bind up than make wounds." However, Walker saw his duty as clear: "But as this cruel rebellion (the legitimate offspring of slavery) is now roabing [sic] our land in mourning I am desirous of seeing them both end as speedily as possible in a manner that will forever settle the question whether man can justly, and safely hold property in man in this country or elsewhere?" Walker wanted to volunteer but hoped that "while the conflict continues, the falling, the wounded and the sick will need to be attended to, in which, or in some other department I may be of service." Walker then listed his reasons for wanting to join the 5th Massachusetts Cavalry. First was his "long and intimate acquaintance with that class of people both North and South, their temperaments dispositions and peculiarities, having lived years among them at the South." The abuse and outrages against "that class of people" naturally attracted Walker's sympathy. He was thus "disposed to share [his] destiny with theirs for the present struggle of their recognized manhood and a government that will sustain it." Second, Walker hoped to be in the South when the rebellion was "fairly crushed" so that he might devote his abilities "(whatever they may be) to the intellectual and moral developments of the freed blacks and poor whites, whom slavery has degraded and polluted." Lastly, Walker wished to go from his native state, "so highly honored now by her representative men, brave, manly, and heroic." Walker noted that his "life heretofore [had] been made up of many pursuits, in which I have had much dear bought experience. The ocean, the workshop, the forest, the prairie, the lecturefield, the sick chamber &c, &c, have by turns furnished me with employment, and I am by no means idle now, but if you say the word Governor I will go with the 5th Regiment, Mass. Cavalry Volunteers to rebeldom and do my best." After expressing regret for having troubled the governor and wondering whether he should have written directly to Colonel Russell, Walker reminded Andrew that he was "known in the city and throughout the state by nearly all the antislavery people, at least, those that were antislavery twenty years ago, and doubtless you have not forgotten the circumstances that fired Whittier's pen to write the poem here enclosed."

Inside Walker's letter was a pamphlet from 1845 titled "The Branded Hand." An antislavery tract, the pamphlet explained that Jonathan Walker had lived in Florida from 1836 to 1841. He then returned to Massachusetts "because he would not bring up his children among the poisonous influences of slavery." While in Florida, Walker had treated his African American employees like family. When he returned to Pensacola in 1844, in his own vessel, he was persuaded to bring seven of them north. Walker was pursued and captured. "Prostrated by sickness, he was confined in a dungeon, chained on a damp floor without table, bed or chair." Walker was showered with filth while confined in a pillory, branded SS—"Slave Stealer"—on the palm of his right hand, and served eleven months in prison. Walker's ordeal inspired John Greenleaf Whittier, the Quaker poet. One stanza will suffice to give the tone:

> Welcome home again brave seaman! With thy thoughtful brow and gray,
> And the old heroic spirit of our earlier, better day—
> With that front of calm endurance, on whose steady nerve in vain
> Pressed the iron of the prison, smote the fiery shafts of pain!

Jonathan Walker was not commissioned into the regiment. Governor Andrew wrote that he appreciated his comments but feared that the rigors of active campaigning might be too much for him.

Perhaps the best example of how not to apply for a commission is a letter written to Governor Andrew by Charles E. Tucker on 6 January 1864. Tucker was a first lieutenant in the 54th Massachusetts Infantry, then encamped on Morris Island, near Charleston, South Carolina. As a veteran officer in Massachusetts's most prestigious black unit, Tucker had a great deal going for him. Tucker had "the honor to address [Andrew] on a subject that may be presumptuous to communicate so directly," but he knew of "no other way" that he could accomplish what he wished, and "please pardon if not in the common way of doing business." Tucker wanted the governor to give him a captain's commission, the command of a company. The lieutenant had "the impression that [he] could bring good recommendations from [his] regimental commander." Tucker also believed he had the experience: "I have commanded a company in the regiment for some five months including the Assault on Wagner." In addition, Tucker mentioned the recommendation of Colonel Henry Lee of the 44th Massachusetts Volunteer Militia, which had helped gain his commission into the 54th. It is possible to be too honest, however: "The objective I have for joining the cavalry is I think I would like it better than infantry, second, the difference in the pay is an item as I have nothing left but what I earn in the army, the war having destroyed all my prospects." Tucker finished his letter by noting that he had always "had a great interest in the people over whom I have the honor to command and am willing to sacrifice all for there [sic] prosperity." The damage was done, though. Tucker's letter was endorsed by Albert Browne: "Ansd. by returning to Lieutenant T, —Jan 21/64[.] Col. Russell reports that he should have the rec. of his superior officers, and that after buying horses, etc., he would find that the increase of pay of a cavalry officer would be no privilege to him."

Of course, if Charles Tucker had been instead Charles Bowditch, Secretary Browne and the governor might have been more receptive. Charles Pickering Bowditch was Henry Pickering Bowditch's younger brother. Luckily for us, Charles Bowditch's war letters were donated to the Massachusetts Historical Society. Bowditch wrote, "On May 22nd, 1863, I joined the Fifty-fifth Massachusetts Volunteer Infantry as Second Lieutenant, and went into camp at Readville on the easterly side of the railroad, the Fifty-fourth Regiment occupying the better camp on the other side." The 55th was ordered to the seat of war in July 1863. Originally proposed for the Virginia theater, the regiment was sent by sea to North Carolina because of the antidraft and antiblack riots in New York and the supposed prejudice in the Army of the Potomac. Bowditch, who had been promoted to captain, described the departure: "In our march through the city, [Boston] we carried loaded guns, fearing an attack on the black troops, but nothing occurred, and we discharged our guns into the dock before embarking on board the transport."

The 55th arrived in Newbern, North Carolina, on 27 July but was ordered to take part in Union operations around Charleston, South Carolina, on 30 July. There the regiment was engaged in fatigue and picket duty in support of the investiture of the Confederate forts defending Charleston. Toward the end of August, Captain Bowditch became sick with what he called "chronic diarrhoea." Bowditch wrote his mother on 30 August 1863 from "Folly (very appropriately named) Island." He tried to allay her fears, "for I'm not so confounded sick as I might be by a long chalk." He reported that he was taking medicine that contained quinine. He also expressed disappointment that his brother Henry had refused a majority in the 54th Infantry. "It is a great disappointment to me personally for I have been expecting him and looking forward to his coming by every steamer." Bowditch explained in notes accompanying his letters that he became ill on 25 August, "which pulled me down badly, at the time, made it necessary for me to have a furlough about a month after this date, and was one of the principal reasons for my exchanging into the 5th Mass. Vol. Cavalry so that I might have a horse to ride, for walking was not easy in my weakened condition."

Bowditch was sent home on sick leave at the end of September 1863. He "was pretty sick and had lost a great many pounds of flesh. Mine was one of the last sick-leaves which allowed officers to go North. Frank [Francis Lee] Higginson, [Captain in the 54th Massachusetts Infantry] was sent [on sick leave] South to Florida." Captain Bowditch had his sick leave extended, so he did not leave Massachusetts until "just before Thanksgiving, when I started South taking with me a lot of men of the 54th and 55th who had been left behind sick." On 15 December 1863, Captain Bowditch wrote his father from Folly Island:

> *Don't you think that it would be a good idea for me to try to get into the negro Cavalry Regiment which Governor Andrew has received permission to raise in Massachusetts? I should then get a horse and the objection which occurred to you when I thought of a Captaincy in the First Mass. Cavalry, that it would look like deserting the cause of the blacks, would be entirely obviated. I think the negroes will make very good horsemen, though perhaps, not graceful ones. They will be able to stick on a horse's back if they are not able to sit up straight. I wish Henry would apply for a Majority in the regiment and I could get a Captaincy.*

Later in this letter, Bowditch reported on the visit of a Major Sturgis, who was on Governor Andrew's staff: "I have just seen Major Sturgis who tells me that the new regiment of cavalry is to be commanded by Henry Sturgis Russell, which is rather a come round, since he did not use to be quite right on the negro question. He also informs me that N. I. Bowditch of the cavalry was slightly wounded. Of course, it must be Henry that is meant. I hope it will be slight enough for him to enjoy his Christmas." Bowditch wrote "of course" because his first cousin, Nathaniel Ingersoll Bowditch, first lieutenant and adjutant of the 1st Massachusetts Cavalry, had been killed in action on 17 March 1863 at Kelly's Ford, Virginia.

On 19 December, Bowditch noted in a letter to his sister Lucy that "Mr. Sturgis tells me that he has got a furlough for Frank Higginson of which I am very glad indeed." In his next letter, written Christmas Eve 1863, the young captain (he was twenty-one) inquired again about the 5th Massachusetts Cavalry. Bowditch was a good correspondent. On 30 December, writing to his mother, Charles seemed very glad to hear that he was going "to have a commission in the Cavalry with Henry." Bowditch reported a conversation with the 55th Massachusetts's colonel, Alfred Stedman

Hartwell, who "spoke very kindly indeed and said he was sorry to have me go and that I could do a great deal of good by staying here, and in fact a great deal of nonsense and ended off by saying that he could not say anything against my going, especially as it was a promotion and he thought he should leave if he were in my place." Bowditch still had to wait, however, for the slow wheels of the administrations in Boston and Washington to turn. On 21 January, still on Folly Island, Bowditch wrote his father, reporting that he had received his letter "informing me that Governor Andrew had written to Washington for an order for me to report to him." Neither the order nor the commission had yet arrived. Bowditch wrote to his mother on 29 January 1864 to explain: "I have as yet received no orders from Washington. . . . The trouble is you see, that the orders have to be transmitted through all the various headquarters that there are around here." Captain Bowditch ran down the list of his various department, division, brigade, and regimental commanders: "First to Gen. Gillmore, and then successively to Gens. Terry, Gordon, Foster, Colonels Beecher and Hartwell, down to me." Bowditch explained the delay with his tongue firmly in his cheek: "And so taking into consideration the probability, almost amounting to a certainty, that some of the Generals or at least their Adjutant Generals will be found drunk, it is not wonderful that I should have to wait a little while."

February 1864 found Captain Bowditch and the 55th Massachusetts Volunteers on their way to Jacksonville, Florida. Charles wrote his brother Henry from "On board Steamer Peconic, Feb'y 14th, 1864" that the regiment had been under marching orders for a week and had finally gotten off after a day of loading the baggage, unloading the baggage and standing in formation in the hot sun. "We have got the mail on board," Bowditch wrote, "so that we shall have to stop at Hilton Head, which will delay us for some four or five hours or so, and we shall not probably arrive at Jacksonville till tomorrow morning." If one is a believer in fate or destiny, then fate stepped into Bowditch's life. He noted, "My recollection is not very distinct about what happened, but I think I found my orders at Hilton Head to go North." By leaving the 55th at Hilton Head, Bowditch missed the ill-fated 1864 Union expedition to Florida. He continued, "I went before some U.S. officer and was probably mustered out and in again for I left the regiment there and started North. On some accounts I regretted leaving the Fifty-Fifth, but I was not in a condition to do marching and the opportunity to have a horse and to be with Henry was too good a one to be lost." Captain Bowditch's experience shows not only the influence of family but also how difficult it was to obtain the detachment of men who were out of state. Colonel Russell, certainly at Henry Bowditch's urging, had first asked for Charles P. Bowditch on 9 January, along with several other men, among them Lieutenants C. Chauncy Parsons and Charles A. Longfellow of the 1st Massachusetts Cavalry. Longfellow, it turned out, was too badly wounded to serve again in the war.

The requests for Bowditch, Parsons, and Longfellow are easily explained, but one wonders where Russell had met or heard of Sergeants Peter J. Rooney, Company K, 1st U.S. Cavalry, and Rienzi Loud of the 1st Michigan Cavalry, who were also requested on 9 January. Company K, 1st U.S., was then serving as Major General Meade's escort. Perhaps Rooney had impressed a Massachusetts officer on Meade's staff. But how did Sergeant Loud of the 1st Michigan come to the colonel's attention?

When Russell wrote to the governor on 25 January to request again the discharge of C. P. Bowditch, Peter Rooney, and Rienzi Loud, he noted, "the First Michigan Cavalry is at home on furlough." We also do not know where Russell had heard of Private George Rogers of the 1st Vermont Cavalry. He had written to Rogers sometime in December or January. On 9 February, Governor Andrew received a letter on official stationery from J. Gregory Smith, governor of Vermont. Smith wrote that Rogers, "now a paroled prisoner [of war,] has received a letter from Lieutenant Colonel Russell of your Fifth Cavalry Regiment promising [sic] to recommend him for a commission in that regiment so soon as he shall be exchanged." Rogers had applied to "Hon. Porter Baxter, M.C. [member of congress]" for help, and there was "but little doubt of his soon being able to obtain his exchange and transfer." From one governor to another, Smith wanted Andrew to inform Russell of the efforts being made on Rogers's behalf, "in order that the place may be held for him as long as possible and Mr. Rogers acquitted of any negligence in the matter." The reciprocal, connected nature of the relationship between petitioner and petitioned is again apparent. Governor Smith put this concept succinctly to Governor Andrew: "Any assistance you can render which will enable Mr. Rogers to accept this commission will greatly oblige me." Colonel Russell evidently really wanted Private Rogers in the regiment, for he endorsed this letter by stating that he had already issued the commission and informed Congressman Baxter.

The "mysteries" of Rooney, Loud, and Rogers are interesting, but they raise more questions than can be answered due to the lack of available information. Occasionally, if the records have been saved, the subjects speak through them, and such mysteries are solved. An example is the case of Curt Gersdorff.

On 12 January, Colonel Russell "respectfully recommended Corporal Curt Gersdorff Third U.S. Artillery" for a second lieutenant's commission. Two days later, Samuel Breck, assistant U.S. adjutant general, telegraphed Governor Andrew to inform him that Corporal Gersdorff had received his discharge from the 3rd U.S. Artillery for appointment in the 5th Massachusetts Cavalry. Further on in the records, however, is a package of recommendations that shows how a corporal of artillery could become a lieutenant of cavalry. Captain H. G. Gibson, commanding Light Company C, 3rd U.S. Artillery, wrote on 9 August 1862 from Harrison's Landing, Virginia, to recommend Gersdorff "for an appointment as a commissioned officer in any corps of the volunteer service." Gibson found Gersdorff to be a "capable and excellent soldier" and a "gentlemen by birth and education." On the back of Gibson's letter is the concurrence of Colonel Henry J. Hunt, who commanded the artillery of the Army of the Potomac. "I have the highest assurances independent of those of Captain Gibson of his qualifications and respectability," Hunt wrote. The next piece of evidence is a letter a Mr. R. K. Darrake wrote to Senator Charles Sumner from Boston on 20 September 1862. Darrake forwarded Gibson's and Hunt's recommendations of Gersdorff and also gave a clearer picture of the man. Darrake referred to him as "Curt von Gersdorff now acting as a private in Gibson's Battery in the Regular Army." According to Darrake, Von Gersdorff was "a German by birth—a gentleman of character and education, speaking our language perfectly, having been in the country fifteen years." When the war started, Gersdorff was living in San Francisco. He joined a California infantry regiment in which he was commissioned lieutenant. When that regiment was ordered to Oregon, "heartily desiring fighting service, he exchanged with a private in the Regular Army whose company had been ordered to Virginia." Darrake believed that Von Gersdorff was a "true lover of our institutions," for he had "enlisted on principle" and "served faithfully for more than a year. . . . Under these circumstances his friends think he certainly deserves promotion."

R. K. Darrake's letter to the senior senator from Massachusetts received no less than five endorsements as it shuttled between the senator, the artillery brigade, the Adjutant General's Office, and the Headquarters of the Army of the Potomac. The first endorsement, undated, was from Sumner: "I call attention to the within strong case for promotion from Corporal in the regular army to Lieutenant." This was received by the adjutant general of the artillery brigade on 18 October 1862 and forwarded to the Adjutant General's Office in Washington. The brigadier general in charge of the Adjutant General's Office was Lorenzo Thomas, who on 20 October "respectfully referred [the letter] to the Headquarters Army of the Potomac, for information why this man is recommended thus, and not through the regular official channels." Darrake's letter then went back to Captain Gibson. The following explanation was sent to Army of the Potomac Headquarters on 23 October 1862. Captain Gibson wrote that Gersdorff "was recommended by me, as my letter will show, for a commission in the Volunteer service, and not in the Regular Army." Gibson was not aware that recommendations for volunteer commissions had to go through official channels. Captain Gibson had "given the recommendation at the request of his brother, Dr. Gersdorff of Salem, Massachusetts, who represented that he could obtain him a commission in the Mass. Vols—and also at the desire of the Comte de Paris who knew the man's family." The Comte de Paris, as Captain Philippe D'Orleans, served as a volunteer officer on the staff of Major General George McClellan, the commander of the Army of the Potomac. There are two more endorsements on Darrake's letter, one sending it "by command of Major General McClellan," on 24 October 1862 from Headquarters, Army of the Potomac, to General Buford, then chief of cavalry for that army. General Buford apparently kicked the letter back to headquarters, for the final endorsement, dated 31 October 1862, reads, "Respectfully returned to the Adjutant General with the request that the paper may be furnished to his excellency the Gov. of Mass. It is hoped the Corporal will be appointed in the Volunteer Service." George Brinton McClellan, "Major General Comdg.," signed this final note. Underneath McClellan's signature is the scrawled comment of some clerk: "Count von Gersdorff—Gibson's (Reg) Battery Rec. by General McClellan for Massachusetts Commission."

While R. K. Darrake's letter to Sumner was making the rounds, a J. W. Gordon wrote the Honorable Caleb B. Smith, secretary of the interior, from

Fort Independence, Boston Harbor. Dated 20 October 1862, Gordon had certainly seen Darrake's letter, because he chose to repeat verbatim the part of it that described Gersdorff. Gordon had never met the man he was recommending, but "those who know him will say that he merits promotion; and will be an honor to the service." Gordon then rather delicately stated the purpose of his letter: "Among [Gersdorff's] friends are many gentlemen of Boston, who ask me to ask your cooperation with others to secure his advancement. In compliance with their wishes I do ask you, if at all compatible with your sense of duty and relations to others, to give him your assistance." Secretary of the Interior Smith sent Gordon's letter, with a positive endorsement, to Secretary of War Stanton. Stanton directed that Assistant Adjutant General E. D. Townshend send the whole package to the governor of Massachusetts, which was duly done on 4 November 1862.

The last link in the chain of how Corporal Gersdorff of the 3rd U.S. Artillery became Second Lieutenant Count Curt von Gersdorff, Company L, 5th Massachusetts Volunteer Cavalry, survives as a beautiful quarto of cream-colored notepaper. Engraved across the top is the legend "Office of Evarts, Southmayd & Choate, No. 2 Hanover Street." In the upper left-hand corner are the names of the firm's partners: "Wm M. Evarts, Charles F. Southmayd, Joseph H. Choate, J. Evarts Tracy." The writer, Joseph H. Choate, was from an old and distinguished family that had had sons in the service of Massachusetts and the republic since the founding of each. Choate wrote from New York on 16 January 1864 to Governor Andrew: "I thank you very much for the commission issued to my friend Gersdorff in whose behalf I made application when last in Boston. He is a worthy fellow and will I am sure do credit to the service." Gersdorff remained with the regiment throughout its service, mustering out as first lieutenant of Company L.

Although the commissioning of officers was proceeding well, there were problems. In the 5th Massachusetts Cavalry, money was almost always the cause of discontent, often—as had happened throughout history—due to the unkept promises of recruiters. Eleven men signed a petition that was sent, in true democratic fashion, not up the chain of command but directly to the governor on 14 January 1864:

Your Honor: we the colored soldiers, composing the Fifth Massachusetts Cavalry do appeal unto you for information respecting our bounty money. We were

*informed by our Recruiting Officer that we were to receive our bounty as soon
as we were mustered into the U.S. Service, but we have found matters to be the
contrary. The reason why we want to know this, is because we want some time to
dispose of it. We have families that are in utter need of it. We would like to know,
if our families, residing out of the state, can receive the state aid of Massachusetts,
by sending their affidavit.*

The eleven troopers were from Company A and incipient Companies B and
C. As in any group, they ranged across the spectrum from miscreants to men
who rose as far as the system let them. Two of the men were mentioned
already in chapter 2: Sergeant John D. Berry, the forty-two-year-old barber
from Watkins, New York, and John E. Mezzeck, the tailor from Charleston,
South Carolina, who deserted on 30 April 1864. James H. Rhoades, a
thirty-nine-year-old farmer from Wilmington, Delaware, also deserted on
15 February 1864.

Of the eleven, only Solomon Peterson, thirty-eight, a farmer from Scio,
New York, had to make his mark. The remainder signed their names. Peterson
remained a private, but he stayed with the regiment until its muster out.
Other privates who signed the petition and soldiered with the 5th Massachusetts
Cavalry until its dissolution were Henry N. Guice, nineteen, a
grocer from Waterproof, Louisiana; Ellis E. Brown, a laborer from Lancaster
County, Pennsylvania; James H. Mann, a twenty-four-year-old seaman
from Boston; and George T. Fisher, thirty-nine, a butcher from Mansfield,
Massachusetts, who was discharged in New York City on 7 November 1865.

The three remaining signers of the petition can be described as natural
leaders. William H. Jacobs, thirty, a hairdresser who gave his residence as
North Bridgewater, Massachusetts, was advanced from sergeant to regimental
commissary sergeant in September 1865 and mustered out with
the regimental noncommissioned staff. Joseph A. Ricker, twenty-four, said
he was from Newton, Massachusetts. Ricker, who wrote "horseman" as his
occupation, mustered out as B Company's first sergeant. Another top soldier
was Bazzel C. Barker, a thirty-seven-year-old barber from Boston. Barker
mustered out as M Company's first sergeant.

The letter went to Governor Andrew who probably sent it back to
Colonel Russell, who must have referred it to the state agency responsible
for paying bounties. Almost six weeks would pass before Colonel Russell

received an answer to the inquiry that began with these men. In the meantime, Russell had a regiment to recruit, muster, and train.

On 21 and 22 January, Russell asked that Governor Andrew and a Major Rogers of the Massachusetts Adjutant General's Office request that Captain Zabdiel Boylston Adams, 2nd Massachusetts Cavalry, be detailed to Boston for promotion to major in the 5th Massachusetts Cavalry. Also on 22 January, Russell respectfully requested a "commission as Major in Fifth Massachusetts Cavalry be issued to Captain H. N. Weld . . . as a battalion is ready for him to be mustered with." Companies B, C, and D were mustered into federal service on 23 January 1864. Captain Horace Weld, with Lieutenant J. Davenport Fisher as acting adjutant of the regiment, issued his first order, General Order No. 1, on 24 January 1864. The task of Horace Weld and the officers under his command was first to turn recruits into cavalry troopers by putting them through the "School of the Soldier." This involved learning how to stand, or, as Colonel Philip St. George Cooke put it in *Cavalry Tactics or Regulations for the Instruction, Formations, and Movements of the Cavalry of the Army and Volunteers of the United States*, the "Position of the Trooper Dismounted: The feet turned out equally, and forming with each other something less than a right angle; the knees straight without stiffness; the body erect on the hips, inclining a little forward; the belly rather drawn in, and the breast advanced; the shoulders square and falling equally; the arms hanging near the side; the palm of the hand turned a little to the front; the head erect and square to the front, without constraint; the eyes straight to the front. When the trooper is armed, the left hand hangs by the side over the sabre."

As of January 1864, four full companies, a battalion of over three hundred men, had been mustered into the 5th Massachusetts Volunteer Cavalry and sworn into federal service. Recruits were learning to form squads, platoons, and companies; facing movements; how to march and how to salute; and who to salute and when. When these rudiments had been instilled, the recruit might be called a soldier. At Camp Meigs, troopers advanced beyond the School of the Soldier to drill and the various details all announced by bugle calls in the cavalry. The majority of the men would be engaged in the dismounted drill of cavalry, learning all the commands and calls to throw out a line of skirmishers, to send out flankers, to go from a column of twos to a column of fours, to columns of squadrons (two companies abreast), to line of battle and back again.

CHAPTER FOUR

"Trained to the Sabre"

Government has telegraphed McKim to buy horses and send to the [Cavalry Depot] Geesborough [Maryland] not furnishing them to our fifth, not even allowing the first battalion to carry those already on hand. Thus they would break it up as cavalry, though now eleven companies full, trained to the sabre and already one third mounted. We have selected officers of the highest character and best experience and carefully selected men to present a model cavalry—all for nought. Nothing but absolute necessity can excuse it.

—GOVERNOR JOHN ANDREW TO MASSACHUSETTS
CONGRESSMAN SAMUEL HOOPER, 30 APRIL 1864

BY THE BEGINNING OF 1864, MEN WHO HAD BEGUN WITH

The Position of the Trooper Dismounted: The feet turned out equally, and form- ing with each other something less than a right angle; the knees straight without stiffness; the body erect on the hips, inclining a little forward; the belly rather drawn in, and the breast advanced; the shoulders square and falling equally; the arms hanging near the side; the palm of the hand turned a little to the front; the head erect and square to the front, without constraint; the eyes straight to the front. When the trooper is armed, the left hand hangs by the side over the sabre[,]

had advanced to marching, the manual of arms, and in general the School of the Soldier.

August Kautz, who was a mediocre general but a productive writer, wrote a treatise during the war called *Customs of Service for Non-Commissioned Officers.* Under "Duties in Camp or Garrison," Kautz wrote that "the various duties to which a soldier is subject are matters of regular detail—each soldier taking his regular tour of each as it comes, and consist, in the main of the following:—1st. Guards. 2nd. Working-parties or fatigue. 3rd. Daily Duty."

Guard mounting involved a great deal of responsibility and ceremony. Veteran troops or regulars would have a first sergeant in immediate command of the guard detail. He would check the uniforms, equipment, and weapons of the soldiers and then march them to the sergeant major or officer of the day, who would inspect them again and divide the guard into three details or reliefs, with each man numbered. This was so that in case of alarm the guard could give his post number and thus location to the corporal of the guard and the officer in charge of the guard detail. Sentinels had to learn not only the proper way to challenge "Halt, who comes there?" and respond "Advance, friend, with the countersign!" but also whom to salute. Sentries had to present arms to officers above the rank of captain but including the officer of the day, whatever his rank. Sentries might have special orders, such as to stand guard over commissary, quartermaster, or ordnance stores.

The general orders of the guard, like the position of attention, are indelible to time. From *Customs of Service for Non-Commissioned Officers*: "I am required to take charge of this post and all public property in view; to salute all officers passing, according to rank; to give the alarm in case of fire, or the approach of an enemy, or any disturbance whatsoever; to report all violations of the Articles of War, Regulations of the Army, or camp or garrison orders; at night, to challenge all persons approaching my post, and to allow no one to pass without the countersign until they are examined by an officer or non-commissioned officer of the guard!" Usually sentries would challenge from Taps until Reveille.

Generally, working or fatigue parties in camp would be charged with "policing" or cleaning the barracks, cookhouses, officers' quarters, and parade ground of the regiment. Daily duty involved soldiers who were detailed as company cooks, clerks, or orderlies. Kautz described orderlies as "soldiers selected on account of their intelligence, experience, and soldierly bearing to attend on generals, commanding officers, officers of the day and staff officers, to carry orders, messages &c." A man on daily duty was excused from guard detail, working parties, and the general drill of the regiment.

Captain Horace Weld's first orders reveal a regiment still in the process of forming, both men and officers becoming accustomed to their duties.

On 24 January 1864, Weld's General Order No. 1 read, "Companies will be formed for Company Inspection at 11 o'clock in front (east) of the Barracks. Company Commanders will see that the men appear properly uniformed and with hair and beard neatly trimmed and that Barracks and Kitchens are put in proper order." Newly promoted Major Weld issued Special Order No. 1 on 26 January 1864 detailing "the order of daily duties for this command." The trooper's day began with "Reveille, 1st call" at 6:30 a.m., "Roll Call" at 6:45, and then "Police in Quarters immediately after Roll Call, orderlies Call, 1st. Sergeants report to Adjutant" at 7:15. Breakfast was at 7:30 followed by "Surgeons Call" at 8:00. At 8:30 a.m. was "First Call" for the guard, and "Guard Mounting" occurred at 8:45. "Camp Police" began immediately after guard mounting. Morning drill began at 11:00 a.m., with "Recall" and "dinner" at 12:30 p.m. After the midday meal, orderlies and first sergeants reported again to the adjutant for orders. Afternoon drill was from 2:00 p.m. until "Recall" at 3:30. "Retreat" and another roll call were held at 4:30. The men were fed supper at 5:00 p.m. "Tattoo," the evening formation, was at 8:00, involving another roll call, with Taps at 8:30 p.m. Major Weld further specified that the "three stated roll calls each day" would be "attended by a commissioned officer."

The holding of three roll calls a day implies that Weld was trying to bring order out of a somewhat chaotic situation, with new recruits coming in daily and being assigned to newly forming companies. This is borne out by the remainder of Special Order No. 1: "Light will be extinguished in the quarters of all enlisted men at Taps. All Furloughs must be sent to Headquarters by 730 a.m. after which time none will be approved. They must in all cases be signed by the commanding officers of all companies and be presented at headquarters by a Sergeant." Anyone far from home, with a group of strangers, would want to meet and converse with his barrack mates, to settle in, to talk politics or women or the war, perhaps to engage in a little roughhousing or horseplay. Also natural was a desire to go on furlough to see the sights of Boston, especially in the handsome uniform of a cavalry trooper. Major Weld wanted to tighten up both practices.

Weld also wanted to increase discipline among his officers. Two orders were issued on 27 January; Special Order No. 2 was for officers commanding companies to report to the "Major Commanding immediately after roll calls." It should have been a given that officers report to the commanding officer for orders and instructions, at least at the start of the day. One wonders whether perhaps there were some officers wandering about, not knowing where they should be or what they should be doing. General Order No. 2 of the same date required company officers to "personally attend to drilling their detail for guard before guardmounting until further orders." Sloppy or unskilled sentries reflected poorly not only on the officer in charge but also on the entire command. Major Weld's General Order No. 3 of 31 January 1864 is further evidence of the rather chaotic state of the nascent 5th Massachusetts Cavalry. Officers commanding companies were to "immediately see that all men rejected from the list of those to be mustered into their respective companies be clothed in citizens dress and their uniforms taken from them and they should be forthwith sent out of camp unless retained as officers servants." Officers were to "pay especial attention to account for all men on their rolls." Enlisted men were required to "quarter in the barrack to which they belong." All newly enlisted recruits were assigned to Company E. This order also made officers responsible for any company property "carried off" by men going on furlough.

The 1st of February, a Monday, saw Major Weld suspend further furloughs until the "Third instant except in cases of sickness or other extreme need, and then only for twenty-four hours." The same day, he also ordered company officers to "give personal attention to seeing that all men in their command are vaccinated without delay." We assume this was for smallpox, although only one man in the 1st Battalion, Private Thornton Hayden of Company A, died of disease in January and February. Hayden, who gave Falmouth, Virginia, as his place of birth, died aged twenty-one on 25 January 1864.

Major Weld held his first battalion inspection at 10:00 a.m. on Sunday, 7 February. Company commanders were ordered to "inspect their commands and respective quarters half an hour previous. There will be bugle calls for both inspections." The major "expected that [the men] appear neatly dressed and that the barracks present a clean, orderly appearance." Weld fine-tuned the daily schedule again on 7 February, revoking Special Order No. 1 and replacing it with Special Order No. 18. There were a few changes. Camp police were to report to the officer of the day, who was not mentioned before, immediately after guard mount (8:45 a.m.). Morning drill was pushed back an hour to 10:00, Recall to 11:00 to allow the battalion to assemble for the noon meal. The biggest change was the introduction of a daily dress parade.

First Call was at 3:30 p.m.; companies assembled at 3:45 and marched to parade at 4:00. Retreat, "when dress parade omitted," was held at 4:30. Three roll calls a day were still being held. Major Weld was reluctant to grant leave, furloughs were "granted to mustered men at the rate of from two to a company daily but long furloughs should not be given without consulting the officer commanding the Regiment and the men should be present for Sunday inspection as far as practicable." Dress parade was a way of further instilling unit identity and pride as well as a sign that Major Weld had growing confidence in the ability of the men to take care of their uniforms and keep in step.

Back in Boston, young men seeking places in the regiment continued to call on Governor Andrew and Colonel Russell. Professor Theophilus Parsons, who had been interested in the regiment from the beginning and had committed his son Chauncy to its success, was now instrumental in sending to the regiment a graduate from the Dane Law School at Harvard. The three men who signed Daniel H. Chamberlain's letter of recommendation had all been his professors at the law school. They all were apparently impressed by Chamberlain and sought to reward merit. The three professors—Theophilus Parsons, former Massachusetts governor Emory Washburn, and retired judge Joel Parker—sent their letter to Governor Andrew on 21 January 1864. It begins, "This will be handed to you by Mr. Daniel H. Chamberlain who does not know its contents, but calls at our suggestion and knows generally the purposes of the letter." They then went on to introduce the bearer: "Mr. Chamberlain came to the Law School from Yale where he took the highest honors of his class. Since he has been here, he has fully sustained the high reputation which he brought with him." His preceptors considered Chamberlain diligent with an unblemished character and "prospects in his profession second to none." The problem, however, was that Chamberlain felt it "his duty to take part in some form in the present national struggle, and so deeply has he felt this that being without patronage or friends to help any claims he might have for a position of more usefulness or influence that he concluded to enlist as a private."

Chamberlain's situation was similar to that of Corporal Curt Gersdorff's in that serving as an enlisted man was a perceived waste of talent. They had intervened "because it really seems to be moral strength thrown away to confirm persons so decidedly superior to the duties of a private soldier." The professors had "remonstrated with him" until they could check with Governor Andrew to see "if there was any office vacant to which you might see fit to appoint him." Parsons, Washburn, and Parker had convinced Chamberlain to "forbear carrying his intentions to enlist into effect until there was an opportunity to ascertain whether there was some wider sphere open." They had asked the young man to deliver the letter in person (never doubting he would be admitted) to introduce him to the governor. It was up to the governor to "converse with him and judge whether he had better be left to carry out his original plans or turn his qualification to some more significant account." The three gentlemen closed by writing that "simply . . . our high estimate" of Chamberlain's qualities had prompted them to write the governor. John Andrew sent this letter to Colonel Russell. "Especial attention," wrote the governor, "is called to the enclosed testimonial from all the professors at the Cambridge Law School."

The matter did not end with Chamberlain's immediate acceptance and commissioning, however. Theophilus Parsons wrote directly to Henry Sturgis Russell on 25 January. Parsons explained that "Governor Washburn (of the Law School) wrote a letter to Governor Andrew which Judge Parker and I signed—respecting Mr. Daniel Chamberlain." Governor Andrew had then urged Parsons to communicate directly with Russell. Washburn had not wanted to see Chamberlain enlist as a private, Parsons wrote. The professor felt that there was "no superior" at the Law School; his praise for Chamberlain was unrestrained: "In all my very wide acquaintance with young men, I have known few who were his equals in quickness and clearness of perception, indomitable energy, and fidelity to all duty. And he is a thorough gentleman in character and manners." Parsons also emphasized the altruistic nature of their actions on Chamberlain's behalf. The faculty had joined in recommending him, "but none of us have the slightest interest in the question, beyond our desire to put 'the right man in the right place.'" Daniel Henry Chamberlain's name was submitted to Governor Andrew the same day Russell received Parson's letter. He was commissioned first lieutenant in March 1864 and took over the duties of adjutant of the regiment from James Newell in February 1865.

The end of January 1864 also saw the commissioning of two scions of the noted Higginson family of Massachusetts. Robert Minturn Higginson was eighteen, the youngest son of Stephen and Agnes (Cochran) Higginson. His brothers were Samuel Storrow (called "Storrow"), who became chaplain of the 9th Regiment, U.S. Colored Troops, and Francis John, who graduated from the Naval Academy in 1861. Robert's first cousin, Francis Lee Higginson, also joined the 5th Massachusetts Cavalry on 30 January. Francis, known as "Frank," was at home on sick leave from the 54th Massachusetts Infantry, where he was a captain. Robert's father and Frank's father were brothers. The young men's grandfather, also Stephen, had remarried after the death of his first wife. A child of this second marriage was Thomas Wentworth Higginson, thus making him the boys' uncle. Robert Minturn and Francis Lee Higginson were the ninth generation to bear that name in America.

Two of Frank's siblings who saw service were Henry Lee Higginson and James Jackson Higginson, both of whom served with the 1st Massachusetts Cavalry Volunteers. Frank was awarded a degree from Harvard in 1863, although he had joined the army before completing his studies. Robert went to Harvard after the war. The prestige of the Higginson name was further enhanced by the fact that, like Charles Bowditch, Frank had previously served with African American troops from the Bay State. The American Civil War saw elites on both sides of the conflict willingly participate.

Harry Russell was almost ready to leave letter-writing and recruiting duty in Boston and move out to Readville. First he had to report to the governor. Writing on official stationery ("Commonwealth of Massachusetts, Executive Department"), Russell on 12 February gave the roster of officers of the "Fifth Regiment Massachusetts Cavalry." Field and staff consisted of himself; Major Weld; Surgeon George S. Osbourne (Harvard AB 1861, MD 1863), formerly assistant surgeon, 1st Massachusetts Cavalry; and Assistant Surgeon Samuel Ingalls. Majors Henry Bowditch and Zabdiel Adams had yet to report for duty. The positions of lieutenant colonel and chaplain were open. There were six captains, leaving six vacancies; ten first lieutenants, leaving five more to be appointed; and eleven second lieutenants, leaving one vacancy. Out of forty-seven possible commissioned officers, thirty-three had been named by the middle of February.

Two days later, the colonel was with his troops at Camp Meigs. Russell issued two written orders on 14 February. His first, General Order No. 7, was a repeat of Major Weld's order of a week before, except that the colonel called for a regimental instead of a battalion inspection. Company E had been mustered into federal service on the 10th of the month and G and H companies were nearly full, so regimental officers had around five hundred men to inspect. The men were to "form in line, on the third squadron in the field on the left of the camp." The men were to fall in without overcoats, presumably so their brass could be checked. Russell expected "that the men will appear neatly dressed, with boots blacked and hair and beards properly trimmed." Colonel Russell also wanted his men to soldier on despite the New England climate. Russell ordered all roll calls to be held "out of doors except in stormy or extreme cold weather." First sergeants were expected "to draw their rolls by heart." As a further disciplinary measure, on 15 February, Russell ordered that no passes were to be issued "for men to be out of camp after retreat."

Now that he was at camp, Colonel Russell wanted to get on with the business of training his regiment. Part of that process continued to be appointing the best available men to be officers. On 17 February 1864, Russell responded to a letter forwarded to him by Governor Andrew: "Jacob Nebrick's recommendations are certainly of the best," Russell wrote, "but, when I tell you that I already have seventeen officers designate, not familiar with the cavalry arm, I hope you will allow me to fill the few remaining vacancies by deserving men from the cavalry regiments now in the field." The regiments Russell had in mind, primarily, were the 1st and 2nd Regiments of Massachusetts Cavalry. To Andrew's credit, except for Henry Hinckley, whom Russell accepted in March, he no longer suggested candidates without cavalry experience. Colonel Russell was on the ground with his regiment and thus able to turn inexperienced officer candidates away.

On 20 February, Colonel Russell received an answer to the 14 January petition of the eleven troopers for their bounty money. Written by Colonel J. F. B. Marshall, paymaster general of state bounties, the letter is a model of bureaucratic patronization. Paymaster Marshall opened his letter with a blanket negative: "In consequence of the numerous fraud and impositions practiced upon the soldiers which have recently come to our knowledge, we have been compelled to decline receiving any order from the volunteers for their state bounties, unless the same shall have been endorsed as having been examined and approved by the town or city authorities on whose quota the volunteer enlisted." Marshall had a response to the obvious objection to the state's policy. "We have several orders presented from the men of your regiment by persons who have represented that it would be difficult to obtain such endorsement, the men being in camp, and not able to vouch for the correctness of the orders. As the colored men who come generally from a distance, are more in danger of being victimized than other volunteers, we do not feel disposed to relax any of our rules in their case, but rather to subject their orders to a closer scrutiny." The "orders" referred to were chits or IOUs against the bounty and pay of the enlisted men. The troopers were advanced cash, for a fee, by "bounty brokers." A more modern term for such men is "loan sharks." Although he was keeping a watchful eye on the bounty brokers, Marshall thus also made it much harder for the men to send money to their families out of state. "I have therefore," he wrote, "informed the parties presenting these orders, that we shall require either the endorsement of the city or town authorities or that of yourself, as Colonel of the regiment, before we can receive such orders."

We cannot know whether J. F. B. Marshall was sincere when he wrote Colonel Russell—if he was truly looking out for the troopers of the 5th Cavalry or if he was a paternalistic bigot who used a strict adherence to rules to avoid paying the men their signing bonuses. According to Marshall, the Office of the Paymaster of State Bounties was acting in the best interest of the troopers of the 5th Cavalry. "As our object is solely to prevent imposition on the men, and restrain them from needlessly squandering their bounties, we feel confident that you will not object to the extra trouble which this requirement may occasion you." Colonel Russell did not waste his time protesting to a functionary like J. F. B. Marshall. Instead, he advanced his own money to the men and requested reimbursement from the paymaster of state bounties.

Paymaster Marshall's letter shows the depth of prejudice still extant in Massachusetts, a state supposedly committed to emancipation and rights for African Americans. Marshall's bigotry is more insidious because of its assumed commonness. Marshall assumed that the colonel of an African American regiment would agree that blacks were unsophisticated and naive—stupid, even—and thus easily victimized. The men should not be paid the full promised bounty, even if it would save their families from poverty, because blacks were profligate and "easily victimized." Marshall assumed that, never having possessed any money, the African American troopers of the 5th Massachusetts Volunteer Cavalry would "needlessly squander" any they received.

As February 1864 gave way to March, Colonel Russell acted to commission deserving white cavalrymen. Patrick Tracy Jackson's father was one of the most influential and successful merchants in Massachusetts. The Jacksons since colonial days had been allied and intermarried with the Cabots, Lees, and Higginsons. Young Patrick had left Harvard at eighteen to take a commission as a second lieutenant in the 1st Massachusetts Cavalry. He was acting adjutant of that regiment and mustering officer in Boston when Russell persuaded him to take a first lieutenant's commission in the African American cavalry regiment. At nineteen, Jackson was one of the youngest officers commissioned, but he had seen more than six months of hard campaigning in Virginia with the 1st Massachusetts Cavalry. Lieutenant Jackson was assigned to Company D of the 1st Cavalry, and it was perhaps at his suggestion that Sergeants George D. Odell and Cornelius Kaler of D Company, 1st Massachusetts Cavalry, were commissioned into the regiment.

George Odell had been a clerk in Sanbornton, New Hampshire, before the war. He had joined the 1st Massachusetts in September 1861. Odell was promoted to corporal in 1861 and sergeant in March 1863. At the cavalry engagement at Aldie, Virginia, fought 17 June 1863, Odell was color sergeant for the regiment. The 1st Massachusetts Cavalry suffered heavily at Aldie, losing 154 men (killed, wounded, or missing) out of a little over three hundred present.

Cornelius Kaler, who at twenty-four was the same age as Odell, had been a shoemaker in Bradford, Massachusetts. Kaler had served in the 5th Massachusetts Infantry, a ninety-day regiment in 1861, and then joined the cavalry that fall. Sergeant Kaler was a resourceful, or lucky, man. At Aldie he had been wounded and captured but escaped. In October 1863, during the Rappahannock Campaign, Kaler was captured again; again he managed to escape. Kaler had reenlisted in the 1st Massachusetts Cavalry in January 1864. He was offered a second lieutenant's commission in the 1st on 1 March but preferred higher rank with the 5th. He came into the regiment as a first lieutenant and was promoted captain, commanding Company M, in April 1864. The 1st Massachusetts Cavalry's regimental quartermaster sergeant, Edward H. Adams, was also commissioned in early March 1864. Adams, twenty-three, had been a saddler before the war, which profession he followed in the army as saddler sergeant until promoted to quartermaster sergeant of the 1st Massachusetts.

On 10 March 1864, Colonel Russell wrote to the governor requesting that "First Lieutenant Erik Wulff, Fifty-Fourth Massachusetts Volunteers be commissioned Captain in Fifth Massachusetts Cavalry." Erik Wulff was in Boston recruiting for the 54th Infantry. Wulff had seen some hard service as a private in the 20th Massachusetts Infantry. He had been commissioned into the 54th in the spring of 1863 but apparently did not leave the state when the regiment left camp on 28 May 1863. There was some confusion caused by the transfer of the 54th's surplus officers and men to the then-forming 55th Massachusetts Infantry. James Bowen noted in his account of the regiment that "Probably at the time of leaving the state the roster of officers was nominally filled; but while some necessarily remained to assist in the formation of the Fifty-Fifth Regiment, others were on staff or detached duty from which they did not return to their places in the Fifty-Fourth, and yet others did not report for service." Lieutenant Wulff was apparently one of those on detached duty, for he was never reported with the regiment in the field.

There were several enlisted men in the same situation as Lieutenant Wulff. Men became ill, remained in Boston to help fill up the 55th Regiment, or went home on furlough and literally missed the boat. One such was the youngest son of African American abolitionist Frederick Douglass, Charles Remond Douglass. Charles and his brother Lewis had both enlisted in the 54th Massachusetts in the spring of 1863. C. R. Douglass was in fact carried on the "company muster in and descriptive roll" of F Company for almost a year. In May and June 1863, he was reported "absent on furlough to go to Rochester, N.Y." and then "absent without leave since June 29, 1863." It's clear that after the regiment left for South Carolina, his company officers weren't sure where Douglass was. The July 1863 company returns list him as "absent at Rochester, New York since May 28, 1863." The December 1863 report lists him at Readville, Massachusetts, as a private in the 54th, "reported as deserter by error." The December 1863 and January 1864 return describes him as "absent sick at Readville, Massachusetts since June 29, 1863 dropped as a deserter by error." Douglass was alternately listed as absent sick at Rochester or Readville until April 1864, when his 54th Infantry muster roll reads, "Discharged for Promotion in 5 Mass. Cav. by SO [Special Order] 122 AGO [Adjutant General's Office] Washington, March 19, 1864." In fact, Governor Andrew wrote to Secretary of War Stanton on 14 March

1864 on behalf of Douglass, requesting Douglass's transfer to the 5th Massachusetts Cavalry. Andrew explained to Stanton that Douglass was the son of the famous Frederick Douglass, who had recruited his sons Charles and Lewis back in February 1863. Charles, because of a "lung complaint," had been prevented from "ever taking the field with the Fifty-fourth."

Charles R. Douglass was enlisted into Company I of the 5th Massachusetts Cavalry. The company was sworn in on 26 March, and not long after, Douglass, who gave "printer" as his occupation and West Roxbury, Massachusetts, as his residence, became I Company's first sergeant. The commanding officer of Company I was Captain Erik Wulff.

Charles R. Douglass was young, just nineteen, when he joined the 5th Cavalry. His few surviving letters home show a young man somewhat impetuous, immature, and seeking the approval of his famous father. Unfortunately, the father's letters to his son are not preserved, so we are left with only half a conversation. From Charles's few saved letters, we can infer that he transferred to the 55th Massachusetts Infantry and then remained behind when that regiment left the state.

On 6 July 1863, Charles wrote his father from Camp Meigs. He had spent the 4th and 5th in Boston, where he had gone to "Mr. Grimes Church and Dr. Rock read a letter that he had received from his wife who is in Philadelphia." Mrs. Rock's letter said that "the rebels were sending the negroes south [into slavery] as fast as they advanced upon our lines and that the colored people were rushing into Philadelphia and that yourself and Stephen Smith and others were doing all you could for them." The son urged his father to "keep out of the hands of the rebels." In his letter, young Douglass also showed his impetuosity. "This morning as I was about to take the train for camp," he wrote, "I saw some returned soldiers from Newbern, N.C. We had just got the news that Meade had whipped the rebels [at Gettysburg] and behind me stood an Irishman." Douglass's vocal support of Meade "made the Irish mad and he stepped in front of me with his fist doubled up in my face and said 'Ain't McClellan a good General . . . you black nigger! I don't care if you have got the uniform on!'" Douglass was enraged, so mad that he "sweat freely." He took off his coat and "went at" the man. While this exchange was going on, a policeman watched from the opposite platform. As Douglass attacked the other man "(he was heavier than me), the policeman came and stopped me and asked what the matter was." Douglass explained, and the cop marched "the other fellow off and that made all the other Irish mad and I felt better." Douglass was not afraid, moreover, because he was armed. "I did not care for them because I had my pistol and it was well loaded." Douglass had made up his mind to "shoot the first Irishman that strikes me—they may talk, but keep their paws to themselves." Douglass ended this letter by writing that the regiment [the 55th] was "a good, healthy looking set of men" and that they were expecting to leave the next week. Douglass hoped to see his father before leaving Massachusetts, but there was apparently no rush, as "the flag has not been presented yet." Douglas instructed his father to send any reply care of Martin Becker, commissary sergeant, 55th Regiment of Massachusetts Volunteers.

September 1863 found Charles Douglass still in Boston. He wrote his father two letters that month, one on the 8th and one on the 18th. Douglass had apparently made some wild statements about the treatment of African American soldiers in camp, for his letter of 8 September is largely explanation. "I have never brought any disgrace upon the family and I never mean to," he wrote. Douglass had never stolen anything, although he had said that he would "take a chicken or anything else to eat when I was hungry, but I have not done so." Douglass had written of soldiers stealing chickens, but he had followed orders and even had "the praise to day of General Pierce [Peirce] of keeping things neat and orderly about the camp." Douglass had pitched in when all were sick except he. Some nights, Douglass was up all night with the ill and "stood over those that died and laid them out[,] wrote to their friends and in fact done most all that was to do except doctor them."

Douglass became sick himself. He "could not drink coffee sweetened with molasses" and had to live on "dry bread alone," for the men were given meat only once a week, and that used to make broth for the sick. Douglass "fell away like a skeleton." When he complained, the doctor, who did not care, for "he had plenty," explained that "hospital rations were small and that we could not draw full rations." To Douglass, that seemed "a funny way to starve a lot of men in a state where there is plenty." Douglass's anger at being "used mean" prompted him to write home and say "anything that came in my head." Douglass resolved to continue to complain. The sick soldiers were "treated like men when the regiment was here, but now they are treated worse than dogs." Douglass's personal situation had improved now that he was on recruiting duty in Boston, and he was happy working with

Lieutenant Wulff: "A man every inch of him, he is a Swede by birth but he is my friend, he has done all he could to have the men satisfied, but there are higher officers then [*sic*] him." Douglass blamed the embezzlement of the quartermaster—"it is for the benefit of his pocket that we don't have our rations." Lieutenant Wulff, Douglass informed his father, was "agoing to establish a new camp, new tents and everything for the fifty-fourth men that we are recruiting and he will have charge of everything, commissary department and all and then our men will have what is right." After a final plea not to "think hard of me for what I said[,] a person will do most anything before they will starve, and say anything." Charles directed his letters sent care of Lieutenant Wulff, Readville.

On 18 September, Douglass wrote his father to bring him up to date on his situation in the army. He had recently had an interview with Colonel Hallowell of the 54th, who told Douglass that he might have "to go down to Morris Island early next month with a batch of conscripts for the 54th, giving me to understand that I must be ready at a moment's notice." Douglass had also seen his "Captain who is on furlough." Although Douglass does not mention him by name, this could only be Francis Lee Higginson. Captain Higginson told Douglass that "Colonel Shaw never told him that I was to report to the 55 [55th Massachusetts Infantry] and after my furlough had passed two weeks" Douglas was reported as a deserter. Colonel Shaw had intervened, however, as "he knew that I was sick and not a deserter." Douglass asserted that he would never desert: "I take a bullet first." Charles hoped to remain in Boston; Lieutenant Wulff was "trying hard to have me stay and help him as I suit him first rate." Charles had written his father "for a couple of your photographs with your name written upon them," one for himself and one for "Lieutenant Wulff whom I esteem as a true friend." Douglass promised to write "as soon as I receive orders to pack my knapsack."

Charles Remond Douglass did not pack his knapsack in September 1863. The only surviving letter from Douglass between September 1863 and May 1864 is dated 20 December 1863. Young Douglass wrote requesting money so he could go home for Christmas. He did not mention Erik Wulff or his activities in Boston, confining his narrative to details of a lawsuit he had pending in the courts. Charles assumed that his brother Frederick had acquainted their father with the details of the case, "but since Frederick has left I have had my defendant rearrested and put under $500 bond so that now he is safe in jail." Douglass had been urged to settle the case (he was not specific about its origins) but refused "because I saw that I had friends to stand by me and to have settled it for a little money would have turned them against me." Charles closed his letter by reassuring his father that he "had some friends here yet." The lack of other letters leaves an incomplete and potentially unflattering portrait of Charles R. Douglass, but his youth should be taken into account. In any case, clearly a man Douglass considered a friend was Lieutenant Erik Wulff of the 54th Massachusetts Volunteers.

Colonel Russell must have welcomed Wulff to the 5th Massachusetts Cavalry. Although without cavalry experience, Wulff qualified for the regiment because, like Charles Bowditch and Francis Higginson, he had commanded black troops. If any difference existed between Erik Wulff and the Higginson and Bowditch youths, it was that Wulff was not a gentleman. Charles Pickering Bowditch made a negative comparison between the officers and men of the 5th Cavalry and those of Massachusetts's two black infantry regiments. His choice of words is interesting: "The men were by no means equal in character to those of the Fifty-Fourth and Fifty-Fifth, and the officers were not of the same class in many cases as those of my old regiment." Bowditch may have been put off by the coarseness of some of the officers—who were self-made men—and by the lack of zealotry among the African Americans who were following the pathfinders of social revolution of a year before. Bowditch, however, failed to mention the courage, self-sacrifice, and tenacity of men who were willing to travel great distances to become soldiers, to leave their families and enlist. These black troopers enlisted and trained knowing the whole time that they would not receive pay equal to that of white soldiers, nor would they have a chance for a commission.

Colonel Russell had sought experienced cavalrymen for his officers, and by and large he was successful. By the end of March, except for Sergeant Robert M. Parker of the 2nd Massachusetts Cavalry, commissioned second lieutenant on 29 April, and a couple of staff officers (surgeons), the regiment's complement of line officers was full. When the 5th Massachusetts Cavalry entrained, by battalion, in May 1864 for Virginia, the regiment was short one captain. A Captain Edward Merrill was commissioned into the regiment, but illness prevented his muster in and he was eventually allowed to resign. A lieutenant colonel had not been commissioned, nor did the 5th Cavalry have a chaplain. A chaplaincy was not within the governor's powers to grant, as he had explained to the (white) Reverend Isaac S. Cushman of Newburyport, Massachusetts: "The enclosed order [expects] the regiments in progress now and hereafter to be entitled to Chaplains[,] the election of which lies with the officers and not with me." The officers of the regiment never did vote on a chaplain, however necessary that figure was to morale. Nor was any "unofficial" preacher from the ranks noted in regimental accounts, although George S. Menoken, thirty-nine, who enlisted on 27 February 1864 in Company K, gave "clergyman" as his occupation.

Of the forty-five officers present in May 1864, thirty-five of them had military experience of some kind. This experience ranged from men who had been privates in the ninety-day regiments of the early weeks of the war to officers who had commanded cavalry squadrons. Of these thirty-five men who had been in uniform, twenty-six of them already bore the yellow piping on the outside seam of their trousers that indicated cavalry. If we break the twenty-six with cavalry experience down further, we see that eleven were previously officers, nine line, and two staff (assistant surgeons). Fourteen of the newly commissioned had been noncommissioned cavalrymen. Colonel Russell referred to one man, Andrew F. Chapman of the 4th United States Cavalry, as "Lance Sergeant," perhaps a temporary or brevet rank. George Rogers, of the 1st Vermont Cavalry, had been a private. The remainder of the white enlisted men who became officers in the 5th Massachusetts Cavalry had been sergeants or, like Sergeant Major George Wilson or Regimental Commissary Sergeant E. H. Adams, noncommissioned staff. Naturally, Russell drew particularly heavily on the two Massachusetts Cavalry regiments in Virginia. Twenty-one of the twenty-six officers with cavalry experience were from the 1st and 2nd Massachusetts Cavalry Volunteers, thirteen from the 2nd and eight from the 1st Massachusetts Cavalry. As important as such factors as previous military experience, hometown, prewar occupation, and average age (twenty-seven) are, it is important to remember that these men were willing to take commissions, and their chances, with an African American cavalry regiment.

Colonel Russell's next priority after securing officers for the regiment was to complete its training. He needed to make sure that the regiment received its weapons and its complement of horses. Before the colonel could move forward on these matters, the problem of bounties and pay for the men exploded with new force. Massachusetts adjutant general William

Schouler wrote the governor on 10 March 1864. Schouler noted that the 8th company of the regiment was full and would soon be mustered into federal service, making two complete battalions. Schouler had received a letter from a "Mr. L. H. Giles of Philadelphia," however, who had recruited a number of men for the regiment in Pennsylvania. Giles "informs me that the families of the men are very anxious to know when the bounty, offered by the State, will be paid." The families of the men were poor and were not eligible for Massachusetts State aid because they were not residents of the state. "Their case appears hard," Schouler wrote, so he respectfully recommended "that the pay rolls of the two battalions be made up, and the men paid." Recruiting would be aided, Schouler believed, and the soldiers were not "bounty jumpers": "The men are of a class who do not desert, and therefore, I think there would be no danger of desertion, should the men be paid." Governor Andrew duly forwarded Schouler's suggestion to Russell, who replied the next day. Part of Russell's endorsement is obscured, the page being torn, but he clearly did not concur with Schouler. "I fear a good many would desert from the Fifth Cavalry," wrote Russell, "were the whole bounty paid now if [the issue?] of the men's families would be removed and temptation for desertion not so great as if the whole were received." Some of the soldiers had brought their families with them. Russell was afraid that if the men received the $325 promised them, they would "go over the hill." However unjust this assessment may have been, Colonel Russell believed it and spoke from familiarity with the men. Russell was in a tricky situation, moreover, because he had personally loaned funds to his troopers. He had the difficult task of recruiting and training a cavalry regiment, a monumental undertaking, while also trying to make sure the state kept its promises.

It should be remembered, also, that recruiting for the Union army was at an absolute peak, a frenzy, in the spring of 1864. You didn't have to be a prophet to know that when the weather moderated and the roads dried out there would be Union armies moving to engage Confederate ones. When those armies met, there would be slaughter. The black man had earned a place in those Union armies, and thus there was stiff competition for African American recruits. A total of 142 regiments of U.S. Colored Infantry were mustered in by 1865, most of them in 1864. In all, 178,975 black men enlisted in the army, beginning in late 1863.

Harry Russell may have been mistrustful when it came to paying his men their entire bounty, but he did not want their families to go to the poorhouse. He had given money to troopers of the regiment expecting the state paymaster to pay him back from the soldiers' wages and bounties. Russell was angry when he learned that others who had lent money to the soldiers, at high interest, were being paid first. He wrote Governor Andrew on 16 March, "I have advanced between $1,500 and $2,000 to the families of my men, charging of course nothing; should not my orders take precedence of those men who have lent the soldiers money for the sole object of gain; even mine have not been filed first at Paymaster's Office." Andrew naturally forwarded the colonel's note to the Paymaster's Office, from which J. F. B. Marshall wrote back the next day. Marshall found "on examination of the orders filed against the Fifth Cavalry, that there are none which invalidate the orders recently filed by Colonel Russell," unless the men chose to accept the fifty dollars down and twenty dollars per month bounty option, "in which case there might be some instances, where the bounty of $50 might not cover the orders." Marshall, then, in his best bureaucratese, turned aside Russell's request: "We shall be most happy to cooperate with Colonel Russell in any plan that shall secure the payment of orders for advances made by him to his men, that shall not involve a breach of faith to other parties who may have bonafide claims, previously entered in our books." Marshall then referred the governor to his letter of 20 February to Colonel Russell as "evidence of our desire to save the men from being victimized by brokers and others, whose only interest in them is a pecuniary and extortionate one."

Governor Andrew sent Marshall's reply to Russell asking that the papers be returned to the executive department files "with any observations he may have to suggest." We can only imagine Russell's frustration at being presented, again, with Marshall's missive of 20 February. Colonel Russell had a problem, though. He had recommended less than a week before that the men not be paid their full bounty for fear of desertion. Colonel Marshall of the Office of the Paymaster of State Bounties agreed, but out of a paternalistic desire not to see the men victimized. Russell, recognizing that half a loaf was better than none, sent a note to Governor Andrew from Readville on 17 March. "I will at once send a list of the men who can choose the $50 and $20 per month," Russell wrote. Colonel Russell, State Paymaster J. F. B. Marshall, and even Governor Andrew apparently thought that the best course was to withhold the promised full bounty of $325. The immediate sufferers from this shortsighted and unjust policy were the troopers and their families.

The regiment and the state of Massachusetts were the ultimate losers, as evidenced by a letter from Boston African American attorney John S. Rock. Rock reminded Governor Andrew in so many words that bad news travels fastest. Rock was in Philadelphia when he wrote Andrew on 18 March 1864. He had been "directly or indirectly connected with recruiting the Fifth Massachusetts Cavalry since December," he wrote. "Unintentionally, I have deceived the men." Rock had told the men, "as Russell instructed," that they would be paid when their companies were mustered in, and "with this understanding they enlisted." The troopers, "who left their families in winter," had waited weeks or even months and had yet to be paid. Many of the soldiers wrote home to their families and friends to complain, "and this has done and is doing much to retard enlistments." To Rock, this seemed particularly harsh because it was winter, "when the wants are more pressing than at any other season." Attorney Rock explained that African Americans who enlisted in Philadelphia received their bounty money immediately and had a more liberal furlough policy. What's more, Rock noted that the stoppage of pay seemed common knowledge. "Though many seem to prefer Massachusetts they don't like to enlist and be without money for months, and this is continually thrown into our teeth." Furloughed soldiers from the 5th Massachusetts Cavalry in Philadelphia "for the sake of getting a little money" had to pay loan shark rates, "say from 25 per cent upwards." Rock had "heard of those who have given (or as they say been obliged to give) dollar for dollar!" Rock gave Private William Vance as an example, whom he had met the day before. Vance was a furloughed man whose leave had expired. His wife was pregnant, "expecting to be confined and he has been trying in vain to get a little money for her and to pay his way back to his regiment. The poor fellow is really in distress." Rock did not point fingers. He politely requested that Governor Andrew "do me the favor to let me know if you please" when the regiment would be paid so that he might let "those who chose to prefer Mass." know what to expect.

William Vance enlisted in the regiment on 11 January 1864 and was mustered into Company C. He gave his age as twenty-five, his occupation as cook, and was credited to Boston. He was listed as a deserter on 1 April

1864. Vance was arrested as a deserter on 28 October 1864, records do not say where, and sent down to the regiment, which was guarding Confederate prisoners of war at the time, at Point Lookout, Maryland. Vance mustered out with the 5th Massachusetts Cavalry on 31 October 1865. The records do not reveal what became of his wife.

Governor Andrew, through his military secretary, Lieutenant Colonel Albert G. Browne Jr., responded to John Rock on 21 March. Governor Andrew, wrote Browne, "directs me to reply that while he regrets the necessity of delaying the payment of the $325 bounty, yet that it is an unquestionable necessity, and that no discrimination is made in respect to it between any corps or classes of troops." Browne enumerated the units then forming in Massachusetts, writing that the policy "applied alike to the 56th, 57th, 58th and 59th Regiments of Infantry, to the new battalions of the 1st and 4th Cavalry, and to the 11th, 14th and 16th Batteries of Light Artillery, as well as to the 5th Reg't of Cavalry." Andrew's reason for not paying the $325 dollars "as soon as mustered" was that "desertions would be frequent between the dates of muster of individuals and the time for their regiment to leave the state." If instead, Andrew contended, the recruit chose the fifty-dollar bounty and the twenty dollars a month extra pay, "there would be no trouble about their realizing at once the pecuniary advantage of the act," for they would receive twenty dollars at the end of their first month's service, and "in all cases in which Colonel Russell should report that it would be prudent to pay the $50 immediately, I should direct such payment." Therefore, Browne wrote, "for the prudential reasons before mentioned, which are founded on experience," the payment of the $325 bounty was delayed for all soldiers "until their regiments leave the state." Having disposed of the issue of having to pay the troopers of the 5th Cavalry their full bounty, at least to his satisfaction, Governor Andrew and Lieutenant Colonel Browne now turned to the issue of the soldiers' orders. This part of the letter gives a clearer understanding of how sordid the practices of "bounty brokers" were, as well as how desperate recruiting was for the Union army in the spring of 1864. At this point in the war, states were competing among themselves and against the federal government for soldiers. If a state did not fill its quota, it would be subject to draft, which during the Civil War meant men being arrested and incarcerated until placed in a unit—even the trains transporting drafted men were locked and guarded. You could buy your way out of service by paying a three-hundred-dollar fee or by hiring a substitute, or you could volunteer and try to protect your family from skyrocketing wartime prices by getting the highest possible bounty. "In respect to the <u>orders</u>, and to the soldiers being shaved on them," Browne wrote,

> *Every effort that can be made, is made here to guard them, but of course if men will not look out for themselves about such things, no one else can fully protect them. Directions from the governor have been given to the Paymasters to require, in all cases of orders from soldiers for a portion or the whole of their bounty, an affidavit from the party holding the order, setting forth exactly how much money he advanced to the soldier, and the paymasters are commanded to pay him on that order only that amount with simple interest,—no matter what amount the order may be on its face,—and to reserve the balance for the benefit of the soldier.*

Upon reflection, one can envision being broke, hundreds of miles away from one's family, with someone offering cash merely to sign (or make your mark on) a piece of paper. Sharp dealing, broken promises, and muddled pay practices led to stories worthy of a Dickens or a Dostoevsky, except that these stories were true. Despite affidavits and paymasters' regulations and every effort being made, "instances of evasion and of shaving cannot be wholly avoided by any human precautions," Browne explained to Rock. However, Lieutenant Colonel Browne added, there had been "less trouble" in the 5th Cavalry than in other regiments, "for from the funds of the recruiting committee, advances in anticipation of the bounty have been made to needy soldiers, to the amount of several thousands of dollars." The recruiting committee referred to was led by John Murray Forbes and consisted of prominent Bay State patriotic businessmen and philanthropists.

John Rock replied to Governor Andrew on 7 April from Philadelphia. He was well acquainted with the governor's "reputation and labors" and did not doubt that Andrew was treating the 5th Cavalry with "the same consideration as other regiments." Rock also agreed that it was not "wise to discriminate in favor of any particular regiment." He even concurred that "desertions would be more frequent" if the men were paid at once. "But the point with me is," Rock wrote, "whether or not it would not be better to lose a few, to gain a great many?" Rock reminded the governor that all great enterprises run risks. "Our ship is in a terrible tempest and it is necessary to throw a part of the cargo overboard to save her. Shall we hesitate to do so?" Rock reiterated his statement of conditions in Philadelphia: African American recruits were immediately paid their bounties and easily granted furloughs. Rock had never heard any complaint about desertions.

By 7 April, the 5th Massachusetts Cavalry had been recruiting and organizing for over sixteen weeks. "They have been enlisting a regiment here [Philadelphia] about every six weeks," Rock wrote. "The last one was filled in five weeks." He then related a story to the governor that must have frustrated Andrew deeply: "Yesterday, I had five to add to our cavalry—they had come 100 miles at my expense. They met here two furloughed men from Massachusetts and learned from them that they had enlisted last December but had not received any bounty except $40 from a bounty broker and for which they were obliged to give orders for $60. They declined to go further." Rock contrasted the situation in Pennsylvania with that of Massachusetts. "The colored soldiers in this state are not permitted to carry the state flag, and copperheadism [racism] is so strong that these (United States) soldiers are not permitted to ride in the city cars or in the same railroad cars with others to the camp, and yet to have colored soldiers here is a great gain." If the bounties had been paid, Rock felt sure he "could have sent three times as many" to Massachusetts because the men "prefer a state that guaranties them nearly every civil right and makes provision for their families which this state does not." Rock found it "exceeding unfortunate that those who are ready and willing to come cannot do so." Rock closed by wishing Governor Andrew continued success and "much honor" for his "untiring & patriotic efforts for the nation" and for Massachusetts.

John Rock was genuinely concerned about the success of the 5th Cavalry and the image of the Bay State. But there is irony, intended or not, in his commending Andrew's honor and patriotism in the same letter in which he laments a pernicious policy. John Andrew led the fight for equal pay for African American soldiers, hammering away in letters to the Lincoln administration, congressmen, and the newspapers. He took every opportunity to speak in public on this issue. Almost simultaneously he was abrogating his responsibility for the troopers of the 5th Cavalry by writing that Massachusetts treated all her regiments the same and that necessity precluded the state from paying a promised bounty.

John Andrew was a man much beset; it could be said that he worked and worried himself to death as governor, since he died at forty-nine soon after the war ended. If it is not too much of an apology for Andrew, he was human, and humans are sometimes noted for their lack of consistency. The governor may have really believed that soldiers would desert if they were paid a large amount of money on muster in. He wanted his state to receive credit for the men recruited there and so sought to keep the men in Massachusetts until their regiments were ready to leave for the front. Sometime between early December 1863, when he received authorization to raise the regiment, and March 21, the governor decided that the state would break its word. Andrew may have been presented with a fait accompli, however. Once he had appointed a colonel, Andrew's usual practice was to leave the running of a regiment to him. Colonel Russell had forwarded the January petition of the men for their pay and had tided many of them over with money from his own pocket. Colonel Marshall's letter of 20 February must have made an impression on Russell because on 10 March he advised Adjutant General Schouler against paying the men the full amount owed them. We do not know how much of that correspondence Governor Andrew saw before 17 March. Russell did not object to paying the men part of their bounty and wages, and neither did Marshall, at least on paper. But the harsh reality was that the men did not receive the $325 enlistment bounty promised them, nor were they paid upon the mustering in of their companies. And that hurt the Bay State's reputation and recruiting for the 5th Massachusetts.

Sometime between 7 April and 12 April, Colonel Russell wrote John Rock. That letter is lost, but it seems likely that Russell had seen Rock's letter to Governor Andrew and wished to comment on that letter and to justify or explain the miserly policy of not paying the men their entire bounties. The correspondence between Harry Russell and John Rock prompted Lewis Hayden to write Governor Andrew from Philadelphia on 12 April 1864. His first sentence echoed John Rock's of 18 March: "In performance of the duty which I have been called upon to perform it now appears that some of the statements which I have made to recruits have not been true." Hayden carefully went over his authorization to act as a recruiter for the state, what the bounty and pay structure for the regiment were to be and who had provided that statement. "I have made the above statements to you," Hayden wrote, "that I may the better state this fact that Dr. Rock, my special and devoted friend has shown me a letter from Colonel Russell in which he states, that I was making the [*sic*] these misrepresentations, knowing them to be false." Hayden was not specific about which misrepresentations he was accused of, but in all certainty they had to do with pay and bounties. "Why he should write such a letter to Dr. Rock I know not, for I was recruiting men, I, not Dr. Rock and the statement was made to him and not to me, and if I were doing wrong why allow me to remain ignorant of that wrong, and address another party[?]" Hayden hoped he did not have to remind the governor "that I have left no stone unturned to promote the best interest of the regiment and the welfare of the state, so far as the colored men of the country are concerned."

The latter part of Hayden's letter deals with a perceived case of parsimony on the part of the 5th Cavalry's commander. Hayden wrote that he had spent his own money to send "every furloughed man" back to camp that was broke. A misunderstanding apparently arose over the extension of furloughs and traveling expenses to two men of Company C, Privates John Hayes and Charles Griffin. Griffin and Hayes were from Delaware. They had gone to Philadelphia to see Hayden about extending their furloughs to allow them to go back to Delaware. They told Hayden that four or five men there also wished to join the regiment. Hayden had "telegraphed [Russell] begging that their furloughs might be extended for a few days, that they might be enabled to accomplish the object, and bring their friends on with them to camp." Hayden had been supporting Griffin and Hayes for almost a week; he saw no recourse but "to advance them the money to pay their expense to camp." Hayden believed Colonel Russell had ignored his generosity. He had thought "that all parties, Colonel as well as everyone else in Massachusetts was anxious to see the cavalry ranks filled, and therefore, they would readily give all the aid they could, but this does not look so to me."

Governor Andrew replied, with some force, to Lewis Hayden on 15 April. He had referred Hayden's letter to Colonel Russell, "because much of it relates to matters which I do not understand." If Hayden had written directly to Russell, "instead of sending an unintelligible telegram," he would have had no trouble. Russell would immediately provide funds to Griffin and Hayes; there was no mention of the potential recruits in Delaware. As far as Hayden being blamed for misleading recruits, John Andrew did not wish to interfere. He repeated his assertion that "the arrangements in all respects touching Colonel Russell's regiments [*sic*] and men are identical with those relating to all other regiments and men at Readville." Andrew just did not want to hear about it. "I perceive nothing else in your letter of which I have any knowledge." Hayden should write directly to Colonel Russell "on matters concerning him, and make them clear," Andrew instructed. He then closed the matter. "I find almost everybody by haste and want of care, getting into every possible scrape with somebody else and then coming to me to get them out, and I rather think this instance of yours is one illustration."

In addition to stiff competition from the federal government, the long-term effect of not paying the full $325 bounty was a drop-off in recruiting. Company A was mustered into federal service on 9 January 1864. Companies B, C, and D were mustered on 29 January, so the 1st Battalion took twenty days to fill up. The 2nd Battalion, Companies E, F, G, and H, was completed on 12 March, after forty-two days, more than twice as long as it took to muster in the 1st Battalion. The 3rd Battalion took even longer. I and K Companies were mustered on 26 March and 1 April respectively; L was filled by 22 April, but the last company recruited, Company M, although not full, was mustered in on 5 May 1864, fifty-four days after the 2nd Battalion was complete.

It took almost six months to fill up the 5th Massachusetts Volunteer Cavalry, substantially longer than the five to six weeks it took to organize regiments of U.S. Colored Troops in Pennsylvania if John Rock is to be believed. Certainly filling up regiments was fine, but one can only wonder about the level of training the Philadelphia recruits received. Whether many troopers would have deserted if paid their full bounty is a matter for speculation. Subtracting men who died and those left behind sick, there were 915 enlisted men in the regiment when it went to Virginia. During the six months the 5th Massachusetts Cavalry was at Camp Meigs, thirty-seven men deserted, 4 percent of the total that went to war in May.

The provost marshal general of the U.S. Army reported in 1866 that desertion in white regiments was 62.51 men per 1,000; for all African American regiments, it was 67 men per 1,000. So, measured against all of their comrades in arms during the entire war, the 5th Massachusetts Cavalry had substantially fewer desertions. Whether this was because of greater love for the Union, unit pride, or lack of opportunity remains unclear. At six, C

Company had the largest number of men "go over the hill" while at Read-ville. Two of the deserters were Privates Charles Griffin and John Hayes. They deserted from Camp Meigs on the same day, 5 May 1864.

With so much time to train, the 5th Massachusetts Cavalry Volunteers should have been the "crack regiment" of African American cavalry that Governor Andrew wanted. They would have been except for one problem: there was enormous demand for horses and an accompanying scarcity of animals. Colonel Russell had moved forward in March to have the regiment armed. As an example of the still decentralized nature of the relationship between the states and the federal government, Governor Andrew for-warded Russell's requisition for weapons not to the War Department or even the Ordnance Department of the army but to Massachusetts's military state agent, Gardiner Tufts, who had an office in Washington, DC. Tufts wrote Governor Andrew on 16 March that he had presented Colonel Russell's request for ordnance supplies "in person" to Captain Balch of the Ordnance Department "and received assurances from him that the matter should have immediate attention." The next day, Tufts forwarded a letter from General George D. Ramsay, chief of ordnance. Ramsay reported, "The sabres and horse equipments for the Fifth Massachusetts Voluntary Cavalry were ordered to be sent to the Watertown, Massachusetts arsenal from New York February 13th. All the articles have arrived except 775 sabres which have not yet been turned in by the contractors, but are expected daily." Brigadier General Ramsay did not mention firearms, but it seems most likely that the 5th Massachusetts Cavalry would have received single-shot breech-loading Sharps carbines, caliber .52, the most widely used cavalry weapon.

The Sharps was a good weapon, combining rapidity with accuracy of fire. The Sharps was loaded with a paper cartridge impregnated with niter, which was fired by a percussion cap. The weapon had several advantages over the muzzle-loading rifles of the infantry. Apart from the fact that breech-loaders could be loaded and fired eight to ten times a minute versus the three for muzzle loaders, they could be loaded when prone or on horseback. The Sharps was also simple to operate; no matter how rattled a soldier got, he could never put more than one load at a time into his weapon. The Sharps consistently outdid the muzzle-loading Springfield in range and was the rifle of choice for the famous Union regiment of Colonel Hiram Berdan, the Sharpshooters. The historian of Berdan's regiment wrote that although the Sharps was open sighted only to a thousand yards, Berdan's men experimented with "whittled sights" that achieved "fair accuracy" at fifteen hundred yards. At Kelley's Ford on the Rappahannock in November 1863, two sharpshooters in different companies aimed at and hit the same retreating Confederate soldier at seven hundred yards.

The regiment was also issued revolvers. The principal handgun of the Civil War was the Colt army model 1860 six-shot revolver. These fired a paper cartridge by percussion caps being placed on each chamber of the cylinder. Colts were .44 caliber. Over 386,000 were produced at Samuel Colt's factory in Hartford, Connecticut, during the war. Cavalry sabers supplied to the 5th would have been the model 1860 light cavalry saber, many of which were made by the Ames Manufacturing Company of Chicopee, Massachusetts.

As March gave way to April, the 5th Massachusetts Cavalry was a regiment that was well armed and equipped, that marched well, and that was efficient at guard mounting and dress parade. The 5th was a regiment that performed cavalry evolutions by platoon, by company or squadron, by battalion, and as a regiment of over eight hundred officers and men. But they did not ride, through no fault of their own.

The problem was a question of priority. The Cavalry Bureau had been created in May 1863, largely to eliminate abuses in the procurement and inspection of horses. Depots were established by the bureau to receive and train new mounts and to "recondition" horses sent there. Still, the Cavalry Bureau could hardly keep up with the demand: it reported that it had purchased 37,412 horses in the first three months it was in operation. The same report, from December 1863, noted that in the six months preceding 30 October 1863, in the East alone, 18,078 horses were reported killed, wounded, or dead of disease. Horses that were turned in as broken down and later returned to their units are not included in this figure. The Cavalry of the Army of the Potomac had alone been issued 35,078 horses in the six months before November 1863. General George Stoneman, in charge of the Cavalry Bureau when the above-mentioned report was written, estimated that at the existing rate of attrition, 435,000 horses a year were required to keep all the federal cavalry mounted.

John Barton, in his article "The Procurement of Horses," wrote of the "most pressing need" in the winter of 1863–1864 for remounts. Horses were bought, but many needed to be broken for riding first before they could be trained as cavalry. "The Cavalry Bureau, having difficulty remounting veteran regiments, tried to discourage the organization of any new volunteer organizations," Barton wrote. Regiments in the field obviously took precedence over an organizing regiment in Massachusetts. Despite the fact that cavalry units were required to pass an examination in horsemanship before federal muster in, the first official mention of the arrival of horses for the 5th Massachusetts does not occur until Regimental Special Order No. 36, dated 18 April, detailing Major Weld to act as inspector of horses for the regiment. This, it will be recalled, was a full four months after Governor Andrew had received authorization to create the regiment.

The mounting of the regiment became the subject of an extraordinary exchange of letters and telegrams between Governor Andrew and the authorities in Washington. This exchange began on 14 April 1864 and continued until 3 May. It is important to remember the context in which this correspondence took place. In the East, the Army of the Potomac and the Army of the James were being readied for Lieutenant General Ulysses S. Grant's 1864 offensive. The simultaneous movement of all the Union armies began the first week of May, the Army of the Potomac crossing the Rapidan River on 4 May. Every regiment and soldier was urgently needed. We can only imagine Governor Andrew's immediate reaction when he saw Assistant Adjutant General Thomas M. Vincent's "bolt from the blue" of 14 April. "To Governor of Massachusetts," it read, "Please forward the battalions of the Fifth Cavalry to Cavalry Depot this City [Washington] where they will be supplied with horses &c. &c. This is sent in answer to a dispatch from General Devens." Major General Devens at this time was commanding the 3rd (infantry) Division of XVIII Army Corps in the Army of the James.

Whatever his initial shock, Governor Andrew moved quickly to stave off this threat. If the regiment was sent by battalion, it might be broken up; if sent without horses, it might never receive them. Andrew thus reacted officially, telegraphing Major Vincent the same day: "Arrangements with Cavalry Bureau made and already work in progress to mount Fifth Cavalry here. Colonel Russell says U.S. Quartermaster McKim will get far better horses much sooner than can be supplied in Washington. General Devens was not fully informed."

Andrew also reached out on 14 April to Brigadier General R. A. Peirce, commander of Camp Meigs, who happened to be in Washington. Andrew wanted Peirce to intervene personally for the 5th Massachusetts: "Vincent telegraphs send Fifth Cavalry to Washington by battalions for mounting," the governor sent. "Do you understand?" Whether it was a result of General Peirce's protests or Andrew's telegram, the next day Assistant Adjutant General E. D. Townshend telegraphed to Governor Andrew, "Upon recommendation of Major General Burnside the telegram of yesterday's date is hereby revoked and the Fifth Cavalry will be mounted before they leave the state." R. A. Peirce sent almost the same information that afternoon: "General Burnside and Colonel Kurtz [Colonel August V. Kautz?] have this day recommended that order for Fifth Cavalry to be sent here be suspended and horses furnished at Readville. Shall know tomorrow—much depends upon horses being furnished promptly. Urge McKim." Burnside, who commanded the IX Army Corps, got involved in this decision because at the beginning of Grant's Overland Campaign, he had a division of African American troops led by Brigadier General Edward Ferrero, under his command. Colonel August V. Kautz, promoted brigadier general on 7 May 1864, was commander of the Cavalry Division of the Army of the James.

A letter published in the *Weekly Anglo-African* gives a good picture of how matters stood in the regiment in April 1864. The correspondent, "A. W.," is presumed to be Amos Webber of Company D. A twenty-seven-year-old laborer from Worcester, Massachusetts, when he enlisted on December 31, 1863, Webber served with the 5th Massachusetts during its entire service. When Webber walked down the gangplank from the troopship in November 1865, he wore the chevrons of a quartermaster sergeant.

From the edition of May 7, 1864:

FROM THE FIFTH REGIMENT MASSACHUSETTS CAVALRY
Camp Meigs, Readville, Mass., April 24, 1864
Mr. Editor: The Twelfth Company of the Fifth Massachusetts Cavalry is now forming. There are 82 men in a company. The most of the men have their sabres. Companies A, B, and C have part of their horses and equipments, and ere long the three battalions will be supplied. The men are fast learning the cavalry drill. They yet have to train the horses to the motions of different exercises.

The health of the regiment is pretty good at present, considering the low lands. The Paymaster called to see us on the 23d inst., and left a few greenbacks. There was some murmuring among the men on account of the pay. Well there might be, for the Sergeants, Sergeant-Major, and Chief Trumpeter are no more than privates as regards pay. However, it is wisdom to wait the action of Congress, as it is working in our favor, so we will hang on that hope.

The officers are much respected, from the Colonel down to 2d Lieutenant, by the men. We can say more than that of Capt. C. C. Parsons of Co. D. He is a gentleman in his manners, and very kind to his men, and takes the utmost interest in them, which, of course, gains for him their affections. A. W.

The issue of whether the 5th Massachusetts would be a cavalry regiment came down to whether U.S. quartermaster Captain William McKim would be able to purchase enough horses to mount the regiment before the exigencies of the 1864 campaign called every available man to the battlefield. The regiment had less than a fortnight's respite. It is interesting to note that when marching orders were sent for the 5th Cavalry, they did not go to Governor Andrew or Adjutant General Schouler or even to Colonel Russell. On 28 April 1864, Major Vincent of the Adjutant General's Office in Washington telegraphed to the "Headquarters, Recruiting Volunteer Service in Massachusetts and of Military Commander" in Boston. Vincent wrote to "Major F. N. Clarke, Superintendent., etc. Boston," that the "General in Chief directs that the Fifth Massachusetts Cavalry be sent immediately to this city to report to General Casey. They will not bring their horses." Major Clark's full title was "major and assistant adjutant general, superintendent of volunteers." Clarke, who was also acting assistant provost marshal general for Massachusetts, was a regular army major, detached from the Adjutant General's Office in Washington to act as the mustering-in officer and recruiting supervisor in Massachusetts. Major Clarke signed Vincent's telegram, marked it "Official," and sent it to William Schouler, who forwarded it the next day to "His Excellency, the Governor, with a request to know whether the Adjutant General will issue marching orders today."

Governor Andrew responded by sending a long telegram to Massachusetts congressman Samuel Hooper on 30 April. The first half of this message is written in the copperplate script of a secretary. "Horses are already delivered to first battalion of Fifth Cavalry (colored regiment) and equipments to the whole regiment, which is thoroughly drilled as dismounted cavalry. I earnestly protest against it being changed into infantry. Its officers are experienced cavalry officers. Eleven companies are full. I hope delegation will unite in protest against this order sent to Major Clarke to forward the regiment without horses. Transportation by water can be furnished next week and horses at new price given can be furnished for whole regiment in three weeks."

Then, obviously not believing that the above went far enough, John Andrew added in his own hand, "And yet Government has telegraphed McKim to buy horses and send to [the Cavalry Depot] Geesborough [Maryland] not furnishing them to our fifth, not even allowing the First Battalion to carry those already on hand. Thus they would break it up as cavalry, though now eleven companies full, trained to the sabre and already one-third mounted. We have selected officers of the highest character and best experience and carefully selected men to present a model cavalry—all for nought. Nothing but absolute necessity can excuse it."

Hooper's reply came the next day, on Sunday, 1 May, but one day earlier, Andrew had received a "hurry up" telegram from Major Nehemiah Brown of the Adjutant General's Office: "How many men is wanted to fill the fifth Cavalry[?] They can be obtained [here] without doubt[.] When will the regiment arrive here[?]"

Congressman Hooper's telegram expressed the urgency of the situation. "In reply to your telegram," Hooper wrote, "I am requested to say that it is not intended to change the regiment to Infantry but to mount them as soon as horses can be procured but there never was a time when they could be more useful dismounted than now and it is earnestly hoped they may be here within four days together with all the heavy artillery that can be sent[.] The secretary [Stanton] is exceedingly urgent that both the troops and artillery may be here with the least possible delay."

Amid this time of martial preparations—men marching in unison, horses pounding across the turf, the clash and swish of sabers in practice— came the reminder that a regiment is not a faceless unit of automatons but composed of individuals. Governor Andrew received a letter on 30 April from a W. Pinkney Ewing of Elkton, Maryland. Ewing was writing on behalf of some of his neighbors: "A colored man named David Gale went from this (Cecil) County sometime in January last as a volunteer in Fifth Massachusetts Cavalry, Colonel Russell, Company H and died a few weeks ago in or near Boston." Gale left two children, both under eight years old. Gale's wife was dead. Gale's father wanted to procure David's state bounty for his children. Ewing requested that Governor Andrew "please inform me what amount of bounty was due deceased, and what course must be taken to obtain it. Will someone have to be appointed and make the application in behalf of the orphan children; and if so, how and to whom?" Governor Andrew forwarded Ewing's letter to Colonel Russell, whom he ordered to "collect immediately the facts concerning the muster in and death of David Gale so that I may endeavor to procure a special notice for the relief of the man's family similar to notice adopted in the case of death after muster before the payment of the volunteer."

David Gale was thirty-one. He gave his occupation as laborer when he enlisted in Boston's Ward Six. Gale joined the regiment on 27 February and was mustered into Company H on 12 March 1864. He was a sergeant when he died "of disease" on 12 April 1864. Governor Andrew could cut the red tape to ensure that a man's orphan children would receive part of their father's pay. Struggling against the War Department bureaucracy was a more difficult task.

Governor Andrew replied to Representative Hooper's telegram of 30 April the next day: "If regiment remains cavalry then Secretary should permit battalion already mounted to retain horses." Andrew "complain[ed] from separating horses from men, and not allowing us to mount remainder." Andrew reported that the first battalion rode well, according to Russell. The governor had gone out to visit the regiment that Sunday. "Excellent men, splendid picked cavalry officers. I want to send horses now ready with regiment and have McKim ordered to mount balance." The governor urged Hooper to "get desired orders keeping our cavalry horses and men together." As a further delaying tactic, Andrew telegraphed a reply to Major Nehemiah Brown, assistant adjutant general, on 1 May: "Fifth lacks about dozen of minimum. Wish to obtain maximum for each company."

Despite Andrew's hope that the "delegation would unite in protest" against injustice to the 5th Massachusetts, he received the following telegram on the afternoon of 1 May from Washington: "Pray send the cavalry and artillery without delay. Don't wait for mounting." The two senators for Massachusetts, Charles Sumner and Henry Wilson, signed this telegram. Andrew replied to Wilson and Sumner's telegram the same day, telegraphing that eight companies of artillery had been sent but that he had to retain a battalion of heavy artillery to garrison Boston's forts. Andrew maintained, in response to mounting criticism, that he delayed no one: "But—I object to separating Russell's cavalry of which one battalion already mounted from their horses." The governor kept hammering away, insisting that the horses accompany the men and the remaining horses be sent to the regiment in Washington. "Read my two telegrams to Mr. Hooper," he wrote the senators. "Stand by justice to a model Colored Cavalry and best selection of Cavalry officers possible." On 2 May, Andrew continued the fight. He sent two telegrams that Monday morning, one to Major Vincent at the War Department, explaining that "every effort [was] being made to hasten forward the Fifth Cavalry. . . . Fear no delay." The other telegram was to Secretary of War Stanton. The governor tried to take a reasonable tack with the irascible secretary: "It will not make an hour's difference in starting our soldiers to accede to my request about Fifth Cavalry." Andrew pointed out that Stanton's proposed plan would "dismount a battalion already mounted and prevents execution of former orders which would mount residue soon." If the government wanted to use the troopers as dismounted cavalry, until all received their horses, "nobody objects." Andrew telegraphed Samuel Hooper and Charles Sumner on 2 May because he had yet to hear back from them about his message of the night before. Sumner and Hooper received a verbatim copy of the telegram to Stanton except for the last line, "accede to my request for justice."

At 12:20 p.m., 2 May 1864, Hooper telegraphed back to Governor Andrew: "The secretary wishes the whole number of men sent at once—those already mounted with their horses, those not yet mounted to be sent without horses. But all the men to come on now." Senators Sumner and Wilson sent a telegram reassuring the governor that "the secretary means that your regiment shall be cavalry but wants them here as dismounted men to take place of men sent to the front." At 2:20 p.m., Governor Andrew and the 5th Massachusetts Cavalry Volunteers got the official word. Already at 11:00 a.m., Assistant Adjutant General Vincent had telegraphed an order from Secretary Stanton ordering the regiment to Washington. Now Brigadier General Edward Richard Sprigg Canby, on Stanton's staff, telegraphed Boston. Andrew's telegram to Stanton had been received. "The men of the Fifth Cavalry who have already been mounted will be sent out with their horses and the entire regiment will be forwarded at once." Quartermaster Captain McKim was instructed to send forward all horses bought for the regiment to Washington. Governor John Andrew of Massachusetts had apparently gotten his way.

On 3 May, Governor Andrew felt it was necessary to set the record straight, at least with the Massachusetts congressional delegation in Washington. Andrew wrote Samuel Hooper to attest to the fact that Colonel Russell was notified of the impending move and preparations were begun immediately. "I did remonstrate with the War Department," Andrew wrote, "by telegraph, by letter and through agents in Washington urging their rights as Cavalry, which are not conceded and confirmed, but the moving of the regiment has never been, by this correspondence, delayed for a single hour." Andrew noted that while Massachusetts authorities had acted promptly to move the regiment, "on the assumption that proper efforts would secure regard for its rights," there was never a direct order from the War Department (until 2 May).

Lest Hooper forget that John Andrew was a lawyer, he wrote that "orders came to Major Clarke, U.S. Acting Assistant Provost Marshal General for this district, (not to me) under the assumption that these troops were under his command: which proceeding is in violation of General Orders of the War Department No. 75 of 1862 and of Paragraph 4 of General Orders War Department No. 131 of 1864." Andrew found it "peculiar" to violate a general order and overlook the rights of the state and then "hold me responsible, just as if the business of the office in Washington was correctly done." Governor Andrew enclosed a copy of Major Vincent's telegram of the day before, "not in form a requisition on me, but being rather an announcement of a decision about the horses, &c., &c. But since it can be tortured into a requisition I treat it as such."

So John Andrew had done his best for the African American cavalry regiment from the Bay State. Fully trained or not, mounted or not, fully recruited or not, their presence was requested at the "seat of war." The men loaded their saddles and tack, their carbines and ammunition, their tents and camp furniture into boxcars. The horses of the 1st Battalion were led up the ramps of the cars and secured, fresh straw put under their hooves. The men of the regiment wore high cavalry boots and short jackets; they carried sabers and holstered pistols. Their trousers bore the yellow stripe of the cavalry branch. On their kepis was the numeral 5 over a pair of crossed sabers. For now—the first week of May 1864—the 5th Massachusetts remained cavalry.

Camp Meigs, or the Camp at Readville, was the most heavily used of the Civil War camps established by the Commonwealth of Massachusetts for training Massachusetts Volunteer Militia (MVM) troops for induction into federal service. Situated adjacent to the Neponset River on a site historically used for militia musters in what was the town of Dedham (now Hyde Park), a camp of rendezvous was first founded near the Readville railroad junction in July 1861 and remained in active service through early 1866. Over time, this camp became the commonwealth's primary training depot and the site of a military hospital.

During those Civil War years, the Readville camps processed and trained at least 29,000 of the 114,000 men who served in the units raised by the commonwealth. Thus, approximately a quarter of all men serving under Massachusetts State colors passed through Readville on their way to war. Those number consisted of fifty-four units, or 40 percent of all MVM establishments, including nineteen of the commonwealth's sixty-six infantry regiments; twenty-one of the commonwealth's forty miscellaneous infantry units; one of the commonwealth's four heavy artillery regiments; eight of the commonwealth's eighteen light artillery batteries; and all four of the commonwealth's state-trained cavalry regiments, including the 5th Massachusetts Volunteer Cavalry. (CREDIT: COA)

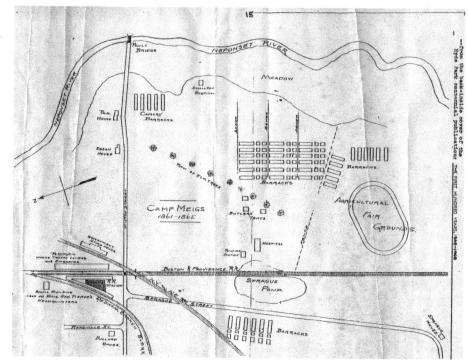

Camp Meigs (CREDIT: SLM)

"In this hour of hope for our common country and for themselves; at a time when they hold the destiny of their race in their own grasp; and when its certain emancipation from prejudice, as well as slavery, is in the hands of those now invited to unite in the final blow which will annihilate the rebel power, let no brave and strong man hesitate."—Governor John A. Andrew, December 26, 1863 (CREDIT: COA)

Patriot Recruiters

Frederick Douglass

Lewis Hayden

John Rock

George T. Downing (CREDIT: COA)

Charles R. Douglass, son of Frederick Douglass, discharged for disability in September 1864 as first sergeant of Company I (CREDIT: BA)

An African American Cavalry trooper, name unknown (CREDIT: BA)

A 5th Massachusetts Cavalry trooper, name unknown (CREDIT: AHEC)

Colonel Henry Sturgis Russell (CREDIT: AHEC)

Major Horace N. Weld (CREDIT: MHS)

Major Zabdiel B. Adams (CREDIT: MHS)

Major Henry Pickering Bowditch (CREDIT: AHEC)

Captain Charles Pickering Bowditch
(CREDIT: AHEC)

Lieutenant Daniel H. Chamberlain
(CREDIT: AHEC)

Petersburg, Virginia: The "Seat of War"

Union Volunteer Refreshment Saloon, Philadelphia (CREDIT: FLIH)

Cavalry depot at Giesborough, Maryland (CREDIT: PHCW)

Brigadier General Hincks (CREDIT: AHEC)

Depiction of the massacre at Fort Pillow (CREDIT: FLIH)

Action of the XVIII Army Corps, 15 June 1864 (CREDIT: FLIH)

Black troops bringing in captured artillery (CREDIT: FLIH)

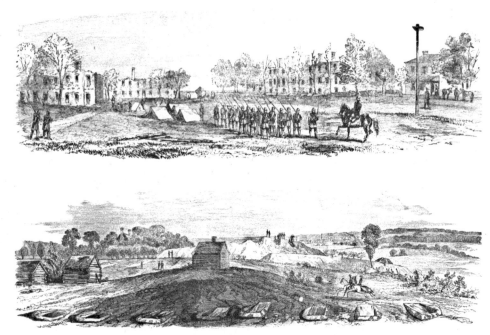

Battery captured by XVIII Army Corps (CREDIT: FLIH)

CHAPTER FIVE

"Actuated by Patriotism"

[*Weekly Anglo-African*, July 9, 1864]

FROM THE FIFTH REGIMENT MASSACHUSETTS CAVALRY

Extract from a letter received by Rev. Amos. G. Beman from his son:

POINT OF ROCKS, Va., June 20, 1864.

DEAR FATHER: I received your letter last night, and was most happy to hear from you, and happy to think that I was still alive and well after our last trying time; for since I last wrote, almost thirty have been killed and wounded. The first notice I had of going into the engagement was at about 1 o'clock, a.m., Wednesday, the 15th. We heard the bugle, and sprang to our arms, and, with two days' rations, we started towards Petersburg, and when about four miles on our way toward that city, at a place called Beatty's House, we came in front of the rebels' works. Here we formed a line of battle and started for the reb's works. I was with some thirty of my Company. We had to pass through a strip of woods before reaching their works. The shell began to come through the woods; but we kept on, while the shell, grape and canister came around us cruelly. Our major and Col. Russell were wounded, several men fell—to advance seemed almost impossible; but we rallied, and, after a terrible charge, amidst pieces of barbarous iron, solid shot and shell, we drove the desperate greybacks from their fortifications, and gave three cheers for our victory. But few white troops were with us. Parts of the 1st, 4th, 6th and 22nd were engaged.

The colored troops here have received a great deal of praise. The sensations I had in the battle were, coolness and interest in the boys' fighting. They shouted, "Fort Pillow," and the rebs were shown no mercy.

*   *   *   *   *

CHARLES TORREY BEMAN

THE 5TH MASSACHUSETTS VOLUNTEER CAVALRY DEPARTED THE BAY STATE by battalions, entraining in Readville, on the Boston and Providence Railroad. The 1st Battalion, designated in military writing as "1/5 Mass. Cavalry" (1st of the 5th), left on 5 May under the command of Major Horace N. Weld, arriving in Washington, DC, on the 7th. The 2nd Battalion, led by Major Zabdiel B. Adams, with Colonel Russell and staff, got underway on 6 May and arrived in Washington two days later. The 3rd Battalion, led by the 5th Massachusetts Cavalry's third major, Henry P. Bowditch, did not depart until Sunday, 8 May, arriving on the 10th.

The train trip south was not without incident. Several troopers took advantage of the confusion of departure to desert. Some, like Privates Charles Griffin and Isaac Hodge of C Company and G Company's Private James Monroe, went over the hill in Massachusetts. Private David Smith, twenty-six, of I Company, who had been a stevedore before enlisting, deserted in Philadelphia, as did Private Robert Miller, a twenty-four-year-old laborer. Miller deserted on 10 May from Company L, 3/5, while Smith's absence was not noticed until 12 May.

Perhaps the most spectacular or desperate act of desertion was that of Private Shadrack Murray, a twenty-five-year-old former coachman from Philadelphia. The "Deserters" page of A Company's record book noted that Murray "jumped from cars while in rapid motion near Baltimore." Nothing further is noted of Private Murray. If he survived, he was never apprehended. Another four men slipped away while the regiment was reassembling across the Potomac from Washington.

The battalions of the 5th Massachusetts Cavalry traveled through the present District of Columbia on the Baltimore and Ohio Railroad, which passed directly in front of the Capitol, down Maryland Avenue, and then crossed over the Potomac on the Long Bridge, near the site of the present Fourteenth Street and Memorial Bridges. Disembarking in what is now Virginia, the battalions marched out on the Columbia Turnpike to Camp Casey, near Fort Albany, which was part of the defenses of Washington.

Camp Casey was approximately a mile and a half from the Virginia end of the Long Bridge and about three miles north of Alexandria, Virginia, just about where the Pentagon stands today. This explanation is necessary because the boundaries of the District of Columbia changed in 1846, at which time Alexandria was retroceded to Virginia. When Colonel Russell reported to Governor Andrew on 10 May, he headlined his letter "Washington, D.C.," even though he was across the Potomac.

Harry Russell had seen his share of ups and downs in three years of army life, and now he received a blow that must have been a hard one to take: "The Fifth Cavalry will, like many other regiments, have to serve their country on foot, for a time at least, as there are not sufficient horses to mount them," Russell wrote. "I trust all the officers of the regiment are actuated by patriotism enough to do their part on foot; of course it is a great disappointment to all; but at such a time as this, we must not consider trifles." Russell then reported on the different elements of his command: "The Third Battalion had not arrived an hour ago; the First with horses has gone to Giesboro, merely to turn their horses over to older troops I think; the Second Battalion is encamped outside Fort Albany, where the whole regiment will probably be tomorrow; or next day." Russell remained sanguine in the face of adversity. "I feel that our infantry service is only temporary, but of course know nothing about it; at any rate let us hope to do our part well whatever it may be." The colonel ended his letter by reporting, "Two or three men of the second battalion were slightly hurt by a railroad accident between New York and here."

Captain Charles Pickering Bowditch, F Company's commander, has left us a vivid picture of that accident. The captain, who wrote his mother from "Arlington Heights, Virginia," on 10 May, first acquainted her with his situation. While he may have been "actuated by patriotism," as Colonel Russell claimed, Bowditch was certainly disappointed. "Just think of our being here in Camp Casey, turned into infantry and about to drill in Casey's tactics. Horrid isn't it? It is all very well to die for one's country but to be turned from cavalry to infantry for one's country is a very different thing." Captain Bowditch, like Colonel Russell, tried to put a good face on the situation: "It is merely a temporary arrangement however, to last only while all the troops are fighting big battles at the front and to prevent any untimely guerilla raid in the rear. The officers are to retain their horses and all have concluded to grin and bear it, since there is nothing else to do." Bowditch then related the story of the 2nd Battalion's trip south: "After our departure from Readville, everything went along quietly till we got to New London, where we had to wait from six till two in the morning before we started. Then at New York, they were entirely unaware of our coming, and we had to wait awhile there, so that we did not get to Philadelphia till six or seven Saturday night, and by a series of delays we arrived at Washington on Sunday evening [8 May]." One of those delays was the train accident, which occurred between Baltimore and Washington. "Our battalion was placed in seven covered cars (common baggage cars fitted with seats lengthwise) and mighty old cars at that," Bowditch wrote. "This made about forty men to a car, which crowded them so that many got on top. Everything went serenely till about twenty miles from Washington, when the axle of the forward wheels of the car which contained my men broke in halves and being pushed back tore off the trucks and wheels of other cars, smashing up two behind and one in front." The battalion was fortunate in escaping with only a few men suffering minor injuries. "Strange to say, no one was killed, though about a dozen got their joints sprained and faces cut. It was the luckiest escape I ever knew," Bowditch related. Despite a scene of destruction, with two of the railroad cars "piled up over the broken wheels and trucks, while another was resting flat on the ground with no wheels at all," the 2nd Battalion was able to clear the tracks in a few hours and resume the journey to Washington.

The 2nd Battalion of the 5th Massachusetts Cavalry spent the night of 8 May in Washington, "and after storing our horse equipment, preparatory to becoming infantry, we were sent to Camp Casey," Bowditch noted. Bowditch also mentioned how the battalion was fed and housed during the forty-eight-hour journey south: "In Philadelphia we went to the Soldiers' Rest and got a jolly good supper and wash and in the morning we had breakfast in Baltimore. While we remained in Washington we were also fed at a Soldiers' Rest. They are great institutions, very refreshing indeed." The "Soldiers' Rest" was a government-run transient barracks. By 1864, there were Soldiers' Rests in Philadelphia, Chicago, and Washington. These institutions supplemented the earlier volunteer run and funded places such as the Cooper Shop Refreshment Saloon in Philadelphia, which was within five minutes' walk of the railroad depot. Similar to the "New England Rooms" in New York City, the refreshment saloon provided wounded, furloughed, and transient soldiers a bed, sanitary facilities, and free meals. Public-spirited citizens of Philadelphia donated the building, the food, and funds to keep the place running. An estimated six hundred thousand men were fed at the refreshment saloon during the war.

On 31 May, I Company's first sergeant, Charles Remond Douglass, wrote his father to describe an accident that happened while the 3rd Battalion was in Baltimore, which had separate North and South railroad stations. Troops bound for Washington disembarked at the North Station and marched or rode across town to the South Station about two miles away. It will be remembered that the 6th Infantry Regiment, Massachusetts Volunteer Militia, was attacked by a mob while moving between stations on 19 April 1861. Douglass's account is reproduced here as he wrote it. Charles had apparently mentioned this incident in a letter to his brother Lewis:

Lew spoke of Captain Wulff shooting a man he did in Baltimore the way it happened is this he ordered all to fall in line which we did except Sergeant [Amos F.] Jackson he stayed out, he was a little drunk but not drunk enough to not know what was right. The Captain fell us in to tell us that he was agoing to let us go around and if we were insulted to go in with a will and defend ourselves, so turning around he saw Jackson out of the ranks. He merely took him by the arm and told him to keep in the ranks when Jackson cursed him, the Captain then ordered him to take off his stripes which he refused to do and to let anybody else do he said if they took off his stripes that he would have to be shot first. The Captain then said I will shoot you then and immediately drew his revolver and shot at Jackson's head, Jackson dodged his head and the ball passed through the heart of Albert White, the one that H. O. Waggoner brought out of bondage no more at present.

The comprehensive roster of Massachusetts's Civil War regiments, published in six volumes compiled by the adjutant general of the Commonwealth of Massachusetts in 1930, lists Albert White of Company I as having "died May 12, 1864, of disease, at Baltimore, Maryland." Therein lies a mystery. Douglass's account has the ring of eyewitness truth. Captain Wulff was apparently able to prevail upon other officers, at the least regimental adjutant Lieutenant James Newell, but possibly his battalion and regimental commanders, to make that innocuous entry in the regimental records, thus exonerating Wulff in the shooting death of Trooper White.

First Sergeant Douglass did not choose to comment further on the accidental shooting of Albert White, although he seems to have been acquainted with the victim. Douglass's blaming the drunken Jackson indicates partial exoneration of his friend Erik Wulff, although Captain Wulff's precipitate action indicates high stress, if not mental instability.

Captain Bowditch wrote to his mother on 9 May that the 2nd Battalion of the 5th Massachusetts Cavalry had turned in its "horse equipments," which included saddles, bridles, hackamores, nose bags, picket pins, saddle blankets, and forage nets. Colonel Russell wrote on the 10th that the 1st Battalion was on its way over to the Cavalry Depot in Giesborough, Maryland, to turn over its horses and horse equipment. The War Department did not issue an order dismounting the regiment until 11 May. Major Weld and the 1st Battalion, with their horses, had reported to "Camp Stoneman," the Headquarters of the Cavalry Division, Department of Washington, by 7 May. Orders were issued to Major Weld and his men at 11:30 p.m., 11 May: "The Major General Commanding Department of Washington [Major General Silas Casey] directs that you immediately turn over to the Q.M. of this Div. [Quartermaster of this Division] all the Government horses in your command and all your horse equipments and arms to the Ordnance Officer and that you report with your Battalion to Maj. Gen. Casey at 10 a.m. [*sic*] tomorrow May 12." The colonel commanding the Cavalry Division further directed that Major Weld "put the order into effect without delay." The quartermaster and ordnance officers had "been notified of the order and will afford every facility for the rapid execution of the same." As a testimony of the dashing of the regiment's hopes, the following words appear in the left-hand corner of this order: "A true copy: Attest [signed] J. S. Newell, 1st Lt. & Adjt. 5th Mass. Cav."

Formal orders may not have come until 11 May, but Colonel Russell and his regiment had been presented with a fait accompli, an action that had its origins in the highest ranks of Union army command. On 2 May, Henry W. Halleck, major general and chief of staff, sent a telegram to Lieutenant General Ulysses S. Grant, then at Culpeper, Virginia. Halleck referred to a message from Grant of 29 April 1864 ordering every possible unit to the armies in the field. "General: I believe all the directions in your confidential dispatch of the 29th ultimo have been carried out, so far as possible. It is a difficult matter to get troops out of the hands of some of the Governors of States, but we are making considerable progress." Halleck reported that Assistant Secretary of War Charles A. Dana had gone out west to "start them off, forcibly if necessary," and that "the five Cavalry regiments so long detained in Indiana have started for Louisville, just as they are, half mounted and half on foot." Halleck wrote that he felt confident that the Indiana regiments could be "regulate[d] when we get them away from the state authorities." What Halleck meant by "regulate" is revealed in his next two sentences: "The Governor of Massachusetts opposes the dismounting of his half-mounted colored regiment and we cannot get their horses. I have to-day ordered the men with their horses here, [to Washington] where we can dismount them in spite of the Governor and send their horses to General Meade."

Although this action was of no comfort because they were unaware of it, the officers and men of the 5th Massachusetts Cavalry were not alone. If there was prejudice involved in the dismounting of the regiment, it was a prejudice against inexperience, not one based on color, for white regiments as well as black were dismounted. Halleck had telegraphed Grant on 1 May: "The Twenty-Second New York Cavalry, now at the depot, is entirely undisciplined and unfit for the field. I have ordered them armed as infantry, and their horses given to the Second Ohio . . . and to detachments of the Army of the Potomac." Grant concurred in Halleck's decision, overriding Major General Ambrose Burnside, IX Army Corps commander, who wanted the New Yorkers to retain their horses. On 2 May, Grant telegraphed Halleck: "The Twenty-Second New York Cavalry were dismounted at my suggestion, that the horses were worth more to mounted veteran cavalry, who have no horses, than men and horses together are. A new regiment will be worth something on foot, but less than their forage on horseback."

In June 1864, General Halleck reported to General Grant that 6,683 horses had been sent to the Army of the Potomac during May. Another thousand horses were awaiting shipment when Halleck was sending his dispatch. These almost eight thousand horses were in addition to the horses supplied to remount cavalrymen at the Cavalry Depot, Giesborough Point, Maryland. Most of these horses were doubtless purchased on government contracts. However, as Stephen Starr notes in his *Union Cavalry in the Civil War* in reference to Halleck's report, "some of these, no doubt, were horses nursed back to reasonable health at the Giesborough Depot. . . . Others were horses taken from new regiments to mount veterans, greatly to the distress of the losers. The Thirteenth Ohio Mounted Infantry, the Thirteenth Pennsylvania, a Massachusetts regiment of black cavalry, the First Delaware, and the Twenty-First Pennsylvania all lost their horses and were made to serve as infantry." Whatever he felt, Colonel Russell did not publicly bemoan his fate and go running to those in higher authority, unlike some of his fellow colonels. Yet, despite General Grant's assertion about value on foot, one is left with the compelling question: What good is a cavalryman without a horse?

The three battalions of the 5th Massachusetts were reunited on 13 May at Camp Casey. The camp, as befitted its namesake, Major General Casey, the author of the Union army's *Infantry Tactics* (1862) and *Infantry Tactics for Colored Troops* (1863) and president of the board of examination for commissions into the U.S. Colored Troops, was a camp of instruction for organizing African American infantry regiments. For Charles Bowditch, writing to his mother, life at the camp seemed bleak and chaotic: "We are allowed nothing but shelter tents here though there is a prospect of the officers living in barracks. There are at present, some 1,200 men in camp here (all colored) besides our own. They are the most undisciplined mob I ever saw. They have no more respect for officers than nothing at all. I have not seen more than a couple of men salute since I have been here. The officers are almost as bad." Despite Bowditch's poor view of the officers and men of the organizing black regiments, someone was on the alert. On 11 May, as 3/5 Mass. Cavalry arrived at Camp Casey, someone recognized Trooper George Murphy of Company M as a deserter from another unit. Murphy's name bears the notation, "retained as a deserter, May 11, 1864, from Twenty-Third U.S. Colored Troops," in the roster of the 5th Massachusetts Volunteer Cavalry. The next day, three men in L Company, Troopers Charles Moore, Anderson Price, and William Smith, were all retained as deserters from another regiment, the 28th Regiment of U.S. Colored Troops. Two more men, Privates Samuel Henly and Thomas Marshall of K Company, were taken up as deserters from the 31st Regiment of U.S. Colored Troops on 13 May. The men arrested as deserters from the 23rd, 28th, and 31st U.S. Colored Infantry regiments had left those organizations and made their way north, drawn by the promises of high bounty and the opportunity (so they thought) of riding instead of walking. We can only imagine their chagrin at being dismounted and marched to a place they might have left only weeks before and having someone sing out, "Isn't that so-and-so with those Massachusetts troops?" Timing was particularly poor for these African American bounty jumpers. All three U.S. Colored Troops regiments soon departed Camp Casey, reporting for duty to the 2nd Brigade of the 4th Division, XIX Army Corps, and combat with the Army of the Potomac.

Two more men were recognized, but not at Camp Casey. When the regiment was brigaded as part of the 1st Brigade, 3rd Division, of the XVIII Army Corps, Troopers Benjamin Johnson and William C. Johnston, both of G Company, were "claimed and arrested" as deserters "from Twenty-Second Regiment United States Colored Troops" on 29 and 30 May 1864, respectively. The 22nd U.S. Colored Troops was in the same division as the 5th Massachusetts.

While at Camp Casey, Colonel Russell was placed in command of a provisional brigade including his regiment and the African American troops assembling there for instruction and discipline. The U.S. Colored Troops at Camp Casey did not benefit from Colonel Russell's experience for long, however. The 5th Massachusetts Cavalry (dismounted) was ordered to join Major General Benjamin F. Butler's Army of the James on 13 May. Butler had begun the 1864 campaign on 5 May, when, with an army of approximately thirty-six thousand men, he had sailed up the James River with a fleet of gunboats, monitors, and transports. On 7 May, General Butler telegraphed Secretary of War Stanton: "We have no news from General Grant. If he has been in any degree successful there, can we not have here ten thousand of the reserves? They can be here in three days after the lieutenant-general gives the order." Stanton telegraphed Butler the next day that he had received no reports from Grant, but that the Army of the Potomac was apparently engaged, as "from six to eight thousand wounded are sent back." Stanton was unable to send Butler reinforcements: "In respect to the reserves mentioned in your telegram, there are none now at the disposal of the department. General Grant has with him all the troops, and you will have to depend only upon such as may have been provided in your programme with him."

Stanton had forwarded Butler's telegram to Lieutenant General Grant, however, and Grant sent it along to Halleck: "If matters are still favorable with Butler, send him all the reinforcements you can." As William Glenn Robertson, in his definitive study of the Bermuda Hundred Campaign, *Back Door to Richmond*, writes, Grant's request for reinforcements for the Army of the James went largely unmet. "With no faith whatsoever in Butler and much personal animosity toward him, Halleck released only the 1,800-man First Connecticut Heavy Artillery Regiment from the Washington defenses for Butler's use." This artillery regiment, familiar with the great guns of siege artillery, was armed with rifles but was restricted from being used in field operations. The only other regiment sent to the Army of the James before its linkup with the Army of the Potomac in mid-June was the 5th Massachusetts Volunteer Cavalry.

Robertson refers to the regiment as "the 5th Massachusetts Colored Cavalry, a green outfit, 1,200 strong." General Halleck was even less precise about the Bay State regiment than Robertson. His dispatch to Butler, dated 12 May 1864, reads:

> *The Fifth Massachusetts Colored Regiment (about 1,200 men) and the First Connecticut Heavy Artillery, Colonel Abbot (about 1,800 men) have been ordered to report to you at Bermuda Landing. Colonel Abbot's regiment has been designated by General Grant for a special service, and in the meantime, will be used by you to hold your defenses, but will not be sent into the field, as the Lieutenant-General may, at any moment, order them to be detached for special service.*

Perhaps Halleck consciously refrained from calling the 5th Massachusetts cavalry; it was he who was responsible for dismounting the regiment. These two regiments, approximately three thousand men, were sent to the Army of the James while the *Official Records* notes that the Army of the Potomac received 24,700 men during the same period.

The 5th Massachusetts assembled on 13 May and marched to Alexandria where they embarked on the transport *Webster*. The regiment arrived off Fort Monroe, at the mouth of the James River, on 15 May and halted for orders. From Fort Monroe, the 5th Massachusetts was ordered to City Point to join the African American 3rd Division, XVIII Army Corps, and arrived on 16 May. Brigadier General E. W. Hincks commanded the 3rd Division.

Edward Winslow Hincks had been born and raised in Maine but moved to Boston in 1849. He was a member of the Massachusetts legislature in 1855 where he made the acquaintance of Benjamin Butler. As Ezra Warner writes in *Generals in Blue*, "probably at the instance of Benjamin F. Butler, under whom Hincks subsequently served, he was appointed a second lieutenant in the Regular Army at the same time he was serving as lieutenant colonel and colonel of a ninety-day regiment of Massachusetts militia." Hincks became colonel of the 19th Massachusetts Infantry in August 1861, one of the regiments that took part in the Union debacle at Ball's

Bluff in October 1861. Colonel Hincks was wounded at Glendale during McClellan's Peninsula Campaign and badly wounded twice at Antietam. Promoted to brigadier general in April 1863, General Hincks served on court-martial and recruiting duty while convalescing. His previous post, before taking charge of the 3rd Division, XVIII Army Corps, was command of the prisoner of war camp at Point Lookout, Maryland, where he served for two months.

Colonel Russell took occasion to write to Governor Andrew from City Point on 17 May to report on the regiment's movements: "The Fifth Cavalry is now under General Hincks, formerly of the Nineteenth Regiment." Russell seemed to think that the posting to an operational command augured well for the regiment: "The men take hold of the muskets very well; but, as General Hincks is anxious for cavalry, I feel our chance for horses is much better than at Washington." The 5th Massachusetts had disembarked from the *Webster* and was getting organized when they were ordered into the trenches. "We were called to arms yesterday before the muskets were unpacked!!! Today we should be better prepared for an emergency," wrote the colonel. Russell also reported that the 5th Massachusetts had received forty-nine recruits during its brief stay in Washington, presumably at Camp Casey.

The 5th Massachusetts had been called to arms on 16 May because the City Point defenses had been stripped; General Hincks and the African American troops of the 3rd Division had been ordered up the Appomattox River to Point of Rocks, part of the defenses of Bermuda Hundred. The white troops of the Army of the James, except for those left holding the Bermuda Hundred defenses, were heavily engaged on 16 May in the Battle of Drewry's Bluff.

Before giving an account of that action, it is necessary to discuss the strategic goals of the Bermuda Hundred Campaign and what had been accomplished prior to the arrival of the 5th Massachusetts Cavalry. In the eastern theater, Grant and the Army of the Potomac had to contend with Lee's well-led army of veterans. An attempted turning movement on the Confederate left, from the Rapidan River to Lynchburg, would have cut Lee's line of retreat to the west and south and possibly created a Vicksburg-style investiture of Richmond. But Grant and the Union army would not have had a supply line, "a very precarious situation," wrote Herman

Hattaway and Archer Jones in *How the North Won*. Attacking from the west meant to gamble that the Army of the Potomac would be able to push back the Army of Northern Virginia into the Richmond defenses, thus breaking Lee's communications and reestablishing their own. The risk of leaving Washington uncovered and being cut off without logistical support was too great. Neither Grant nor his predecessor Meade was willing to try this plan. Instead, Hattaway and Jones wrote, "Grant had no course open but to turn Lee on the east where Grant could base himself on the series of Virginia rivers."

Just pushing Lee back was not enough, however, and Grant knew it. The Army of the Potomac, with superior numbers and excellent logistics, would be able to take the initiative, but there would be no surprise on the part of the Union. According to Archer Jones in *Civil War Command and Strategy*, "the soldiers on both sides well understood this stalemated war of a high ratio of force to space, and they most diligently and adroitly practiced the ancient art of field fortification." Grant was confident that his better-equipped, better-supplied, and numerically superior army would be able to push Lee back into the Richmond defenses. The question was, in sending Butler and the Army of the James up their namesake river, how long it would take for the Army of the Potomac and the Army of the James to link up? Another question, unasked at the time but that has dogged Grant's reputation ever since, is how high a cost in casualties was Grant willing to pay?

Politically attuned, Grant also expected to capture Richmond. Grant knew that the public did not understand strategic turning movements or interior lines of communication. The dramatic defeat or destruction of an enemy army or the occupation of an important city were seen by all as clear-cut victories. To begin the strike at Richmond with an attack by waterborne troops, Grant turned to Ben Butler, who in the spring of 1864 commanded the Department of Virginia and North Carolina, based at Fort Monroe. Grant did not heed the words of Chief of Staff Halleck, who had the innate mistrust of the regular army officer toward the political appointee. In April 1864, Halleck wrote to General Sherman that it seemed "but little better than murder to give important commands to such men as Banks, Butler [and] McClernand." No general was more political than Ben Butler.

Butler had been a prominent attorney and Democratic politician in Massachusetts before the war. He had gained a certain notoriety at the

Democratic Party's convention in 1860, where he cast fifty-seven consecutive ballots for Jefferson Davis as president of the United States. When the war came, he firmly supported the Union, however. Butler took advantage of his position as brigadier general of militia and Massachusetts's advanced state of preparation in 1861 to lead the Union regiments that seized Annapolis and Baltimore, Maryland. Credited with relieving Washington, Butler was commissioned major general of volunteers by President Lincoln on 16 May 1861.

While he commanded at Fort Monroe in 1861, forces under Butler were defeated at Big Bethel, Virginia. In an action more embarrassing than sanguinary, Northern troops making a night march fired into each other. The next day, 10 June 1861, the main body of Union troops milled about as they waited for their officers to figure out what to do. The officers, Butler wrote, "carefully disobeyed orders, which were . . . to go right ahead with fixed bayonets and fire but one shot, and they did not do even that." Little more than a skirmish, federal losses were eighteen killed, fifty-three wounded, and five missing, while the Confederates under command of Colonel John Bankhead Magruder lost one killed and seven wounded. Big Bethel was mostly a publicity victory for the South, as trophies from the fight were displayed in Richmond shop windows.

It will be recalled that it was Butler, while commanding at Fort Monroe, who coined the term (and the legal interpretation) "contraband of war" for escaped slaves who entered the Union lines. General Butler also commanded the successful amphibious assault of Hatteras Inlet in August 1861. The following May, he served as overall commander of land forces in the expedition that captured New Orleans. Named military governor of the Crescent City, Butler's tenure was controversial to say the least. Butler was given the nickname "Beast" by Southerners and declared an outlaw by President Davis for, among other acts, hanging a man who had torn down the national flag and his famous "Women Order," General Order No. 28, dated 15 May 1862: "It is ordered that hereafter when any female shall, by word, gesture, or movement, insult or show contempt for any officer or soldier of the United States, she shall be regarded and held liable to be treated as a woman of the town plying her avocation." Butler was also accused of peculation, a libel that followed him for the rest of his life concerned the theft of silverware from the house where he made his headquarters. He was relieved of duty in December 1862 by President Lincoln because of an altercation involving the foreign consuls in New Orleans. Ezra Warner writes, "That he governed effectively and performed useful service is impossible to deny, but that he lined his own pockets and those of his family and friends seems equally evident." Butler was without a command until November 1863, when he returned to Fort Monroe as commander of the Department of Virginia and North Carolina.

The department "comprised a few square miles of tidewater shoreline and several thousand square miles of water," according to Richard West, one of Butler's biographers. The Yorktown peninsula, the city of Norfolk, and federal outposts in North Carolina at New Bern, Little Washington, Plymouth, and Roanoke Island were included in Butler's command. General Grant met with General Butler at Fort Monroe on 1 April 1864. Grant put the gist of that meeting in a letter to Butler dated the next day. Butler was to concentrate sixteen thousand men from his own department, which would form one army corps (the XVIII). Added to the XVIII Army Corps would be eighteen thousand men from the Department of the South. Major General Quincy Adams Gillmore would command the latter troops, designated the X Army Corps. Grant, at the end of his letter, reminded Butler of his objectives without denoting a specific timeline:

> When you are notified to move take City Point with as much force as possible. Fortify or rather entrench, at once, and concentrate all your troops for the field there as rapidly as you can. From City Point directions cannot be given at this time for your further movements. The fact that has already been stated, that is, that Richmond is to be your objective point, and that there is to be cooperation between your force and the Army of the Potomac, must be your guide. This indicates the necessity of your holding close to the South bank of the James River as you advance. Then, should the enemy be forced into his entrenchments in Richmond, the Army of the Potomac will follow; and by means of transports the two armies would become a unit.

General Butler, in his version of this meeting with Grant, wrote that "General Grant had told me, in conversation, if I could hold the Petersburg and Richmond Railroad cut for ten days, and secure our proposed base at Bermuda and City Point, that by that time he would join me there, or on the James about Richmond, having either whipped Lee's army or forced it into the entrenchments around Richmond, when the combined armies of the Potomac and my command would invest Richmond, the navy holding the James and approaches." Several factors would appear to be at odds in Butler's report of the conversation with Grant and the latter's written orders. Grant may have been confident of success against Lee, but did be explicitly predict that the Army of the Potomac would have driven Lee into the defenses of Richmond in ten days? Also, did Grant mean for the Army of the James to seize and fortify Bermuda Hundred? Butler believed he did, for on page 16 of his appendix in *Butler's Book* is the copy of a dispatch sent by General Grant on 16 April. It reads, "All the forces that can be taken from the coast have been ordered to report to you at Fortress Monroe by the eighteenth inst., or as soon thereafter as possible. What I ask is that with them and all you can concentrate from your own command, you seize upon City Point and act from there, looking upon Richmond as your objective point." In reference to transports, Grant wrote, "Keep what vessels may be necessary for your operations. No supplies are going to North Carolina except such as may be necessary for the troops there. I presume the call for vessels is in consequence of the preparations ordered for supplying our armies after a new base is established." Butler footnoted this last sentence of Grant's by writing, "i.e., at Bermuda Hundred. Called City Point in General Grant's and General Halleck's dispatches." Now presumably Generals Grant and Halleck, who could read a map as well as the next man, would have written "Bermuda Hundred" if they had meant that place, rather than City Point.

Another factor was Grant's omission of any mention of attacking Petersburg. Historian William Glenn Robertson believes "the chief flaw in the federal plan of operations was its fixation upon Richmond." Butler has been roundly condemned for not immediately taking Petersburg in May; this failure is magnified by the more than nine months spent in the trenches around the Cockade City. This is hindsight with a vengeance, however. No one could have anticipated the siege (more properly an investiture) of Petersburg in April or May 1864. As the Army of the James maneuvered, portions of the army were detached to garrison City Point, forts on the James River, and the Bermuda Hundred defenses. As Robertson notes, "to garrison Petersburg against the Confederate brigades arriving by rail from the Carolinas would have required a major portion of Butler's remaining troops and precluded an advance in strength against Richmond as Grant's plan specified." Later, Grant in his *Memoirs* and Grant's aide Horace Porter in his *Military History* asserted, in what may have been hindsight after the campaign broke down, that Butler was instructed verbally to seize Petersburg, but nowhere in his written instructions did Grant refer to that city as either a primary or a secondary goal.

To reiterate, then, these were the goals for the Army of the James: first, to seize and fortify a base as far up the James River as could be effected with naval collaboration; second, to break the Confederate transportation network; third, to distract and divert Confederate units that might otherwise reinforce the Army of Northern Virginia; and fourth and finally, to threaten or seize, if possible, the city of Richmond. All this was to be done, again if possible, during the ten days from 5 to 15 May.

Since a campaign may fail in planning, execution, or both, let us examine briefly the high command of the Army of the James. It is indeed extraordinary that the left wing of Grant's strategic plan, the anvil to his hammer, would be entrusted to an army commander totally without practical training and also completely without experience of moving troops around a battlefield. As Robertson notes in *Back Door to Richmond*, "Butler's actual combat experience was nil, since he had never personally led a large column in field operations. Big Bethel had been a mere skirmish fought by subordinates, the action against the Hatteras forts had been primarily a naval show, and New Orleans had required a police commissioner more than a combat commander." But Grant was stuck with the Bay Stater; for political reasons Butler could not be relieved, and he insisted on taking active field command instead of remaining in Fort Monroe and playing an administrative role.

Grant sought to leaven the untried Massachusetts general with two regular army West Point graduates—William Farrar Smith and Quincy Adams Gillmore. Smith, to differentiate him from other Smiths, was known in the army as "Baldy." Smith was a Grant protégé. Graduated from the military academy in 1845, Smith earned distinction as an engineer officer before the Civil War, returning to West Point to teach that science. A native Vermonter, he had become colonel of the 3rd Vermont Infantry in July 1861. He had served on the staff of General Irvin McDowell at the First Battle of Bull Run and was promoted to brigadier general of volunteers on 13 August 1861. Later, Smith commanded a division of the VI Army Corps on the peninsula and during the Maryland campaign; he then acceded to command of VI Corps prior to the Battle of Fredericksburg. After the Union debacle at Fredericksburg, Smith, whose promotion to major general was before the U.S. Senate, cosigned with General William B. Franklin, the commander of the "Left Grand Division" of the Army of the Potomac, a letter to President Lincoln extremely critical of their commander, Ambrose E. Burnside. This act of disloyalty cost Smith both his corps command and his promotion, as the Senate failed to approve the recommendation that he be promoted to major general. While serving as chief engineer of the Department of the Cumberland with the rank of brigadier general, the Vermonter was able to redeem himself during operations around Chattanooga, Tennessee. General Grant was favorably impressed with Smith, for he promoted him to chief engineer of the Military Division of the Mississippi in October 1863. Grant also sponsored Smith's promotion to major general, writing the secretary of war on 12 November 1863 to request that Smith be "placed first on the list for promotion to the rank of major-general. He is possessed of one of the clearest military heads in the army; is very practical and industrious." When action was not forthcoming, Grant wrote Lincoln on 30 November, once again asking that Smith's name be placed first on the list for promotion. Smith, in his apologia, *From Chattanooga to Petersburg under Generals Grant and Butler*, wrote that by Grant's "invitation I came east with him in his private car when he came to Washington early in March, 1864, to accept the position of Lieutenant-General." Smith was duly confirmed as major general on 9 March 1864 and took command of the XVIII Army Corps, comprising the troops of the Department of Virginia and North Carolina, some sixteen thousand men.

Another eighteen thousand men, making up the X Army Corps, came up from South Carolina under the command of Major General Quincy Adams Gillmore. Gillmore was another West Pointer, the top-ranked student in the class of 1849. His class rank gave him a first assignment in the Corps of Engineers. Like Smith, Gillmore taught engineering at the Military Academy before the war. Unlike Smith, however, Gillmore had never been a line or field officer. His promotions to brigadier general (28 April 1862) and major general (10 July 1863) came about as a result of successful engineering work, most notably his reduction of Fort Pulaski in Savannah Harbor, the capture of Batteries Wagner and Gregg, and the deployment of the eight-inch rifled cannon known as the "Swamp Angel" during federal operations to recapture Fort Sumter in Charleston Harbor.

There were some flaws in the high command of the Army of the James. First of all, Gillmore had held departmental command in South Carolina; he was now in a subordinate position to an unskilled and inexperienced nonprofessional superior (Butler). Added to that, as Robertson notes, was the fact that, "except for some limited, and catastrophic, offensive operations in the Department of the South, Gillmore was as inexperienced as Butler in commanding large units in a campaign of maneuver." Furthermore, Smith had perhaps too much experience to be serving under Butler. Equal in position to Gillmore, Smith could only suggest possible courses to the X Corps commander. Moreover, Butler was too unsure of himself to make the two work together. Further complicating matters was the fact that Smith was opinionated and took orders poorly. Grant wrote that he was "likely to condemn whatever is not suggested by himself." Coupled with Smith's iras-cibility (his protégé and devoted admirer James Harrison Wilson called him a "consciously contentious man") was his slowness to act. Adam Badeau, an officer on Grant's staff who wrote the three-volume *Military History of Ulysses S. Grant*, notes that Smith was overanxious to prepare for every possible contingency. "His skill was great, his judgment cool, but his movements were somewhat too elaborate." In Butler's version of events, written in later life, he wrote that Smith had the "one inevitable regular army failing . . . interminable reconnaissances—waiting and waiting, not going at a thing when he was told, but looking all around to see if he could not do something else than what he was told to do, or do it in a different way from what he was told." It should be remembered, before we are too quick to condemn the high command of the Army of the James that these men did not operate in a vacuum. There were division and brigade commanders, regimental officers and enlisted men; all bore some responsibility for the success or failure of the campaign. Opposed to those men, of course, were over twenty thousand Confederate troops, with the skillful and experienced P. G. T. Beauregard in command.

Several aspects of the Army of the James made it unique among all the Civil War armies. This army was the largest led by a political general and the only one to have a political goal, the capture of Richmond, as its primary objective. Historian Edward Longacre, writing in *Military Affairs*, considers the Army of the James "the most highly politicized fighting force in American history." Part of that politicization was the politics of race. The Army of the James contained the highest number of African American troops in the Union army, "as much as 40 percent of its maximum strength of 40,000 officers and men," Longacre points out. At a time when it was official Washington policy not to pay African Americans the same as whites and not to commission them, and when other armies used them as fatigue details or wagon guards or garrison troops and doubted the capacity of blacks as soldiers and even human beings, Butler welcomed them to the Army of the James. The army commander encouraged the enlistment of African Americans in cavalry and artillery units, willingly accepted black regiments in exchange for white ones, and provided housing, employment, and rations for the women, children, and elderly "contrabands" who came into his area of operations, many of whom were the dependents of troops enlisted in the Army of the James.

What's more, Butler entrusted his African American troops with important operational tasks. While the fleet conveying the Army of the James sailed up the James River on 5 May, the 1,800 African American cavalrymen of the 1st and 2nd U.S. Colored Cavalry regiments paralleled the fleet's advance on the north side of the river. Butler also used black troops to seize and garrison important points on the river, guarding his line of communications. On the same day, the honor of being the first units ashore went to the 1st and 22nd U.S. Colored Infantry regiments and to two sections of Battery B, 2nd U.S. Colored Artillery. These troops, part of the 1st Brigade, 3rd Division, of the XVIII Army Corps, seized a point on the north side of the James River known as Wilson's Wharf, a bluff that commanded the river both above and below. These troops met with no opposition, and the federal fleet continued a few miles farther to another rise of ground.

The Confederates had built a fort there on the south side of the James and named it Fort Powhatan. The remaining units of Brigadier General Edward A. Wild's 1st Brigade; the 10th and 37th U.S. Colored Troops; and two sections of Battery M, 3rd New York Artillery, stormed ashore to find empty emplacements. Butler felt that Fort Powhatan was "the weak point of my whole position. For, although it was some twelve miles below City Point on the James, yet if it were once in possession of the enemy, it would be impossible to get any troops or supplies up the river, as the channel ran close under it."

The general deliberately chose African American troops to garrison the captured fort because, he wrote, "I knew that they would fight more desperately than any white troops, in order to prevent capture, because they knew—for at that time no measures had been taken to protect them—that if captured they would be returned into slavery, under Davis's proclamation, and the officers commanding them might be murdered. So there was no danger of a surrender." Butler also designated black troops to seize City Point. Hincks's 2nd Brigade of the 3rd Division, comprising the 4th, 5th, and 6th U.S. Colored Troops, did this.

Thomas L. Livermore, a young officer on General Hincks's staff, has left an account of the seizure of City Point on 5 May. The steamer with Hincks and his staff came up with the naval vessels under Admiral Samuel P. Lee, which were halted at Harrison's Landing about four miles below City Point. According to Livermore, "our signal officer communicated with one on Admiral Lee's ship and asked what the navy proposed to do, and received for answer that 'the Admiral was about to go on board an ironclad and go up.'" Admiral Lee was apparently fearful of striking a floating mine, called a "torpedo" in the Civil War. General Hincks, Livermore wrote, "thought this rather contemptible in the admiral" and "ordered the army transport to go ahead." There was a Confederate flag flying at City Point, and Captain Livermore was determined to seize it: "Without waiting to look at surroundings much, I jumped ashore with an ax in one hand with which to cut down the rebel flag, and in company with some of our headquarters orderlies and guards I ran up the bluff." Livermore and his party had soon captured the flag and driven off the few Confederate soldiers, who put up no resistance. Most of them were soon captured. "A rebel Captain or Lieutenant walked up to me at this juncture," Livermore continued, "and with great asperity of manner said this was a flag-of-truce station and demanded my name. I paid him the attention of seeing that he was taken prisoner, and that was all." City Point was indeed used as an exchange point for Confederate prisoners of war. Even as Hincks's staff was securing the place, a steamer full of exchanged Confederate prisoners of war arrived from the Union prison camp at Point Lookout, Maryland. However, as Livermore wrote, "if they wished to be treated as if under a flag of truce they should not have had a broad rebel flag flying without any, or at least with an insignificant, white flag out, for if there was a white one we did not see it until our attention was called to it."

Captain Livermore described City Point as a fifty-foot-high bluff rising at the point where the Appomattox River flows into the James. There were the piles of a wharf, which had been burned; "at the foot of the bluff a few shabby houses ranged along two or three short lanes or streets; and the spacious grounds and dilapidated house of one Dr. Eppes." All the white people of the town had left, and after a scout of about a mile down the railroad track, which ran from City Point to Petersburg, the three regiments of Hincks's 2nd Brigade began to entrench. The general and his staff appropriated the Eppes mansion as their headquarters.

The remainder of the Army of the James sailed up to Bermuda Hundred, a landing about a mile farther up the James, north of the Appomattox River. The James River bends south at Richmond. In 1864, the river passed two strongly held and well-sited Confederate emplacements at Chaffin's Bluff on the north and Drewry's Bluff on the south, about four miles from the Confederate capital. Meandering until it makes almost an oxbow at a place called Farrar's Island, the James makes two more abrupt bends before it widens and deepens and joins the Appomattox and thence flows to the sea. The area directly across from City Point bounded by the James on the north and the Appomattox on the south is Bermuda Hundred, a "hundred" being the term for a Virginia political subdivision of colonial times, somewhat smaller than a county. From Point of Rocks on the Appomattox, about three miles upriver from its mouth, to Farrar's Island on the James was a distance of a little over three miles. This western edge of Bermuda Hundred formed the famous neck of the "bottle." Livermore, certainly with the benefit of hindsight, roundly condemned Butler's decision to disregard Grant's instructions and land troops at Bermuda Hundred, speculating that the Bay Stater chose Bermuda Hundred "because he supposed the approach to Petersburg from City Point would be strongly opposed." This was certainly not the case, as the seizure of City Point shows. The captain rightly sketched out what his general might have done instead:

> [Butler] might have occupied high and easily defended ground at City Point for his base, might have had a railroad in running order between that point and Petersburg, might have from that point approached Petersburg on the arc of a circle only nine miles long, and might have had as fair an opportunity to approach Richmond and destroy the railroads as he could have. In operating

from Bermuda Hundred, he chose in Bermuda Hundred low ground and a point at least fourteen miles from Petersburg as the road runs, without railroad communication, and separated from Petersburg by the Appomattox, which is not fordable and Swift Creek, which proved a formidable obstacle to his advance.

Unfortunately for Ben Butler and the Army of the James, history is not made up of "might have beens." Butler's poor decision making would mean hot work for the troops under his command, including the 5th Massachusetts Cavalry.

The amphibious operation had gone flawlessly, and Butler wanted to push on the night of 5 May and seize Drewry's Bluff, about fourteen miles away. Both Smith and Gillmore strongly objected to this idea. Since the federal cavalry under Brigadier General Kautz had been sent south of Petersburg to break up the railroads into that city, the two corps commanders felt that without cavalry reconnaissance, with only a portion of the troops landed, and during full darkness, such a plan was too reckless. "One of them," Butler wrote, "intimated that he should feel it his duty to refuse it even if it were ordered." As for Butler, he wrote that he "was tempted to go myself, but I had Kautz out before the enemy, and West with his Negro cavalry out making a demonstration on the Chickahominy. I had all the details of the army only under the personal supervision and knowledge of my staff, and I thought it was my duty not to go." Smith and Gillmore later denied that this incident occurred, although historians Bruce Catton and Alan Nevins believe Butler. Whether or not it did, we are left to wonder whether Richmond might have been cut off on the first day of the Bermuda Hundred Campaign.

From 6 to 9 May, the Army of the James was engaged in digging fortifications across the Bermuda Hundred neck and operating against the Petersburg and Richmond Railroad and the turnpike that ran between the two cities. The Bermuda Hundred defenses were within two miles of the railroad. Brigadier General Charles A. Heckman's 1st Brigade of the 2nd Division, XVIII Army Corps, was sent out on 6 May as a reconnaissance in force. Heckman was instructed to ascertain Confederate positions and numbers but not to bring on a general engagement. Heckman's brigade consisted of four regiments, some 2,700 officers and men, and was accompanied by two guns (a section) of Battery L, 4th U.S. Artillery. This force was met by around six hundred South Carolinians—three companies of the 25th South Carolina and the entire 21st South Carolina under Colonel Robert Graham—at Port Walthall Junction, where a railroad line branched off the Richmond and Petersburg road to Port Walthall on the Appomattox above Point of Rocks. The South Carolinians took advantage of a sunken road and screening woods to mask their numbers, and volley fire turned back the advancing Union troops. Heckman's troops outnumbered the enemy over four to one, but the general chose neither to flank the Confederate force nor to break the railroad. The Confederates considered this a victory, for they had saved the railroad from a veteran Union brigade supported by artillery. Their accomplishment is all the more impressive given that half of the Confederate force arrived by train from Petersburg as Heckman was forming his brigade into a line of battle and preparing to advance.

Baldy Smith suggested to Butler that a more concerted effort to cut the railroad and engage the enemy be made on 7 May. General Gillmore had been ordered to detach troops to support Heckman's probe on 6 May but had refused, perhaps because some X Corps units were still disembarking at Bermuda Hundred and some were still marching from the landing to the trenches. Gillmore, however, chose not to explain why he refused Butler's order. Instead he wrote, "The project of striking the railroad to-night with a detachment from this command has been abandoned for what I deem good and sufficient reasons." In order to continue work on the unfinished trenches, Smith suggested that a brigade be detached from each of the (white) divisions of the X and XVIII Army Corps, allowing five brigades for what Butler called "a demonstration in my front to destroy the railroad as far as possible between Petersburg and Richmond." General Smith was placed in overall command of this detachment, with tactical command under the direction of Brigadier General William T. H. Brooks, the commander of the 1st Division, XVIII Army Corps. Butler reported that Gillmore was still uncooperative: "Although my order to Gillmore was explicit, yet he claimed that his troops which I had ordered should report to General Smith, were still under his own command; and because of his unofficer-like interference it became necessary that I should issue a general order placing General Smith in command of the detached forces of the Tenth and Eighteenth Army Corps, which had been ordered to operate toward Petersburg and Richmond on the railroad." On only the third day of the campaign, the Bay

Stater became disgusted with Gillmore's poor leadership and lack of cooperation and determined to fix the X Corps commander. Ever the politician, Butler chose political means to punish Gillmore: "Finding it impossible to get on with Major-General Gillmore's tardiness of movement, and knowing that he was before the Senate for confirmation to the grade which he filled, I wrote a note to the Chairman of the Military Committee of the Senate [Senator Henry Wilson of Massachusetts], asking that he bring his name before the Senate at once and have it rejected by that body, giving my reasons for making the request."

Brooks's five brigades, numbering some eight thousand men, made contact with the Confederates on the same field as the day before. Confederate troops had been rushed to the spot, however, and now two weak brigades comprising some 2,600 men defended Port Walthall Junction. Brooks maneuvered his troops poorly. Attacks were made piecemeal and were not pressed with vigor. Of nineteen regiments in this force, only six came under fire. While true that it was brutally hot (Heckman's brigade lost nearly a hundred men to sunstroke) and the terrain was difficult—tangled woods cut by ravines and creeks—the turnpike and the railroad should have given sufficient orientation to Brooks and his brigade commanders. The end of the day saw a federal withdrawal to the Bermuda Hundred defenses. Once again, a Confederate force, outnumbered this time by more than three to one, had beaten off the federal attackers. William Glenn Robertson, having sifted through the *Official Records*, sums up the results of the expedition: Total Union losses "amounted to 24 killed, 268 wounded, and 53 missing. In exchange for this sacrifice, Brooks had been able to place upon the railroad only half a regiment. The results amounted to one hundred feet of track ruined, one small trestle burned, and several telegraph lines broken."

While Major Generals Butler, Gillmore, and Smith were apparently satisfied with the results of the Union demonstration on 7 May since they allowed the entire Army of the James to remain quiescent on 8 May, the lesson of Port Walthall Junction—that the Confederates were able to quickly concentrate men by rail—appears to have been lost on the high command of the Army of the James. The lower ranks of the army, however, were not so self-deluded. S. Millet Thompson, who was an officer of the 13th New Hampshire and the regiment's historian, referred to the second battle of Port Walthall Junction more pointedly: "Possibly the nearest answer ever made to the question: 'How to fight without winning?' 'How to advance without going ahead?'" Thompson reported another rhetorical question that was soon going around the Army of the James: "How long will it take to get to Richmond if you advance two miles every day and come back to your starting point every night?"

Part of the reason that Butler persisted in demonstrations against the railroad and chose not to drive immediately upon Richmond was his lack of any encouraging news from General Grant. All Butler knew was that the Army of the Potomac was fighting heavily in the Wilderness. Until he could coordinate his movement with Grant, he made no concerted advance on the Confederate capital.

The plan for 9 May used the largest federal force yet to move against Confederate communications. Only three brigades were to be left in the Bermuda Hundred defenses. Smith and Gillmore were to make two strong probes to the railroad: Gillmore and most of X Corps to Chester Station, north and west of Port Walthall Junction, Smith and most of XVIII Corps to move against Port Walthall Junction again. The two corps were then to join and turn to the south and strike the road and rail bridges over Swift Creek.

On 9 May, Union troops reached Swift Creek, skirmished with the Confederates, and pushed them back into their entrenchments across the creek. A probe from City Point led by General Hincks was ordered to coordinate with Smith and Gillmore's advance from Bermuda Hundred. Thomas Livermore described this movement: "As I have said, General Hincks had orders only to take and occupy City Point, and although no enemy came in sight of our pickets we were allowed to remain without moving for two days after the 6th of May. On the 9th, we moved out with such troops as we had brought to City Point, four or five regiments of infantry, the battery, and possibly the 5th Massachusetts, and a company of one of the before-mentioned Negro cavalry regiments (1st and 2nd U.S. Colored Cavalry) mounted, under Captain Dollard."

Livermore is mistaken about the 5th Massachusetts; the regiment did not arrive at City Point until 16 May. According to Livermore, Hincks was ordered to "move up toward Petersburg and to attack that city" while the white troops drove down from north of the Appomattox River. Hincks's advance went well for some four miles, until shots were heard. General Hincks had ordered Captain Livermore to accompany the black cavalry, who were well in advance of the infantry. Captain Dollard had put out three scouts, one of whom, riding back, "reported, with eyes sticking out, that 'de rebels in our uniforms' were firing on him and his companions." Livermore, believing that only a picket force was before them, suggested that Dollard and his troopers charge. The Union cavalry galloped down the road between twin rows of junipers, bullets flying all around them. "We were at their post in a minute or so, and found ourselves halting in a farmhouse yard on the brink of the river, which flowed in front of and forty or fifty feet below us." In the middle of the river lay Union gunboats; fleeing down the bank was a detachment of U.S. Marines. The marines, Livermore wrote, "had been posted at this point, where the road on which we approached ran into that leading from Point of Rocks to Petersburg on the east side of the river, and, not knowing which way to look for rebels, had, in a panic, mistaken our dusky-faced men for rebels, and fired at them."

Livermore and his party were lucky that the marines were such poor shots, for no one was hurt. The Union gunboats, under the command of Brigadier General Charles K. Graham, who had been a naval officer before the war, were supposed to operate against an earthwork on the north bank of the Appomattox known as Fort Clifton. When Livermore and the company of black cavalry arrived, Graham's gunboats and Fort Clifton were exchanging fire. There was no sign of Union troops on the other side of the river, which, Livermore wrote, "embarrassed General Hincks, who had been told to cooperate with their advance, and aided him in the change of route which he now determined upon." Hincks was concerned about being confronted with infantry supported by artillery (for there were Confederate skirmishers out now and civilians had confirmed intelligence that the Confederate Washington Artillery of New Orleans was in the vicinity), while leaving his flank exposed to fire from Fort Clifton. Hincks therefore marched his troops south to the City Point railroad, "determined," according to Livermore, "not to trust his force of two thousand or so raw troops to advance on Petersburg alone." The men marched on beside the railroad tracks until gathering darkness called a halt. Captains Livermore and Dollard continued on and, with a small party of cavalrymen, chased off a party of the enemy's pickets at the farm of a man named Baylor. The party continued on until the watch fires of the Confederate pickets were seen. They were within half a mile of the Petersburg defenses. Livermore returned to General Hincks and reported in, but General Butler had ordered Hincks's force to return to camp, "which we did, very much disgusted with the result of our first advance." This was only the first of several advances from City Point led by General Hincks and the African American troops of the 3rd Brigade, XVIII Army Corps.

While true that, as Livermore noted, Butler had issued orders for the recall of all the elements of the Army of the James, this did not occur immediately. Butler met with Smith and Gillmore late in the afternoon of 9 May. The generals conferred and, having heard nothing from Grant, decided to continue their attack to the south on Petersburg, this time with a determined, coordinated assault, not a demonstration. Orders were duly sent to General Hincks at 6:35 p.m., 9 May, to advance at seven o'clock the next morning, "so that all the force may be drawn to the advance of General Smith. When you hear his guns and have word from him, engage the enemy and push on." Butler asked his generals whether they had any questions or comments, and when none were forthcoming, he rode off to his headquarters. Butler was hardly out of sight when Quincy Gillmore laid out an alternative plan to Smith. Gillmore proposed that the Army of the James withdraw from Swift Creek that night and move back to the Bermuda Hundred line, destroying the railroad as the army retreated. The Appomattox would then be crossed by a pontoon bridge east of Petersburg, which would, Gillmore wrote, "cut all the roads which come into Petersburg on that side. Such a bridge can readily be constructed in one night, and all the work of cutting the road, and, perhaps, capturing the city, can be accomplished in one day, without involving us in heavy losses." Gillmore put this proposal in writing, and both corps commanders signed it; the time of writing was 7:00 p.m. General Smith later recorded this incident in *Battles and Leader of the Civil War*. For some reason, Smith omitted to mention the previous conference with Butler:

> *After several hours spent in ineffectual efforts to find a crossing place [over Swift Creek] which offered a fair prospect of forcing a passage, General Gillmore, commanding the Tenth Corps, and myself met for consultation, and united in a letter advising General Butler that if Petersburg was to be taken, the proper way was to throw a bridge across the Appomattox behind our lines and, crossing there, to assault the works at Petersburg from the east. General Butler's written answer disapproved of the suggestion; his spoken criticism was of such a character as to check voluntary advice during the remainder of the campaign.*

According to Smith, again in *Battles and Leaders*, Butler "said he was not going to build a bridge for West Point men to retreat over." Whether Butler made the remark or not, it seems in character. Perhaps the more important question is not whether Butler held professional officers in contempt, for that was well known in the army, but *when* he made that remark. Butler had solicited the opinions of Smith and Gillmore on the proposed attack for the next day and, believing all in agreement, had ridden off in the dusk. The two corps commanders should have gone to see Butler and sold him on the new attack. If Gillmore and Smith truly believed that their proposal would succeed, and save lives in the bargain, should they not have ridden the few miles to Butler's headquarters to confer with him in person? Offering advice, "put[ting] everything in writing," is overcautious punctilio and shows a lack of initiative; sulking when the advice is not taken is unprofessional and childish. Ben Butler certainly gave Gillmore and Smith the rough side of his tongue in his dispatch replying to theirs, but the tactical picture was changed by the time he sent his reply. Butler had received communications from Secretary of War Stanton that brought about a complete change in plan. Butler, in the first part of his responding dispatch, called Smith and Gillmore out for what he saw as their diffidence:

> *While I regret an infirmity of purpose which did not permit you to state to me, when I was personally present, the suggestion which you made in your written note, but left me to go to my headquarters under the impression that another and far different purpose was advised by you, I shall not yield to the written suggestions, which imply a change of plan made within thirty minutes after I left you. Military affairs cannot be carried on, in my judgment, with this sort of vacillation.*

Butler then continued his dispatch, giving his orders for 10 May and explaining, albeit without specifics, his reasons for the change in plan. "Information," Butler wrote, "received from the Army of the Potomac convinces me that our demonstration should be toward Richmond, and I shall in no way order a crossing of the Appomattox for the purpose suggested in your note." Butler had faith that General Kautz's cavalry raid (5–10 May) south of Petersburg would break communications into the Cockade City. The Army of the James would therefore withdraw from Swift Creek while "attempting, in the first place, to destroy the railroad bridge, and then complete a thorough destruction of the railroad as we return to our position, with the intention of making a subsequent early demonstration up the James from the right of our position [at Bermuda Hundred]." Butler had received information that the anticipated linkup with the Army of the Potomac was near at hand.

The information Butler wrote of had come in the form of three dispatches he had found waiting for him at his headquarters. These were from Secretary of War Stanton, reporting on the Army of the Potomac. The first, sent at 10:00 a.m., 9 May, read, "Advices from the front give reason to believe that General Grant's operations will prove a great success and complete victory. On Saturday night the enemy had been driven at all points, and Hancock was pushing forward rapidly to Spottsylvania Courthouse, where heavy firing was heard yesterday. It was reported yesterday by a deserter that the enemy's only hope was in heavy reinforcements from Beauregard."

A second dispatch was sent at 3:20 p.m.: "A bearer of dispatches from General Meade has just reached here by way of Fredericksburg. States that on Friday night Lee's army was in full retreat for Richmond, Grant pursuing with his army. Hancock passed Spottsylvania Courthouse before daylight yesterday morning."

The last telegram from Stanton to Butler was sent at 4:00 p.m.: "A dispatch from Grant has just been received. He is on the march with his whole force; army to form a junction with you, but had not determined his route. Another dispatch from him is being translated."

If Stanton's information was accurate (and why should Butler doubt it?), then the time had come for the Army of the James to join with the Army of the Potomac and drive on to Richmond. The Army of the James spent 10 May in returning to the Bermuda Hundred defense line. A sharp action took place in the late afternoon near Chester Station, as Confederates under Major General Robert Ransom attacked a blocking force left by Butler. On 11 May, as he had done on the 8th, Butler allowed the Army of the James a day of rest. He justified this decision in his autobiography with this line: "Wishing to have the assistance of General Kautz's cavalry in the contemplated movement I gave them rest, and to put the lines in the best possible order to be held with a small force, I rested on the 11th, making ready to move by daylight on the 12th."

Granting that when the days of torrid heat finally broke on 12 May and that when the Army of the James did move it marched, maneuvered, and fought in the pouring rain, the Union advance was still slow and cautious. It took three days for the Army of the James to advance and assault the Confederate works at Drewry's Bluff. The outer line of Confederate trenches was taken on 14 May, but the intermediate and inner works were intact. A proposed assault by two brigades and two regiments of General Smith's corps on 15 May rested on the detachment of a brigade to guard the flank of the attacking column. When that brigade could not be spared, Smith persuaded Butler to call off the attack. As William Robertson wrote in *Back Door to Richmond*, "with that decision, the Army of the James passed to the defensive."

When the rebels counterattacked, screaming the rebel yell in the dawn fog on the morning of 16 May, Union troops had already lost the initiative. Despite Baldy Smith's assertion that "not a man was driven from their lines" in the 1st and 2nd Divisions of XVIII Army Corps, it was Smith who decided to withdraw his artillery and later retire his entire corps. It was General Butler, however, who ordered the withdrawal of the entire Army of the James. Butler in his book agreed with Smith that except for Heckman's brigade, the XVIII Army Corps "maintained a steady fire, inflicting upon the enemy a very terrible loss." Butler had ordered Gillmore to attack with the X Corps in a dispatch sent at six o'clock on the morning of 16 May. Gillmore delayed, inhibited by a few Confederate skirmishers on his front and by his own indecision. Butler cited this hesitation as the rationale behind his forces' eventual withdrawal: "Meanwhile, having left to General Gillmore's discretion, after several hours' delay, whether he should make an attack, and he having informed me that he was falling back, and for other reasons that I have in part stated, came to the conclusion that it was my duty, Grant not having met me 'in ten days' from the time of his crossing the Rapidan, to proceed to carry out the rest of his instructions by ordering a withdrawal of my force from the enemy's front. This was done leisurely, and without any attack or interference by the enemy."

As Smith, in his *Battles and Leaders* piece, snidely observed, albeit with the benefit of hindsight, "without further molestation, both corps reentered the historic bottle, which was at once carefully corked by a Confederate earth-work."

One cannot help but feel sorry for Ben Butler, for just as with the legend of the New Orleans spoons, he would be forever after known as "Bottled-Up

Ben Butler." While Butler's withdrawal of the Army of the James to the Bermuda Hundred defenses certainly lessened his offensive options, it did not eliminate them. The Army of the James was blocked only from going due west. For example, by throwing a pontoon bridge over the James, Butler's army could have struck north toward Chaffin's Bluff and Richmond. According to William Robertson, "on Bermuda Hundred neck itself there was approximately one mile of unfortified territory between Ashton and Swift Creeks. This sector was later fortified, but during May and early June it was lightly held by Confederate forces." Perhaps the best possibility for offensive operations lay south of the Appomattox in an attack from City Point. Union troops had also seized a rise of ground that overlooked Point of Rocks called Spring Hill. An attack from Spring Hill and City Point could have struck Petersburg from the east, along the same route that General Hincks's African American troops took on 9 May.

If Butler and the Army of the James were going to act, however, they would have to do it soon, for Butler's leisurely retirement to the Bermuda Hundred lines was only one of many disappointments confronting Grant in mid-May. In his memoirs, Grant remembers 18 May as the culmination of discouraging developments. After the Army of the Potomac had spent two weeks in futile and bloody assaults on Lee, its II and VI Corps had again that day made unsuccessful attacks on entrenched Confederates. Also that day, as Grant related, "news came that [General] Sigel had been defeated at New Market, badly, and was retreating down the [Shenandoah] Valley." Grant had at once requested Sigel's replacement. In Louisiana, General N. P. Banks had been defeated and relieved, his Red River Campaign a complete failure. "Further news from Butler," Grant continued, "reported him driven by Drury's Bluff, but still in possession of the Petersburg road. . . . All this news was very discouraging."

Accordingly, Grant wrote Halleck on 21 May to try to get some answers as to why the Army of the James was on the defensive: "I fear there is some difficulty with the forces at City Point which prevents their effective use. The fault may be with the commander, and it may be with his subordinates. . . . I wish you would send a competent officer here to inspect and report by telegraph what is being done, and what in his judgment it is advisable to do."

Halleck sent two generals, Quartermaster General Montgomery C. Meigs and the chief engineer of the U.S. Army, Brigadier General John S.

Barnard. Impatiently, Grant now moved to supersede the mission of Barnard and Meigs. Before those officers (whom Butler called in a letter to his wife "a sort of smelling committee") arrived at Bermuda Hundred on 23 May, Grant telegraphed Halleck: "The force under General Butler is not detaining 10,000 men in Richmond, and is not even keeping the roads south of the city cut. Under these circumstances I think it advisable to have all of it here except enough to keep a foothold at City Point. . . . Send Smith in command."

Generals Meigs and Barnard, unaware of Grant's order to Halleck, investigated the Army of the James in good faith. Arriving in the early morning of 23 May, they met with Butler and then with his corps commanders in turn. This "smelling committee" (presumably the generals traveled with their escorts and staffs) inspected the Bermuda Hundred defenses and then crossed the Appomattox to City Point. After inspecting General Hincks's garrison, which included the 5th Massachusetts Cavalry (dismounted), the two generals recrossed the river and composed an interim report. Despite Butler's denial, Meigs and Barnard thought it possible "that very recently, and since our force has been entirely on the defensive, rebel troops have gone to Lee." They approved of the Bermuda Hundred lines and saw possibility in Butler's position: "General Butler's position is strong; can be defended, when works are complete, with 10,000 men, leaving 20,000 free to operate." The two generals also expressed satisfaction with the logistics of the Army of the James and found "the troops in good spirits." Therefore, they concluded, "We think that this force should not be diminished, and that a skillful use of it will aid General Grant more than the numbers which might be drawn from here."

The next day, after another meeting with Generals Gillmore and Smith and another tour of the trenches, Meigs and Barnard prepared their final report. The two generals listed first the accomplishments of the campaign: the occupation and fortification of a base; demonstration upon and diversion of a strong force of Confederates; temporary interruption of the enemy's communications; and the collection of large supplies of forage, ammunition, and rations. Meigs and Barnard saw two choices facing the Army of the James. The generals proposed that the army either take the offensive, cut railroads, fight the enemy, and draw troops from Lee, "with a chance of capturing Petersburg," or "remain purely on the defensive, sacrifice the water communication by the James River for a time, and spare 20,000 men for transfer to the Army of the Potomac." Barnard and Meigs also looked into the problems of the high command in the Army of the James. Again, there were two courses of action: "What in our opinion ought to be done is either, first, to place an officer of military experience and knowledge in command of these two corps, thus making them a unit for field operations, and then assume the offensive; or, second, to withdraw 20,000 men to be used elsewhere. General Butler is a man of rare and great ability, but he has no experience and training to enable him to direct and control movements in battle. . . . General Butler is satisfied with the ability and aid of General William F. Smith. He does not appear to be satisfied with General Gillmore." General Meigs and Barnard inferred that General Butler "evidently desires to retain command in the field. If this desire must be gratified, withdraw Gillmore, [and] place Smith in command of both corps under the supreme command of General Butler. . . . Success would be more certain were Smith in command untrammeled and General Butler remanded to the administrative duties of the department in which he has shown such rare and great ability."

While Meigs and Barnard's assessment of the problems besetting the Army of the James was very astute (perhaps their only error was a perceived amity between Butler and Smith), General Grant had already decided differently.

It is hard to put an exact date on when the Bermuda Hundred Campaign ended. It may have ended when Butler and the Army of the James were "bottled up" at Bermuda Hundred on 17 May after their "leisurely withdrawal," or on 22 May, when Grant decided that he must have the immediate detachment of 17,000 men from the Army of the James. Although William Robertson writes that "by 23 May the military situation on the Bermuda Hundred peninsula gave every indication of having become a stalemate," the 5th Massachusetts Cavalry was finding plenty to do garrisoning City Point. General "Baldy" Smith, writing for *Battles and Leaders of the Civil War*, rather sneeringly referred to "the colored troops, Hincks's division of infantry, nominally attached to the Eighteenth Corps, and some cavalry" who "were left at City Point for what purposes unless to keep the letter of the order of April 2nd, it is hard to understand." Completely inaccurately, Smith wrote that "in the movements of the campaign they might as well have been back in Fort Monroe." Although Smith characterized the

African American troops of the City Point garrison as "wanting in drill, discipline and actual service in the field," he had some praise for the "many excellent officers and a division commander who united to great bravery much experience and the ability to take advantage of it."

Captain Thomas Livermore, Hincks's aide-de-camp, described the defenses at City Point, where the 5th would see its first action. "The General caused a redoubt and a line of works to be thrown up extending from river to river and thereby enclosing ourselves complete. . . . Our picket line was drawn up half a mile or so beyond the works in a line which commanded the country well." Livermore's pleasant vignette of the life of a staff officer shows how well the officers of the 5th got on with the rest of the command: "At headquarters, we led a comfortable life." General Hincks and staff dined in one of the rooms of the Eppes mansion, "and here at meal-times we all assembled with our servants marshaled by Moses, the general's boy, ranged behind us as waiters, and with many a jest and story our meals were merry enough; and as we had frequent communication with Norfolk and Baltimore we had a very good cuisine, as well as good ale." When not busy the officers would take their ease "on the lawn under the trees, whose shade, with breezes from the river, delightfully tempered the heat; and there, with the broad James and the Appomattox and the busy fleet plying their waters before us, affording a changing and enlivening view with the meadows and woods in the distance, we took solid comfort in our siestas, or with the iced julep, and tobacco for those who liked." During the evening, a regimental band might play, and "the officers of our command, particularly of the 4th and 5th Massachusetts Cavalry, came there to chat or make merry with us."

A battalion of the 4th Massachusetts Cavalry, under Colonel Arnold A. Rand, was also posted at City Point. Of course, it was fine for staff officers to take siestas and sip juleps when not working. Captain Charles Bowditch, commander of F Company, found life somewhat more full. Bowditch wrote his father on 23 May from City Point: "For a little while at any rate, we are definitely established here and we are endeavoring to make ourselves as comfortable as possible." This was difficult, for "regularly every morning we have to get up at three a.m. and turn out our companies under arms." After a roll call, the men stacked their arms and slept near them, "one officer remaining with the men and keeping awake." The men were allowed to sleep, in full kit, until 5:00 a.m., when another roll call was held and the trenches occupied until 7:00 a.m. "Then there is an order for five hours drill, which makes nine hours a day for the men to keep their equipment on."

Despite the fine food and drink afforded the officers and Bowditch's quest for comfort, the regiment had certainly been deployed to a combat zone where tensions ran high. During an alert, as on 20 May, when Confederates under Beauregard attacked the Bermuda Hundred defenses, the men were in the trenches and on the picket line all night. In this, their first battlefield deployment, the raw troops of the 5th Massachusetts sometimes made mistakes. Bowditch recorded in his letter one accident that had deadly consequences: "Last night we sent out a picket of 300 men and this morning one of my corporals is brought in wounded in the thigh. The bone is broken and I don't suppose that he will ever get well." The wounded man was Corporal John Gambol of F Company. A thirty-one-year-old former cook from Baltimore, Maryland, Gambol died on 23 May 1864 "from wounds received from a sentinel under his charge." We do not know the circumstances, whether Gambol was shot by a nervous trooper while making his rounds in the dark, or perhaps at dawn, when the men were discharging their pieces preparatory to returning to camp. (The Springfield rifle could be unloaded with a device called a worm that screwed onto the ramrod, but the fastest and simplest way to get a charge out of the weapon was to fire it.) In any case, Corporal Gambol's death was the first in the regiment while in the field.

First Sergeant Charles R. Douglass, in a letter to his father from City Point dated 31 May, left a record of life at the seat of war. He reported heavy firing "just above our picket line." Expecting to be called into the line of battle at any moment, Douglass wrote, "We have been fighting ever since our Regiment came here, I mean our forces." Douglass mentioned seeing Brigadier General John H. Martindale, a division commander in the XVIII Corps who also happened to be from Rochester where the Douglass family lived, as the general passed by with his troops on the way to the transports. Listing the three regiments of U.S. Colored Troops infantry sent to the Bermuda Hundred defenses (interestingly, he referred to these regiments by the states in which they were raised, viz. "the Twenty-Second Pennsylvania, Fifth Ohio and Fourth Maryland"), Douglass identified these as the troops "that whipped General Fitch [Fitz] Lee up the river the other day." Continuing his letter, the sergeant gave his account of taking the regiment's first prisoner.

The week before, while on picket, Sergeant Douglass had "espied a man in grey clothes dodge behind a tree. . . . In a moment, I had my piece to bear on him, I was only about a dozen yards off and the old wild cat had go[t] so near me without being perceived." Douglass related how he ordered the man to "step from behind the tree or I would knock a hole through him." Once the man did as ordered, the first sergeant saw that he apparently had no rifle. When Douglass ordered the man to precede him back to the Union lines, the prisoner "very reluctantly" complied; "as soon as he had passed in front of me I cocked my piece, which went click, click. He stopped stone still and wanted to know if I meant to murder him." Douglass assured his prisoner in a "harsh tone" that "if he stopped before I ordered him . . . I would shoot him." Douglass took his prisoner to Captain Wulff, who ordered the man searched. The first sergeant pitched into the task, "making him strip off every rag, for he was covered with them." Douglass's prisoner had a pepperbox revolver, a "dirk knife," and a quantity of currency: "$50 in rebel money, $15 in gold and some silver coin and greenbacks." Douglass's prisoner turned out to be the man who owned the land where they were picketed. The first sergeant noted that he kept the pepperbox pistol while making no mention of the disposition of the man's cash. Douglass wrote proudly that he had "had the praise of bringing in the first prisoner." Douglass also mentioned, in a single sentence that begs for elaboration, that he had "also brought in six contrabands from a farm house." He chose not to write about the age, sex, or condition of his fellow African Americans, whom he had brought out of slavery. They were apparently less exciting than a white skulker in gray rags. In other news, First Sergeant Douglass noted, "This morning I had chicken for breakfast." Explaining that his company had gone on picket duty the day before, Douglass told how his close companion "Captain Wulff made a raid on an old farm house outside our picket lines and shot seven chickens," one of which he sent to his friend the first sergeant.

Life for officers and men on the regimental level was a long way from the problems of the high command. Two days after his letter of 23 May, Charles Bowditch's circumstances had improved remarkably. Bowditch wrote his friend Lucy that he was recovering from having "got a little sun-struck on board the transport," which made him feel "headachy and all-sort-of-over-ish-you" for a week or so. Bowditch now expected to enjoy himself and "not to have much hard work to do, since General Hincks has just shown that he possesses a large amount of sense by putting me upon a General Court Martial for the trial of whatever cases come up and of which Colonel Russell is President." Bowditch found this "very jolly as it relieves me of all duty of all sorts in the regiment." Bowditch was excused from picket duty, from roll calls, and from being named officer of the day. The young captain felt that City Point was "reasonably secure," as "entrenchments have been thrown up here and there with pickets." Charles reported that his brother, Major Henry Bowditch, had been placed in charge of the pickets.

Except for a few videttes (mounted pickets) of the 4th Massachusetts Cavalry, the 5th Massachusetts was doing all the guard duty at City Point. "Our men being new," Bowditch wrote, "are of course seeing things where there is nothing to be seen, and last night there was a continual firing all along the line." Bowditch also reported a Confederate attack on Wilson's Wharf, which was being held by Brigadier General Edward A. Wild and two African American regiments of his 1st Brigade. This was the attack Charles Douglass referred to in his letter. "They sent down reinforcements from here, and altogether had a lively time." Bowditch then drew a "pen portrait" of the major general commanding the Army of the James, who had recently paid a visit to City Point. "[Butler] is by all odds the most shocking and disreputable looking man I ever clapped my eyes on. He had his hat perched sideways on his head and looked more like a New York 'Blood-tub' or a 'Plug-ugly' than anything else."

Life in garrison gave plenty of opportunity to send and receive letters, and Charles Bowditch was a good correspondent. As the Bay Stater's letters demonstrate, for officers and men, life was made up of passing the time in camp, dealing with the demands and temptations of occupation, spending time in the trenches or on picket, organizing the arrival and departure of troops, and listening to rumors. Lulls in the action gave old friends a chance to reunite and take advantage of the local amenities, such as they were. As Bowditch reported to his mother, General Hincks invited him on Thursday, 26 May, for tea: "I found the General playing euchre with Captain John White (his expected brother-in-law) [and an officer on Hincks's staff]." The general, it will be remembered, was also a Bay Stater. Bowditch found "General Hincks very sociable," and they had a pleasant chat. Bowditch was struck by Hincks's resemblance to the first leader of the Army of the Potomac: "He has very much the look of McClellan though without the scowl which McClellan has on his forehead." Bowditch was also pleased to find "Bob Verplanck, one of my classmates [at Harvard]," on General Hincks's staff: "It was very nice to have a chance to talk over old times." Though impressed by the Eppes mansion, which must have been a lovely place, the captain lamented its current state: "Now it is pretty effectually used up by shot and shell." By way of example, he remarked that one could look at the front of the house and see clear through to the other side, following the tracks of the shells. Bowditch also marveled at the way Dr. Eppes and his forebears had landscaped the grounds, thinking them "very handsome though evidently kept in the usual careless Southern style. The roses are in full bloom all around and I have a bunch in my tent which one of my men brought me."

Bowditch was also a witness to the challenges of occupation. Reporting on some trouble that arose with Dr. Eppes, who could not be accused of being short on gall, Bowditch wrote that he was "disgusted to see the mild way that the secessionists" were treated. Bowditch wrote of "Dr Reps (or some such name)," who was taken to Fort Monroe when City Point was seized on 5 May. From Fort Monroe, Eppes was sent to Richmond; as a noncombatant Confederate sympathizer, there was no reason to hold him, but he could not return home. From Richmond, the doctor sent "a schedule of the property which he says he had which he wishes to be sent after him and General Butler has ordered General Hincks to collect all the property and have a report made on its condition preparatory to turning it over to the doctor." Eppes included in his list four slaves and a Confederate flag. Bowditch found humor in relating his commander's policy regarding these items: "General Hincks says that these two articles will not give him much trouble, since he does not recognize slaves as property and he has no knowledge of there being a Confederate nation which has a right to have a flag." One can only wonder at the reception afforded Dr. Eppes if he had happened to live in Georgia or South Carolina, somewhere within the area of operations of General William T. Sherman's troops.

For all the coddling of Dr. Eppes that caused Bowditch annoyance, the captain's letters give evidence of some casual appropriation of Confederate stores, not all of which were war related. Charles Pickering Bowditch could only reflect his background and education. When in the field, he took tea with the general, he wrote letters and sat on courts-martial, and he socialized with staff officers who were Harvard classmates. Other officers had risen from the ranks, and when in the field they, too, reverted to type. Curtis Whittemore was the second lieutenant in Bowditch's company. He had been an enlisted man before joining the 5th Cavalry, and now Lieutenant Whittemore showed himself to be adept at the unthinking theft for which cavalry on both sides of the war were notorious. Bowditch sent home a "protractor taken by Lieutenant Whittemore from a rebel house just outside our picket lines." Bowditch considered Whittemore "a very good hand at foraging." He had foraged a "medicine chest, a chair, coffee pot, salt cellar, a saddle and half a dozen novels, which latter are very acceptable indeed." Although Bowditch acknowledged in his letter an order prohibiting foraging, he noted that, since Whittemore had turned the medicine chest over to the 5th's regimental surgeon, "who pronounced it exactly what he wanted, as his had not come," there probably would be no trouble over the other items Whittemore had appropriated.

Rumors abounded in the camp. As Bowditch wrote his mother on 28 May, "the 22nd colored troops and the 4th I believe have come here, which fill up the small space which we have inside the entrenchments pretty closely." He added that the regiment had to move its camp within the lines because of the newly arrived troops and a change in the trench line. "Yesterday the news came," Bowditch further reported, "that 'Baldy' Smith was crossing the Appomattox on the way to Petersburg and had advanced four or five miles on his way without a shot." On top of this news came a new rumor that evening to the effect that Smith was going to cross the James to Malvern Hill and join his corps with the Army of the Potomac. Like all good rumors, these two had elements of truth in them. General Butler wanted to try and capture Petersburg before the transports arrived to bear Smith's troops to Grant. Later, Butler would write in his book, "Having also learned that there was in Petersburg a possible aggregation, including reserves, militia, and convalescents, of some two thousand men, of which not more than two thirds would be substantially effective, I organized an expedition of eleven thousand men under General Smith, and put them in column at Bermuda Hundred to attack Petersburg on the 29th of May. They were ready to march the very next morning, but on the evening of the 28th the transportation to take them away arrived with positive orders that they should at once go to Grant."

Regimental life was perhaps simpler and the routine more straightforward than on the staff or in the high command, but it was the subject of much caprice and little or no explanation. On 28 May around 4:00 p.m., the 2nd Battalion of the 5th Massachusetts Cavalry was ordered to be in marching order with two days' cooked rations by 6:00 p.m. As Bowditch reported on 29 May, the 2nd Battalion was put on board a transport ship at the appointed time, with "one wagon for our baggage." Rumor, soon confirmed, was that the regiment was headed up the Appomattox River. The 5th Massachusetts sailed up the Appomattox about five miles until the pontoon bridge that crossed from Point of Rocks to Spring Hill was reached. Unbeknownst to the officers and men of the regiment, the 5th Massachusetts made up part of the force General Hincks was to use to cooperate with an attack by General Smith's troops on Petersburg on 29 May.

Bowditch recorded his disappointment at what happened next. At the pontoon bridge, the officers of the regiment "had got all the companies ready to land, when up comes a dispatch boat from City Point ordering us back again to camp." Officers and men were pretty disgusted at the mix-up, particularly because as they were preparing to unload, there went the white troops of XVIII Corps in the opposite direction, crossing the pontoon bridge on their way to City Point and the transports that were to carry them to the Army of the Potomac.

Having been in the army long enough to know that "there was nothing to be done except to obey orders, though it did make us feel, as Colonel Russell said, like 'a shirt collar with all the starch taken out,'" Bowditch resignedly concluded, "Thus ended the first cavalry, steamboat, infantry raid of the Fifth Massachusetts." After Smith's troops had passed through City Point, the 4th, 5th, and 22nd U.S. Colored Infantry Regiments were sent to Bermuda Hundred to take the place of the detached troops. This left only the 5th Massachusetts and the battalion of the 4th Massachusetts to garrison City Point. Colonel Rand of the 4th Massachusetts was in overall command of the defenses of the post. "This regiment," Bowditch wrote, "does the whole picket duty for this point which is keeping them pretty constantly employed." Bowditch expressed his confidence in the earthworks surrounding City Point. He thought that the 5th Massachusetts "could make quite a fight" from the trenches, "though I must say I should prefer that the rebels should not bring more than 40,000 or 50,000 men against us." The captain, referring to the Confederate attack on Wilson's Wharf, where, on 24 May, a large force of cavalry under Major General Fitzhugh Lee first requested the surrender of that post and then were handsomely repulsed, wrote that Brigadier General E. A. Wild and his two African American regiments, the 1st and 22nd U.S. Colored Troops, knew that, although outnumbered by more than two to one, surrender was out of the question: "The colored troops fought very well, they say, at Wilsons Creek [*sic*]," Bowditch wrote, "and gave the chivalry an idea of what the negroes can do, when they have freedom and Fort Pillow to nerve them."

The massacre of African American troops at Fort Pillow, Tennessee, on 12 April 1864, was also much on the mind of I Company's first sergeant, Charles Remond Douglass, as was the affair at Wilson's Wharf. In the young first sergeant's letter to his father of 31 May, Douglass wrote, "Our boys are very anxious for a fight. I think their wishes will be complied with shortly." As for himself, Charles wrote his father that he was "not over anxious but willing to meet the devils at any moment and take no prisoners. Remember Fort Pillow will be the battle cry of the fifth Mass. Cavalry."

At the end of May 1864, the 5th Massachusetts Cavalry (dismounted) was in the trenches at City Point. At times the entire defense of that vital post was their responsibility. Each evening a battalion, some three hundred men, went out on picket. Each dawn the regiment came under arms and then filed into the trenches for two hours to await a possible Confederate attack. The men were drilled in the intricacies of the infantry under the broiling sun.

For the officers, life was routine unless some special duty broke up the daily round. Officers could be detailed to sit on a general court-martial, like Colonel Russell, Captain Bowditch, and Lieutenants Edward H. Adams and Robert M. Higginson. Others might sit on a board of inquiry, like the one that met on 17 May "to investigate all the circumstances connected with, the responsibility for, and the conduct of, an affair [a picket skirmish apparently] in which Private James Dickenson, Company 'G', Fifth United States Colored Troops was killed, and several other members of the same regiment were either killed, wounded or captured on the 16th inst." Major Weld and Lieutenants Davenport Fisher and Rienzi Loud were detailed to that board. On 19 May, a board of survey consisting of Colonel Russell, Lieutenant Colonel N. G. Chamberlain of the 37th U.S. Colored Troops, and Major J. H. Terry of the 5th U.S. Colored Troops was convened to "investigate the circumstances attending the loss of ordnance stores for which the Company Commanders of the Fifth Massachusetts Cavalry are responsible." As far as we know, neither of those two boards issued any recommendations or findings in writing that has survived. Any record of reprimand (or explanation of circumstances) has been lost. Other officers might be detailed for responsible positions like First Lieutenant Charles E. Allan, who on 22 May was "relieved from duty with his regiment and assigned to duty as Assistant Provost Marshall for the division." These special details were not about assaulting enemy works, forming lines of battle, or coolness under fire. But they had everything to do with the maintenance of good order and discipline, and with keeping the great machine that was the 3rd Division and the Army of the James running smoothly.

Lest we carry the machine image too far, it is important to remember that this was an army made up almost exclusively of volunteers, and then still subject to the interference of state officials and civilians. One such case concerned the promotions of officers within the regiment. Governor Andrew received a letter dated 2 June from a Henry J. Taylor of New Bedford: "Understanding that the captain of Company 'L' Fifth Massachusetts Cavalry has resigned, I would respectfully ask that First Lieutenant F. L. Gilman now in charge of said Co. be appointed to the vacancy. I would refer your excellency to Bridgadier [*sic*] General R. A. Peirce who is personally acquainted with him, for the requisite information as to character and ability." Peirce's endorsement was written on 8 June. Peirce thought Gilman "a very worthy young officer," but since the regiment was in the field "under an officer in whose judgment I have the highest confidence," Peirce suggested that Russell be first sounded "in regard to the promotion of Mr. Gilman, who has never seen service, except in the 5th Cav." There is an interesting anomaly here, for in the records of the adjutant general of the commonwealth, no officers of the 5th Massachusetts Cavalry resigned until July. Taylor and Peirce must have heard that Captain Edward Merrill, who had remained in Boston on recruiting duty and who was never mustered in with the regiment, had resigned. Francis Gilman would not be promoted until that vacancy was confirmed.

Captain C. P. Bowditch wrote his father a brief note on 7 June. The regiment had moved its camp again, one can only wonder why, on 5 June. The new camp "afford[ed] a very nice swamp for our men to live in, though the officers' quarters are on higher ground. A ditch runs diagonally across the company street, which in our street has been covered over with boards." The men had board floors for their tents, however, which must have given some comfort from the mud. Bowditch was tiring of court-martial duty: "Yesterday we had a very long session from eight in the morning till after one and I do not think that any of the members were very sorry to adjourn over to-day." The garrison at City Point had heard little cannon or rifle fire for the last few days "in the direction of Grant, while previously the firing was very distinct and heavy." The distinct and heavy sound of warfare was doubtless from Grant's assaults on the Confederate lines at Cold Harbor, only about four miles from Richmond and about fourteen from City Point. Bowditch was not hopeful about the Army of the Potomac: "We can hardly look for the evacuation of Richmond yet awhile however. Lee isn't a man to give up easily."

There were signs for the astute observer that the quiet days in the trenches of the Bermuda Hundred front were soon going to end. The troops at City Point may not have been aware of Grant's strategy, but Ben Butler certainly was. After the failure of the frontal assaults against Lee at Cold Harbor on 3 June, Grant determined that he must shift his army to the south side of the James. On 5 June 1864, Grant sent the following dispatch to General Halleck outlining his plans:

> I will continue to hold substantially the ground now occupied by the Army of the Potomac, taking advantage of any favorable circumstances that may present itself until the cavalry can be sent west to destroy the Virginia Central Railroad from about Beaver Dam for some twenty-five or thirty miles west. When this is effected, I will move the army to the south side of the James River, either by crossing the Chickahominy and marching near to City Point, or by going to the mouth of the Chickahominy on the north side and crossing there. To provide for this last and most possible contingency, several ferry-boats of the largest class ought to be immediately provided.

The day after this dispatch, Grant sent a pontoon train to Bermuda Hundred Landing, along with two staff officers who were to prepare maps and pick the best site for the pontoon bridge. He also informed Butler on 6 June that the Army of the Potomac would soon be crossing to the south side of the James River.

Major General Butler saw the end of the independence of the Army of the James in Grant's dispatch; if his army were to achieve anything, it would have to do so before becoming a truncated subsidiary of the Army of the Potomac. Therefore, Butler renewed his plan for a raid into Petersburg. The general's plan called for Hincks to use his reserve brigade at Bermuda Hundred (the 4th, 5th, and 22nd U.S. Colored Troops), as well as troops from the river forts and City Point. The African American troops were to assault the thinly held Confederate earthworks, while Kautz's cavalry were to loop around to the west and break into the city.

While Generals Hincks and Butler were making their plans, General Gillmore arrived at Butler's headquarters. "When the condition of things at Petersburg was disclosed to [Gillmore]," Butler wrote, "and when he learned that I proposed to send General Hinks in command of the expedition, he became very strongly impressed with the great probability of its success, and insisted that he ought to command it, being senior officer." Butler could hardly turn down Gillmore's request, although he had strong doubts about his subordinate. Butler also knew, as Livermore wrote, that General Hincks had a "great contempt for General Gillmore" and "had expressly stipulated with General Butler, on taking command under him, that he should never be put under the command of General Gillmore." A brigade of white troops from X Corps was substituted for Hincks's Bermuda Hundred brigade, and the 3rd Division commander was reduced from leading the main force of some thirty-five hundred men to less than two thousand from the river forts.

The 5th Massachusetts remained at City Point on 9 June, when General Hincks and his black soldiers marched on Petersburg, taking the same route that they had on 9 May. Livermore described the advance of Hincks's force: "Early in the day, having passed the ground I had on the former expedition selected for the night's bivouac, our skirmishers encountered the pickets in front of the rebel works, which works were in plain sight, and pretty soon the artillery opened on us. . . . We got our lines all in shape ready to assault, and it was so reported to General Gillmore, whose other troops joined our right, but he did not dare to attack and ordered a retreat." Livermore noted that "General Kautz actually penetrated the works with cavalry on the south side of Petersburg, but was obliged to retreat." Hincks was so incensed at Gillmore's temerity that he sent Captain Livermore by steamer "up the river again to tell General Butler that if he would give him the same force which

Gillmore had had he would give him Petersburg on his commission." Livermore found Butler and delivered the message, "to which he replied that the next time Petersburg was assaulted it would be by an army corps." So ended the ill-fated Kautz-Gillmore raid of 9 June. For his inaction, Butler relieved General Gillmore on 14 June. William Glen Robertson, who wrote his master's thesis on the attack, assessed it thus: "Bold in conception although rather hazy in its ultimate goals, the operation was a fiasco from the beginning."

On 14 June, Colonel Russell wrote Governor Andrew from City Point to inquire whether "any steps [had] been taken towards providing the Fifth Cavalry (?) with a Lieutenant Colonel?" The bulk of Russell's letter dealt with this issue, but he closed with these words: "We are all well, still behind fortifications. Officers and men have taken hold of the new arm with praiseworthy energy." Sometime before 15 June, Colonel Arnold A. Rand of the 4th Massachusetts Cavalry wrote to Brigadier General R. A. Peirce, the commander of Camp Meigs. On 20 June an officer on Peirce's staff, Charles C. Dunbar, forwarded extracts of this letter to Governor Andrew, for his information. "At present, I am in command of defenses at this post with troops among whom are the Fifth Massachusetts Cavalry ordered to me," Rand wrote. Rand could "not repress my admiration of the manner in which officers and men bear their dismounted condition." Colonel Harry Russell, in his enduring way, "behave[s] nobly, and only says 'if it is necessary, for the present we must bear it [and] will do the best we can.'" Rand described the officers and men as "animated" by Russell's example, taking "hold of their infantry drill with a vigor which ensures success." The 5th Massachusetts had been "hard worked," Rand reported, "on fatigue at fortifications— almost constantly on picket duty—and yet have managed to get into such condition as to hold a Dress Parade on Sunday evening, which would have shamed many a white regiment." Colonel Rand, as the overall commander of the picket line at City Point, could "speak understandingly of the value of their service, and now that they have got through shooting each other, they are most satisfactory." This last is an obvious reference to the shooting of Corporal Gambol on 23 May. These extracts of Colonel Rand's letter concluded with some fulsome praise: "One thing I can say, the spirit and cheer of these men under their disappointment is worthy of officers, men, and Massachusetts. If there are rewards for merit they will be splendidly mounted by and by."

Colonel Rand's letter could not have been written after 15 June, for the 5th Massachusetts was no longer posted at City Point after that date. What's more, it seems likely that Rand would have mentioned that the 5th Massachusetts had been in a battle. Ben Butler was entirely correct when he told Captain Thomas Livermore that the next assault on Petersburg would be by an army corps. Butler, in his *Book*, noted, "At my suggestion the remainder of the Eighteenth Corps was marched to the White House on York River and placed upon transports and landed at my Pontoon Bridge at Bermuda Hundred, arriving there on the night of the 14th of June."

Baldy Smith wrote that he "arrived at Bermuda Hundred with my aids about sunset, and was told that I was to have Kautz's cavalry and Hincks's division of colored troops added to my force, and that I was to proceed at two o'clock a.m. to attack Petersburg [on 15 June]." General Andrew A. Humphreys, in his book *The Virginia Campaign of '64 and '65: The Army of the Potomac and the Army of the James*, went into greater detail about the plan of attack: "General Butler's Cavalry under Brigadier-General Kautz, 2,400 strong, and the available part of the division of the colored troops under Brigadier-General Hincks (3,700 officers and enlisted men, infantry and artillery), were assigned to General Smith, in addition to his own infantry, 10,000 enlisted men."

Kautz's cavalry was to "cross the river at one o'clock in the morning, and threaten the entrenchments near the Norfolk and Petersburg Railroad, and at the same time protect the left flank of the infantry." General Hincks and the African American troops were to march down the road parallel to the City Point railroad until they reached the crossroads at Baylor's Farm, whence they were to take a side road down to the Jordan's Point road, which ran parallel to the City Point road to the south and west. Hincks's black regiments, Humphreys wrote, were to "take a position across the Jordan's Point road as near as possible to the enemy's works." The 1st Division, XVIII Corps, under General Brooks was to "follow Hinks," Humphreys wrote, "and form on his right, and General Martindale [2nd Division, XVIII Army Corps] to proceed on the river-road to a point near the City Point Railroad and await orders." Humphreys reminded the reader "that the Petersburg entrenchments encircled the city at the distance of two miles from it and consisted of a series of strong redans or batteries connected by infantry parapets with high profiles, all with ditches." General

Smith's troops had a march of about seven miles to get to the trenches outside Petersburg.

It would only be fair to General Smith to let him describe the day's events. "Owing to delay caused by the cavalry," the march did not begin until after daylight. "We met the enemy about six a.m.," Smith wrote, "but we fought our way, capturing rifle pits and one piece of artillery, and formed our lines in front of the fortifications of Petersburg." Smith ordered up his artillery but was forced to move his batteries back when the Confederate cannon opened up. Smith "found from the great strength of the fortifications, the wide open spaces along the entire front, and the heavy and well directed artillery fire of the enemy, which prevented our getting any artillery into position to do any service, that we could not hope to capture the works by regular assault." According to Smith, "the only course left was to make a reconnaissance of the enemy's line to discover its weak points." General Smith conducted this reconnaissance himself, on foot, sometimes crawling on his hands and knees. This scout naturally took a while; Smith estimated it at about two hours. He "then determined to make an attack by throwing forward heavy bodies of skirmishers along my whole line at the same time, to be supported during the brief period of the assault by artillery." The artillery, however, was temporarily immobile because Smith's chief of artillery had ordered the horses to be taken to water. It took another hour or so to get the horses back and hitched up to the limbers. Time was also spent "to make it sure that the skirmishers of all three divisions of Martindale, Brooks and Hincks would advance simultaneously." Smith rather defensively wrote that "every moment until seven o'clock p.m. was spent in preparing to make the assault a success." When the attack was finally made, "the whole force moved at the same moment and the success was perfect." Smith reported that the white troops of Brooks's division took ten guns. Hincks's African Americans captured six cannon. "It was nearly nine o'clock before the fight was over," Smith wrote. "We had taken the principal fortifications which the rebels had erected to protect what they considered the key to the Confederacy."

General Humphreys's description of the assault of the XVIII Army Corps substantially concurs with Smith's account:

About seven o'clock the skirmishers advanced, and the artillery opened upon the salient (Redans 5 and 6), which made no reply. The skirmishers met a sharp infantry fire, but carried the works, taking between 200 and 300 prisoners and four guns. The lines of battle followed and occupied the entrenchments. General Brooks was formed to resist an attack, while General Martindale on the right, and General Hinks on the left, were following up the advantage gained. Five of the redans on the left, from number 7 to 11, both inclusive, which commanded the position at the centre, were captured by Hincks's division, the last number 11, at the Dunn House, about nine o'clock in the evening. Artillery was captured in each. A mile and a half of the entrenchments, with sixteen guns, were thus captured, and this showed that the infantry force defending Petersburg was very small.

Captain Thomas Livermore was a great deal closer to the action than either Humphreys or Smith. "We left City Point on the morning of June 15," Livermore wrote, "soon after daylight, and, preceded by Kautz's cavalry, took the same road on which we had traveled in Gillmore's expedition a few days before." Around 9:00 a.m. the cavalry came under fire, and General Smith rode up and "ordered General Hincks to push on without delay and clear the enemy from our front." General Hincks and staff rode at a gallop to the head of the infantry column. Livermore described an accident that occurred during their gallop: "On the way we had an occasion to cross a ditch, and the general in his haste attempted to jump his horse over it, but she plunged her fore feet into it and the general was thrown." Hincks was badly hurt, but he climbed back into the saddle and rode on. In 1862, General Hincks had been wounded at Glendale, a bullet going completely through his body, cutting an intestine. He had survived, but this fall from his horse had wrenched that wound, causing him great pain. Hincks was too tough to turn over operations to another officer, though, and he stayed with his division all day. "We found the cavalry withdrawing," continued Livermore, "and greeted Colonel Mix, of the [3rd] New York Cavalry, as he passed us." Mix "wore a merry face and rode away in high spirits," Livermore wrote, but that was "the last we saw of him, for he was killed that day."

General Hincks now formed his troops into two lines of battle by brigade. The 1st Brigade "under Colonel [Samuel A.] Duncan, comprising the Fourth, Fifth, Sixth and Kiddoo's Regiment, [22nd U.S. Colored Troops] in advance," and the 2nd Brigade under "Colonel [John H.] Holman, comprising the First Infantry and Fifth Massachusetts Cavalry, dismounted, following at a distance of about a hundred yards." General Smith wanted no delay in this advance, so no skirmishers were thrown out. Livermore recalled carrying Hincks's orders to Colonel Duncan, "who was to see in this his first battle," finding him "rather pale but determined" as he set about forming his line. The lines were formed stretching across the road, and the order was soon given to attack. "Our infantry entered a piece of woods about a quarter of a mile wide, through which the road ran, and crossed these woods under a very severe artillery fire which the enemy, who were posted in open ground beyond the woods out of our sight, poured into us," Livermore wrote. The young captain asked General Hincks to let him ride forward "to see how our lines were getting along." Taking his fellow staff officer Bob Verplanck with him, Livermore galloped down the road. "The shot and shell tore by, rending the trees and bursting with disagreeable ferocity, and our wounded or dead were pretty frequent." Livermore and Verplanck could hear the shouts of the black troops as they advanced, and all seemed to be going well when, as the two rode back to General Hincks to report, "to our astonishment a portion or perhaps all of the Fifth Massachusetts Cavalry came retreating in great confusion, and I am not sure we did not also see some of the Sixth Infantry, a part of which also broke."

Almost simultaneously, according to Livermore, the 1st Brigade, cheering loudly, swept up to a rebel earthwork. Hincks and his staff "about a hundred yards beyond the woods rode up to [the] first brigade, which was scattered along a line of earthworks, which with a piece of artillery it had captured with a charge on emerging from the woods, the rebels running away incontinently before our men could get to the works and even before they were fairly out of the woods." Livermore described the African American soldiers as being in "high glee" and recorded this exchange: "The General said to one black fellow who stood near by, on the broad grin, loading his rifle: 'They ran before they saw you; what do you suppose made them?' The fellow laughed, 'Yah! Yah! I reckin dey thmelt uth.'" Livermore described this, justifiably, as a "handsome victory" and "a good beginning for our division." He also gave an explanation for what happened to the Bay State regiment. "The officers of the Fifth Massachusetts Cavalry said that their men were demoralized by the conduct of one of the field officers in the first brigade, who, as they alleged, just as that line emerged from the woods turned to the rear and madly gesticulating urged them to retreat or halt, and I think the Sixth Regiment was affected by his conduct." Livermore also wrote, "We had great charity for the Fifth Massachusetts Cavalry. It was officered by a gallant set of men, but was indifferently drilled for foot service and was discontented and spiritless because it was not mounted."

This action, prior to the assault on the main works at Petersburg, was called "Baylor's Farm" because it occurred near that house. As a final note, Livermore mentioned in his book that the "orders which General Hincks received did not admit of the delay which a flank movement would have necessitated, but if we had been able to spend the time we could have approached the breast work in flank and not lost many men in clearing it." By a frontal assault, about three hundred men out of thirty-five hundred became casualties.

From the major general commanding to the staff captain of a brigadier general, we come finally to the line officer of a regiment. Captain Charles Bowditch wrote his mother from "somewhere near the Appomattox" on 18 June 1864. "We have had our first fight and I have got out all right," he wrote. "Wednesday morning (June 15th) we started out a half past one o'clock [a.m.] from City Point, marched till about six or seven with an interval of two or three hours rest." Sometime after 7:00 a.m., Bowditch continued, "we were formed in line and marched through fields and over a railroad gully and through dense woods till we came to an open field, where we found a line of infantry drawn up some little way in front of us." The regiment from the time it had formed a line of battle was taking shellfire, with what Bowditch called "a rather disagreeable accuracy."

The 5th Massachusetts now moved into a clearing, and after "having a few shells pitched at us, the line in front of us moved on and we followed suit." The troops entered a "thick wood, just as full of underbrush as it could be, rendering it almost impossible to keep in line." Bowditch wrote that the men did their best to keep their dressing in the dense woods. "In the mean time the front line had driven the rebs out of the woods and they began to play pretty sharply with grape and canister, and the sharpshooters letting us have a good share of rifle bullets, while the shell burst round altogether too freely to be amusing." Captain Hiram E. W. Clarke, commanding G Company, was hit in the leg soon after entering the woods. He was able to continue, however, and remained with his company. "The first thing that I saw on emerging from the woods was a mass of men in front of me firing apparently at random and now and then cheering," Bowditch wrote. Before the 2nd Brigade could come up to this "mass of men," they had "turned round and ran for the woods." Captain Bowditch asked his mother to imagine the effect "such a course would have upon our men, just coming out of the woods, and seeing others running helter skelter back upon them."

The troops who broke were the 6th Regiment of U.S. Colored Infantry. It took some time, and probably a certain amount of shouting and cursing, to get the men separated and formed back into line. "We got them up again and out of the woods, and formed line again in the open field, but in the meantime Colonel Russell had been shot in the shoulder and Major [Zabdiel Boylston] Adams in the breast and we were all under the command of the Lieutenant Colonel of the Sixth, who was more like a fool than anything else." Remember, the 5th Massachusetts had no lieutenant colonel at that time. The regiment moved up behind a hedge, a good position to charge the rebel artillery, and then they were moved forward "where there was not a mite of cover and where the rebs had a slanting fire on us." The men formed a line of three or four ranks and stood there in the Virginia sun "while the battery played on us like the old Harry," Bowditch wrote.

Instead of charging the Confederate artillery, the commanding officer of the 6th U.S. Colored Troops had the 5th Massachusetts lie down in ranks while he, apparently, deliberated what to do. The regiment was eventually moved by the flank to attack the rebel works. This attack was not made, for by the time the 5th Massachusetts got into position the battery had been assaulted from the other side and the Confederates had retreated. Bowditch reported the capture of a brass twelve-pound howitzer to his mother and assured her that "Henry will probably give you a better drawing of the field than I." Bowditch then gave the following assessment: "In the beginning the men were exposed to a severe cross-fire, while sharpshooters in the woods around made it extremely nasty. Only one of my men was wounded and that not seriously. Our men behaved very well indeed though it is not the most favorable way of going into a first action with another regiment breaking through them."

So ended the Battle of Baylor's Farm, the regiment's first fight. Sixteen troopers and three officers of the 5th Massachusetts Cavalry were wounded: Captain Clarke, Major Adams, and Colonel Russell. Those who made the ultimate sacrifice were Private Thomas Williams, Company D, a twenty-four-year-old seaman who had enlisted in January at New Bedford; G Company's

Private William Edwards, twenty-one, who gave "servant" as his occupation and claimed Boston as his residence; Daniel Carter, thirty-one; and Henry Johnson, twenty-seven, who were, respectively, a forge man and a teamster before the war. Carter and Johnson were in Company I. These men had emphatically answered the question of whether African Americans would fight. The officers and men of the 5th Massachusetts Cavalry believed they had done well; they had advanced under fire and carried a Confederate position. Unfortunately for the dismounted troopers of the 5th Cavalry, others were not so sure of the regiment's success.

Omenhausser Watercolors

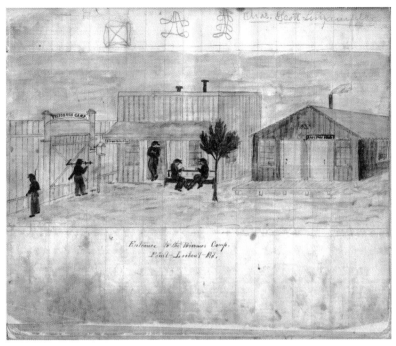

Entrance to Point Lookout (CREDIT: SCUA-UMD)

Prisoners arriving at Point Lookout (CREDIT: SCUA-UMD)

Lady visitor at Point Lookout (CREDIT: SCUA-UMD)

Barrel jacket, Point Lookout (CREDIT: SCUA-UMD)

Bottom rail on top, Point Lookout (CREDIT: SCUA-UMD)

No change for you, Point Lookout (CREDIT: SCUA-UMD)

Stolen knapsack, Point Lookout (CREDIT: SCUA-UMD)

Note the intermingling of Confederate prisoners and Union soldiers (including an officer), coming together despite being enemies, at this show put on by Confederate prisoners dressed in blackface. Note also that the artist did not include any African American troopers of the 5th Massachusetts Cavalry, who apparently refused to be humiliated in person. Omenhausser's handwriting can be somewhat difficult to read. The man on the extreme right says, "I feel so good I can almost taste myself." (CREDIT: SCUA-UMD)

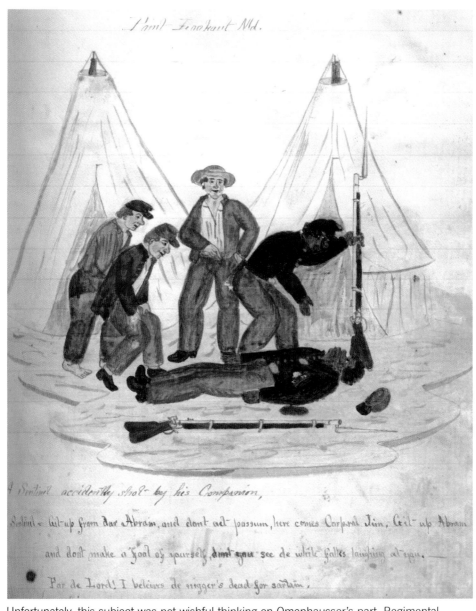

Unfortunately, this subject was not wishful thinking on Omenhausser's part. Regimental records note that Private William Brooks, Company H, was "accidentally shot and killed, March 18, 1865 at Point Lookout, Md." (CREDIT: SCUA-UMD)

"Doublequick, sah!" Point Lookout (CREDIT: SCUA-UMD)

Rebels running in place, Point Lookout (CREDIT: SCUA-UMD)

Pray for Abe Lincoln, Point Lookout (CREDIT: SCUA-UMD)

CHAPTER SIX

Cavalry in Fact as Well as Name

My Theodore: Is the big "Injun" approachable to-day? If he be and is good naturedly disposed to the little papooses, one of the smallest of that, I would like to wait on him in a matter of business. Time with me grows short and precious, and I shall be relieved if you would designate some hour to-day at which it would be well for me to grovel in the pine cuttings of the great man's tent.

—Captain Charles Francis Adams Jr. to
Lieutenant Colonel Theodore Lyman, August 1864

The 5th Massachusetts Cavalry (dismounted) spent the remainder of 15 June 1864 under the command of Major Henry P. Bowditch. General Hincks and the 1st Brigade's commander, Colonel Holman, evidently were not sure what to do with the regiment, as Charles Bowditch wrote: "We were marched and counter-marched and at last were ordered to support a battery of ten guns which was going to take part in the attack on the Petersburg entrenchments." Wherever they went, it seemed to Bowditch, they were forced to move because of enemy cannon fire. In one place, a rebel shell hit the ground and rolled down the first rank of the regiment without exploding. "At another time an elongated shell ricocheted and, bouncing over and over, made a jump across the gully through which the road ran, just escaping by six inches Captain [Cornelius] Kaler, who dodged in time, and passing through his company." The men were able to scatter before anyone was injured. The 5th Massachusetts remained with the battery until nightfall, hearing the cheers, the screams, and the heavy firing as XVIII Corps took the Confederate earthworks. After dark, the regiment marched up to the newly captured works and encamped.

This was not a pleasant place to bivouac, as Bowditch recorded in a letter dated 18 June from "Near Point of Rocks, Virginia." The young captain began his letter by mentioning the mass attack of XVIII Army Corps on 15 June. The men "rushed on over a long open plain on which they were exposed to a cross-fire from three batteries and charged the center fort." Bowditch expressed amazement at the success of the attack and concluded that the works must have been lightly held. Bowditch explained that the regiment had camped that night "outside the left fort," or Redan No. 11, near the end of the line of captured trenches. "The ground in front of the fort," Bowditch wrote, "was covered over with tall weeds and some underbrush, and in places it had been impossible to bury the dead, and the result was the most awful stench." The morning of 16 June, the regiment formed ranks and marched down toward the Appomattox, from the left to the right of the Union line. The officers and men of the 5th Massachusetts "lay on a ridge till about noon," after which the regiment was again put in motion, this time away from the river.

In the afternoon, the regiment stopped in an orchard near the house "of some people calling themselves Union, and whose property was therefore respected," wrote Bowditch. This family had evidently been bypassed by the war, for they had plenty of provender to sell the Union troops: "We bought some hens . . . and potatoes and eggs and had a jolly chicken stew and roast chicken. Then I bought a large pailful of milk and had two or three jolly tumblers full of milk fresh from the cow, going down to see the cows milked for the purpose." Perhaps the fact that the young daughter of the household accompanied Captain Bowditch prompted him to "go down to see the cows milked." The family, by name Rushmore, featured in several more letters of Bowditch in June and July.

After the noon meal, which Bowditch described as a "pretty good dinner," the regiment moved back up to the front and "acted as reserve for a skirmish line and to guard against a flank attack which of course never came," Bowditch wrote. On 17 June, the regiment marched west down the Appomattox and crossed over the pontoon bridge that ran between Spring Hill and Point of Rocks, going into camp at the latter place as part of the defense forces of the Bermuda Hundred line. Bowditch reported that

General Grant "had demanded the surrender of Petersburg on threat of shelling it and we certainly heard some very heavy firing in that direction." Heavy firing also continued all day on 18 June as the Army of the Potomac attempted to exploit the limited success of XVIII Army Corps of 15 June and capture the Cockade City.

The failure of the Union army to capture Petersburg became one of the long-standing controversies of the war. Indeed, Smith's failure to capture Petersburg largely prompted his writing *From Chattanooga to Petersburg under Generals Grant and Butler* in order to justify his failure. On the other side of the controversy, Thomas L. Livermore was one of a vociferous group that included Generals Hincks and Butler. Livermore, in his account of his military life, *Days and Events*, described the moments after the Confederate earthworks had been taken, around 9:00 p.m. on 15 June: "The spirits of all men were very high and we were willing to move on at once. I asked General Hincks if we should not set about arranging our line to advance, when to my utter surprise he said that the orders from General Smith forbade a further advance, and we actually made no advance that night and one of the best opportunities for capturing Petersburg was lost, for the rebel army, which had not then reached Petersburg, hurried down there in the night, and on the next morning we found the iron veterans of Lee's army in our front between us and Petersburg, which lay not over a mile ahead of us."

Livermore speculated that perhaps Smith's receipt of a dispatch from General Grant notifying him that II Corps of the Army of the Potomac was on its way to support Smith "led him to delay his attack in the hope that Hancock might join his left in the charge." If this was true, General Smith did not take the opportunity of requesting the troops of II Corps, for two divisions of that corps had arrived on the battlefield, according to Livermore, by 7:00 p.m. This was just about the time (or not long after) XVIII Corps attacked.

General Humphreys, in *The Virginia Campaign of '64 and '65*, gave General Smith the benefit of the doubt about when II Corps arrived, while still judging him harshly:

> [Smith] knew also, he says, that some portion of the Army of the Potomac was coming to aid him; and therefore, the troops were placed so as to occupy the commanding positions and wait for daylight. Upon the arrival of General Hancock he

requested him to relieve his troops and allow them to rest, which request General Hancock complied with. It is probable that an immediate advance of the whole of Smith's force when the salient was carried, or at nine o'clock, when it would have been supported by two divisions of the Second Corps, would have resulted in the capture of Petersburg and possession of the north bank of the Appomattox.

General Grant, for his part, wrote in his report that "for some reason that I have never been able to satisfactorily understand, [Smith] did not get ready to assault his main lines until near sundown." According to Grant, Smith's troops should have been able to walk into the city: "Between the line thus captured, and Petersburg there were no other works, and there was no evidence that the enemy had reinforced Petersburg with a single brigade from any source." There was a full moon and the skies were clear, "but instead of taking these troops and pursuing at once into Petersburg, he [Smith] requested General Hancock to relieve a part of his line in the captured works, which was done before midnight."

So Lee's veterans arrived in time to deny the city, with its vital rail network, to the Union army. Despite concerted and strong Union attacks on 16, 17, and 18 June, the Confederates stabilized their line and fought off the Armies of the Potomac and the James. The Bermuda Hundred Campaign was effectively over on 16 June, as Grant wrote in his report: "By the time I arrived the next morning the enemy was in force." The Siege of Petersburg, more properly an investiture, had begun.

Livermore, in *Days and Events*, recorded his impression of the days following the Union victory of 15 June: "I recollect riding along the crest on which the rebel works were which our division had taken on the morning of June 16, and seeing a portion of the Army of the Potomac move down toward Petersburg and engage the enemy, who seemed to be in strong force and whose bullets flew around my vicinity." Livermore also recorded the positioning of XVIII Corps, thus giving us a clearer picture of the movements of the regiment than that provided by Captain Bowditch or the regimental compendia. James Bowen, for instance, in *Massachusetts in the War* merely noted "being armed as infantry, the command was industriously drilled in that branch of tactics, performing guard and picket duty meantime, and taking part in various expeditions." Livermore wrote that "the Eighteenth Corps occupied a line from the Friend house to the river, its right striking the river at least a mile below Petersburg." Between the Friend house and the river, the Confederates had an earthwork, "a redan or lunette . . . which was still held by the rebels and which it was determined to take." The task of assaulting the rebel earthwork was assigned to General Hincks and his 3rd Division. Hincks in turn, reported Livermore, "accordingly selected Colonel Ames's regiment [6th United States Colored Infantry], with the view, I believe, of giving it an opportunity to restore its reputation, which, as I have said, suffered at Baylor's Farm on the preceding day."

That limited attack was called off, however, in favor of a general advance against Petersburg itself. XVIII Corps, therefore, threw out a reinforced line of skirmishers connected on the left with the skirmishers of a division of the Army of the Potomac. The whole line advanced on 16 June seeking to drive the Confederates out of positions they still held. The black troops of the Army of the James, not long after the general assault of 16 June, which was unsuccessful, went into reserve. Livermore wrote that "our division soon took position on the bluffs near Beasley's house, and there we remained for a few days without being engaged in line of battle, though picket work and night alarms kept us busy."

Captain Bowditch, writing to his father from "Headquarters Fifth Massachusetts Cavalry in the field" on 22 June 1864, mentioned that "we had hardly got into camp at Point of Rocks and got our tents all pitched before we were ordered to be ready to start." The regiment was under orders on the evening of 21 June to be ready to march the next morning at 2:00 a.m. But they "did nothing but lie around and wait till seven or eight, when the column really got started and, marching very rapidly, crossed the Appomattox and directed our course towards Petersburg." The 5th Massachusetts broke for lunch in the woods near the river, in plain sight of the enemy, who fired an artillery shell that fortunately passed overhead and exploded harmlessly in the rear.

"In the afternoon," Bowditch continued, "we were again set in motion and this time our regiment marched back exactly the same track that they had come, for some mile and a half or two miles, and are now on picket along the river this side of Petersburg and opposite the rebel batteries, which are in plain sight from our pickets." Bowditch reported that they had as yet not exchanged fire with the Confederates. Bowditch closed his letter by lamenting the hard hand of war. The country round about "would make an agriculturist's mouth water," with open fields for pasturage and others planted with corn and oats. "There is one piece close by the house where we are bivouacked (the same one I spoke of in a former letter occupied by the Rushmores) in which the corn is planted with the most mathematical accuracy. It seems rather hard to spoil such fine fields of grain by marching through them with horses and men, smashing down the grain without compunction, but it has to be done and can't be helped." Despite Colonel Rand's assertion that the regiment had "got through shooting each other," there was a casualty during the 5th Massachusetts's stay across the Appomattox. Private Joseph Jackson was accidentally shot on 20 June while at Point of Rocks. Private Jackson died 18 July 1864 in XVIII Army Corps hospital at Fort Monroe, Virginia.

In the meantime, while the 5th Massachusetts moved across the Appomattox and then back again, the high command was submitting its reports. General Smith submitted his report on 16 June. He reported first on the action at Baylor's Farm:

About 4:00a.m. the head of my column left Broadway. Near Baylor's farm our cavalry came upon the enemy's artillery and infantry. General Kautz being unable to dislodge them, General Hincks was ordered to make the attack. The rifle-pits were gallantly carried by General Hincks' command and one piece of artillery captured. My command was then ordered to move forward according to the original orders of the day, and got into position around the enemy's works at Jordan's house about 1:30p.m.

General Smith, after describing the taking of the enemy's earthworks at Petersburg, had these words for his soldiers: "Too much praise cannot be awarded to the troops for their gallantry of yesterday, and the colored troops are deserving of special mention." Smith thought the conduct of XVIII Corps worthy of notice. He sent a circular on 17 June wishing "to express to his command his appreciation of their soldierly qualities as have been displayed during the campaign of the last seventeen days." The general commended his men for enduring "all the hardships of a soldier's life" and facing up to all of its dangers. "Marches under a hot sun have ended in severe battle; after the battle, watchful nights in the trenches gallantly taken from the enemy." Smith felt that "the crowning point of the honor they are entitled to" was won on 15 June when the soldiers of XVIII Corps carried "a series of earth works, of most commanding positions and of formidable strength," along with cannon, prisoners, and Confederate battle flags.

This victory was "all the more important" because the troops had been hastily summoned and quickly put into brigades and divisions; they had "never been regularly organized in camp where time has been given them to learn the discipline necessary to a well-organized corps d'armee." The honors won by XVIII Corps, wrote Smith, "will remain imperishable." Once again, Smith singled out the African American troops: "To the colored troops comprising the division of General Hincks the general commanding would call the attention of his command, with the veterans of the Eighteenth Corps. They have stormed the works of the enemy and carried them, taking guns and prisoners, and in the whole affair they have displayed all the qualities of good soldiers."

On 20 June, Brigadier General Hincks sent in his report to General Butler. Of particular note is his description of the advance on the Confederate earthwork at Baylor's Farm:

> *Having reported the state of affairs to General Smith, I was ordered to deploy in two lines of battle, with skirmishers in front, and force a passage of the swamp. Considerable delay was occasioned by the difficulty in getting the Fifth Massachusetts Cavalry into line by reason of its awkwardness of maneuver, it being composed of new recruits, and drilled only in Cooke's single rank cavalry formation, which entirely unfitted it to act as infantry in line.*

Hincks described the woods and swamp as "extremely difficult of passage," and when the lines advanced they were "furiously assailed by spherical case, canister and musketry along the whole line." As for the 6th U.S. Colored Infantry breaking ranks, Hincks reported that "some confusion, however, arose among the regiments upon the left of the road, and a few of the men fell back to the open space of ground." Hincks described the rebels as being in a "hastily constructed work, occupying a very strong position in Baylor's field, with four pieces of artillery and some force of infantry in the field-works, and two pieces of artillery, with supports, upon the crest of the hill on the right." Hincks estimated the distance from the edge of the woods to the Confederate position as "400 yards over open, rising ground." The

African American troops charged over the open ground, upon which "the enemy fled towards Petersburg, leaving in our hands one 12-pounder gun."

The subsequent movements of the 5th Massachusetts can be traced in Hincks's report. Hincks's command marched down the Jordan's Point road until they came up to the Confederate works at Petersburg around 11:00 a.m. Skirmishers engaged the enemy, and General Hincks "now directed Colonel Duncan, with Captain Angel [James R. Angel, commanding Battery K, 3rd New York Light Artillery], to bring a portion of our guns to bear upon the enemy's works, if possible." This, as Captain Bowditch confirmed in his letter, "was found to be impracticable, on account of the complete sweeping cross-fire maintained by the enemy's batteries upon every portion of the crest, until later in the day," when two sections of artillery were put into position near the Peebles house, about half a mile from the Petersburg defenses. After the morning assault of 15 June, which was "executed with great gallantry and promptness," the 3rd Division was moved to the right of the Union line, near the junction of the Spring Hill and City Point roads and not far from the river. Colonel Holman's 1st Brigade was on picket duty along the river, while Colonel Duncan's 2nd Brigade was employed in constructing earthworks for the Union forces. "On the 19th," Hincks reported, "the division was relieved by [Brigadier] General [David A.] Russell's [1st] division, of the Sixth Corps, and, marching over the pontoon bridge near Spring Hill, went into camp during the afternoon near Point of Rocks." General Hincks expressed satisfaction with his soldiers, whom he felt had proved their worth:

In the gallant and soldierly deportment of the troops engaged on the 15th instant under varying circumstances; the celerity with which they moved to the charge; the steadiness and coolness exhibited by them under heavy and long-continued fire; the impetuosity with which they sprang to the assault; the patient endurance of wounds, we have a sufficient proof that colored men, when properly officered, instructed, and drilled, will make most excellent infantry of the line, and may be used as such soldiers to great advantage.

Hincks enclosed a list of casualties and noted that "among the wounded were Colonel H. S. Russell and Major Z. B. Adams, of the Fifth Massachusetts Cavalry, who fell while gallantly leading their regiment in the charge at

Baylor's farm." General Hincks also reported on the state of his health: "By reason of severe disposition, under which I was suffering when the movement commenced, and of injuries received by an accident during the fight on the morning of the 15th aggravating disabilities, I was physically unable to take so active part in the operations before Petersburg as I desired to." General Hincks's illness had implications greater than the relief of that officer.

In addition to the official reports, there was newspaper reporting and letters from African American soldiers. Among the last are letters sent to the black owned and published newspaper in New York, the *Weekly Anglo-African*. Known affectionately by the men simply as "the *Anglo*," a rather heated correspondence ensued in the pages of that newspaper between "Africano" of the 5th Massachusetts Cavalry and black soldiers from other regiments, whom Africano accused of breaking ranks and running away. The controversy began with the 25 June 1864 issue of the paper, in which an anonymous trooper from the 5th Massachusetts Cavalry, "Africano," reported on events in Virginia. The letter is worth quoting in its entirety, as it is an authentic voice from the ranks and gives an idea why it engendered controversy:

> New York, June 25, 1864
> FROM THE 5TH Massachusetts Cavalry
> Camp Hamilton, City Point, VA.
> June 15, 1864
> Dear Anglo:
> On the evening of the 13th inst., an orderly of the 4th Massachusetts Cavalry (of course, one of the members of the would be superior race, one of those Anglo-Saxon men whose unequalled *courage, coolness* and *self-possession* (?) unlike the negro, can always be seen even in the most trying circumstance) made his appearance in camp. If the furies of the Plutonic Empire were riding their winged steeds in his pursuit, he would not have been more terrified. Mr. Editor, had it been a negro, had it been a poor slave, whose manhood was crushed by the degrading influence of slavery, the white folks who witnessed the scene would have had fun for a month, but the object of laughter being the *all-competent*, the *all-intrepid*, WHITE MAN nothing was said, their ivory teeth found nothing worthy of displaying their pearly whiteness. But, enough of that. What was the object of his coming? Two or three straggling rebel cavalry came in contact with him, and with electric speed he was home to raise an excitement which is always

necessary for the enjoyment of we dwellers in tents. The negroes were on the alert as usual, ready for the march. We were called out, assigned and took the road with cheerfulness. After a recreative march which only tended to relax our stiffened veins we were ordered back to camp without having the pleasure of unloading our rifles. Night made its lonely appearance, fruitless of an engagement and nothing transpired worthy of attention. The morning of the 14th opened to us and instead of Aurora decking the sky with her rosy fingers, it was sultry, and for Virginia in this season of the year, we could call it cool. Sol's appearance was delayed and for a while the azure sky was enveloped in smoky clouds. The boys were sent out reconnoitering. After marching the short distance of about four miles we halted near a farm where an old "Greyback" was seen ploughing, he was flanked and he soon had received the "shades," Lincoln's "black *clouds*," he sent for his horse by one of his "nigger" boys vainly trying to make his exit, but he was halted, and though with reluctance he surrendered. He was taken to those high in office, and feigning to be a Union man was, on that plea, set at liberty. Oh! When will we learn to discern foe from friend, disloyal from loyal? It was with pains that they succeeded in keeping the boys from shooting the "wolf in sheep's clothing." A rebel signal corps, at least, the captain and lieutenant were captured and safely taken to camp; the others fleeing, their horses were secured. We returned to camp laden with trifling spoils only to assure our tent-confined comrades that we had really encountered the grey backs. As is customary in camp we gathered around our fires each one relating or discussing some topic.

The bugler's call—the assembly—and we were in ranks. The roll is called, taps sounded, lights ordered out and we laid on our rubber blankets ruminating over this day's adventure; listening to the distant sound of the destructive cannons dealing out God's retributive justice to the oppressors of humanity! Ere Morpheus his weighty fingers o'er our weary form had placed, our commissary sergeants were ordered to prepare two days rations for the men. In the twinkling of an eye, the campfires were blazing, officers' horses were prancing, and men were ready for the field. At 2½ o'clock in the morning of the 15th, the boys marched with the enthusiasm of veterans, and on nearing the rebel city, Petersburg, by three miles, encountered the foe in an intrenched position with masked battery, opening a most terrific fire of shot, shell, grape, and canister, which poured like hail upon us. We halted, formed in line of battle, amid the thunder of this exterminating shower of deadly missiles. Our line was broken but through the unparalleled coolness and bravery of our gallant Colonel, we again rallied, formed our line, and poured upon them the deadly contents of our rifles. Strange to say, Mr. Editor, on nearing the field we could perceive thousands of our Saxon brethren, but when we were engaged, they were withdrawn, leaving us to fight our way through the superior numbers of our enemy, which, we are proud to say, we nobly did. The troops engaged were the 1st U.S. Colored Troops, the 4th, the 6th, the 22nd Pennsylvania, Battery B, (colored), and the 5th Massachusetts Cavalry, dismounted. The 4th U.S. Colored Troops were deployed as skirmishers, and being in the advance, suddenly came on the rebels in their intrenchments. They were fired upon as soon as they were within shooting distance, but, failing to sustain themselves, fell back in confusion on the heroes of Massachusetts, who, though for the first time in open engagement, and with rifles, with which they are not familiar, not only proved themselves valorous men, but added fresh laurels to the already imperishable laurels of the glorious Bay State. In the engagement our beloved Colonel was wounded in the shoulder, and notwithstanding the excruciating pain it must have undoubtedly caused him, he dismounted, rallying the boys, still leading them onward to victory. The indomitable Adams, Major of the 2d Battalion, was also wounded in the breast. It is supposed serious, and may prove fatal. The gallant 5th, confiding in the undaunted courage of their heroic commander who stood the storm like a statue of iron, rallied with the coolness of veterans, took the rebel works by storm, capturing two twelve pound howitzers, and other implements of war.

The Spartans of the 1st, 4th, 6th, 22nd and Battery B were active co-workers in the sanguinary encounter and by their experience and bravery won a glorious name, of which the country and even the negro-hating Copperheads will be proud when peace shall have spread her olive branch of freedom o'er this wide domain of freedom.

One of our boys, being wounded, fell, and as an officer neared him, he stretched out his hand, exclaiming, "Massachusetts boys, give 'em hell!" He died a hero's death, leaving his body to bleach on southern plains.

The indomitable courage of our gallant commander won for himself the affection and confidence of his men, the gratitude of his country, and a name among the noble defenders of human rights. May the God of battles, with His invincible shield, spare his valuable life for the further advancement of his men, the comfort of his numerous friends, and for the upholding of the banner of freedom. The casualties are small. It is very mysterious, but we can account for it. The protecting hand of Providence guides the oppressed and showers His wrath upon the oppressors.

AFRICANO

Africano's letter was answered in the 2 July edition of the *Weekly Anglo-African*.

A MISSTATEMENT

Before Petersburg, Va., June 28, 1864

Mr. Editor: Over the signature of "Africano" writing from the 5th Regiment Massachusetts Cavalry (dismounted), so gross a misstatement appeared in your paper of June 25th that I would have answered it sooner, but that our occupation in the trenches prevented; but I now avail myself of the first opportunity to do so.

"Africano" states that the 4th U.S. colored Troops, unable to sustain itself against the fire of the enemy, fell back in confusion upon them (the 5th Cav.), and that they (the 5th) rallied and carried the works. This statement is simply a falsehood.

The advance upon the rebel works was made in the following order: The 22nd U.S. Colored Troops on the right, the 4th in the centre, the 6th on the left. The 5th U.S. Colored Troops and 5th Massachusetts Cavalry formed the reserve.

Our regiment was the first to clear the woods and met with heavy enfilading fire from the rebel work which was discovered on our right. Nevertheless our boys charged at a double quick until our reserve, the *5th Massachusetts Cavalry*, who were *not yet out of the woods*, fired a heavy volley, which took effect upon the rear of our left wing, which, with the fire of the enemy, threw it into confusion. We were then ordered back into the woods to re-form, and fell back again accordingly, reformed, and again advanced, in time to lose several more men killed and wounded, before the final capture of the work. Next, it was the 22nd U.S. Colored Troops that took the work when we fell back, and not the 5th Cavalry.

"Africano" expresses surprise that their loss was so small. Perhaps the fact that they did not come out of the friendly shelter of the woods until after the action was over, may partly account for their loss being so small, while ours summed up to one hundred and sixty killed and wounded out of less than six hundred, in the short space of ten minutes.

Through all the subsequent fighting of the day, our regiment still held its position in the front, and wound up the day by carrying the last rebel on the line, charging through a swamp knee-deep.

In justice to our regiment, I trust you will give this an insertion.

C. A. Fleetwood

Sergt. Maj. 4th U.S.C.T.

"Africano" was not finished, however. He responded in the 23 July 1864 edition of the *Weekly Anglo-African*, writing from Point Lookout, Maryland, where the 5th Massachusetts was guarding Confederate prisoners of war.

THE FIFTH MASSACHUSETTS CAVALRY BEFORE PETERSBURG.

Point Lookout, Md., July 12, 1864.

DEAR ANGLO: Reading in your issue of the 9th inst. an article headed, "A Misstatement," from the pen of a Fleetwood, alias, Fleetfoot, of the 4th U.S. Colored Troops, I cannot, in justice to my regiment and self, allow it to remain unanswered. The writer, after indulging in expressions unbecoming a gentleman, says that "the advance upon the rebel works was made in the following order." As I am not accustomed to indulge in falsehoods, I disagree with the writer in this respect. The 6th was not on the left with us; they were on the right. The 4th U.S. Colored Troops and 5th Massachusetts Cavalry were the only regiments on the left. We were not, as the Sergeant-Major asserts, "in the reserve," for when they (the 4th) came out of the woods, we (the 5th) followed, and were not seven yards distant. They (the 4th) yelled like wild Indians, saying, "*It's no use, boys, we have been under fire before, and when we fall back, it's time for everybody to fall back.*" Nothing could stop the fleetfeet, for with the swiftness of electricity, they were in the woods, and did not show their faces until the 5th and gallant 22nd had taken the works.

At the time the running match commenced we were obliquing to the left, our regiment forming the second line of battle. The 4th, panic-stricken, fell back, charging upon us, and we were ordered to advance and take the ground they had evacuated. The infuriated officers of the 4th, seeing us advancing to take the lost position of the 4th, cried out, "Soldiers of the 4th, are you going to disgrace yourselves?" They pointed their revolvers at their affrighted men, threatening to shoot them if they did not advance. Threats were vain; for the men themselves vehemently cried out: "Retreat boys of the 5th, Retreat!" Our Colonel, pained at their confusion, and thinking that we were going to follow their example, rushed to the front, crying, "No cowards in the 5th! Rally, boys, rally!" These are facts that can be substantiated. Several of the men composing our regiment are well acquainted with the writer, who was just going front, and spoke to him. That being the case, he knows nothing about how the lines were formed. The 4th, being deployed as skirmishers, had no other alternative than to be first out of the woods; but did they long sustain the position they took and could have held[?] They (the 4th) had no charge to make. They could not charge; for the Johnnies had driven them away from the ground they held, and which they had not *pluck* enough not to run from. The 5th Massachusetts Cavalry, "not yet out of the woods," as the writer says, was in position, and had the honor of taking and holding the ground which the skeddaddling 4th had so ingloriously abandoned.

We will not excuse ourselves for the fire, which, as the writer says, took effect upon the rear of his left wing; for advancing as we were, we could not but suppose that the 4th had changed their base, and that the rebels were precipitating their force upon our second line of battle. They (the 4th) were so confused that they took our regiment for theirs, not withstanding the yellow stripes.

The rebel works, after the 4th had fled, were to our front, and as we and other colored regiments comprising the line of battle charged, they were abandoned. It is more than surprising to "Africano" that the 4th re-formed and again advanced. Such is not the case; for the officers could not rally them in time, even to form the reserve of the 5th Massachusetts Cavalry, that had so gallantly recovered the lost honor of the skeddadling 4th.

"Africano" would like to ask the writer where were his wounded—in the field or in the woods? We agree with the writer when he says he "led the advance"; but did he keep it? No! he ran back in confusion, and the 5th Massachusetts Cavalry, taking them for rebels, fired into them, killing a great many. The rebs had no time to slaughter them for their fleetness would not allow them (the rebs) the chance; but we are sorry to say the murderous fire of the 5th done the damage, which we sincerely regret. Africano.

Sergeant Major Fleetwood did not respond to Africano's last until much later in the summer. The 4th U.S. Colored Troops was actively engaged as a duly brigaded regiment in the 3rd Division, XVIII Army Corps, and saw heavy fighting.

From the 13 August 1864 edition of the *Weekly Anglo-African*:

SERGT. MAJ. FLEETWOOD IN REPLY TO "AFRICANO"
Camp 4th U.S. Colored Troops,
Before Petersburg, Va., July 25, 1864
Mr. Editor: I trouble you once more upon the "vexed question" arising from the incidents of June 15th.

In your last issue, the redoubtable "African(o)" of the Fifth Massachusetts Cavalry, attempts to sustain the misstatements made in a former letter, by others equally gross; and still sheltering his cowardly head under a *nom de plume*, as on that day he did his body behind the trunk of some forest king, avails himself of his security to indulge in personalities, and attempts at witticisms only laughable on account of their failure.

The cognomen of *Fleetfoot* I am perfectly willing to accept, as neither Africano or any other can say I have ever yet availed myself of my fleetness of foot in getting away from the vicinity of the rebels. To this he bears, no doubt, unintentional witness, by saying that several members of his regiment saw me *going to the front*.

Notwithstanding that he "disagrees" with me, my statement regarding the formation of the line of battle was correct. If not, and as he says, were the 4th U.S. Colored Troops and 5th Massachusetts Cavalry the only regiments on the left, and the 5th Mass. Cavalry "not in reserve," how does he account for their being seven yards in our rear? In only one way can he possibly place the 6th on their right, viz: by the admission that he had faced by the rear rank, and was marching to the rear, *which I do not doubt*. Were it not so, what need for their Colonel to rush to the front and cry, "Rally! Boys, rally!" Is it such as these he means when in the next sentence he adds, "These are facts that can be substantiated"? It is conceding more than I asked.

The utter absurdity of having an entire regiment deployed as skirmishers to cover a line of battle front of only two other regiments, is too apparent for even this passing notice. But two companies—A and B—of our regiment were deployed as skirmishers, and covered our battalion front.

Africano says that we "had not pluck enough *not* to run from" our ground. It is to be hoped that we never will, as such *pluck* is decidedly at a discount in the army. And again: "The 5th Mass. Cav., *not yet out of the woods, as the writer says*, was in position, and had the honor of taking and holding the ground which the skedaddling 4th had so ingloriously abandoned." What more did I assert than that they held the ground that we had abandoned, viz: the woods from which we charged. O Africano! Oh inglorious skedaddle!

"Judge ye between us, oh, ye people."

Africano states that our men were so confused as to be unable to distinguish that regiment from ours; and in another sentence says, "The 5th Mass. Cavalry, taking them (the 4th) for rebels, fired into them." By his own standard, which were the most confused: those who failed to notice a yellow stripe on a collar or cuff, or those who, seven yards distant, under the brilliant light of the morning sun, and, as he claims, in the *open field*, could not tell *black* men in *blue* uniforms from *white* men in *grey* uniforms?

Out of thine own mouth, O Africano!

As he has come down so far as to admit that the 22nd Regiment assisted them in taking the works which, in his first letter, he claimed to have been taken by his regiment alone, and has made so many other contradictory assertions, no person possessing the organ of comparison can fail to perceive that he belongs to that class of personages of whom it is said they "should always have good memories."

Furthermore, this fight took place in the morning, and was all over by 9 o'clock a.m. How then does Africano account for a regiment which displayed such coolness and valor being left in the rear for the remainder of the day, while the "ingloriously skedaddling 4th" held, through the remainder of the day, the post of honor—the right of the line—and participated in the battle and triumph of the evening, which has added the brightest star yet to the galaxy with which this war is crowning our nation.

How will he account for their (5th Mass. Cav.) being returned to a *school of instruction* at peaceful Point Lookout, Md., while the 4th remains in the front, adding daily to her roll of honor the names of her brave men who have fallen a sacrifice to their race, and whose names shall shine with still increasing brightness when the name of Africano has descended to its deserved oblivion?

He dares to ask where were our wounded—in the field or in the woods? I had charge of the party who went back over the ground hallowed by the blood of our fallen braves, and found them wounded, dying and dead, *both in the field and in the woods*, the majority of the wounded in the woods, where they had dragged themselves for shelter, though some fell from the effects of the shelling of the woods; but nearly all of the dead in the open field. Let no dastard *dare* attempt to cast the mantle of dishonor over the corpse of the humblest hero who "Sleeps for the Flag."

Were it not to vindicate the honor of my regiment, traduced by your nameless correspondent, in the eyes of the people, I would not have condescended to notice this second thrust from behind a screen.

I shall not again do so. To the truth of my assertions I can bring those to witness whose testimony cannot be doubted. To back the false assertions of Africano none can be found, save those who, like himself, are *nameless*.

Regretting deeply this bickering among those who should be *brethren*, I can only say, "Woe unto him by whom the offense cometh." Hoping it may not inconvenience you to give this an insertion, I remain, very respectfully, yours,

C. A. FLEETWOOD,
Sergt. Maj., 4th U.S.C.T.

As noted above, in June 1864 General Hincks closed his report to General Smith by writing that he had been injured on June 15. On 26 June, Major General Smith telegraphed to General John A. Rawlins, Grant's chief of staff. Besides bypassing General Butler, Smith's dispatch proposed a restructuring of the Union armies in the east. Hincks's ill health, Smith wrote, would "compel him to give up his duties for a while, if not permanently, and I am left without a proper officer to command a division, the value of which will depend upon the ability with which it is led." Smith considered Brigadier General Edward A. Wild, the second in command of the division, as "entirely unfitted for the command"; Wild was under arrest for insubordination. The 3rd Division, XVIII Army Corps, comprised about five thousand men according to the field returns of that day, Smith reported. "Of this there are four regiments, three of dismounted cavalry and one of infantry, yet undrilled in loading their muskets, numbering in all about 2,200 men, and General Hincks reports them unfitted by reason of ignorance of drills for service in the field." Smith therefore proposed that the four regiments mentioned (Smith did not specify the units, but the cavalry are obviously the 5th Massachusetts and the 1st and 2nd U.S. Colored Cavalry) "be sent back to some point where they can be instructed and aid in holding entrenched lines or positions which will have to be held wherever the main army may be." Removing the four regiments, which Smith "dare[d] not trust in any responsible position," would leave General Hincks with less than three thousand men. Hincks's depleted division would then be joined to the African American troops (some four thousand men) in the 4th Division of IX Corps, under the command of Brigadier General Edward Ferrero. Smith thought Ferrero should take overall command and that "the consolidated division, be assigned to the Ninth or Eighteenth Corps, as the General-In-Chief may judge best for the interest of the service." Smith also recommended breaking up the "light battery with colored cannoneers, which is expensive and worse than worthless," although the commander of B Battery, 2nd U.S. Colored Light Artillery, Captain Francis B. Choate, was well recommended to Smith, and "it might be judged good to allow him to fill up his battery from [white] volunteers from the heavy artillery in this corps."

Edward Winslow Hincks sent two dispatches on 26 June, one to General William F. Smith, reporting his health and strength as too poor to "give that personal attention to the conduct of my division that its inchoate condition requires," and predicting that he would not soon return to the field, and a second message to Major William Russell Jr., assistant adjutant general, XVIII Army Corps. Hincks reported on the condition of his command, stating that, out of the ten regiments in his division, he considered only five regiments of infantry, the 1st, 4th, 5th, 6th, and 22nd U.S. Colored Troops, "to be effective for duty in line of battle." Hincks then listed the faults of the remaining regiments:

> *The Tenth and Thirty-seventh Regiments of Infantry are largely composed of new recruits, and but partially organized; the Fifth Massachusetts Cavalry (dismounted) is also composed of new recruits, and not drilled in infantry formations; the First and Second United States Colored Cavalry (dismounted) are unskilled in the use of arms, untaught in infantry formations, and without drill and proper discipline.*

Hincks was unwilling to risk the above-named regiments in battle until they had spent some time in a camp of instruction. He felt that justice to the troops and the good of the service required further training.

Now, General Butler, when he found out about it, was somewhat miffed that a corps commander who was supposed to be working for him would write directly to Lieutenant General Grant's chief of staff, thus airing a problem in the Army of the James for others to comment on. Butler sent a response to Smith's dispatch at 11:00 p.m., 26 June, and subjected Smith to the full force of his skill as a cross-examiner. Butler first called attention to a discrepancy in Smith's numbers: "Your field return of the 23rd instant gives 7,852 colored troops for duty. In this dispatch you say you have now nearly 5,000. What has become of nearly 3,000 of these troops in three days?" As for Choate's African American artillery, Butler felt that this was a personal vendetta on the part of Smith's chief of artillery, and, wrote Butler, "as that officer is of that class who do not trust any colored troops, and has since proved his own inefficiency by deliberately riding into the enemy's lines in a fit of drunken or other delirium, as I am informed, and been captured by them, I am not inclined to base much official action on his judgment." Furthermore, it seemed impossible to Butler "that the three regiments of colored cavalry are yet undrilled in loading their muskets, as one of these regiments was in the charge for which you have publicly so highly complimented the colored troops, and took the works they were ordered to do." If the troops who had successfully carried the Confederate earthworks at Baylor's Farm and Petersburg were not dependable, then Smith had few black troops that were, Butler pointed out. The major general commanding also noted that while he held Brigadier General Hincks in the highest esteem, he "should hardly advise the disorganization of his division because of his loss."

As far as consolidating the African American troops, Butler mentioned that Grant had made a similar suggestion some days before, only stipulating that white troops be sent also from XVIII Corps to IX Corps to replace the black soldiers detached. Butler knew Smith did not want to lose white troops, and he now wrote with a tinge of sarcasm: "Supposing, however, until now that this was against your wish I have objected, but will now withdraw it and allow the change to be made so far as it rests with me." As a final backhanded reminder to consult his army commander and use the chain of command, Butler wrote that he would send a copy of his dispatch to General Rawlins, "so that he might have our views before him at the same time, although as a rule I would not send forward such communications without an interchange of views."

Major General Smith apparently did not like the tone of Butler's dispatch. Therefore, he paid a visit to General Hincks on 27 June and asked him to respond in writing to Butler's various assertions, which Hincks did that day, his last communication in the service of the United States, as it turned out. Hincks numbered his paragraphs so as to give a careful, however damning, assessment of his division. His first point dealt with troop numbers, the discrepancy in which "was probably made in transmission through your headquarters." The division on 27 June comprised 5,063 officers and men present for duty; Hincks thought he had had less than 5,500 men at least since 19 June. Second, while Captain Choate may have been a good officer, his battery had "not realized [Hincks's] hopes," proving "inefficient and unserviceable," and Choate had applied for infantry soldiers to work as gunners "as the colored gunners were incompetent." Third, the three regiments of dismounted cavalry were "unskilled in the use of muskets and entirely unfitted for operations in the field, by reason of having been taught only the single formations of ranks as prescribed by Cooke's Tactics, and it is impossible to move them in line of battle with any precision, steadiness, or effectiveness in action with their limited knowledge of the school of the company and battalion." Hincks also pointed out that "most of the officers of these regiments have no knowledge of infantry tactics." Hincks's fourth point dealt specifically with the 5th Massachusetts Cavalry:

The Major-General commanding misapprehends the facts concerning "one of these regiments" and its action on the 15th. In forming line of battle in the morning, for the attack upon the enemy's works near Baylor's house, I placed the Fifth Massachusetts Cavalry (dismounted) on the left of the second line of battle, and its awkwardness in maneuvering delayed my movement fully three-quarters of an hour, and finally when it advanced, though nobly and heroically led, it was but little other than an armed mob, which was held up to its work by the almost super-human effort of its officers.

According to General Hincks, the 5th Cavalry's "losses were heavy, among them being its gallant commander (Colonel Russell) and Major Adams, while its power to inflict injury upon the enemy was nominal. I could but commend its gallantry, but considering its inefficiency, decided that to further engage it with the enemy would be a reckless and useless exposure of life to no purpose, and accordingly withheld it from participation in the final attack upon the enemy's works, which were carried by the five well-drilled infantry regiments of the division."

Hincks further reported that two infantry regiments, the 10th and 37th U.S. Colored Troops, had been recently recruited and organized, and having had little opportunity for drill, "though not so entirely useless for field service as the dismounted cavalry, are yet far from being effective regiments." Hincks, however, noted that the five efficient regiments of his division, the 1st, 4th, 5th, 6th, and 22nd U.S. Colored Troops, had afforded "conclusive evidence that colored men, when properly officered and drilled, will not only make soldiers, but the best of soldiers of the line." There was a caveat in that success, though, that perhaps the social agenda of advancing the cause of African Americans was obscuring common sense: "But in our exuberance of satisfaction at their deportment, we should be cautious lest we imperil the success of the project of arming colored men, as well as the success of our armies, by assuming that the negro is a soldier ready made, rather than that he will make a soldier by patient, persistent, and intelligent drill and instruction." On the whole, Hincks thought his officers intelligent and that they would improve with experience and instruction. The officers of the dismounted cavalry regiments were at a decided disadvantage, however, being unfamiliar with infantry tactics, "and many of them would prefer to leave the service to remaining in an arm for which they feel themselves so entirely unfitted by instruction and experience." Hincks thought it proper that those cavalry officers deserving to resign should be allowed to do so and the remainder be given the opportunity "to acquire a proper knowledge of the arm they are now required to serve with."

General Smith forwarded Hincks's dispatch of 27 June as an enclosure to a dispatch of his own to General Rawlins on 28 June, this time sending his communication through Butler's headquarters. Smith addressed himself to Rawlins, full of pomposity and injured pride: "The Major-General commanding Department of Virginia and North Carolina [Butler] having done me the honor to forward to me a copy of his endorsement on a letter of you of the 26th instant, with reference to the colored troops, I deem it due to myself and the interests of the service, which I was honestly endeavoring to promote, to forward for the information of the Lieutenant-General commanding, communications upon the subject from Brigadier-General Hincks, commanding colored division." Smith explained that the discrepancy in his field returns came from counting one of Hincks's brigades twice.

Smith also wished to refute Butler's attack on Smith's artillery commander, but he chose a rather tortuous way of doing it: "In my letter to you [Rawlins] I made the assertion therein contained, giving no authority and therefore taking the responsibility as to the correctness of the statement upon myself, therefore the Major-General commanding . . . had no warrant for his assertion that my statement was based upon that of my Chief of Artillery." Smith stood by his statement that four regiments of Hincks's division were untrained and inefficient, using Hincks's report as evidence. "That testimony may be corroborated by my own observations on the field of battle." Smith wanted to "particularly call attention to the Statement of General Hincks with reference to the Fifth Massachusetts Colored Cavalry (dismounted), and the part of the action in which that regiment was engaged." However much Smith wanted to consolidate the black units of the Army of the James, he certainly did not mean for that consolidation "to entirely break up the two white divisions of the Eighteenth Corps, or to have white regiments transferred from a corps where they were well contented to a corps where they had no association." But Smith, rather sanctimoniously, wrote that if his proposed consolidation did occur, and "that reorganization should carry with it the disorganization of the two white divisions of the corps," he would "rest satisfied" that General Grant "judged it best for the interest of the service."

While these dispatches were being sent and received and the efficiency, or lack thereof, of the 5th Massachusetts was being discussed, the regiment was doing its duty as a duly brigaded regiment of the 3rd Division, XVIII Army Corps. As far as we can tell, neither Major Bowditch nor any other field-grade officer in the division wrote a report of the 5th Massachusetts's part at Baylor's Farm or the assault on Petersburg. In addition, there is no record of General Hincks ever soliciting a report from the regiment. Hincks also apparently did not bother to share his conclusions about half the troops of his division with their respective regimental commanders, nor did he seek to rectify the situation other than to suggest that they be sent to a camp of instruction and that the officers of the dismounted cavalry be allowed to resign. It would appear that it never occurred to Hincks to ask that his dismounted cavalry receive horses and continue their cavalry training. We are left to speculate on the good work that General Kautz's Cavalry Division of the Army of the James might have done if it had the addition of the almost three thousand officers and men of the 1st and 2nd U.S. Colored Cavalry regiments and the 5th Massachusetts Volunteer Cavalry.

From 22 to 29 June, the 5th Massachusetts was on picket, along the Appomattox River, anchoring the right of the Union line. Captain Charles Bowditch wrote his mother on 25 June, the letter headed "On picket on the Appomattox." Bowditch was having a difficult time placing his men. There was a swamp between the regimental picket line and the river, and Bowditch had been ordered to place his troopers on the banks of the river itself. "Some of the posts could be placed easily, but three of them, which I had to post, had to be pushed through a dense jungle with grape vines and all other sorts of vine intervening, which had to be cut away with a knife in order to make any progress."

The young captain succeeded in placing his men, but it took two hours for them to hack their way through the swamp and the men were dangerously exposed, in plain view of rebels across the river. At night, they suffered from the miasmic fogs of the river and the torments of a myriad of insects. Bowditch wrote his sister Charlotte on 27 June to report that the regiment's tents had finally arrived from Point of Rocks.

The 5th Massachusetts, still on picket, held the river line while Union and Confederate batteries on either side of the river fired over the heads (sometimes) of the African American troopers. Bowditch wrote that he had seen their corps commander, General William F. Smith, on the 26th. "[Smith] has rather a round face with a light colored mustache and imperial and is a very substantial sort of man, one who lives well, I guess, when he is able," he noted. The Union artillery was fired for Smith's "edification, he being desirous of shelling a bit of woods where a rebel battery was supposed to be; but as half the shells did not explode and the other half burst up in the air, no great harm was done." Bowditch noted that as he was writing there was "quite a scrimmage in the way of artillery firing" going on, but as no shells had come near him, he chose to ignore it.

Bowditch closed his letter by requesting that his sister "tell my paternal that lately I have had too much to do to pay any attention to Miss Julia and that owing to the large influx of troops the number of cows belonging to her family has decreased so sensibly that it is impossible to get milk, even by paying great attention to milking and the young lady." Bowditch explained in a footnote to the above passage that Julia Rushmore was the daughter at the house where he had obtained fresh milk. Charles's brother Henry and his father "were inclined to make fun of my devotion to her, but it was worth any amount of devotion to get the milk."

Bowditch also noted that his pickets were the last ones posted in the swamp on the riverbank: "It was folly to post the pickets on the river banks, for an alarm could have been given much more quickly if a rebel advance had been formed to make their way through the swamp. My picket was the last one placed there and the order was withdrawn." More important, though, Bowditch noted, "shortly after this the regiment was sent to Point Lookout to guard rebel prisoners. I never knew why this was done, for our men had been discharging their duties very well."

General Butler did not want to break up the regiment; to allow the mass resignation of the 5th Massachusetts's officers would have been a severe blow to the morale of other officers in the 3rd Division and would have confirmed the prejudices held about the capacity of African Americans for military service. Instead, Butler transferred the regiment to the prisoner of war camp at Point Lookout, Maryland, where the Potomac River meets Chesapeake Bay. Point Lookout was in the District of Saint Mary's, Maryland, which until 31 May had been in Butler's District of Eastern Virginia. The District of Saint Mary's and the Point Lookout prison camp had been transferred to the District of Washington and XXII Army Corps, under the command of Major General Christopher C. Augur. There was a bit of a mix-up at first because Butler's headquarters had neglected to inform the commander at Point Lookout, Colonel Alonzo G. Draper of the 36th U.S. Colored Troops, of the regiment's transfer. General Butler wanted to swap his dismounted cavalry for a regiment of (hopefully) trained black infantry. Colonel Draper sent this message to Secretary of War Stanton on 1 July: "The Fifth Massachusetts Dismounted Cavalry (colored), 1,000 strong, have reported here to relieve the Thirty-sixth United States Colored Troops, 1,000 strong, who are ordered by General Butler to report to his headquarters. I am in doubt whether to obey the order. The transports are here waiting for the Thirty-sixth." Draper received the following reply, on the same day, from Major General Augur: "You will relieve the Thirty-sixth United States Colored Troops by the Fifth Massachusetts Dismounted Cavalry, and send the former regiment to General Butler." Colonel Draper was to remain in command at Point Lookout until relieved by Brigadier General James Barnes, who was en route.

Charles Bowditch wrote his mother on 3 July, contrasting the luxury of fixed quarters at Point Lookout with his previous life in the field. Bowditch had a wall tent to himself with a board floor and a piece of carpet. "A door on hinges hangs at the front of the tent, while in the door a frame holding four panes of glass turns on its hinges and allows me to sleep with my window open or shut. An arm-chair and my army chair, which is also an arm-chair and a pine table stained red add to the luxuriousness and comfort of my apartment." The regiment had just completed a Sunday evening inspection "instead of a morning one, and finished off with a dress parade and a bath in the sea." Bowditch reported the water as "very pleasant" as it was brackish and thus did not give the sticky feeling one got from saltwater. Bowditch was also "very well off" in terms of food. He bought two quarts of milk each day and had bread and milk each morning and evening. "The people come down from up country with berries, chickens, onions, etc., so that we shall be able to live like fighting cocks." Captain Bowditch supposed "that we are pretty permanently established here."

On 6 July, Bowditch wrote two letters, one to his friend Lucy and one to his father. To Lucy, Bowditch wrote that "the best thing you can do is to persuade your parents to come down to Point Lookout, St. Mary's district, State of Maryland, and pass a week or so, bringing you down with them." As an incentive, Bowditch described the places "worthy of notice," among them a "large swamp, occupying a good sized piece; a large enclosure, called by outsiders a 'pen', in which 15,000 rebel prisoners are penned up"; a large unfinished hotel and a "small hotel or eating house and boarding place"; the Provost Marshal's Office; and several hospital buildings. Bowditch considered Point Lookout "altogether a very nobby place and has some very pleasant pieces of woods near by." The young captain sent home a box containing five wooden fans, each carved out of a single piece of wood. These were examples of the handcraft of the Confederate prisoners, who also made rings, watch chains, and other objects out of wood, metal, bones, oyster shells, or gutta-percha. Bowditch noted that some of the Confederates had been prisoners since Gettysburg. He saw one man who had been taken on 4 July 1863 working as a carpenter on the new hotel. The prisoners did not have to work unless they wanted to. The men received extra rations or tobacco if they did. This was "rather a contrast to the way our men have been treated in Richmond," Bowditch observed. Bowditch also found it "very pleasant . . . to see these rebels working under the charge of negro guards."

Charles Bowditch was still getting teased by his brother Henry about Miss Julia Rushmore and the milking incident, for he explained in his letter to his father that "she and I went down to see the cows milked and not to milk them ourselves. She sat on a stile on one side of the fence and I on the other while a minion named Winnie milked the bovine animals." An apparently alcoholic punch made with the milk "was the effort of Captain Parsons *et aliorum* and not of myself." Brother Henry had been "stuffing" their father, "but I should judge that he had been drawing largely on his imagination." Bowditch noted that General Barnes had arrived, which he took to mean, "We shall have to be reviewed, inspected and tortured in every way his imagination can devise to keep us employed." Bowditch found that the "only objection about this place is that the water is not good at all, giving almost all the diarrhoea. The land is so low that there is not much drainage and so the water gets polluted with the surface water I suppose."

The transfer of the regiment to Point Lookout was not without incident, however, as an anonymous letter to the *Weekly Anglo-African* attests. The writer's rather florid style is similar to that of "Africano." Note that the accidental deadly shooting by Captain Erik Wulff is alluded to. Worth quoting entire, it is from the 16 July 1864 edition:

MONSTROUS BARBARITY IN THE 5TH MASSACHUSETTS CAVALRY

Mr. Editor: Away from the battle field, where we hear nothing but the savage booming of merciless cannons pealing out destruction on friend and foe; where men, dead, wounded and dying, are falling, with friends trampling on their lifeless and mangled carcasses without the chance of assisting them. Away from all these and once more comfortably encamped on a beautiful point in the State of Maryland bordering on the sea shore, I again address you.

We were, a few days ago, eye-witnesses of an act, a most atrocious crime perpetrated on an inoffensive creature, a private of this Regiment— George Washington, of Company L. The poor fellow was tied to a pole by his two thumbs, his feet scarcely touching the ground. The distance was not less than seven inches. All his efforts at stretching to gain a resting place for his expanded body in order to keep his weight from severing his thumbs, were vain. His arms and legs ached from his exertions. He felt that his strength was gradually passing away—his stern heart and stout resolutions refused sympathy with the approaching weakness of his outstretched form. The little strength which trench-digging, throwing up breast-works and heavy marches had left, soon became exhausted. The new sea-grass twine cleaved to his thumbs, pressing them like a vice, cutting with razor sharpness. The pain becoming so excruciating, he struggled vainly to release himself; his mouth became opened; his eyeballs were almost forced from their sockets by the great agony he suffered. He felt as if he could live but for a few moments longer. A horrible pain it was, for his own bodies weight seemed to be against his having . . .

[line obscured]

. . . soldiers! How tightly wrapped it was! Agony—heart-rending agony! He was taken up insensible, and the Doctor arriving, his wound was dressed; his consciousness, his natural sight, sense and feeling returned, and he felt relieved. The murderer, the carnivorous miscreant whose savage intentions was gratified was present, and with fiery eyes gazed upon the foul work he had so cowardly done. A cold shudder would have run through the veins of the most hardened mortal witnessing the scene.

The reason alleged by the American torturer—the *Christian criminal* (!) was that "he had tried to commit *a rape on the person of a contraband woman!*" This is mere fabrication—a *lie*, the criminality of which is unparalleled in the annals of falsehoods. The atrocious villain, abashed of his crime, could find no other way of evading censure but by pronouncing a most damnable falsehood.

The real cause of this punishment was that the poor worn out creature had hid himself, or could not be found when wanting to go on duty. The Regiment had just arrived from the front and had gone into quarters, which the 36th U.S.C.T. had just vacated, the men were busily engaged in removing the rubbish which had accumulated.

The officer who ordered this punishment is one of those "wolves in sheep's clothing," whom the world call *Christians* (!). O Christianity, how long will thy name be thus made the mantle of crime! How long will it be trampled under foot, covering merciless fiends who seek refuge under thy banner for the sole purpose of evading the retributive justice of civil and moral law?

If Colored soldiers are to be commanded by such Christians (and there are many more of these in this Regiment), why we had better be deprived of everything, aye, freedom itself. May God in his providence, hasten the day when man will not only be free from his chains, but from under the scurrilous contempt of *Northern footpads.*

These Northern hide-pinching "nigger" drivers, these shoulder-strapped boot blacks and midnight assassins, who, before negro regiments were formed, could not even hide their nakedness; aye, many we have seen lounging around the steamboat landings and railroad depots, waiting to grasp the satchel of some weary traveler, in order to procure life's necessaries, are now the war-like aristocracy composing the negro-commanding officers! These, I say, instead of trying men by Court Martial, as is customary in the army, take the law in their own hands. Already one WULFF—one of Switzerland's bearded lobsters, has been a devouring *wolf* in our sheepfold. Baltimore was the theatre in which the tragic scene was enacted. Yes, innocent men have been shot down like mad dogs in this regiment composed of Northern freemen, some as prominent as these *pocket-filling, negro-elevating pale faces.*

The 5th Massachusetts Cavalry is supposed to be from a Christian State—is supposed to be commanded by Christians—by men of uncontaminated morals and good standing, but we see daily occurrences of crime. At the moment of my writing, many are suffering living deaths—aye, worse than crucifixion! These offenders—these American criminals, worse than those engaged in the massacre of St. Bartholomew, are permitted to continue their duties in defiance of Justice! Oh Goddess of Justice! Will thou not hasten the time when these may be brought to know that thine edicts must not be trampled under foot with impunity! Yes! me thinks I hear the distant roar of thy chariot wheels! Methinks thy annihilating thunderbolts are near and ready to fall. Withhold not thy power, but come with the destructive strength of the whirlwind, and save us from the havoc which these lawless miscreants have inaugurated.

It would be far better to be in the bonds of accursed slavery, than to breathe the breath of freedom in such a withering atmosphere. It would be better to be in the State Prison than to be soldiers sustaining the banner of a country that has always kept us for its union aggrandizement—that has always used us only because the etoffe [Fr. fabric?] was genuine.

It becomes our duty to denounce such glaring facts. We denounce such *christian* and *humane* officers, that the world may know that on American soil the barbarities of an uncivilized Africa are carried on to its greatest extent, and, unfortunately, to the shame of those in power, who wink the eye, just because these outrages, these crimes, are committed on negroes.

It is enough that we have been taken to Washington, half drilled in Cavalry tactics (organization for which we enlisted), dismounted, deprived of the arms we knew but little about, sent to the front with inexperienced officers to be made *pontoon bridges* of—sheep for the slaughter—to be treated as dogs by would be *Christian men*, whose purpose it is to brutalize as much as possible those who, having no country, even in the land of their nativity, volunteer and sacrifice home, its tender . . .
[line obscured]
. . . *of the inferior!*

Is it not more than hard that free-born citizens, hailing from the *free State of Massachusetts*, endowed with all the facilities which the Divine Maker, in his bounty, has given to his creatures, should be thus brutally treated? We call the Governor's attention to this, and if government does not see that justice is done, we shall not only resent the outrages, *but shall be under the painful necessity of turning our arms against these demagogues, who daringly, insult and trample on our manhood without just cause only to satisfy the hateful passion of prejudice!*

After escaping rebel bullets, railroad iron and harrow teeth, are we, Mr. Editor, and you Christian people of the North, to be thus mangled, brutalized and degraded by men calling themselves Christians, holding commissions in the regenerative army of American Freedom? Are we no better off than those whose fate it is to be born in Egypt's land, hunted down by rebel bloodhounds?

This *gentlemanly* and *Christian* officer, about whom too much cannot be said, bears the name of F. L. Gilman, Liet. Comd'g Co. L, 5th Massachusetts Cavalry.

We are satisfied that nothing will be done that this denunciation will be of no avail, yet we are desirous that our friends at home, that all true Christians may know how *kindly* and *humanely* the brave men who are sacrificing their lives, for the upholding and perpetuation of American institutions, are treated by those having authority over them. As *"the pen is mightier than the sword,"* we trust that they shall not always domineer over us, allowing passionate hatred to be their only guide.

In conclusion, Mr. Editor, I must confess that I was never so moved in my life, as I was when I witnessed the heart-rending scene. Moved for the poor creature who suffered the torture—moved for the *hobgoblin* perpetrator of the atrocious crime—moved to see God's image, his most perfect and glorious work, abused, outraged, barbarously treated as it was, and for such a small offence—shirking from fatigue duty. Moved for the hobgoblin, I say, because God has granted him so many advantages, even the *command* of His *creatures*, vested him with a reasonable soul, which according to our Anglo-American brethren, is not given to the poor negro, the object of their scurrilous contempt. Though we have no souls, we have arms, which they crave for the defence of their divided country, and if anything is worthy of respect and attention, these men are.

The government for which our life's blood is being spilt, to water the scorching plains of Virginia, ought at least to give us something better than the sordid, brutish beings for to lead us, whose hellish propensities shock nature itself!

* * *

This incident went unreported in the regimental records. Nor was there any mention of it in any of the officers' letters. Indeed, such casual brutality as bucking and gagging, being made to carry a log or fence rail, standing on a barrel, or even being tied up by the thumbs were common nonjudicial punishments in white regiments on both sides during the Civil War. What is uncommon here is the reaction by men who were seeking to prove themselves as men and soldiers, men whose memories of the humiliation and torment of slavery were all too fresh.

There are three George Washingtons in Company L of the 5th Massachusetts Cavalry as listed in *Massachusetts Soldiers, Sailors and Marines in the Civil War*. George Washington, 1st (so listed), was a twenty-one-year-old private who enlisted in Boston on 4 April 1864, giving laborer as his occupation. This George Washington mustered out with the regiment on 31 October 1865. George Washington, 2nd, was a twenty-two-year-old farmer from Boston who enlisted on 15 April 1864. Private George Washington, 2nd, died of disease in Point Lookout, Maryland, on 15 July 1865, a full year after the barbaric punishment described in the anonymous letter had taken place. George Washington, 3rd, gave Vicksburg, Mississippi, as his hometown and laborer as his occupation when he enlisted at age nineteen on 21 June 1864. Records do not show where Washington enlisted, but it will be recalled that the 5th Massachusetts Cavalry was in Virginia at the time. Washington, 3rd, mustered out with the regiment on 31 October 1865.

Private Washington's punishment apparently did not reflect poorly on Lieutenant Gilman, for that officer was promoted to captain, commanding Company L, on 24 July 1864. Furthermore, the *Weekly Anglo-African*, which published the anonymous letter, had this missive from the regiment's sergeant major, Gustavus Booth, published in the 30 July 1864 edition:

FROM THE FIFTH REGIMENT MASSACHUSETTS CAVALRY
Point Lookout, Md., July 15, 1864
Mr. Editor: We are very comfortably quartered here, occupying the tents, etc., of the 36th U.S. colored Troops, who left here about a week ago for the front. The spot where we are located is one of beauty and romance—the ocean breezes sweep across the island the whole day, making it agreeable in this warm weather. The boys, when not on duty, are engaged in fishing for oysters, crabs, rock or tailor fish, of which there are not a few.

Our boys are doing guard duty here at the Prisoner Camp. We have here about twelve or fifteen thousand rebel prisoners. Brig.-Gen. James Barnes is in command of this district. Our details from the regiment are large, the boys doing picket and guard duty. They do their duty cheerfully.

We have a splendid brass band, led by the celebrated Kimball, of Boston. We were pleased yesterday to see some ladies from Boston. Away from the merciless bullets of the enemy we enjoy the harmonious sounds of our band, and nothing is here wanted to make our camp the resort of happiness—a modern paradise—but the softening and consoling influence of woman. It is announced in camp that in a few days we will be mounted. Then we shall show ourselves one of the best cavalry regiments in the service.

G. Booth, Sergt.-Maj.

In July 1864, the commander of the post at Point Lookout was Brigadier General James Barnes, who happened to be a Bay Stater. He had been graduated from West Point in 1829 and served seven years in the regular army, mostly as an instructor at West Point. Barnes had pursued a career in civil engineering until war broke out. He was appointed colonel of the 18th Massachusetts Infantry in July 1861 and brigadier general of volunteers in November 1862. Barnes held division command in V Corps at Gettysburg but seems to have lost control of his troops, according to Ezra Warner in *Generals in Blue*. After Barnes was wounded at Gettysburg, he was posted to garrison and prison camp duty. General Barnes was commandant of Point Lookout from July 1864 until June 1865 when the camp was closed down.

Besides the newly arrived 5th Massachusetts Cavalry, General Barnes had under his command two regiments of the Veteran Reserve Corps. These were troops who had been wounded or discharged for disability yet still wished to serve. Originally designated the Invalid Corps, the name was later changed, perhaps in part because quartermasters in the army also used the initials "IC" to designate goods or animals "inspected and condemned." The 139th Regiment, Ohio National Guard, was also at the Point until 21 August 1864, when that regiment was relieved from duty, its term of enlistment having expired. There was one battery of artillery, the 2nd Wisconsin, at the post. The regiments on duty at Point Lookout are enumerated here because the regiment was to be here quite a while, until March 1865, and from July 1864 on, when rebel prisoners wrote in their diaries and letters home of being guarded by African American soldiers, only one regiment was meant, the 5th Massachusetts Cavalry.

There were many men, thousands, who would not agree with Charles Bowditch's description of life at Point Lookout as luxurious. Point Lookout in 1864 was a sandy tract of land on the southern end of the western shore of Maryland. The point was formed by Chesapeake Bay on the east and the Potomac River on the south. In the northern part of the peninsula was Tanner Creek, a tidal inlet that made Point Lookout almost an island. Across this inlet were the smallpox hospital and the graveyard, which the Confederates called the "Peach Orchard." Union troops had constructed a fort and a fence across the narrow neck of land, effectively enclosing the entire post. From Tanner Creek to the tip of the peninsula was about a mile and a half. About three-quarters of a mile from the neck, on the eastern side of the peninsula, were three prisoner of war camps, one for enlisted men, one used as a hospital, and one for rebel officers. These enclosures were made of planks fourteen feet high, with a sentry walk or gallery constructed about three feet below the top of the palings and eight feet wide.

The largest camp, for enlisted men, was known as the "Bull Pen." This enclosed some twenty-three acres of land in the shape of a parallelogram, being 1,024 feet on the north side, 1,400 feet on the south, 919 feet on the seaward side, and 1,194 on the land side. Near the western end of the enclosure were eight single-story buildings, each 22 feet wide by 145 feet in length. Seven of these were cook and mess houses; the eighth was used for commissary stores. The prisoners were housed in Sibley tents, which were bell shaped and had an opening in the top to let smoke escape. The tents were placed back-to-back in two rows, with streets fronting each row. A prisoner coming into the camp was assigned to a row of tents, called a division, each division containing a thousand men. There was not a bush or a tree or hardly a blade of grass in any of the prison enclosures. During cold weather, the prisoners drew firewood, which was delivered to the Point by boat. Rations for the prisoners were not overly generous, to say the least.

Anthony M. Keiley, who was taken prisoner on 9 June 1864, left an account of his experiences at Point Lookout. "Between dawn and sunrise a 'reveille' horn summoned us into line by companies for roll-call," he wrote. After roll call, the men were marched by companies to the mess hall, "where a slice of bread and a piece of pork or beef were placed on the tables at intervals about twenty inches apart. The meat was usually about four or five ounces in weight." This meat, whether salt pork or beef, "was seized and consumed greedily." For "dinner," the noon meal, the men were again formed by companies, "and following the same routine we marched to the mess houses where another slice of bread, and over a half-pint of watery slop, by courtesy called soup, greeted the eyes of such as could find comfort in that substitute for nourishment." That was all the food the prisoners received for the day.

Perhaps even more life threatening than poor rations or scarce firewood in winter was the lack of fresh water. Less than two weeks before the arrival of General Barnes, on 23 June, U.S. Surgeon James H. Thompson, in charge of the Confederate prison hospital, which was also composed of tents, felt compelled to submit a report to Colonel Draper, then commanding the post. Dr. Thompson pointed out the extreme crowding at the Point, "and as sanitary officer of the camp" respectfully protested against the addition of further prisoners, "there being now fully 14,000 within the prison camp, and near 20,000 on the Point in all, including the United States Hammond General Hospital, with 1,300 wounded men [federal soldiers], the contraband camp of indefinite numbers, the quartermaster's department, and troops of the garrison." Thompson was "urged to make this protest" for the following reasons: first, the general overcrowding of the Point, and second, "the already insufficient quantity and injurious quality of the water." Thompson noted that "the water of some of the wells is already unfit for use, and to this state of the water I attribute largely the increased amount of and fatality of disease during the last month." Surgeon Thompson was concerned that overcrowding and poor water would make preventative measures "futile, and we may see ere the summer is past an epidemic that will decimate not only the ranks of prisoners, but affect alike all the inhabitants of the point." Dr. Thompson recommended that condensers be brought to Point Lookout to convert saltwater to fresh; that no further prisoners be added to the fourteen thousand already present; that fresh vegetables be added "in consideration of the scorbutic tendency and character exhibited in the majority of diseases occurring in camp"; and that barracks be built for the two hundred ill Confederate prisoners. Colonel Draper approved Thompson's report and forwarded it up the chain of command, but there was only so much that lay within his authority. Draper responded to Dr. Thompson that he had "forwarded an application to purchase a condenser capable of producing 17,000 gallons of fresh water daily." He also reported the requisition of lumber for a prison hospital, but only enough material was sent to erect one ward. An increase in rations or the addition of antiscorbutic vegetables, however, was in the hands of the U.S. commissary general of prisoners of war, not in Colonel Draper's.

Besides the problem with drinking water, there was a similar problem with water for bathing. Anthony Keiley observed, "The eastern face of each of the 'pens' fronted the bay, and the gates led from the enclosures to a narrow belt of land between the fence and water, which was free to the prisoners during the day. Piles were driven into the bay on either side to prevent any dexterous reb from 'flanking out.'" Keiley noted that the same enclosure of water held the latrines, or "sinks," as the men called them. "Most of the prisoners readily availed themselves of the opportunity of bathing, but I must admit my own squeamishness at this prospect, prevented me from utilizing this privilege during my stay," Keiley wrote. He also recorded the arrival of the 5th Massachusetts Cavalry on 1 July: "Today one of the negro regiments that has been guarding us, the Thirty-Sixth, United States Colored, left this point for the front. Their places were taken by the Fifth Massachusetts Colored Cavalry, ordered here, it is said by Butler, for cowardice in the presence of the enemy." Keiley's statement shows the power of ugly rumor to travel quickly. That malicious falsehood must have come from the Union side, as Keiley had no way of knowing the circumstances surrounding the regiment's transfer. There was just enough of a grain of truth in this rumor to make it believable to Union backbiters and rebel bigots.

Friday, 1 July, also saw the arrival at Point Lookout of a medical inspector, Surgeon C. T. Alexander, U.S. Army. Alexander reported to Colonel W. Hoffman, commissary general of prisoners of war, on 9 July. The body of Alexander's report to Colonel Hoffman was embodied in the forms used for the purpose. Alexander inspected not only the prison camp but also the large hospital for Union soldiers at the Point, as well as the medical staff. A brief quote will give the flavor of this report:

> 1. Camp, name and geographical position—Point Lookout, Saint Mary's County, Md. 2. Topography of surrounding country—peninsula formed by Potomac River and Chesapeake Bay. 3. Topography of locality, soil, drainage—flat, soil sandy, drainage not naturally good. 4. Water, source, supply, quality, effects—pumps, deficient, quality bad, diarrhea and dysentery. 5. Fuel, whence obtained, kind, supply—by boat, oak and pine, abundant. 6. Local courses of disease, removal, mitigation—bad water, deficiency of vegetables.

At the end of this report, which went on for another forty-seven points, Surgeon Alexander appended a paragraph with the following recommendations: "First, the water, being brackish and scanty, is causing a large increase of disease. This should be remedied at once by a sufficient supply of fresh water being furnished by boats until condensers suitable for the purpose are obtained." Second, Alexander pointed out "a misunderstanding in reference to the construction of a hospital." Insufficient material had been ordered; the medical inspector felt that the large number of Confederate sick would require "at least six wards, with laundry, mess room, kitchen and sinks." Lastly, Dr. Alexander recommended that the daily boat between Baltimore and Fortress Monroe, Virginia, deliver vegetables sufficient to "correct the scurvy and tendency thereto now existing."

Despite Dr. Alexander's report and Colonel Draper's requisition of a condenser before his relief, the water situation at Point Lookout continued to be difficult. Anthony Keiley recorded in his diary for 7 July, "The supply of water is getting very scant, and the quality infamous. Guards have been placed over some of the pumps to prevent waste. With every precaution, the amount is still so insufficient that a waterboat had to be sent down from Baltimore today to furnish a supply to the hospitals." The necessary condensers were apparently never delivered. A first sergeant of the 52nd Georgia, N. F. Harman, arrived at Point Lookout on 3 October 1864. "Our supply of water was from six wells with pumps," Harman wrote. "Of these, only one well could be used for drinking purposes. . . . If the water from the other wells was allowed to stand even one night, a thick green scum formed, as if copperas was in it, and the water was unfit to drink. The death rate was heavy."

Point Lookout's most celebrated prisoner of war was probably the poet, composer, and literary critic Sidney Lanier. Born in Macon, Georgia, in 1842, Lanier served in the 2nd Georgia Battalion from June 1861 until mid-1862, when he, along with his brother Clifford, transferred to the Confederate Signal Corps. The Lanier brothers became part of a "mounted field squad" of signalmen stationed at Burwell's Bay near the mouth of the James River. While at Burwell's Bay, Lanier began his novel *Tiger-Lilies*, which is based on his experiences there in the winter of 1863. The advance of the Army of the James left Lanier's unit behind enemy lines. In a letter to a Northern friend written after the war, Lanier noted, "Our party was ordered to remain, acting as scouts in the rear of Gen. B.'s [Butler's] army. By dint of much hiding in woods, and much hard running from lair to lair, we managed to hold our position and rendered some service, with information of the enemy's movement." The two brothers were transferred in August 1864 to Wilmington, North Carolina, to serve as signal officers on blockade-runners.

Wilmington was the last open port of the Confederacy, and the blockade was tightening. Lanier gave an account of his and his brother's experiences running the blockade: "Cliff made three delightful and adventurous trips: from Nassau to Wilmington: was wrecked, on the last voyage, and just saved his life, getting on a federal schooner just in time to see his steamer go down." Clifford Lanier somehow made his way to Bermuda and was about to board the blockade-runner *Maude Campbell* as signal officer when he heard of the capture of Wilmington in February 1865. Clifford "went to Havana, thence after a pleasant time of a month with friends in Cuba, to Galveston, Texas, whence he walked to Macon, Georgia: arriving just in time to see our Mother die." Sidney successfully ran the blockade at Wilmington "but was captured, in the gulf-stream, by the federal cruiser *Santiago de Cuba*, carried to Norfolk, thence to Fortress Monroe, and Camp Hamilton, and at last to Point Lookout," where he spent four months.

Lanier, in *Tiger-Lilies*, has left us the impressions of a gifted writer about what it was like to be a Confederate prisoner of war at Point Lookout. "To go into a prison of war is in all respects to be born over," Lanier wrote. He explained that "for, of all the men in all the prisons of the late war, it might be said, as of births in the ordinary world,—they came in and went out naked." In the prison camp at Point Lookout, Lanier wrote, "were born, at a certain time, of poor and probably honest parents, twelve thousand grown men." All these men had as an inheritance at this second birth were each individual's capabilities of body and soul. "And so, in this far littler world, which was as much separated from the outer world as if it had been in the outer confines of space, it was striking to see how society immediately resolved itself into those three estates which invariably constitute it elsewhere." Those estates, according to Lanier, were the aristocrats, "who lived well but did not labor"; the artisans, "who lived well by laboring"; and the "drones, who starved by not laboring."

Moreover, each of these classes were subdivided in the same ways as occur "in the regions of crowded civilization":

For instance, of the aristocrats, there were the true-gentlemanly sort, the insulting-obtrusive sort, the philanthropic sort, the fast sort; of the artisans, there *were the sober-citizenly sort, the mind-your-own-business-and-I-mine sort, the gloomy, brooding-over-oppression sort, the cheerful workers, the geniuses, together with those whose labor was spiritual, such as the teachers of French, and arithmetic, and music, including those who lived by their wits in the bad sense; and of the drones, the kind who swear that the world owes them a living, but who are too lazy to collect the debt; the sentimental-vulgar kind, whose claims are based upon a well-turned leg or a heavy mustache, and are consequently not appreciated by a practical world; the self-deprecatory sort, who swear that Nature has been unkind in endowing them, and who then must starve for consistency's sake or forswear themselves; and lastly, the large class of out-and-out unmitigated drones, who, some say, serve the mere purpose of inanimate clay chinked into the cracks of this great log-cabin which we all inhabit, and who, poor men! Must endure much bad weather on the wrong side of the house.*

So it seems to Lanier's autobiographical character, Philip Sterling, as he arrives inside the "Bull Pen" and gazes out over the camp. He recognizes and greets several old army comrades but notes how prison had changed them: "They did not crowd to shake joyful hands with him and hear the news from outside, but met him with smiles that had in them a sort of mournful greasiness, as if to say: 'Ah, old boy, mighty poor eating in here!'" Divided into squads, Sterling/Lanier's group arrives in front of a tent, where the corporal in charge inquires as to the number of occupants: "Bout a million, countin' lice and all!" is the response from a voice, "whose tone blent in itself sorrow, anger, hunger, and the sardonic fearlessness of desperation." Outside of this tent is a "long, cadaverous man," stripped to the waist, who held his ragged shirt across his knees, "toward which he occasionally made gestures very like those of a compositor setting type." The man, who is crushing lice in the seams of his shirt, says of the louse hunt, "'Fords me a leetle amusement. Jest gittin' well o' the fever: cain't git about much yet!" Inside the tent, Sterling encounters a huge individual seated cross-legged on the ground before a bench on which sits "a rat-tail file, a beef-bone, a half-dozen gutta percha buttons, a piece of iron barrel-hoop, two oyster shells, and a pocket-knife." For the clothes of this man, who is polishing a gutta-percha ring with a rag dipped in bacon fat, the narrator observes, "those three thieves, grease, dirt, and smoke, had drawn lots; but not content with the allotment, all three were evidently contending which should have the whole suit. It appeared likely that dirt would be the happy thief."

Rather than have his character give in to despair and melancholy, Lanier has Sterling find humor in the "ludicrous phase of the situation." His artisan tent mate admires his pluck and with a merry eye thrusts his head through the tent fly and ejects "from his mouth a surprising quantity of tobacco juice. It was his manner of laughing." Later, Sterling and a friend meet up and stroll over to the camp bulletin board. A large crowd is gathered around a man reading a list of names from a paper tacked to the board. "Letters from Dixie," explains Sterling's friend. They arrive at the bulletin board, which is "covered with a thousand strips of paper, bearing in all manner of chirographies a thousand items of information." Men who had changed their residences in the camp advertise the fact; others have space to rent to set up shops or to make a "splendid stand for the unwanted bean-soup trade"; a J. Shankins possesses a blanket "which he would swap fur a par of britches, please call at . . ."; a company of blackface minstrels announces its new program, "admission ten cents. No Confederate money received at the door"; men "advertised to meet the eye" of their brothers or cousins, who if in the prison were to call at . . . ; Jaines Haxley inquires "if any gentleman in the 64th regiment seed his son with his own eyes killed at the sharpsburg fite"; one poor individual has drawn a pair of shoes of two different sizes and "wished to know if enny gentleman had a shue, size number 10, pleese call at . . ."—all the sardonic humor of men in difficult circumstances. One note inquires "if Dixie and the Yanks was still a-havin' high words. Let dogs delight." Another "facetious individual, blushing to reveal his name, and therefore writing over anonymous, perpetrated the enormous joke of 'Help wanted, to assist me in eating my rations. None need apply except with the most unexceptionable reference'; to which was appended the replies of a hundred different applicants for the situation." Such was prisoner of war life at Point Lookout, Maryland.

The 5th Massachusetts Cavalry settled into the routine of life at Point Lookout, adjusting to the contrast between life in the field and duty as prison camp guards and garrison troops. After the excitement and harshness of life in the field, there was a certain amount of letdown. Two officers, K Company's Captain Erik Wulff and Captain Edward R. Merrill of L Company, put in for leave to go to Washington. Wulff requested ten days and received three; Merrill requested five days and also got three. Both officers then sent in their resignations while on furlough.

We are left somewhat in the dark as to what reasons they gave for their resignations because the letters requesting them have been lost. Later cases show that General Barnes required that officers wishing to resign give sufficient reasons. The resignations of several officers were turned down or returned for further amplification; one could not simply quit and go home. Whatever their reasons—and we could speculate about their dismounted condition, unhappiness about serving as prison camp guards or lack of active service, or even Captain Wulff's mental stability—those reasons were sufficient for the general commanding St. Mary's District and General Augur in Washington to release them from duty.

Other officers availed themselves of an easy access to alcohol. While records reveal that enlisted men obtained alcohol and drank to excess, these soldiers are only encountered in the records when they appeared before a military court. For officers, there was access to a supply of commissary whiskey. In the National Archives, as part of the records of the District of St. Mary's, XXII Army Corps (Record Group 393), is a lined notebook bound in green cloth. This ledger of "Whiskey Orders Approved" lists by date, name, and amount the commissary whiskey obtained by officers. From 4 July 1864 to 28 March 1865, the names of twenty-four officers of the 5th Massachusetts Cavalry appear in this book. Several officers received alcohol only at the beginning of the regiment's posting to Point Lookout, in July or August of 1864. Surgeon Harlow Gamwell, for instance, who may have needed whiskey for "medicinal purposes," received alcohol four times, one canteen each time, on 21 July and on 1, 11, and 13 August. A Civil War–era army canteen such as the M 1858 model held about a quart of liquid. Regimental quartermaster Lieutenant Windsor Hatch was another who did his drinking during the early part of the regiment's stay. Lieutenant Hatch requisitioned whiskey over an eight-week period, but he either was doing a great deal of entertaining or had brought a great thirst in from the field: Hatch drew a gallon each time on 9, 19, and 26 July and on 1 and 10 August. Other officers who felt the boredom of garrison duty in July and August did not space out their orders like Quartermaster Hatch. Captain Peter Rooney's name appears only three times, for a gallon each time on 25 and 30 July and a quart on 4 August. Lieutenant Rienzi Loud's drinking was also binge-like: he received a quart on 15 July, a gallon the next day, and three pints on 18 July.

Officers availed themselves of commissary whiskey in July and August and then received no whiskey until the spring, perhaps to celebrate the arrival of better weather or in anticipation of taking the field once more. Such officers include Lieutenants Abner Mallory and George Odell. Mallory requisitioned whiskey, a gallon at a time, on 4, 18, and 28 July, 1 and 4 August, 12 September, and 16 February. Odell received a quart on 5 July, a gallon on 9 July, and another gallon on 16 February.

The officer whose name appeared most in the "Whiskey Orders Received" book, Lieutenant Daniel Chamberlain, also took a hiatus after the summer. Chamberlain ordered three pints on 25 July, a gallon on 28 July, three pints two days later, a gallon on 2 August, three pints on 8 August, three more on 12 August, and three more on 13 August; then he did not order whiskey until New Year's Eve 1865, when he received a gallon. Chamberlain slowed down in the spring, for he ordered whiskey only twice more before the 5th Massachusetts took the field: a gallon on 20 January and a gallon on 7 March.

The drinking of commissary whiskey was not confined to the junior officers. Major Horace Weld succumbed to the same temptations as the younger line officers; he received a gallon on 20 July, two quarts on 28 July, a gallon on 4 August, and two quarts on 29 August. Weld did not drink the government's whiskey again until 6 January, when he ordered a gallon. This apparently lasted until 25 February, when he ordered another gallon. Major Zabdiel B. Adams, who was absent wounded until autumn, limited his drinking of U.S. whiskey until the winter and spring. Adams rang in the new year on 31 December with a gallon of whiskey and then received a gallon on 9 and 20 February and on 13 and 25 March. Major Adams was president of a general court-martial the latter part of March, so perhaps he was entertaining. There is a notation for "Captain Parsons et al.—2 gallons" on 28 March. Parsons also served on the court-martial; it seems that there was a party to celebrate the court's adjournment and the receipt of marching orders for the regiment.

The regiment had one scare as it settled into the routine of garrison life in the middle of July 1864. Captain Charles Bowditch wrote his father on 15 July that the 5th Massachusetts had been ordered to move, on 13 July, across the neck of land, inside the stockade that stretched across the northern end of the Point. Union gunboats were ordered to lie close offshore in anticipation of a Confederate cavalry raid to free the prisoners at Point Lookout. This raid was part of Confederate general Jubal A. Early's march on Washington, DC, in July. In *Battles and Leaders*, General Early noted his instructions from General Lee: To move his corps, with two battalions of artillery, "to the Shenandoah Valley; to strike Hunter's force in the rear and, if possible, destroy it; then to move down the valley, cross the Potomac near Leesburg . . . or above Harper's Ferry, as I might find most practicable, and threaten Washington City."

The forces under Early defeated the scratch force sent out from Washington under General Lew Wallace, but the Union troops had cost the Confederates a day. Interestingly, as a secondary objective, Early mentioned in *Battles and Leaders* that "a letter from General Lee had informed me that an effort would be made to release the prisoners at Point Lookout, and directing me [to] take steps to unite them with my command." By the afternoon of 11 July, Early's corps, less than ten thousand men, had penetrated the District of Columbia, halting in sight of Fort Stevens near Rock Creek. Early continued his account: "After abandoning the idea of capturing Washington I determined to remain in front of the fortifications during the 12th, and retire at night. [Confederate brigadier general of cavalry Bradley T.] Johnson had burned the bridges over the Gunpowder, on the Harrisburg and Philadelphia roads, threatened Baltimore, and started for Point Lookout; but the attempt to release the prisoners was not made, as the enemy had received notice of it in some way."

Charles Bowditch recorded the excitement at Point Lookout: "A little while ago an orderly came in from the front, (the idea of our having a 'front' down here in this corner of the world!) announcing that the rebs were within twenty miles of here. Immediately a great hubbub among Headquarters people and a fortification which they are building was immediately hurried up."

Bowditch surmised that the camp was in no danger; a large Union warship had arrived to provide further security. "The 'Minnesota' steam frigate has steamed up abreast the fortification and is prepared to throw broadsides into any rebs that may appear." Bowditch also reassured his father that his health was good. The young captain had not availed himself of commissary whiskey, but he had managed to find something to drink. "My health and internal economy have improved very much lately, owing as much as anything, I suppose, to our having fresh milk and berries and very good eating in general, to say nothing of the good effect of port wine, three bottles of which I have already disposed of," Bowditch wrote his mother on 23 July. He had woken early and gone for a swim and then sat down at 6:00 a.m. to take pen in hand. The day found Bowditch in a reflective mood. After describing the weather, he wrote, "Just a year ago yesterday I started from Boston in the 'Cahawba' in the Fifty-Fifth Regiment. I didn't believe then that the war was going to last as long as it has and at present I don't see much chance of its cessation." Bowditch doubted, however, that the North would be the first to give up. General Barnes's inspector general had inspected the 5th Massachusetts the day before, Bowditch noted: "The men look as well as could be expected considering the amount of hard duty they have had to perform. Their clothes were pretty dirty and worn but new ones can be got for them and then they will make quite a reputable appearance."

On 28 July, Charles Bowditch wrote his friend Lucy. The night before, there had been another alarm, which provided a break in the routine. "We got under arms, sent out reinforcements for the pickets and then went to bed." It did not take much, Bowditch wrote, "to get up a scare on the most improved style, rebels and other fixins complete." Bowditch did have one important piece of news: Captain Charles Francis Adams Jr. of the 1st Massachusetts Cavalry had been appointed lieutenant colonel of the 5th Massachusetts. Captain Bowditch supposed that this was "Col. Russell's doings but I should not think that Captain Adams would wish to join the regiment until it is mounted." According to Bowditch, "most of the [former] officers of the First are delighted to have him come here."

Harry Russell and John Andrew's search for a lieutenant colonel had begun almost at the regiment's inception. The first candidate brought to Governor Andrew's attention was Major Samuel Emery Chamberlain of the 1st Massachusetts Cavalry. Chamberlain had led a colorful life before the Civil War. Born in Center Harbor, New Hampshire, in 1829, the family moved to Boston in 1844. That same year, Chamberlain's father died, and he went out alone to a relative's farm in Illinois. In 1846, Chamberlain, not yet seventeen, joined the 1st Regiment of U.S. Dragoons. Chamberlain fought throughout the Mexican-American War and made his way to California in 1850. He was three years in California, continuing a career of adventure and escapade that included the 1853 filibustering expedition of William H.

Walker to Baja California. Chamberlain sailed back to Boston around the world by way of the Philippines, India, and Scotland, reaching the Bay State in 1854. His extraordinary experiences are recorded in his copiously illustrated diary, published in 1956 as *My Confession: The Recollections of a Rogue*.

Chamberlain became a policeman in Cambridge before the war. He was commissioned first lieutenant of a three-month regiment in April 1861. After joining the 1st Massachusetts Cavalry five months later as a private, his experience was recognized, and he was commissioned captain in November of that year. Chamberlain was wounded and captured at Poolesville, Maryland, in September 1862. While at Libby Prison in Richmond, incidentally, one of his fellow prisoners was Harry Russell.

Captain Chamberlain was commissioned major on 30 October 1862. Exchanged in December 1862, Chamberlain was on the staff of Brigadier General W. W. Averell until he was severely wounded during the cavalry action at Kelly's Ford, Virginia, on 17 March 1863. That same action, it will be recalled, saw the mortal wounding of Henry and Charles Bowditch's cousin Nathaniel Bowditch. A bullet smashed through Chamberlain's left cheekbone and took a downward trajectory, lodging between his shoulder blades. After recuperating from his wound, Major Chamberlain returned to the 1st Massachusetts in June 1863 and participated in the regiment's actions at Brandy Station and Aldie on 9 and 17 June, respectively. During the autumn and winter of 1863, Chamberlain commanded Camp Parole at Annapolis, Maryland, a depot for dismounted cavalrymen. Samuel Chamberlain must have made the acquaintance of Theophilus Parsons during his stint as a Cambridge policeman, for Parsons took it upon himself to sponsor Chamberlain's advancement into the 5th Massachusetts.

Parsons wrote to Governor Andrew on 10 December 1863. The professor had obviously already broached the subject of Chamberlain's appointment to both Andrew and the major, for he was awaiting a reply from "Chamberlin," as Parsons spelled it. Parsons made a point of reassuring Governor Andrew about Chamberlain's correct attitude toward enlisting blacks. "Before almost anyone, he was earnestly in favor of enlisting Negroes," Parsons wrote. Parsons noted that Chamberlain was "thoroughly acquainted" with African Americans and thought "them better adapted for cavalry, in some respects, than infantry, though good for either." As a further inducement, Parsons reported that Chamberlain had told him "many months ago" that he felt sure that he "could bring a regiment of mounted colored men into such condition, and do such work with them, as to make them acknowledged as one of the best regiments in the service." Parsons's son Chauncy had served with Major Chamberlain and would "take care that Colonel Russell understands Chamberlin perfectly." Parsons was certain that Colonel Russell would get along well with Lieutenant Colonel Chamberlain.

Over the next four months, Parsons pressed his sponsorship of Major Chamberlain. The major, for his part, was not averse to being courted by the governor. On 16 December 1863, Parsons wrote that Chamberlain had turned down the lieutenant colonelcy of the 5th Massachusetts because he felt that his presence was crucial to the 1st Massachusetts Cavalry. "He feels wedded to his Regiment, he may exaggerate the importance of his remaining in it, but I think he does not," Parsons wrote. Parsons had heard (not from Chamberlain, he was quick to add) that the major had refused a colonelcy in an Iowa cavalry regiment. Chamberlain was also well thought of by general officers. According to Parsons, Chamberlain had "received the strong assurances of Generals Hooker, Stoneman, Averill and Dufee [Duffié], of their decided approbation, and their disposition to favor his advancement." Parsons expressed extreme regret at Chamberlain's refusal; the professor felt that Chamberlain "would have brought into the Regiment, energy, experience, skill, perfect temperance on his own part, (to which his surgeon says he owes his recovery) and a really patriotic fidelity to duty."

A month or so later, however, Major Chamberlain's name was still in play. Governor Andrew had evidently asked Theophilus Parsons about Chamberlain's health. "I have no doubt that Major Chamberlin is perfectly well," Parsons wrote on 20 January 1864. "For months he has been fit for service, troubled only with some times of neuralgia where a bullet shattered his nerves—but it is now—or was when I heard from him—nearly gone, and was never more than a troublesome annoyance." Parsons informed the governor that Chamberlain was on detached service at Camp Parole and could not leave without orders, presumably "from some department in Washington." The professor had missed Andrew at the State House and promised to call the next day. Parsons's information about Chamberlain's presence at Camp Parole and his presumed complete recovery from his wounds prompted Governor Andrew to write to the War Department to have the major sent to Massachusetts. Governor Andrew, who should have known better after more than two years of war, did not follow the correct procedure in ordering Chamberlain north, as the following telegram from the War Department, dated 24 January 1864, shows: "Major Chamberlain cannot be ordered to report as requested[.] [P]lease state date at which you wish him discharged to accept promotion[.] [S]uch action will then be taken immediately as [to] allow him to report promptly. [Signed] Thomas M. Vincent A.A.G."

On 3 February 1864, Theophilus Parsons took occasion once more to praise Samuel Chamberlain to Governor Andrew. The officers appointed to the 5th Massachusetts were "an excellent set," all, with the exception of Major Weld, "young, and all full of energy and determination." According to Parsons, Chamberlain's presence "might be just the difference between having the regiment be a good regiment and its being a very good regiment; so good as to exert a powerful influence." Chamberlain possessed experience and understanding of both the cavalry soldier and the African American, Parsons felt. The major was intelligent and energetic, was well thought of as an officer by "the best judges," and meant "to be a soldier as long as he lives—his success in making this Regiment all we desire would be eminently useful to him." All these factors, the professor added, would "join to make him throw his whole heart into the work."

Theophilus Parsons also wrote to Major Chamberlain on 3 February, urging him to come to a decision on whether to join the 5th Cavalry or remain with the 1st. Chamberlain wrote back on 7 February 1864. He did not directly come to a decision, for he found it "extremely difficult to decide, to which regiment, inclination, duty, and the greatest good for the service, calls me." Chamberlain had a "firm belief in the efficiency of Negro Cavalry." Then Chamberlain, for all his vaunted understanding of blacks, wrote a paragraph-long generalization:

> The negro is a natural horseman, fond of horses, and the horse fond of him; easily brought under discipline, obedient and prompt to orders, full of hot blood and brute courage, which makes him terrible and ferocious in battle, choosing close hand-to-hand conflicts to long range, which quality will render well drilled Black Cavalry, irresistible in a charge; and I have great confidence and faith that the Fifth can be made, not only a model, but one of the most efficient of Regiments; and if it should please his excellency to appoint me to the Fifth, I will by close attention to the drill, discipline and comforts of the men, endeavor to make it a crack regiment, and in that way, prove that I am not unmindful of his confidence in me.

There was a mitigating factor, however: Chamberlain asserted that cavalry should not be sent into the field until the men had had at least six months' continuous drill. Mounted troops without proper training in horsemanship and firearms, he felt, could not be depended upon and were "liable to panic, offering great inducement to the foe, to replenish their used up horses and arms." As illustration of this fact, Chamberlain mentioned the "large number" of cavalry regiments from Pennsylvania and New York that were sent into the field as soon as they were formed: "During the entire year of '62, the Rebel Cavalry kept themselves supplied with horses and arms, from the cavalry of those two states." The 5th Massachusetts should not be sent into the field until fully trained, Chamberlain felt, "and in consequence will lose the spring campaign, which undoubtedly will be the most brilliant of the war, and which I don't wish to miss." So Major Chamberlain left the matter up to Governor Andrew, for "whatever his excellency in his wisdom, thinks is best for the cause, I as a soldier will cheerfully cooperate, and endeavor to do my duty in any position, he may order me to fill."

Governor Andrew did not take any action about the lieutenant colonelcy of the regiment until the second week of March 1864. He received the following reply from Assistant Adjutant General Thomas Vincent to his request that Major Chamberlain be ordered to Massachusetts for promotion: "In reply, I am directed to inform you that the interests of the service will not permit the request to be granted. Major Chamberlain is now on detailed service and he cannot be spared from his duties at the present time." This was not the end of Samuel Chamberlain's connection with the 5th Massachusetts however, because in July 1865 he would be promoted to full colonel of the regiment.

Colonel Russell was not informed of the War Department's action, for on 16 April he wrote to Governor Andrew to propose his own candidates "in case Major Chamberlain is appointed Lieutenant Colonel in the First." Captain Charles Francis Adams Jr. was Russell's next choice after Major Henry Lee Higginson, who was still at home recovering from wounds received at Aldie, Virginia, on 17 June 1863. Colonel Russell hoped that Governor Andrew would "see fit to learn from him the facts as to his [Higginson's] recovery." Harry Russell did not articulate his feelings about Samuel Chamberlain, but we can infer that he preferred an officer of the same social background as he, who had gone to the same schools. Samuel

Chamberlain was an excellent soldier, but he was no gentleman. Russell considered Higginson as standing "first rate" in his regiment, and there were "many personal reasons" why the colonel preferred him above all. The 5th Massachusetts had yet to take the field in April, so Higginson's "actual services in the Fifth would not be wanted as soon as in the First and he may be ready in time."

As April 1864 gave way to May, Russell tried again to have Major Higginson commissioned into the regiment. Russell had written Higginson also on the sixteenth of April to recount a recent conversation with Governor Andrew:

> *The Governor asked me whom I should like for Lt. Col. and I said you; he said that, if you could not take the field with the 1st., you probably could not with the 5th, and spoke of Charley Adams as a good person for it. I told him I liked Adams, but was sorry about you. Now, Henry, I should prefer you to anybody else and I wish you would at once take steps about it; what kind of position can we take to oppose the Governor's theory that, if you are not well enough for one, you are not for the other? I am sincere in what I say; I would rather be without any Lt. Col. for many months, if I can have you in the end.*

On 2 May, Russell wrote to the governor. He had seen Higginson and believed him sufficiently recovered to take the field: "As I believe that Major Henry Lee Higginson, First Massachusetts Cavalry will soon be fit for active duty, I would respectfully ask that he be commissioned as Lieutenant Colonel of Fifth Massachusetts Cavalry," Russell wrote. Three days later, as the 1st Battalion entrained for Washington, Harry Russell wrote to Henry Higginson. The governor was still undecided about the state of Higginson's health. Russell urged Higginson to call on the governor at once; "whatever the Governor does about the Lt. Col. of 5th Cavalry, I know that he is actuated by his desire to help the regiment in this hour of trial; I wish you were ready for work, for then there would be no hesitation," confided Russell.

In the end, Henry Higginson did not take the post. Higginson's wound was too severe to allow him to ride at anything but a walk, and he could not sustain that. Major Higginson did try to take a position on General Francis C. Barlow's staff in July 1864, but he came back after a few weeks. Instead, Governor Andrew chose Captain Charles Francis Adams Jr. of the 1st Massachusetts Cavalry.

It took a while for the governor to make up his mind, however, and Colonel Russell was writing as late as 14 June to inquire, "Have any steps been taken towards providing the 5th Cavalry(?) with a Lt. Col.?" Russell had not "heard a word" from Henry Higginson since leaving Massachusetts and was now prompted to write to him. Colonel Russell hoped that Higginson's condition would give him the promotion: "There is no one whom I should prefer to him." Harry Russell was wounded the next day on 15 June, and the matter was taken out of his hands. When Governor Andrew did move to promote Captain Adams, on 15 July 1864, he did so independently, without even communicating directly with Adams. It took Charles Adams a full four weeks before he could be detached from his duties as commander of the Cavalry Escort of Headquarters, Army of the Potomac.

In the meantime, Governor Andrew received an extraordinary petition, signed by many of the noncommissioned officers of the 5th Cavalry, which provides good insight into the morale of the men, particularly when it came to being dismounted. This petition, written out by its first signer, Acting Sergeant Major Alfred Froward (Gustavus Booth, who signed the letter to the *Weekly Anglo-African* as sergeant major that month had apparently reverted to his prior rank of sergeant), came directly to the point:

> We, the undersigned, non-commissioned officers of the Fifth Regiment Massachusetts Cavalry Volunteers, in behalf of our respective companys of the regiment respectfully beg leave to call your attention to the few remarks you made to the Fifth Massachusetts Cavalry on your last visit to the regiment a few days before the regiment left Readville for the seat of war, wherein you pledged your faith personally on behalf of the Commonwealth of Massachusetts that we should in all respects be justly dealt by, and, that we should be a regiment of cavalry and not infantry.

Although the troopers did not blame Governor Andrew for their being dismounted, "we hope and trust that you will remain firm to the promise you made us."

One of the reasons the men wrote the governor was his promise that they would remain cavalry. There was also, however, the humble plea that "there are a great many of us who are incapable by reason of physical disability and other causes to perform the duty of an infantry soldier and therefore would, if reorganized as infantry be discharged the service." The men did not want to be discharged, "but only beg to be what we enlisted for, and as a Regiment of Cavalry in the field of battle we believe that we can maintain the proud name that Massachusetts bears today." The petition ended with the final hope that Andrew would give a "careful perusal" to their request.

Fifty noncommissioned officers of the 5th Massachusetts signed their names to this letter. Alfred Froward, whose promotion to sergeant major would be confirmed in September 1864, was joined by the rest of the senior noncommissioned officers of the regiment. Also still unconfirmed were Acting Ordnance Sergeant John Malone, Acting Quartermaster Sergeant John Grayson, Acting Commissary Sergeant William Jacobs, and Acting Hospital Steward George Whitzell. All signed in the order listed, directly below Froward's name. The next name below George Whitzell's was that of Sergeant Amos Webber of D Company. Webber must have wanted to confirm the petition's statement about physical inability to serve as infantry, for he wrote, "Rejected: March 25, 1863 from the Fifty-Fourth Regiment." In all, sergeants from Companies C, D, E, G, H, I, K, L, and M signed, as did "First Corporal" James Kelley of G Company, Regimental Clerk A. D. W. DeLeon, and six members of the regimental band. The troopers had not used the chain of command in sending their petition to Governor Andrew, but this was hardly unusual; the governor had made his promise, and he would be held to it. Andrew was accountable, not a federal department, the national administration, or an unfamiliar general officer. Besides, the one officer the men might have brought their grievances to was Colonel Russell, and he was absent wounded. Major Weld, in command, was one of three majors and lacked the prestige (or connections) of Russell. But what could Governor Andrew do for a regiment in federal service hundreds of miles away?

As July gave way to August, even Charles Bowditch repeated the rumor that the 5th Cavalry was to be permanently assigned to the infantry service. Morale certainly suffered from the transfer to Point Lookout. There was no longer the excitement and need for the discipline and alertness of field service. Also, without a colonel or lieutenant colonel, the regiment lacked both a leader and a mediator. Point Lookout was indeed a long way from active operations. Bowditch wrote his father on 3 August asking, "Do you hear anything at the North of this regiment being irrecoverably turned into infantry? There are rumors here of it." Bowditch doubted that many officers would stay with the regiment if it were permanently dismounted. He "couldn't stand the service on foot."

Perhaps in part prompted by those camp rumors, two days later Captain Charles Bowditch made an important decision. He wrote to his mother to explain: "I have taken a step today, my dear Mother which I hope I shall not have to look back upon with regret (or at least with regret for having done wrong)." Bowditch had sent in his resignation after carefully discussing the matter with his brother, Major Henry P. Bowditch, who concurred in his decision. "At the same time, it is impossible to prevent feeling unpleasantly at the thought of leaving the regiment where I have many friends, and especially in giving up Henry's company for the sake of which I left the Fifty-Fifth." Nevertheless, Bowditch felt that he should resign, "not on account of myself (for I do not think that I ought to take myself into consideration), but on account of the service."

Bowditch had had what he called "chronic diarrhoea" for almost a year, a condition that "seems to take away all the energy which I used to have in bringing my men to the proper state of discipline." Bowditch was debilitated, and "the simplest duties seem to require a great exertion." He admitted that he was "unable to properly attend to the duties of a company and this has induced me to resign."

It took twenty days for Charles Bowditch's resignation to come through. His paperwork had to go to Major Weld, commanding the regiment, and after approval was sent on to General Barnes. Barnes was not satisfied with Captain Bowditch's first letter and sent it back to him on 8 August with a request for more specificity. Bowditch responded not long after with a surgeon's certificate of disability signed by Regimental Surgeon Dr. Harlow Gamwell. "Chronic diarrhea for nearly twelve months" won Barnes's approval and forwarding to Washington.

Other officers were not as successful as Captain Bowditch. Lieutenant James S. Newell, regimental adjutant, received a letter from First Lieutenant Andrew F. Chapman on 5 August 1864 tendering his resignation, "for the reason that I consider myself incompetent to hold my present position in an infantry regiment, as I cannot instruct men in what I know nothing of myself," Chapman wrote. He had served "since the commencement of this war in the regular cavalry" and was "perfectly willing" to be transferred back to his "old regiment, the Fourth Regular Cavalry as a private, not wishing in any way to get out of the service, but merely to vacate a position I do not feel myself fit to hold." Major Weld approved and forwarded Chapman's resignation to General Barnes. Barnes approved the lieutenant's request but added this endorsement:

> *The Fifth Massachusetts Cavalry is dismounted and there is a general want of knowledge of infantry tactics among the officers. This officer appears to be sincere in his desire to remain in service even if he goes into the ranks of the cavalry arm. His resignation is therefore approved and his transfer to a cavalry regiment recommended as private.*

First Lieutenant Chapman's resignation was approved at the regimental and district level but turned down, without explanation, by Major General Augur. Under the printed words "Headquarters Department of Washington, Twenty-Second Army Corps" and the written date (August 9, 1864) are the words "Respectfully returned to Brigade General Barnes. Disapproved." It was plain that unhappiness or incompetence was not an adequate excuse, at least for the major general commanding the department.

Another officer, not looking to depart the 5th Massachusetts for good but to get a thirty-day sick leave, was Captain Horace B. Welch of C Company, who requested leave based on a surgeon's certificate signed by a compliant Dr. Gamwell. Unfortunately for Welch, Gamwell's certificate had to be countersigned by Surgeon A. Heger, medical director at Point Lookout. Heger was a regular army doctor, not a volunteer surgeon, and after examining Welch, he dismissed his application in July with a terse "No necessity for leave is apparent." On 10 August 1864, Captain Welch tried again for a thirty-day furlough, this time being more specific in his application: "Physical disability arising from inflammation of spinal cord, caused by an injury received in front of Petersburg." This time Welch's sore back gave him the leave he requested, but he was unable to extend his stay at home and was back with the regiment by the end of September.

The officers and men of the 5th Regiment of Massachusetts Cavalry Volunteers had no way of knowing, but the choice of Captain Charles F. Adams Jr. as lieutenant colonel would dramatically improve the status of the regiment, at least when it came to horses. Adams wrote to Governor Andrew on 5 August ostensibly to express his gratitude. "Though I have not as yet received any official communication of the fact," Adams wrote,

"I see by the papers that you have done me the honor to commission me as Lieutenant Colonel of the Fifth Massachusetts Cavalry." Adams was, however, extremely reluctant (if not averse) to being dismounted. "In the first place, I would like to say in regard to this commission, it would be useless, or worse than useless, for me to be mustered into this regiment as Lieutenant Colonel unless it is, in fact, to be a mounted regiment; for me now to go into the dismounted service would be, not only to throw away whatever of useful training I have got in three years of the cavalry, but I should stand in the way of other officers far more competent that I to fill that position." Therefore, Adams, warming to his true aim, proposed a plan to Governor Andrew, "the only available means, which suggest themselves to me, of remounting that regiment." Adams did not expect the 5th Massachusetts to be "mounted on the same footing as the old and tried regiments of the Cavalry Corps." He noted that "fifty percent of the effectiveness [effectives]" of his own regiment, the 1st Massachusetts Cavalry, were "doing dismounted duty, or none at all," because the War Department could not get horses for them. It would be presumptuous to think that newly bought horses would be furnished "to a new and inexperienced organization like the Fifth." Instead, Adams pointed out that, although the "consumption of horse flesh by our armies in the field is enormous, but a comparatively small proportion of this is lost by death." A great number of horses were condemned by inspecting officers and turned in to the Quartermasters' Department for "rest and treatment." Adams proposed mounting the regiment on horses turned in as unserviceable by other commands. Adams saw the advantages of this plan as "multifarious"; there would be a great savings to the government because often horses so turned in received poor care and ended up dying. If issued to the 5th Massachusetts, the horses "would receive the utmost care, as, on recruiting them, would depend the regiment's only chance of a mount." The mounting of the regiment would be helpful in its duties at Point Lookout, Adams felt, and the horses would find the Point salubrious. "Finally, without the issue by the Government of a single serviceable horse, I feel justified by experience in saying that, in two months, an effective and well mounted cavalry regiment could be placed in the field ready for active service, and upon horses not one in three of which would ever in any other way be made useful to the Government."

If Governor Andrew and Colonel Russell approved his plan, and Captain Adams trusted that they would forward that approval to the War Department, Adams, for his part, as soon as he received approval of the plan and his commission from the governor, would "wait upon Generals Meade and Grant in relation to the matter, and immediately thereafter obtain leave to go to Washington for to press it upon the attention of Secretary Stanton and General Halleck." If Adams's proposed interviews with Messrs. Meade, Grant, Stanton, and Halleck seems brash for a mere captain of cavalry, it should be remembered that he was in command of the cavalry escort for the Headquarters of the Army of the Potomac and thus in daily contact with Generals Grant and Meade. He was also, after all, an Adams from Massachusetts and son of Lincoln's ambassador to Great Britain. Adams thought that in any case, he would force the issue and "discover whether it is the intention of the Government to do anything toward mounting the regiment or not." His proposal seemed to him the best course and "but a slight recognition of the gallant and universally acknowledged service of the regiment" on 15 June. As may be expected, Governor Andrew was quick to "heartily condone the suggestion and approve the course proposed by Lieutenant Colonel Adams."

While Captain Adams was waiting for promotion and approval of his plan and reaching out for every string he could pull, matters got somewhat lively at Point Lookout. Captain Charles Bowditch wrote his sister Charlotte on 11 August. Bowditch had heard nothing as yet about his resignation, although General Barnes had forwarded it to Washington. Despite his illness, Bowditch was still able to ride a horse. He reported that he was "acting as Field Officer of the day, whose duty it is to ride round and round the point from morning to night and from night till morning, with an orderly tagging on behind." Actually, Bowditch was too self-deprecatory. The position of field officer of the day was a responsible one, not only in command of the defenses of the post but also overall command of the guard detail. All was routine, but a few days before, that routine had been interrupted: "One of our men shot a rebel prisoner the other day for refusing to obey the prescribed regulations." The trooper had been "entirely exonerated" by the officer in command of the guard detail, and yet the soldier was put in the guardhouse while the matter was investigated. "It is a pretty way to urge men to do their duty," Bowditch wrote.

Two Confederate prisoners recorded the event in their diaries. Sergeant Bartlett Yancey Malone, Company H, 6th North Carolina Infantry, was captured on 7 November 1863. His diary is noted for its brevity, lack of emotion, and phonetic spelling of speech patterns. Malone recorded, "The knight of the 7th a Negro Sentinel shot one of our men and killed him for no cause attal." Private Charles Warren Hutt of Westmoreland County, Virginia, wrote on "Sunday, August 7, 1864. Clear and very warm. For breakfast beef and chocolate. The latter made me very sick. A man belonging to the Twenty-Fifth Virginia Infantry was shot this evening by the Negro Sentry killing him instantly for no provocation whatever."

It was perhaps natural that a few of the guards at Point Lookout would abuse their authority. It is natural that a few among many would be bullies or quick tempered or interpret their instructions with absolute literalness. Perhaps more natural was the very human desire for revenge—revenge against the perceived oppressors of one's very race. Revenge, what's more, that carried no fear of retribution and little condemnation from one's superiors—that is, so long as that revenge (or literal obedience to orders) was not abused. Sergeant Malone made another entry in his diary three weeks later: "The 28th of August a Senternal shot a nother one of our men wounded him very badly it is thought that he will die." These two shootings prompted General Barnes to take action. He issued General Order No. 46 on 29 August 1864. Barnes felt the need to reiterate the army's policy toward shooting prisoners:

While the sentinels on post are to be held to a strict responsibility for their obedience to the orders they may receive, they will also be held responsible for any unauthorized act which they may commit. The wanton and unnecessary shooting at prisoners of war for slight offenses will be severely punished. The general good order which the prisoners of war at this post have observed entitles them to the protection of the Government, and any trifling or unimportant disobedience of a sentinel's orders on the part of a prisoner can be corrected in some other way than by shooting at him, by which the lives of others entirely innocent of any offense are endangered. Firing upon a prisoner can only be justified in extreme cases, and when the offense is of a serious nature, leading to mutiny or disorder among the prisoners. The officer commanding the guard will be held responsible that the sentinels are fully instructed in all their duties, and in this respect particularly.

It is possible to find some humor in this situation, not in the murder of helpless prisoners of war, but in the dramatic role reversal of black guards and white prisoners. William Wells Brown, the African American writer whose *The Negro in the American Rebellion: His Heroism and His Fidelity* provides many fascinating songs and scenes from the war, related this anecdote: "A Virginia rebel, who has issued a book giving his experience as a prisoner in the hands of the federals at Point Lookout and Elmira, tells the following story:—'The boys are laughing at the summons which S., one of my fellow-Petersburgers, got to-day from a negro sentinel.'" The Confederate's friend had on a tall beaver hat when captured, a hat "of the antique pattern considered inseparable from extreme respectability in the last decade and for many a year before." While wandering about the Bull Pen, seeking no doubt "something to devour," said friend

> *accidentally stepped beyond the "dead line," and was suddenly arrested by a summons from the nearest negro on the parapet, who seemed to be in doubt whether so well-dressed a man could be a "reb," and therefore whether he should be shot at once.*
>
> *"White man, you b'long in dar?"*
>
> *"Yes."*
>
> *"Well, ain't you got no better sense dan to cross dat line?"*
>
> *"I did not notice the line."*
>
> *"Well, you had better notice it, and dat quick, or I'll blow half dat nail-kag off!"*

Sergeant N. F. Harman of the 52nd Georgia, who arrived at Point Lookout in October 1864, told another story. Describing the guard details at night, he reports that there were two African American soldiers, armed with rifles and revolvers, for each division of a thousand men. "Every one had to be in his tent when 'taps' was sounded and all lights had to be put out, and talking was not permitted." Sometimes, Harmon writes, "these negro patrols call[ed] men out of their tents and chas[ed] them up and down the streets until they were exhausted." Harman claimed that "one night," two of these patrols, "after running one poor fellow until he could barely move, ordered him to his tent, but before he reached it, one of them called out:

Hold on dar, hold on; come back here!
[The 5th Massachusetts trooper then said to the prisoner:]
What's your sister's name and wher she lib? I want to write to her."

Harman also notes a more serious incident, although once again he does not record the date: "One night one of these patrols shot into a tent and killed two men. When the officer came rushing in to see what was the matter, the negro said he shot into the tent to make the prisoners stop talking." Harmon asserts that the men in the tent were asleep and that "nothing was ever done to this negro patrol for the murder of two men who were asleep when shot."

Confederate soldiers in general felt humiliated and enraged by the very presence of African American soldiers. Evidence suggests that the ones driven most wild by the existence of black troopers were the rebel officers. One such was Captain Robert E. Park of the 12th Alabama Regiment. Park was wounded and captured at the Battle of Winchester, 19 September 1864. Transported first to Baltimore, Park arrived at Point Lookout on 23 November 1864. Captain Park kept a diary, which was published by the Southern Historical Society in the 1870s. In his diary entry of 9 December 1864, Park noted the visit of an enlisted man to the officers' enclosure: "Alfred Parkins, of Winchester, a prisoner in the 'Bull Pen,' as the quarters of the privates is designated, came to see Lieutenant Arrington, having as a guard over him a coal-black, brutal-looking negro soldier, an escaped 'contraband'; as Beast Butler styles the stolen and refugee slaves from the South." Parkins acquainted the Confederate officers with the bad conditions in the Bull Pen—poor food, few blankets, men in rags, and little wood provided for fires. Parkins told Captain Park that "several of the negro soldiers guarding them were once slaves of some of the prisoners, and have been recognized as such." Some of these former slaves were still "respectful, and call their young owners 'master', and declare they were forced to enlist," Parkins related. A majority, however, were proud of what Captain Park called "their so-called freedom." The Confederate captain condemned them as "insolent and overbearing." According to Captain Park, the African American troopers of the 5th Cavalry "frequently" fired into the prisoners "upon the slightest provocation." A few days before, Park noted, a prisoner had been shot by a black soldier as the prisoner "walked slowly and faithfully from sheer debility away from the foul sinks to his tent, simply because he did not and could not obey his imperative order to 'move on faster dar.'" Instead of being court-martialed for this "wanton murder" (no record of which exists, by the way), the "villain" was seen a few days later "exulting in his promotion to a corporalcy." Captain Park believed that the posting of black troops to Point Lookout was a deliberate policy of the War Department and the Union government. "This employment of former slaves to guard their masters is intended to insult and degrade the latter. Such petty malice and cowardly vengeance could originate only in ignoble minds."

It seems a far stretch to believe that the War Department would purposefully send men known to be former slaves to guard men known to be their former masters who had been taken prisoner, particularly when the 5th Massachusetts was raised in the North and arrived at Point Lookout, it would seem, by chance. Perhaps it is as far a stretch as believing that freedmen, in the uniform of the U.S. Army and carrying weapons, would be respectful and use the term "master."

Captain Charles Adams, still commanding the cavalry escort (Company D of the 1st Massachusetts Cavalry) of Generals Meade and Grant, had not been idle while Charles Bowditch and others recorded the incidents of life at Point Lookout. On 8 August, he obtained an interview with the commander of the Army of the Potomac, Major General George Meade. His manner of obtaining that interview is once more indicative of the closely connected nature of nineteenth-century society. Lieutenant Colonel Theodore Lyman was a Bay Stater from an influential and affluent family and a Harvard classmate of Adams. Lyman was also on the staff of General Meade. Adams was all informality when he sent a note to Lyman requesting the meeting:

> *My Theodore: Is the big "Injun" approachable to-day? If he be and is good naturedly disposed to the little papooses, one of the smallest of that, I would like to wait on him in a matter of business. Time with me grows short and precious, and I shall be relieved if you would designate some hour to-day at which it would be well for me to grovel in the pine cuttings of the great man's tent.*

Adams's interview with General Meade went well, for he left for Washington not long after. Captain Bowditch, for one, eagerly anticipated the arrival of the two senior officers of the regiment. Writing to his father on 14 August, he noted of Adams, "I shall be very glad to see him again, for, though he is rather quick in his manner, he has always been very kind and pleasant to me." The Bowditch brothers were well acquainted with Adams before the war. Charles Bowditch also inquired as to the health of Colonel Russell. "I hope he will recover soon so that he may come here, for the regiment needs him exceedingly." Morale in the regiment was not good due to its dismounted status as well as an absence of officers. The regiment had only half its complement of officers present. "This system of detailing officers is carried to an outrageous extent," Bowditch wrote. The difficult job of leading a company of troopers was hard enough with three line officers; it was more of a burden when one or more were absent on other duties. "From our regiment at the present time," he noted, "there are detailed away from the regiment, so that they do not attend to regimental duties, the following officers: four on court martial, one on building stables, one as Assistant Provost Marshal, one as Recruiting Officer, one as Commissary of prisoners, one as General Barnes's staff, while eleven are sick or away from the regiment, and there are two or three vacancies, making twenty-three or twenty-four officers who are unable to do any duty in this camp."

Charles Adams had been quite successful with General Meade, for as he wrote to his mother, the general "not only approved it [the plan] himself but gave me a letter of introductions to General Grant, with which I next day went down and presented myself to the Lieutenant General." Adams met Grant the following morning sitting in front of his tent chatting with a few of his staff. "He told me to be seated," Adams explained, "read my letter, thought an instant puffing at his eternal cigar and stroking his beard as he listened to what I had to say and then replied in a short decided way: 'I will approve your plan and request the secretary to issue you the horses and have an order made out for you to go to Washington to attend to it yourself.'" This was, as Adams wrote, "three times what I had expected to get from him."

All was not so smooth in Washington, however, as Adams continued in his letter: "Then, and for the next week, I went through all the disgusting routine of one who waits upon those in power, dangling my heels in anterooms, on the walls of which I patiently studied maps and photographs, and those in high places shoved me from one to another as is their wont in such cases." Adams saw Colonel James Hardie, chief of staff to Secretary Stanton, who sent him to Assistant Secretary of War Charles A. Dana. Major Weld was ordered to Washington on 21 August to report to Assistant Secretary of War Dana, doubtless to inform him of the condition of the regiment and to strengthen Adams's case. "Dana suggested Colonel this or General that," Adams wrote, "but distinctly disapproved of my scheme." Stymied at Assistant Secretary Dana's, Adams hung around outside Secretary Stanton's office, hoping to be admitted to the "holy of holies." Colonel Hardie, wearying of Adams's presence, suggested he request an interview with General Halleck. "In an evil moment," Adams noted ruefully, "I allowed myself to be beguiled into stating my business to General Halleck." That "crusty cuss" gave Adams rather short shrift: "In about one minute he signified an emphatic disapproval of me and of my plan, and of General Grant and of everything else, and concluded an emphatic statement that he wouldn't give me a horse, if he had his own way, without a positive order, by slamming the door in my face." Another man would have been offended, perhaps have given up, and while true that Adams felt "somewhat depressed in spirit," he felt no animosity toward Halleck. On the contrary, Adams "derived a grim satisfaction from the reflection that if such was my reception by General Halleck, what must be the fate of the harpies and vultures who flock round the War Department[?]" Possessed with more than a modicum of vinegar in his own character, Charles Adams wrote, "It isn't pleasant to be roughed out of a man's office and it's decidedly unpleasant to have one's pet scheme trampled under foot before one's eyes, and then kicked out of doors; but I do like to see a man who can say 'no' and say it with an emphasis, and for old Halleck's capacity in this respect I can vouch."

Nevertheless, Adams had no other recourse but to return to Secretary Stanton's office and hope that Colonel Hardie would be weary enough of him to show him mercy. Eventually Adams's patience and Grant's letter won him Stanton's endorsement, although he never did get in to speak to the secretary. On 27 August 1864, Special Order No. 299 gave First Lieutenant Windsor Hatch, regimental quartermaster, "permission to visit Washington for the purpose of procuring ordnance and ordnance stores, and quartermaster's stores, necessary to remount the Fifth Massachusetts Cavalry." Lieutenant Colonel Adams turned over his cavalry escort command and took the U.S. Military Railroad from the Army of the Potomac Headquarters to City Point, whence he took a steamer to Point Lookout. He took command of the regiment on 8 September 1864, almost concurrently with the arrival of the first draft of horses. After almost four months of service in the field, the 5th Massachusetts was cavalry in fact as well as name.

CHAPTER SEVEN

"He Had No Effects"

Cavalry Crossing a Ford
A line in long array where they wind betwixt green islands,
They take a serpentine course, their arms flash in the sun—hark to
the musical clank,
Behold the silvery river, in it the splashing horses loitering stop
to drink,
Behold the brown-faced men, each group, each person a picture, the
negligent rest on the saddles,
Some emerge on the opposite bank, others are just entering the ford—while,
Scarlet and blue and snowy white,
The guidon flags flutter gayly in the wind.
—Walt Whitman

THERE WAS AN ALMOST TIDAL ASPECT TO THE EBB AND FLOW OF OFFICERS
and men into the 5th Massachusetts Cavalry. A large batch of recruits had
been added to the regiment in May and June 1864; as the summer wore
on and gave way to autumn, men were leaving. Captain Charles Pickering
Bowditch spent days in Washington working on getting out of the army.
Prior to his discharge he visited the Pay Department, the Adjutant General's Office, the Quartermaster's Office, and the Ordnance Office. Bowditch
went to some of these offices more than once because he had to account for
government property issued to his company as well as settle all his personal
accounts. He finally cut through all the red tape on 23 August. His letters
reveal much of his nature: hardworking, cheerful, an essentially decent young

man. His conscientiousness and good eye for detail surely made him a solid officer. Respectful but with an unforced, natural affection, he was a good son, brother, and comrade.

First Lieutenant Jacob Cook of Company D also resigned in August, citing physical disability. Major Weld approved that resignation "for the good of the service," which leads one to believe that Cook's resignation may not have been completely voluntary. Lieutenant Cook left in mid-September, around the same time that a group of troopers were recommended by the regimental surgeon (those recommendations in turn approved by the Point Lookout post surgeon) to be discharged for disability.

The afflictions of the men ran the gamut. The most serious appears to have been Private George W. Gool of Company A, who was discharged for a cancerous tumor on the back of his neck. In what seems a far less serious matter, Private George Wilson, Company A, got his discharge for obesity. These group discharges also occurred in October, November, and December. Men were certainly becoming ill to the point that, for the good of the service, they should be discharged, but one does wonder how long some of those conditions had persisted. Troopers were also discharged individually for disability. The Adjutant General's Office issued Special Order No. 301 discharging First Sergeant Charles Remond Douglass, Company I, 5th Massachusetts Volunteer Cavalry, on 10 September 1864. Douglass, like many of his fellow soldiers in the regiment, succumbed to dysentery. He was honorably discharged on 15 September.

Lieutenant Colonel Adams sent his first letter to his family from Point Lookout on 18 September. Charles Adams had had three years of the most difficult service, and he held himself to the highest and most rigorous standard as an officer and a gentleman. He did not suffer gladly those who could not meet the standards he set for discipline and efficiency, whether officer or enlisted man. Moreover, Adams certainly never expected that his private letters to his parents and siblings would end up in print for the whole world to see. In the 18 September letter to his brother Henry, Adams confessed that the week had not been exciting; they rarely were at Point Lookout. Adams had taken command, was busy, "and so kept contented." He was "organizing" and saw matters "daily growing and improving," which kept him "quiet and satisfied." He was happy with his officers, who knew "their duty and are well disposed and zealous." Adams then chose to poke fun at his African

American troopers, writing with a biting sarcasm, "As for the 'nigs' they are angelic—in all respects. I am now convinced the race is superior to the whites." Adams found his soldiers' philosophy of life "sounder in that it is more attainable." All the men wished for was plenty to eat and plenty of sleep. "Send a Corporal to take charge of a working party and go down in ten minutes to see how they're coming on, you'll find them all asleep and the Corporal leading the snore." Adams also found the physical appearance of his men amusing: "Then they're built so much better than white men. Their feet—you never saw such feet!" The feet of some of his men were so large, Adams related, that they preferred to walk in the fields as the roads were too narrow. The heads of his men were also huge. "A white man's head is flat, but they—sometimes when they uncover in the sacred precincts of my quarters I think that the highest pinnacle of their sugar loaf craniums will never be exposed."

As commanding officer of the regiment in Harry Russell's absence, Lieutenant Colonel Adams was necessarily removed from contact with the majority of his men. He thus saw them in the general mass, not as individuals. It is to his detriment, however, that he chose in an attempt at humor to repeat the bigoted stereotypes of his era about blacks. Colonel Adams did check himself and made a more serious and reasoned assessment of his new command to his brother: "Jesting apart, however, my first impression of this poor, humiliated, down-trodden race is both favorable and kindly. They lack the pride, spirit and intellectual energy of the whites, partly from education and yet more by organization; but they are sensitive to praise or blame, and yet more so to ridicule. They are diffident and eager to learn; they are docile and naturally polite, and in them, I think, I see immeasurable capacity for improvement."

Adams admitted that these were only his first impressions, but it seemed to him that his men were better approached with kindness and affection than by the "rugged discipline which improves whites." Adams wrote that the easy course would be to "crush them into slaves, but very difficult by kindness and patience to approach them to our own standard." This seemed a tall order to Adams, who knew himself well. "Patience, kindness and self-control have not been my characteristics as an officer, any more than they have been characteristics of ourselves as a dominant race." Time would tell, but Adams had "little hope" for African Americans "in their eternal contact with a race like ours."

As Lieutenant Colonel Adams had noted to his brother, he was busy "organizing" the 5th Massachusetts Cavalry. Adams issued Special Order No. 160 on 22 September, "for the government of company commanders in making out morning reports, to insure an equal division of duties among the companies of this command." Some officers, apparently, were not sure how to account for their men. Blacksmiths were to be reported under the head of "Farriers." Tailors and saddlers were supposed to be reported under "Artificers." There seemed to be some confusion about the morning report form, particularly the difference between the categories "Present for Duty" and "Present, on Daily Duty." The former meant present in the company and thus under the orders of the line officers—that is to say, present as a cavalry trooper, ready to fight. The latter meant present on regimental detail and therefore not under the orders of company officers. "Two cooks in each company, a company clerk and such enlisted men as company officers employ as servants, (including mess cooks) will be reported as 'present' and on 'daily duty' and no other men will be reported as on daily duty except such as are detailed by orders from Regimental Headquarters such as hospital attendants, members of the band (musicians) orderlies of field and staff, etc." Reporting procedures must have become rather lax, for Adams felt it necessary to order "all enlisted men incapacitated physically or mentally, from regular [duty] will not be reported as 'cooks' or otherwise but will be examined by the surgeon and reported 'present.'"

Having clarified the reporting procedures and presumably brought detailed and detached men back to the regiment, Colonel Adams now did his own detailing in Special Order No. 161, 23 September 1864. Four privates were detailed to the post surgeon as hospital attendants, Corporal John L. Brown of Company H was detailed as regimental forage master, and Adams chose Private George Washington, Company E, to act as his orderly. The most important assignment handed out in Special Order 161 was that given to Sergeant J. F. Brooks of Company E, "to act as Regimental color bearer until further orders." Brooks was exempt from all other duties. This was a good way to build morale: to give a man a prestigious and dangerous job, because the enemy would be keying on and hoping to capture the colors, and to let unit pride grow through him.

Charles Adams wrote to his brother Henry on 23 September, mostly to crow over Sheridan's recent victory at Winchester and Sherman's successes in Georgia. He did give an idea of the state of the 5th Massachusetts Cavalry, however: "Here everything is quiet all day long, and every day I live surrounded by my 'nigs' and very busy, for everything is to be done and be done by me." Adams lamented the lack of skills among his men; he first had to teach himself a job before showing his men how to do it. "For instance, with 700 horses here I didn't have one tolerable blacksmith. Before a horse could be shod I had to go to work and show the smiths what a good horseshoe is." Adams felt that Colonel Russell's long absence and his own delay in arrival had let the regiment "fall into arrears, and the officers have never been under one able commander long enough to become homogenous." Adams was bringing organization to the regiment by "pulling things to pieces and building up" with all his might. Left alone, he was convinced of his ultimate success. Colonel Russell was due to report back to the 5th Massachusetts any day, however, and "he may go to work anew in his way, perhaps better than mine, but still another and unfortunate change."

Adams's intelligence on Colonel Russell was reliable. He reported back to the regiment on 29 September, three and a half months after his wounding. Major Zabdiel Adams, who had been shot in the chest at Baylor's Farm, had returned to the regiment in mid-August. By the beginning of October 1864, for the first time since the 5th Massachusetts was authorized, the regiment had its full complement of officers: colonel, lieutenant colonel, three majors, twelve captains, and twenty-seven lieutenants. Several officers joined the regiment at Point Lookout, balancing resignations and promotions. The Reverend Isaac Cushman, who had tried unsuccessfully to secure the chaplaincy of the regiment the previous winter, was appointed assistant surgeon on 6 September, replacing a doctor who had resigned in May. Lieutenant Colonel Adams got Governor Andrew to commission two sergeants from his old squadron of the 1st Massachusetts in late September: John H. George, who had been a spinner in Salem, New Hampshire, and William A. Hatch, a clerk in Boston before the war. Both became second lieutenants. Hatch was twenty-five; George, who had survived three years of war, had just turned twenty. Even younger than John George was Robert S. Oliver, who was only seventeen. It is not clear who sent Second Lieutenant Oliver, a Massachusetts native, to the 5th Massachusetts, whether it was Governor Andrew, the Adjutant General's Office, or at his own request. Lieutenant Oliver, who had service in the regular army after the war, began his military career with a volunteer regiment of black cavalry.

Soldiers in garrison are notorious for getting in trouble; that is, those inclined to stray—and there are always a few—are almost certain to find temptation in some form. St. Mary's District Special Order No. 314 of 17 September gives a glimpse of one such temptation. General Barnes ordered, "The following named colored women living near the camp of the Massachusetts Cavalry and reported as disreputable, are required to leave this district without delay." The order named Harny Queen, Rose Garden (surely noms de guerre?), Betsy Barnes, Amy Vicerrse, and Mary Ford. Provost Marshall Brady was charged with executing the order.

Colonel Russell put himself firmly in the saddle upon his return, immediately promulgating a fourteen-paragraph order, "Regulations for the Stable." The fourteenth paragraph of this order demonstrates its tone: "The proper cleaning of a horse will occupy a good groom about thirty minutes. There is much ignorance of what good grooming is in this regiment at present and awkward and unsystematic ways of going to work on a horse, combined with a most improper use of the brush and comb are of constant occurrence. Men are daily seen, currying horses knees and hocks. In view of the great importance of making good grooms of the men of this regiment a careful recurrence to and study of the best theoretical treatise on grooming which can here be procured is strongly recommended to aid officers."

With a full complement of officers, men, and horses, the 5th Massachusetts now began training in earnest as cavalry at Point Lookout. There was no immediate prospect for action, but the regiment trained hard, stood guard duty over prisoners, and defended the post. Colonel Russell was meticulous, but he was no martinet. One officer who testified that his African American troopers truly loved Harry Russell was a newly minted second lieutenant from Concord named Edward Jarvis Bartlett. "Ned" Bartlett, as he was known to his family, had had an interesting war prior to 2 October 1864 when he reported to Company E, 5th Massachusetts. Bartlett was twenty-two years old in 1864; he had already served as an enlisted man with the 4th Battalion of Massachusetts Rifles in 1861 and the 44th Massachusetts Infantry, a nine months' regiment, in North Carolina. Bartlett spent the fall and winter of 1863 on the staff of Major George L. Stearns recruiting African American troops in Nashville, Tennessee. Although he was a paid civilian volunteer, Bartlett had had some experience marching and bivouacking with black troops as they moved about the countryside collecting suitable men for the U.S. Colored Troops. Bartlett had applied for a commission in the 5th Massachusetts Cavalry in January 1864 but was turned down. He had sponsors among his friends in Concord, notably the Emerson family, but no cavalry experience, and he was not even in the Bay State at the time. Major Stearns resigned from recruiting in February 1864, and Bartlett transferred to the U.S. Sanitary Commission in Washington, DC. Bartlett worked through the terrible summer of 1864 as a clerk in the Sanitary Commission's office on H Street in Washington, on hospital transports and in the hospitals, as a stretcher bearer, writing letters for wounded soldiers, dispensing tracts and Bibles, and giving out crackers and coffee.

Governor Andrew signed Bartlett's commission in July, but he did not join the regiment as second lieutenant of Company E until October, perhaps because he was so needed at the Sanitary Commission or because it took so long for his commission to reach him. In any case, the young lieutenant adjusted well to life with an African American cavalry regiment at Point Lookout. Bartlett was a faithful correspondent, usually writing home once a week. He wrote his second letter to his family from Point Lookout on 15 October. Bartlett wrote of the small incidents that made up the days and weeks at the Point. After a spell of rain and cold, the weather had moderated. Bartlett had had his hut, a shelter tent on top of a timber square, sheathed in preparation for the winter. He had "lined the inside with shelter tents, so the sides are white and clean; the fire place is opposite the door, the bed and wood box on the right side; opposite is my table and wardrobe that I constructed out of an ordinance box." The previous night a hard rain had fallen. His roof had proved "tight as a drum." He was well pleased with his living quarters; everything was "as jolly as I could wish." Bartlett was acquainted with fellow Concord residents Lieutenants Charles P. Wheeler and Robert Oliver. There was also an acquaintance known to the folks at home: "I wrote to you that there was a Captain Welch in the regiment, he is the oldest man among us and we call him father. He used to know Jim in Lowell and is all the time talking about him and more particularly about his wife. . . . He used to think that she was the best girl living." Captain Horace B. Welch was not the oldest line officer at thirty-two, just one of them. Welch, it will be recalled, had enlisted in San Francisco in the "California Battalion" of the 2nd Massachusetts Cavalry.

Lieutenant Bartlett seemed to enjoy the cavalry. He had thrown himself into training his horse to respond to knee and rein pressure (this left the trooper's hands free for his weapons) and found moonlit rides along the beach "glorious." Bartlett had availed himself of one of the perquisites of white soldiers, not always officers, south of the Mason-Dixon Line: "I have procured a stricker [striker] (camp phrase for servant). . . . He is a very black boy, about fifteen years old named John Goff." Young Goff took care of Bartlett's living quarters, shined his boots and brushed his uniform, fetched wood and water and ran errands. "For this I pay him $12.00 per month and I assure you he is a most useful arrangement."

One duty that his servant did not do for him was groom his horse. This did not bother Bartlett greatly since he liked that time of day and the surroundings. "Just at sunrise, we are on stable duty and the stables are near the shore. . . . Yesterday the sea was splendid, the surf ran very big as a strong wind was blowing." The waves made him think of his sister Martha, who loved the seashore. He thought of her often, "as I have the water before my eyes all the time." Bartlett watched the sun rise out of the ocean every morning, "and it is a glorious sight though I wish some of the cold mornings that I was in bed." On the whole, however, Ned Bartlett made little complaint. He did ask his family to send him a Boston paper and any magazines they were done with at home. "Reading matter is scarce here, and although my chief reading matter is Cook's Tactics & the Army regulations, which are very well in their way, but then a little light reading would be acceptable."

Bartlett wrote his sister Martha on 23 October. He had not written his usual midweek letter as a consequence of coming off guard duty, and he "spent the little of the morning that was left resting and cleaning up." He reported that Secretary of War Stanton, Major General Augur, and General Barnes had reviewed the 5th Massachusetts and the other regiments at Point Lookout on the 19th. Interestingly, Bartlett did not comment on the inspection, but rather on the picket detail (a corporal and three men) he took out after the inspection. Bartlett's picket post was up the road in a pine grove about half a mile from the 5th Massachusetts camp. "It is not posted to guard against the advance of the enemy, but to guard against an enemy almost as fatal as the rebels: it is to prevent whiskey being brought into the camp."

The men had found ways of getting alcohol into camp, and Colonel Russell was determined to put a stop to it. Bartlett and his detail stopped everyone coming toward the post but made only one arrest. "In one wagon I found four bottles, I froze to them [a curious nineteenth-century phrase probably derived from hunting] and sent them down to the Colonel." Bartlett "enjoyed the day very much in the woods." The detail camped overnight near their post, and Bartlett found the experience "quite like old Newbern [North Carolina] times—at night sleeping on the ground with plenty of blankets and a large fire—I never rested better."

The days were getting colder and shorter at Point Lookout; Reveille, at 5:30 a.m., was pitch dark and chilly. "It's going to be cold enough here this winter," wrote Bartlett. He was pleased with his hut, though. Lieutenant Bob Oliver came over every night after Taps, and "we sit and tell tales over the fire, talking over old times and speculating on new ones." Oliver had been promoted to first lieutenant after less than a month with the regiment, which speaks well of him as well as of any military training he had prior to his appointment. Bartlett was learning about being an officer: "I am fast learning the names of my men and also their characters and dispositions, who are the good soldiers and who are the shirks—for there are some of the latter, even in the Fifth Cavalry." Bartlett had a couple of generalizations about the men of Company E. The troopers could "bear being treated well and kindly but they must be kept at a distance," as they were more prone than white soldiers to "take advantage of a favor." Bartlett and his fellow company officers, Captain James Wheat and First Lieutenant Edward H. Adams, were "fortunate in having a good company—a set of men as a class who are disposed to do well." Bartlett was not too impressed with Captain Wheat; he thought he lacked force. Lieutenant Adams he liked. Lieutenant Adams was a "fine fellow and officer—but," he noted to his sister, "this is against regulations to talk of superiors."

Despite regulations, Bartlett felt he must tell Martha how popular Colonel Russell was. Russell was "loved by the officers and worshipped by the men—I have never heard a word of complaint against him since I have been here." Colonel Russell was never seen "except in line of duty. He is very quiet and reserved but he sees and knows all that goes on." Bartlett reported that Colonel Russell was having a house built "out of real boards" and that before long, Mrs. Russell would come to Point Lookout. "This is the rumor and no doubt it is the truth." Bartlett felt that he and his fellow officers would be glad to see her, not that they would come in contact with her, but the sight of any woman would be welcome. "I should not be surprised," Bartlett wrote, "if some other of the officers would follow his example."

Charles Francis Adams was considering marriage, as he described in his autobiography how he traveled to Newport, Rhode Island, in the winter of 1864 and became engaged. However, as the autumn of 1864 wore on, Adams was ill, probably with dysentery, possibly with malaria: "I went to the Headquarters [Army of the Potomac] a perfectly well man; but the seeds of malarial disease were, I imagine, implanted, and during the summer of 1864, I began slowly to break down." Adams attributed his illness to "incessant feeding on hard-tack and meat freshly killed and fried in pork-fat, and the inordinate drinking of black coffee—quarts of it, each day. We all did so; we and the medical men evincing an equal lack of either knowledge of or regard for the most elementary rules of hygiene." At Point Lookout, Adam's illness "grew rapidly on me." He took sick leave in November, returned in December, and left again in January. It was on that January leave that Adams became engaged to Miss Mary Ogden of Newport. He married her in 1867.

Adams wrote his father on 2 November, about two weeks before he obtained his first sick leave. His father had evidently asked him to describe life at Point Lookout. "A safer residence or one to my mind less inviting could not well be found," Adams wrote. Point Lookout was a "low, sandy, malarious, fever-smitten, wind-blown, god-forsaken tongue of land dividing Chesapeake Bay from the Potomac River." Adams found Point Lookout "remarkably well adapted for a depot of prisoners, as it is not only notoriously unhealthy, but most easily guarded." Adams wrote of the peninsula that was almost an island, of the Union gunboats, and of the Confederate prisoners who did not seem to have a strong desire to escape. "To be sure they do not here live in luxury, but neither do they starve, and judging by appearances, for they look tough and well, imprisonment does not disagree with them." Adams described the stockades for the prisoners as "large enclosures, containing several acres, surrounded by a board fence some fifteen feet high, round the outside of which sentinels are posted. From this vantage ground they observe the proceedings of our deluded brethren and shoot them, if necessary." Adams noted that many of the prisoners arrived at Point Lookout wounded or sick. There were presently some 2,800 patients in the

Confederate hospital, but he had no idea of the rate of mortality. "Heavy or not [the death rate], with a view to encourage new comers, I presume, there is always kept piled up close to the main entrance some eighty or one hundred ready made coffins."

The camp of the 5th Massachusetts was further up the point about a mile from the prison pens. "Here we look after our horses, build houses, dig wells and stagnate." Perhaps because of that inactivity or his illness— or because he had a naturally patrician and philosophic turn of mind— Lieutenant Colonel Adams wrote some rather unflattering things about his African American troopers. "I'm gradually getting to have very decided opinions on the negro question; they're growing up in me as inborn convictions and are not the result of reflection. . . . The conviction is forcing itself upon me that African slavery, as it existed in our slave states, was indeed a patriarchal institution, under which the slaves were not unhappy, cruelly treated or overworked." Adams was quick to point out to his father that this conclusion did not approve of slavery, the effects of which were "ruinous and demoralizing to both races and because swine may be well fed and happy in their filth, I do not argue that it is good to be hog-reeve or hog." Adams based his opposition to slavery on the "broader principle, that, happy or unhappy, it is not good for either that one man should be master and another slave; that such an arrangement is diametrically opposed to the spirit of modern progress and civilization." Nevertheless, history had shown that "no mortal people of any known race or color" would long endure "systematic cruel treatment." Sooner or later an oppressed group or race would "break out at last and always with a fierceness proportioned to the length and severity of previous ill-usage." As proof, Adams pointed to the French peasant uprising of 1789, the Haitian Revolution of 1798, and the Indian Mutiny of 1857. No such rising, no race or (in the case of France) class war had occurred in the United States. "Here, after all sorts of efforts to stimulate them, after arms are thrust into their hands, as the last result of two hundred years of slavery, they are as supine as logs or animals." Adams concluded that either African Americans did not possess even the spirit of "the lowest order of known animals" and could not be "tortured into resistance to oppression" or "the two hundred years of slavery through which they have passed was that of the patriarchal type which left the race as a whole, not overworked, well fed and contented—greedy animals!" Adams pointed to his own regiment and "the ugly characters in it" to support his explanation "of this wonderful supineness."

Having satisfactorily explained (to himself, at least) the state of the black race in America, Adams turned to the effects of the war on African Americans. He saw military service as their "only chance of salvation." Blacks made good soldiers, "particularly in those branches of the service where a high order of intelligence is less required. Negro infantry, properly officered, would I believe be as effective as any in the world." As far as cavalry was concerned, Adams was less sanguine. Like most bigots, self-confessed or not, he used generalizations and isolated examples to portray an entire group. These brutal generalizations are all the more striking coming from the grandson of John Quincy Adams, who as president and congressman threw Southerners into fits when the subject of the "peculiar institution" came up. Adams wrote:

> *After all a negro is not the equal of a white man. . . . He has not the mental vigor and energy, he cannot stand up against adversity. A sick nigger, for instance, at once gives up and lies down to die, the personification of humanity reduced to a wet rag. He cannot fight for life like a white man. In this regiment, if you degrade a negro who has once tried to do well, you had better shoot him at once, for he gives right up and never attempts to redeem himself. So his animal tendencies are greater than those of the whites. He must and will sleep; no danger from the enemy and no fear of punishment will keep him awake. In infantry, which acts in large masses, these things are of less consequence than in cavalry; but in the service which our cavalry does, where individual intelligence is everything, and single men in every exposed position have only themselves and their own nerve, intelligence and quickness to rely on, it is a very different thing.*

On the whole, which seems to be the root of his problem, Adams found blacks excellent soldiers in units, "but individually unreliable." We can only wonder what had prompted Adams to take the commission into the 5th Cavalry. What were his motivations? Perhaps we can imagine a scene in which Lieutenant Colonel Adams witnessed an enlisted man or men resting rather than working, thus invoking his wrath and leading him to stigmatize an entire race.

Lieutenant Colonel Adams's comments on the "negro question" and the suitability of African Americans for cavalry service were put aside as he neatly contradicted himself when he described the army as the "proper school of the race" in the latter part of his letter. Through necessity, soldiers in the 5th Massachusetts had to become competent "jacks of all trades." A day spent in the regiment's camp would amaze his father, Adams felt. "You cannot realize the industry, versatility and ingenuity called forth." With only axes and nails, the troopers cut down trees, split rails, rove shingles, and built both stables and houses. "Every blacksmith, every carpenter, every shoemaker, every tailor and every clerk is constantly busy, and those who can do nothing else dig and carry until they can do something better." Wells were being dug and pumps made for those wells. Bricks were being baked and chimneys constructed with plaster and mortar made of mud. "The large, open fireplace in my quarters evinces no little ingenuity and skilled labor. Such, in little, is what I hope to see the army become for the black race, a school of skilled labor and of self reliance, as well as an engine of war."

Adams, like Theophilus Parsons so many months before, saw the army as a potential educational institution and vocational school and hoped that fifteen to twenty thousand African Americans would be retained in the service after the war. After commenting on the excellent work his men were doing on fatigue duty, Adams assessed the troopers as soldiers, again contradicting his previous statements:

> Of the men here my conclusions are decidedly favorable. They are docile and take readily to discipline and a large percentage of them, fully as large as of the whites, are decidedly soldierly in their bearing. As horsemen, I think they are at least as good as the whites—better, if I might judge by the surprising manner in which our present lot of horses have improved in condition. We now have the best lot of horses, without exception, that I have ever seen in Virginia. Of the courage in action of these men, at any rate when acting in mass, there can no doubt exist; of their physical and mental and moral energy and stamina I entertain grave doubts. Retreat, defeat and exposure would tell on them more than on the whites. So far, as a whole, they more than fulfill every expectation which I entertained.

At Point Lookout, the topic of the first week of November was not the place of African Americans after the war but the presidential election. Captain Horace B. Welch, Lieutenant George D. Odell, two officers of the Veteran Reserve Corps, and several VRC enlisted men obtained leave to go home to New Hampshire to vote. It is presumed that other officers took advantage of home leave to vote as well. The 1864 election marked the first time states allowed soldiers in the field to vote. The black troopers, of course, had yet to receive this right. One of Governor Andrew's staff officers, J. H. Ware, who signed himself "Major, Asst. Adjt. Gen'l., Secretary," wrote on 19 September 1864 to "Priv. John D. Berry, 5th Mass. Cavalry, Point Lookout, Md.," in reply to his letter of the 15th (now lost) to "His Excellency the Governor," that "no provision has been made by law in this state for soldiers voting in the field." The *Weekly Anglo-African* weighed in with an editorial on the front page:

October 8, 1864

ARE COLORED SOLDIERS TO VOTE?

This question has often been put to us and we have invariably answered it this wise:

We have no idea that *all* colored soldiers are to be permitted to vote, though that they deserve the privilege and would exercise it in defence of freedom as well as they have the musket, we have not a shadow of doubt. Many persons seem to believe that the President can confer the right upon those who have heretofore been deprived of it; but this we look upon as a great mistake. Only those can be voters whom States through their Legislature or constitutional Conventions make such; and if this be the case, only those who were voters in their States before they enlisted for the war, can be voters now. We do not think that all Massachusetts soldiers can claim citizenship in that noble State; but her 54th and 55th Regiments, the 14th Rhode Island, now the 8th United States, and the 20th and 26th United States, do contain a great many legal voters; and we earnestly hope that the government will see to it that a poll is opened in these, and other colored regiments, that every legal vote may be secured.

We will not insult the intelligence of our colored soldiers by asking them to vote for ABRAHAM LINCOLN, for we know they will do that. They went to the South to fight for liberty and the Union, and we doubt that there exists a single man among them who would withhold his vote from the only man who now represents their principles in the canvass. Many of our soldiers have felt bitter toward the government, because they were kept so long without their pay; but *we know* that neither Mr. Lincoln or Mr. Stanton could help it. There were questions which had to be settled by Congress before the colored soldiers could receive their pay; and the moment those questions were settled and the government could make proper arrangements, the payment of the colored troops began. So let our gallant fellows have a chance to cast their votes; and we have no doubt that they will vote solid for LINCOLN and JOHNSON for LIBERTY and the UNION.

Ned Bartlett wrote his family on 13 November. He was "greatly delighted at the result of the election and think that it is a great thing that Lincoln carried the day." Bartlett also reported the arrival of Harry Russell's wife, Mary, with their baby and a nurse on 11 November. Russell had gone up to Washington, leaving all three installed in his newly completed house. "She won't see much female society here," Bartlett wrote, "but I suppose she won't be lonely with her husband, for she must love him a great deal to come down and live on this sandy point for the sake of being with him." A week later, Bartlett wrote his sister Martha from the "General Guard House." He was officer of the guard that day and had "charge of the ten thousand prisoners of war, also of my guard of over two hundred men which of the two is much the hardest to take care of." Bartlett was excited about the regiment's plans for celebrating Thanksgiving on 24 November. There was to be a "general holiday and the camp guard . . . taken off." Major Henry Bowditch, Assistant Surgeon Dr. Frederick G. Parker, and Captain C. Chauncy Parsons were the "committee of arrangement and they have got up a stunning programme," Bartlett noted. Reveille was to be replaced by music provided by the full band. From 10:00 a.m. to noon there was to be horse racing, both trotting and running, but only among the officers, as no government horses were yet to be risked at a gallop. Thanksgiving dinner with turkey and all the trimmings was to be served at noon to all the officers and men. The afternoon was filled with sack and wheelbarrow races, a jig-dancing competition, foot racing, a turkey shoot, and the climbing of greased poles. "A greased pig is to be let loose every half hour during the afternoon—whoever catches him has him." Prizes were offered for each competition, music was to play all day, and at 5:00 p.m. there was to be another regimental meal. "So you see that we are going to try to have a real New England Thanksgiving—and try to take off some of the disagreeableness of being here on that day."

Bartlett wrote his friend Edward Emerson almost two weeks later on 26 November. He was once again officer in charge of the guard and took the time to write and assess for him the past two months he had spent at Point Lookout. "I think that I have now been here long enough to render you an account of myself, to let you know how I get on as an officer! What I think of the regiment, etc. For I think that you are sufficiently interested in my military career to listen to my story, and my complaints also, if I have any to make." Edward Waldo Emerson was Ralph and Lydia Emerson's son. Born in 1844, he and Bartlett were contemporaries. In a few days, Bartlett would be two months as second lieutenant of Company E. "I had no idea how much I had to learn and how much more there is to be learnt."

Bartlett had arrived believing he knew what it meant to be an officer but soon realized he was mistaken, so he "set to work heart and soul and am still at it." Despite Lieutenant Bartlett's coming "green among a set of good officers, I have never enjoyed myself so much as I have for the past two months." He had "received kindness on every hand and have found aid whenever I wanted it." Bartlett arrived Sunday morning, 2 October 1864, walking through the sand to report to Colonel Russell. He had not walked since and resolved not to as long as there was a horse in E Company's stables. He was immediately assigned to his company and went with the men on water call that noon. "Next day, I went on drill which luckily happened to be simply marching in column so I had nothing to do but ride in my place and see how they did it."

For the first few weeks, Bartlett was completely ignorant of cavalry tactics and, worse, "I mixed it up in my mind with the little infantry tactics that I remembered." Soon "the light broke upon me," Bartlett wrote, and he had learned rapidly, to the point where he could take the troop out alone for drill. He enjoyed drill immensely, putting his men "through all the hardest evolutions we have learnt, at the walk, trot and gallop." Bartlett thought the company's horses "a fine lot—better than was expected." Colonel Russell had had the horses assigned by color to the different companies. "We have the blacks and there are not a better looking lot in the regiment." The regiment had stable call mornings and evenings, water call at noon, and conducted mounted drill in the afternoon. This made the regiment cavalry. "Now comes a complaint—A detail of over two hundred men go down every morning to the Point to guard the rebs." The regiment was infantry when it did this duty, as it continued to use infantry rifles and equipment. "Hurrah for the day that we shall throw aside our muskets for our sabres."

Bartlett also felt that the 5th Massachusetts had been "worked harder than any regiment that ever left the state." Officers and men had been "thrown right into the front and did fighting and outside picket duty." At Point Lookout the troopers continued to work hard. Enlisted men had guard duty every other day. A trooper rose at Reveille and had half an hour for breakfast, followed by stable duty for an hour before water call. If a man was going on guard duty, he had to clean his uniform and equipment preparatory to guard mount at 9:00 a.m. The guard detachment marched a mile and a half through the sand to the stockades and stood guard for twenty-four hours, "posted on the top of a high stockade with nothing to break the wind sweeping across from the bay to the river." (We can assume that only a portion of the entire guard detail was on duty at one time.) The guard was relieved the next morning but did not rest, marching back to camp in time for noon water call. Companies were inspected at 1:30 p.m., did mounted drill from 2:00 until the 3:30 stable call, which lasted until 5:00 p.m. A trooper's time was his own from the evening meal until Reveille the next day. "Of course this is nothing compared with what the regiments are doing at the front," Bartlett explained, "but then I only write it that you may see how little time we get for cavalry drill."

Life for the officers was somewhat less monotonous. Lieutenant Bartlett had received a "very polite invitation" from Mrs. Russell to call for tea. He reported her "very cordial and the Colonel idolized by both his officers and men." There were also opportunities for evening rides along the shore and in the pinewoods. Bartlett noted that his horse, Billy, suited him very well, "though I had a hard time learning and training him." He had taught the horse "army life—to reign [sic] perfectly, and to face a line of bayonets and not to run when he hears musketry—all of which he was sadly deficient in." The camp was still buzzing with the great success of the Thanksgiving festivities.

Four days later, on 30 November, Bartlett received a letter and package from his sister Martha, which prompted him to write. Everyone in his family at Concord had contributed to a Thanksgiving letter, and he thanked them for that and for the reading material they had sent him. More important, he had received a bundle made up by the Bartlett women as a present to his company. At Tattoo, the evening formation, he "told the men that I had received from home a bundle of towels sent as a present to the enlisted men of Company E. The men were formed into line by the first sergeant and marched up one by one to receive their gift. The troopers "all seemed pleased and grinned and said 'thank you.'" Afterward, First Sergeant Isaac Watson made a short speech thanking Lieutenant Bartlett on behalf of the company. "Such a little thing as that goes a great way and does a deal of good for them to see that they (although they are black) are not forgotten by the people at home. In behalf of the company, I thank all who assisted in procuring, making, marking and sending them."

Bartlett had become a good officer. His company commander had gone on fifteen days' leave. First Lieutenant E. H. Adams had been named regimental quartermaster, so First Lieutenant Rienzi Loud temporarily took command of Company E. Loud was usually on guard detail, so it was Bartlett who really ran the company. "The men come to me for everything and I am bound that the company shall lose nothing while Captain Wheat is away." Bartlett had directed the mounted drill that afternoon. "I wish I could always do it," he wrote. He was conscientious, attentive to duty, and considerate of the welfare of his men.

Appearing in the 3 December 1864 edition of the *Weekly Anglo-African*, "A. W.," presumably Sergeant Amos Webber, wrote with news from Point Lookout:

FROM THE 5TH REG'T MASS. CAVALRY

From the 5th Mass. Cavalry, Point Lookout, Md., Nov. 12, 1864.

Mr. Editor: It has been long since you have heard from the 5th, as my friend, "Africano," has stopt his masterly pen from furnishing the news to you on account of the pressure of business. Permit me to give you an item or two. Since we left the front near Petersburg, the regiment has been doing guard together with other regiments, guarding those gentlemen (rebels) who have come up to pay us a visit, and take a peep at their former slaves with Uncle Sam's clothes on, and armed with the instruments of war, glaring him in the face. Sometimes they meet in spite of the bitter feeling entertained toward each other. The regiment has pretty heavy duties to do. It is part infantry and part cavalry.

The number of men from this regiment daily is from one hundred and fifty to two hundred, going and coming to the rebel pen. Then there are some in the woods cutting down trees, making boards, building stockade for their tents, covering the stables and guarding the camp. They keep the boys at home being afraid we will go too far. But they murmur not, but wait patiently till they are relieved of infantry business.

The afternoon of each day is set apart for drilling, of which the men are getting a pretty good understanding; together with the art of managing a horse. The band men have all white horses. Speaking of the band it has improved much since they left Readville last May, and would improve more if they did not handle their axe and pick so much. Election day the boys were alive with the hopes of Lincoln being re-elected. Amid the booming of cannons they would send a shout from the headquarters to our camp.

The health of the regiment is pretty good at present, and there are but a small number in the hospital.

We have lost one who was beloved by all who knew him, quartermaster Sergt. William H. Skene. He died at the age of 32 years. He was a resident of Cambridge, Mass., where he left a wife and family to mourn his loss. There cannot be too much said in praise of Regt. Com. Sergt. William Jacobs, and Quartermasters Sergt. William D. Curtis of Co. D, who nobly went forth and had the body embalmed that it might be sent to his family, and arranged to some extent for the funeral, to the satisfaction of the family. There is credit also due to his captain, Capt. Emery, who accompanied the body to Baltimore, to have it conveyed safely to Cambridge, Mass.
A. W.

Life ground on quietly for the 5th Massachusetts through the winter of 1864. Colonel Russell ordered his majors to institute battalion drill on 4 December, a sign that the regiment's training was progressing. Ned Bartlett "went out and did as well as I knew how and nobody found fault so I suppose that it was all right." Bartlett was still de facto commander of Company E in December, as First Lieutenant Loud turned out to be "one of the laziest fellows in the regiment," doing "no more than he can help." Bartlett did not mind; he was glad of the experience. The Point was enjoying an unusual period of warm weather the first week of December. Bartlett found the weather "glorious" and "as mild as summer," so much so that one night while officer of the guard he had paused in his midnight rounds. "I sat for some time on the top of the stockade looking out at the sea, enjoying the night without an overcoat."

Several officers had followed Colonel Russell's example and brought their wives to the post. Captain Gilman, commanding L Company, had brought his wife, a "very fine looking lady," Bartlett reported, to live with him "in his rather small house built of logs and covered with tents." Bartlett knew of two captains who wished leave to go home and get married, with the intention of bringing their wives to Maryland.

Bartlett wrote his sister on 23 December, "Furloughs is the great excitement here now." Both officers and enlisted were trying to get leave. "Ten days is the longest furlough given, but the dodge is to get sick at home and get an extension." Captain Wheat had done this. He had been gone thirty days when Bartlett wrote. "How much longer he will stay I do not know, or care much for we get along very well without him." Enlisted men had to have a good excuse, but they too could get their ten days. Corporal Lewis Morris of Company E sent a letter to the Secretary of War on 10 December requesting a furlough "to provide his two sisters with a home, their mother having recently died." General Augur sent this request to General Barnes, who referred the matter to Colonel Russell who gave Corporal Morris a ten-day furlough (with perhaps a lecture on the chain of command) on 23 December. Sergeant John A. Williams, serving on detached service with the 2nd Wisconsin Battery at Point Lookout, preferred to have his wife come visit him. Colonel Russell would not allow her to remain permanently at the Point, but he allowed her visit.

As Ned Bartlett had mentioned, a way for an officer to extend his leave was to get sick, or to claim illness and obtain a surgeon's certificate. An officer could thus stretch out an original furlough to a month or more. There was a point, however, beyond which it was not wise to go, when a leave of absence became absence without leave. First Lieutenant Edgar Blanche, Company G, twenty-five, had been a wagon maker in Pennsylvania before the war. He had been a sergeant in the 2nd Massachusetts Cavalry before his promotion into the 5th Massachusetts on 8 February 1864. Blanche had gone on furlough on 15 September 1864. At the end of November, he sent a letter to Colonel Russell saying that he would not be returning to the regiment. Lieutenant Blanche's letter has been lost, so we do not have his justification for remaining more than sixty days away from his company. Colonel Russell evidently felt Blanche's reasons inadequate; he forwarded Blanche's letter to General Barnes with a request that the first lieutenant be dismissed from the service. On 15 December 1864, the Adjutant General's Office issued Special Order No. 449, paragraph 12 of which read, "By direction of the President, First Lieutenant Edgar M. Blanche, Fifth Massachusetts Cavalry, (Colored), is, upon the recommendations of his superior officers, hereby dishonorably dismissed the service of the United States, for absence without leave, with condition that he shall receive no final payments until he has satisfied the Pay Department that he is not indebted to the Government." Lieutenant Blanche was the only officer so dismissed in the regiment.

Unlike officers, who had the option of resigning, enlisted men had a much more difficult time leaving the regiment. During its stay at Point Lookout, from July 1864 until the end of March 1865, one or two troopers left on furlough and never came back and a few deserted, but most of the soldiers who left the 5th Massachusetts did so through disability discharges. Sometimes the post surgeon was not cooperative with this process. Five men were recommended for discharge in October, but only one, Private Francis Richardson, Company M, who had "phthisis" (a term associated with tuberculosis), was sent home. Private Betsy Smith of Company G ("dementia"); Private Thomas Grant, Company G ("rheumatic"); and Private Jones A. Lockley, Company K (chronic rheumatism), were all recommended for treatment. Surgeon Heger disapproved Private John Walker of Company K, who had a "false aneurysm of radial artery of left arm, the result of a wound" received at Baylor's Farm. "Ball passed between bones of arm without fracture. Recommended for treatment," was Heyer's dry notation. Four troopers were let go in November: two for chronic rheumatism, one for inguinal hernia, and one for a tumor in his left side. The examining board discharged five men in December. Three had the following ailments: "dropsy from hepatic disease," internal piles, and "loss of his left thumb, the result of a gunshot wound." As for the other two, the board finally came through for Private Thomas Grant, Company G, for chronic rheumatism, and Private John Walker, Company K, for "old fracture of left arm, result of a gunshot wound."

For most people, the ending of an old year and the beginning of a new one is a time of reflection about the past and hope for the future. Lieutenant Colonel Charles Francis Adams Jr. was no different. Holed up in his hut with a fire blazing in the hearth and a gallon of commissary whiskey at hand, he wrote his father. He was back with his regiment, at least for a time, although his health had not improved. Adams wrote as the clock ticked toward midnight on New Year's Eve. The year 1864 had been good for him: "Whomever else it has mis-used and left the worse for its events, it certainly was a pleasant, kind and beneficent year to me." The year had been one of "almost unmixed success"; he had accomplished all that he had set out to do. "To be sure my mark was not high but I struck it." The year had begun with him hoping for a visit to see his family in England, "so long the pleasant dream which made hardship bearable." That dream had been made possible by his company of the 1st Massachusetts Cavalry, and his alone, reenlisting, earning the company and Captain Adams a thirty-day furlough.

Adams had spent his leave in Europe pleasantly; he did not look forward to returning to his regiment. "When my vacation was over and the old life of hardship, now rendered doubly hard in contemplation and almost unbearable by contrast with the present, when this again stared me in the face, then I made one little effort, just pulled one little wire, and again the whole scene changed." It was Theodore Lyman who had been the "little wire" that helped Companies C and D of the 1st Massachusetts Cavalry become General Meade's cavalry escort.

During the spring and summer of 1864, Adams's squadron had had some arduous riding and had done some scouting, but no real fighting. "The terrible campaign which killed so many of my friends and was one succession of increasing hardships and privations to those whom it spared, was to me a summer picnic and pleasure excursion." Then came the unsought promotion into the 5th Massachusetts. When he accepted the offer and reported in to the regiment, Adams had not come empty-handed: "I brought them their horses, and again my attempt had been successful." Adams had wanted to go home in October, but "November saw me at Quincy." Adams thought that his father would agree that 1864 had come to him "full handed" and had been "a pleasant and a prosperous year." He could not foretell the future but hoped that "all blessings were not expended in the past, and that the power which has so well looked after that, will supply its cakes and ale in quantity also in the future."

Adams's stay at Point Lookout was not long, only about a month. He was just not physically fit enough to remain, as he explained in a letter to his father on 16 January 1865.

I told you some weeks ago that I looked upon my return to Point Lookout at present as a mere experiment. Gradually, I have become persuaded that the experiment was not a success, and accordingly I have broken up my establishment and am off to reestablish myself. I don't know that I am much less well than when I

*returned from Boston, but I certainly am no better. Accordingly, I have now set-
tled up all my affairs in the regiment, broken up my household, packed up all my
traps and am now on my way home for an indefinite period of time—certainly,
I think, forty days and perhaps sixty. I shall get to Boston tomorrow evening and
shall at once take steps to get myself put on some detached duty.*

Lieutenant Ned Bartlett, Company E, had not stayed up to ring in the
new year. He wrote to his friend Annie Andrews in Concord that the old
year "would go out just as well without my watching it and I did not care
to lose the sleep." It had snowed at Point Lookout, a few inches not long
after New Year's Day. "It put a stop to all drill for the horses [hooves] are
not caulked and consequently cannot stand on the slippery snow and ice."
Bartlett wrote in a letter to his sister on 22 January, "It's just about a year
ago when I tried and failed to get a commission in the Fifth Massachusetts
Cavalry, and here I am today an officer in the same regiment. How strangely
things do work out for the best!" By the third week in January, the snow
was gone and drill had resumed. More important, a shipment of sabers had
arrived and was issued to officers and men. "We have sabre drill every morning (dismounted) and in the afternoon mounted battalion or regimental
drill, the men wearing their sabres." Until his departure, Lieutenant Colonel
Adams conducted drills, "who is by no means popular with us," wrote Bartlett. Colonel Russell led the drill when the whole regiment turned out. The
parade ground at Point Lookout was too small for almost a thousand men
and horses to maneuver, so formations were compressed—"close columns,"
or larger units acting as smaller—squadrons acting as troops and troops
as platoons. The officers of the regiment had had two verbal examinations
on how to handle cavalry troopers in different situations, "Colonel Adams
presiding and making everyone feel uncomfortable by his method of catechizing us as if we were a parcel of school boys."

After he left Point Lookout in January 1865, Lieutenant Colonel
Charles F. Adams Jr. had quickly been taken on the staff of Governor
Andrew. Adams's brother, John Q. Adams, was already a lieutenant colonel
on Andrew's staff and primarily responsible for his brother's promotion into
the 5th Massachusetts Cavalry. Adams wrote in a letter to his father on 30
January 1865 that once again fortune had smiled upon him: "Since I sat
down to write this letter all my future prospects have undergone a change."

A messenger had arrived with an offer from Major General Andrew A. Humphreys, in command of the II Corps of the Army of the Potomac, naming Adams assistant inspector general of the corps. Humphreys had paid him "a very high compliment," Adams wrote, as an assistant inspector general held the highest field-grade rank on the staff, usually lieutenant colonel. There was opportunity for promotion, moreover, as Adams noted to his father. His predecessor in II Corps had been promoted to brigadier general, chief of staff. An inspector generalcy was "a position which I formerly greatly coveted," Adams admitted. "I shall accept this offer, at least for a time and return to a new and more influential life nearer Headquarters."

Adams's expected life of comfort and prestige was not to be, however. In February 1865, Colonel Russell decided to resign for urgent personal reasons. We can never know exactly why, because the reason has vanished with Russell's letter. It went to General Barnes at Point Lookout and then to General Augur at Washington before becoming lost. Barnes endorsed Russell's resignation, received at St. Mary's District Headquarters on 4 February: "Respectfully forwarded. Colonel Russell's services are important to the regiment but he represents the case as urgent. As a matter of form it is approved but the exigency must be determined by the Major General Commanding."

Second Lieutenant Bartlett speculated as to why Harry Russell resigned. "He says that he leaves for family reasons. I suppose that he does not care to take the field again or perhaps his wife does not care to have him." According to Bartlett, the regiment was truly taken aback by Russell's decision. "This is a sad day for the regiment," Bartlett wrote his sister Martha on 5 February. "Everybody feels blue and downhearted and with good reason too, for we have lost our colonel." Russell had announced at the evening meal on 4 February that he would be leaving in two days' time. "It was a great surprise to all of us," Bartlett wrote. "When I was first told of it I thought it was a lie, until at last I was made to believe it." Bartlett admitted that Colonel Russell "had done his duty" in serving for almost four years, but his departure would be a "sad blow" to the 5th Massachusetts Cavalry and the regiment's officers in particular, "for ever[y] one loved him." Loved he may have been, but, Bartlett wrote, Colonel Henry Sturgis Russell was also "just" to his officers. "He was never know[n] to favor one more than another and treated all alike." Nor was that love demonstrably reciprocated: "He was never familiar with his officers and it was impossible to feel at ease in his presence, but for this they respected him."

Bartlett's use of words and phrases reveals a great deal about his conception of leadership. Charles F. Adams was "not popular" and "not well liked," as if leadership was a form of contest or election. Harry Russell, by contrast, was "idolized," "worshipped," and "loved," but not because he was affectionate or good-humored. He was not popular, in other words, but was loved because his combination of fairness and authority had earned the respect of everyone in the regiment.

The 5th Massachusetts was a modern organization in the sense that the absence of its senior leadership (colonel, lieutenant colonel) did not destroy the effectiveness of the organization. As Lieutenant Bartlett wrote, the regiment continued to perfect its drill. Wooden stakes had been set up on one side of the parade ground. Bartlett called them "polls." Troopers and officers did a saber drill called "running at heads," which involved galloping by the polls and slashing at bags of hay (the "head") fixed on their tops. "It is not so hard to do with the cuts but the point is to hit straight," he wrote. "It's good practice and great fun." Hurdles had also been constructed and ditches dug for jumping, so the training of horses and men continued.

Harry Russell's decision to resign left Lieutenant Colonel Adams with a difficult choice. He wrote his mother on 14 February, "In my last I was comfortably disposing of myself for a summer's enjoyment in a snug, pleasant staff place." Adams received a "cool letter" from Harry Russell the next day informing him of the latter's resignation. "This makes me full Colonel, and in so far is pleasant enough, but I regard it as decidedly a promotion down stairs as between the command of my regiment and the position I might have held in the Second Corps staff." It took Adams some time to make up his mind, and more time for him to feel better and then to get his gear together. In the end, Adams's sense of duty and obligation sent him from Massachusetts back down to Maryland and the 5th Massachusetts Cavalry.

Before he left, he wrote a cordial note of thanks to Governor Andrew on 9 March 1865. "I cannot leave here for my regiment once more, without expressing to you my great sense of obligation to you in the matter of my late 'tour of duty' in Boston and vicinity." Governor Andrew's interference on his behalf had enabled Adams to sufficiently recover his health to give him "a fair chance of once more showing myself an efficient officer." What's more,

Adams also thanked the governor for making his marriage engagement possible. Adams believed himself "always a fortunate officer, but, certainly, I have found the time during which I looked to you for orders and received [them] more, the most agreeable of my military life." He concluded what for him was an effusive letter by reiterating his thanks "for that friendly interference which has not only restored me to health and efficiency but furnished to me one of the pleasantest episodes of man's life."

Even before he left Boston and Newport, Colonel Adams had moved forward to promote up the officer corps of the regiment. Major Horace N. Weld was promoted to lieutenant colonel to replace Adams. Captain Albert R. Howe, Company A, was promoted to major to replace Weld. First Lieutenant James S. Newell, regimental adjutant, was promoted to captain for Howe. First Lieutenant Daniel H. Chamberlain became regimental adjutant, and Second Lieutenant John G. S. White was promoted to first lieutenant for Newell.

There was a problem, however, with two of these promotions. Adams received a letter from Major William Rogers, assistant adjutant general for the commonwealth, written on 3 March 1865 on behalf of Governor Andrew. "His excellency directs me to write to you, in relation to the promotion to the Majority, made vacant by Major Weld's promotion, that, unless some very strong reason exists to the contrary, of which he has not been informed, he thinks Captain Parsons is clearly and decidedly entitled to the promotion." In other words, Governor Andrew was asking, "Who on earth is this Albert Howe when I practically promised Theophilus Parsons that his boy Chauncy would be a major?" Andrew believed Parsons entitled to promotion, Rogers explained, because there was an understanding that after Horace Weld, Parsons was to be senior captain. Parsons was also deserving of higher rank because he had an "early prospect of promotion" from first lieutenant to captain in the 1st Massachusetts Cavalry; therefore, unlike "most officers" of the 5th Cavalry, Parsons had joined the regiment without, in effect, receiving a promotion. His commission was earlier than any other captain in the regiment, but the date of his swearing in, or muster, was the same as Albert Howe's: 9 January 1864. Also, Rogers noted, Second Lieutenant George B. Farnsworth was senior by date of commission and muster to Second Lieutenant White. "In all cases of departure from the order of seniority, his excellency wishes to have the reason specifically stated."

Colonel Adams responded two days later with a couple of painful truths. Captain Howe was promoted to the vacant majority "in pursuance of the suggestion of Colonel Russell and for the following reasons." Howe had always been considered senior captain and had commanded a battalion before, as when Major Zabdiel Adams was absent wounded. With the promotion of Major Weld, Captain Howe was presently in command of the 1st Battalion, to which both he and Captain Parsons belonged. "The vacancies among the field officers of this regiment at this particular time it is especially desirable should be filled by the best ability in it," Adams wrote. In Adams's opinion, Captain Howe was "decidedly the most energetic and efficient of the two officers named—by regimental usage he is the senior of the two, and he is mustered of the same date." If that was not clear enough, Adams wrote, "the appointment of Captain Parsons to fill this vacancy will be opposed to my best judgment, and in my opinion, will not conduce to the efficiency of the regiment." Adams disposed of the Reverend George B. Farnsworth even more quickly than he had Chauncy Parsons: "Second Lieutenant George B. Farnsworth . . . has unfortunately a reputation for inefficiency and has been recommended to resign." Adams believed that Farnsworth had decided to either resign or transfer. "I cannot recommend him for promotion," Adams wrote.

Back in Maryland, the newly promoted officers settled into their duties. The regiment had been paid off to include 31 December 1864, and the troopers were flush with greenbacks. "The sutler is reaping a heavy harvest," Lieutenant Bartlett noted to his sister. "Some of the men send their money home but the greater part of them stuff themselves with good things until the cash is gone." The regiment was the beneficiary of the congressional act, passed the summer before, increasing the pay of African American units to equal white ones. There had been a mounted dress parade on Sunday instead of the usual inspection, with the entire regiment drawn up and passing in review before Colonel Adams. In the midst of these events, Colonel Adams wanted to address regimental discipline. "A general court martial is sitting in camp," Bartlett wrote on 19 March, 1865. "Adjutant Chamberlain being judge advocate."

General Order No. 6, 14 March 1865, Headquarters Saint Mary's District, ordered that a general court-martial meet at 10:00 a.m. on 15 March 1865 at Headquarters, 5th Massachusetts Volunteer Cavalry, "for the trial of such prisoners as may be brought before it." Besides First Lieutenant Chamberlain, judge advocate, there were nine members of the court. Majors Zabdiel B. Adams and Henry P. Bowditch were the senior officers, Adams acting as president. Major Albert R. Howe and Captains Hiram E. W. Clarke and Francis L. Higginson of the 5th Massachusetts sat on the court, as well as First Lieutenant Davenport Fisher. Captains A. W. Shaffer and M. Egan of the 20th Regiment, Veteran Reserve Corps, and Second Lieutenant I. F. Watkins, 11th Regiment, Veteran Reserve Corps, completed the court. Major Adams and his court tried ten troopers who took part in five separate incidents, occurring from 15 December 1864 to 25 January 1865. There were two types of courts-martial in the army during the nineteenth century. One, the field officers' court-martial, made up of officers of a regiment, dealt only with the men of the regiment and with cases that were minor or perceived to be minor: punishments included forfeiture of pay, confinement in the post guardhouse, special fatigue duty, or sometimes all three.

General courts-martial dealt with more serious cases, could sentence men to military prison or to be executed, and required the endorsement of a general officer. The accused in general courts-martial had to answer not only for a charge but also for the specification of that charge and could be found guilty or innocent on one or both.

For instance, Private John Hackett, Company K, 5th Massachusetts Cavalry, was brought before the court on the charge of "resistance to a superior officer." The specifications stated that "on or about December 15, 1864, at the General Guard House, Point Lookout, Hackett brought his gun to a 'charge bayonet' on his superior officer, Second Lieutenant John K. George while he was in the execution of his office, as Officer of the Guard and used the following language: 'God damn you, you would not strike me that way.'" Private Hackett pleaded not guilty but was found guilty of both the charge and the specification. He was sentenced to forfeit all pay and bounty and to be confined at hard labor for six years. For the final sentence, though, General Barnes had to add his endorsement. The post commandant approved the proceedings and findings in Private Hackett's case but found that "the evidence in the case does not justify the sentence, and it is therefore modified to a forfeiture of $10 a month for six months." General Barnes expected that this punishment would be "sufficient punishment to warn Private Hackett as [to] the danger of making even a show of resistance to his superior officers, to warn him of the great danger to which he is exposed by insubordinate conduct."

The pattern in Private Hackett's case, that of a stiff sentence handed down by the general court-martial and then modified by General Barnes, was followed in six of the ten cases. A ringleader in a particular case was usually recognized and punished more severely. This was so in both the cases of Privates Butler and Underhill, 14 January, and Privates Strafford and Bolden, 25 January. Private George Butler, Company D, had two charges lodged against him: assault and battery with intent to commit rape, and conduct prejudicial to good order and military discipline. Both charges stemmed from an incident that occurred during the small hours of 14 January at Point Lookout. Trooper Butler, possibly drunk, broke into the house of civilian telegraph operator James E. Carns and attempted "to commit a rape on the persons of Eliza J. Carns and Anna M. Carns [the wife and daughter, respectively, of Carns]." The specifications of the second charge read that Private Butler absented himself from the camp of the 5th Massachusetts Cavalry "without authority and did enter the house of James E. Carns, a citizen of St. Mary's District and did then and there behave in an indecent and disorderly manner." Private William A. Underhill, Company E, was charged with the same crimes as Butler. Underhill was found not guilty of the first charge, and while found guilty of the second, the words "without authority" were stricken. The court sentenced Private Underhill to forfeit six months' pay, which General Barnes modified to ten dollars a month for six months. Private George Butler, by contrast, was confined to the Hard Labor Prison at Norfolk, Virginia, for twenty years. General Barnes felt that the court was too easy on Butler: "The evidence in this case would have justified a charge of higher character, for which the highest penalty known to the law would have been appropriate punishment."

Privates Joseph Strafford and Fielding Bolden, both Company F, 5th Massachusetts Cavalry, were accused of mutiny. The specifications read that "having been ordered by Sergeant William Carter, Company C to 'fall in' while returning to camp from duty as provost guard willfully refused to obey said order, the said Privates Stafford [and Bolden] willfully and unlawfully struck with a musket the said Sergeant Carter, January 25, 1865." Both men were found not guilty of the charge but guilty of conduct prejudicial to good order and military discipline. Stafford was found guilty of the specification of striking Sergeant Carter, but the words "with a musket" were excised. Private Bolden was found guilty on the specification of striking Sergeant Carter with a musket, but he too was acquitted of willful disobedience to orders. Stafford was sentenced to forfeit one year's pay and to be confined at hard labor for one year; Bolden forfeited ten dollars a month for ten months. As in Private Hackett's case, General Barnes modified Stafford's sentence to forfeiture of pay (ten dollars a month for a year) rather than a prison term. "It is to be hoped that Private Stafford can render a better service to the country, by a proper performance of his duty as a soldier for the future, than by his confinement at hard labor."

Lieutenant Ned Bartlett had written to his friend Annie Andrews on 5 January 1865. He wondered where his brother Bradford and his friend Sam Hoar had heard there had been a mutiny in the regiment. "It's a great mistake as nothing of the kind ever happened or was ever thought of." There had been a little trouble three weeks before, Bartlett admitted. "One of the Sergeants of Company F was reduced [to the ranks] and he insulted his Lieutenant and struck at him, for which he was handcuffed in the guardhouse." That night, 16 December, some of the confined man's friends attempted to gain his release. Lieutenant Robert M. Parker, Company M, the officer of the guard, fired three shots from a revolver over their heads and scattered the crowd. The ringleaders were arrested and confined to the guardhouse until they came before the court-martial in March. "This is all that occurred," Bartlett wrote. "It amounted to very little and nobody thought of it two days after."

It is interesting to note that news of this mutiny reached the Bay State so quickly. The men of the 5th Massachusetts Cavalry were not different from those of any other organization. Most, the great majority, did their duty and followed orders to the best of their ability. There were a few lazy men, a few liars and thieves, and one or two sexual predators. A few men drank on duty and could not hold their liquor. Any regiment in the Union army had its share of discipline problems. The difference between the men of the 5th Massachusetts Cavalry and other regiments lay in how the African American troopers expected to be treated when they broke the rules.

Three charges were lodged against Private (then Sergeant) Abraham H. Williams, Company F, for his actions on the afternoon of 16 December 1864. The first charge was drunkenness on duty. The specification read that

Williams "did appear on the company drill in such a state of intoxication as to cause disturbance during the drill." The second charge was contempt and disrespect toward his superior officers—specifically, "having been ordered by his superior officer Captain C. E. Allen Company 'F' to keep quiet in the ranks and stop talking, did reply to Captain Allen in a disrespectful manner, in words to wit: 'No man shall make me stop talking.'" Captain Allen ordered First Lieutenant Abner Mallory, with at least one noncommissioned officer, to arrest Sergeant Williams, take his stripes, and lock him up. The third charge against Williams was mutinous conduct, that Williams "did, while being shackled by Lieutenant Mallory use the following mutinous language, 'No God damned white son of a bitch shall put irons on me'; or words to that effect and did use force to prevent himself from being shackled." Captain Allen and Lieutenant Mallory had made a bad mistake. By fetching handcuffs and forcing Williams into them, they turned a difficult situation into an ugly, dangerous, and potentially explosive one.

Charles Francis Adams's ignorance of the men under his command, revealed in his comments about the "supine" nature of African Americans, is dramatically illustrated here. No black man, once free and in uniform, would ever allow himself to be subjected to the trappings of slavery again. Williams went wild at the sight of the shackles, and in their outrage at the use of handcuffs, his fellow troopers overlooked his drunken and disrespectful behavior. Williams was the only defendant who pleaded guilty at this court-martial. Lieutenant Chamberlain advised him to admit guilt to being drunk on duty but to plead not guilty to the other two charges. Williams was found guilty of the first two charges (drunkenness and disrespect) and their specifications and guilty of the third specification (mutinous language) but not the charge of mutiny. Abraham Williams was sentenced to spend a year at hard labor and to forfeit six months' pay. Like the cases of Privates Hackett and Strafford, General Barnes thought that little would be served by sending Private Williams to prison and modified his sentence to forfeiture of ten dollars a month for a year. Barnes made sure to note that drunkenness was no excuse for a crime. "It is to be hoped," Barnes wrote, "that Private Williams understanding now fully the danger to which he is exposed by the use of intoxicating drink, will appreciate the importance of sobriety to him, and will show by his conduct hereafter, that he can make some amend for the offense, of which he has been [found] guilty, by a correct performance of his duties as a soldier of his country."

Sergeant James H. Cornish, Company F, suffered more for what he didn't do than what he did. Cornish was charged with disobedience to orders and contempt and mutinous language to his superior officer. Captain Allen had ordered Cornish to arrest Williams, but he "refused to do so and instead allowed the man to go to the Colonel, H. S. Russell, Fifth Massachusetts Cavalry." Russell may have been sympathetic to Williams, but he did not intervene on his behalf, and Captain Allen again ordered Cornish to arrest Williams; again Cornish refused. The specification of the second charge read, "Said Cornish, when a Sergeant, when Lieutenant Mallory attempted to tie up the said man did interfere, and did use the following words, to wit: 'Mallory don't strike that man, don't touch him,' or words to that effect." The court found Cornish, who had spent three months in the guardhouse and lost his stripes, guilty of only the second charge and specification and sentenced him to forfeit three months' pay. General Barnes also was inclined to go lightly on Cornish, given "his long confinement and his good character" and ordered him released and returned to duty. Cornish's "objectionable language" ought to have been considered an "involuntary appeal to his officer in a moment of excitement" rather than mutinous talk, Barnes wrote. The general suggested that a soldier should never be struck except in self-defense. "This can rarely be the case, and it is particularly incumbent upon the officers of colored troops to perform their duties with dignity, and without giving way to passion, the consequences of which might be fatal and for which they would be responsible." Barnes's words seem sadly too late to help those for whom they were intended.

Two men were charged with mutiny arising from the events of the night of 16 December. Private James Finley, Company H, was alleged to have used the following words in the presence of other enlisted men: "Boys, come get your equipments, we are going to the guard house to release that man." The specification noted that Finley appeared in the company street with his rifle and equipment, "with the intention of releasing an enlisted man of the Fifth Massachusetts Cavalry then undergoing punishment at the guard house of the Fifth Massachusetts Cavalry." Finley was found guilty of the charge, but intention could not be proven and the guilty verdict on the specification struck out the words "and did shortly afterwards appear in the company street with his arms and equipment, with the intention of releasing an enlisted man, etc." Private Finley's language earned him a hard-labor sentence, without pay, for the remainder of his term of enlistment. General Barnes set aside the sentence of the court, however, due to insufficient evidence. Finley's language "tended to excite mutiny," but Barnes thought he should have been accused of a lesser offense, "for which he might have been properly punished." Barnes expected Private Finley to take the court's sentence as a warning and to "conduct himself with more propriety hereafter."

Private Albert Jones was also charged with mutiny. The evidence against him was more specific than against Finley and the sentence consequently harsher. There were two charges, actually: mutiny and conduct prejudicial to good order and military discipline. The specifications are worth quoting for the full effect: "In this, that he, the said Private Albert Jones, Company 'H', Fifth Massachusetts Cavalry (colored) on the evening of the 16th of December, 1864, approach the guard house of the Fifth Massachusetts Cavalry and demanded that the irons should be taken off Private Abraham H. Williams, Company 'F', then undergoing punishment, thereby causing a mutiny in camp." The second specification reads, "In this, that he, the said Private Albert Jones, Company 'H' did in the presence of the enlisted men of Company 'H' use the following language to wit: 'I don't care a damn about shooting shoulder-straps [officers],' and when ordered to be silent by the First Sergeant of Company 'H', Fifth Massachusetts Cavalry, continued to talk in a mutinous manner." Private Jones was found guilty on both charges and specifications. As the specifications were worth quoting, so, too, is the sentence of the general court-martial: "And the court does therefore sentence him, the said Private Albert Jones, Company 'H', Fifth Massachusetts Cavalry (colored) to be shot to death with musketry, at such time and place as the competent authority may direct: two-thirds of the members of the court concurring."

It seems that Jones was chosen as the example for the others. Albert Jones was not executed, although the men of the 5th Massachusetts probably never knew that. General Barnes approved and forwarded the court's sentence to President Lincoln. As he had done for so many others, Lincoln commuted Jones's death sentence on 10 April 1865, four days before he was assassinated. Jones was not sent to the Hard Labor Prison in Norfolk but instead served his time in Petersburg, Virginia, a city liberated on 3 April 1865.

Colonel Adams had prevailed upon his friend Lieutenant Colonel Theodore Lyman twice before, once to have his squadron of the 1st Massachusetts Cavalry named headquarters escort and again to have his new regiment remounted. Now he turned to Lyman once more. Major General C. C. Augur, commanding the XXII Army Corps, which included the District of St. Mary's, received a message from Lieutenant General Ulysses S. Grant on 20 March 1865: "Is the Fifth Massachusetts Colored Cavalry longer needed at Point Lookout? If not, send it to the army of the James." General Augur telegraphed General Grant the next day: "The Fifth Massachusetts Cavalry (Colored) will be sent, as you have directed, as soon as they can exchange their muskets for carbines and transportation be obtained." Just to make sure, General Augur telegraphed on 21 March to General Barnes at Point Lookout, "General Grant wants the Fifth Massachusetts Cavalry. Can you spare it?" Barnes replied the same day: "I should recommend that the Fifth Massachusetts Cavalry be ordered to the front. I will make the best disposition of the force left here, and if necessary it would be far better to fill up the regiments of the Veteran Reserve Corps. As cavalry the Fifth Massachusetts are of no use here. It will make a good regiment in the performance of their regular duty as cavalry." In reply to another message, General Barnes telegraphed to General Augur that the regiment numbered "1,200 men and 900 horses, camp and garrison equipage, and six wagons."

Lieutenant Ned Bartlett wrote his cousin Ripley on 23 March from Point Lookout. The regiment was under marching orders, ready to move, and had been since 21 March. Colonel Adams and Quartermaster Edward H. Adams were in Washington, drawing carbines and pistols for the regiment (the men already had their sabers). As soon as the colonel and the quartermaster returned, the regiment would turn in its infantry weapons and accoutrements. Bartlett did not know where the regiment was to be posted but assumed it would be to the XXV Corps of the Army of the James. Bartlett also had no way of knowing when the regiment would leave: perhaps tomorrow, perhaps in a week. "I am glad enough of the chance to see some active service before the war is closed up for I am sick of this inactive life and this hard guard duty and muskets," Bartlett wrote.

The XXV Army Corps was formed in December 1864 by consolidating all the African American units of the IX Corps, Army of the Potomac, and the XVIII Corps, Army of the James. The white units of the X and

XVIII Corps, Army of the James, were consolidated into the XXIV Army Corps. Major General Godfrey Weitzel acceded to command of the XXV Army Corps upon its formation. General Weitzel promulgated an order on 20 February 1865 creating the XXV Army Corps badge, a square, which was worn on the kepis of all officers and men of the corps. Headquarters and division flags also bore this emblem. General Philip Kearny, who had invented the "Kearney Patch" as a morale builder, had instituted the use of distinctive corps badges in 1862. General Weitzel's order—more an oration, really—shows not only his romanticism and youth (Weitzel was twenty-nine) but also how he felt about commanding an army corps of near thirty thousand black men.

> In view of the circumstances under which this corps was raised and filled, the peculiar claims of its individual members upon the justice and fair dealings, of the prejudice, and the regularity of the conduct of the troops which deserve those equal rights that have been hitherto denied the majority, the commanding general has been induced to adopt the square as the distinctive badge of the Twenty-Fifth Army Corps. Wherever danger has been found and glory to be won, the heroes who have fought for immortality have been distinguished by some emblem to which every victory added a new luster. They looked upon this badge with pride, for to it they had given its fame. In the homes of smiling peace it recalled the days of courageous endurance and the hours of deadly strife—and it solaced the moment of death for it was a symbol of a life of heroism and self denial. . . . Soldiers: To you is given a chance in this spring campaign of making this badge immortal. Let history record that on the banks of the James thirty-thousand freemen, not only gained their own liberty but shattered the prejudice of the world and gave to the land of their [birth] Peace, Union and Glory.

By 24 March, elements of the regiment had traveled to Deep Bottom, Virginia, by company and by squadron [two companies] because of the small size of the transports. Deep Bottom is on the north side of the James about eight miles from Richmond. It lay back about a mile and a half from the XXV Corps trenches on the extreme right of the Union line, a line that stretched well west of Petersburg. It was fairly quiet in their sector, with occasional artillery fire and sniping going on, but in other areas of the line elements of the Union army were on the move. The II and V Corps were in support of the movement of the ten thousand cavalrymen of the Army of the Potomac under Major General Philip Sheridan. Sheridan's force was marching all the way to the extreme left of the Union line and beyond, seeking to stretch the Confederate line to breaking and draw the Army of Northern Virginia out its trenches. Sheridan's troopers would meet the Confederates in the Battles of Dabney's Mill on 31 March and Five Forks on 1 April.

Ned Bartlett wrote his sister Martha on 30 March, reporting the beginning of Union operations on the left of the line. At dusk the night before, "we could hear cannonading plainly and see the flashes of the guns." A heavy rain began falling at midnight and continued for twelve hours, leaving the camp "a perfect mud hole." Bartlett had slept in a mud puddle, and as he wrote, the rain was dripping down his back. Colonel Charles F. Adams Jr. wrote his father on 10 April, describing his regiment's return to the field: "Grant's great movement was already under way and General Weitzel, to whom I reported, ordered me to get out to the front with no delay." The regiment needed to be concentrated in one place to finish the issue of Sharps carbines and Colt pistols and to rid itself of excess baggage, the accumulated junk of almost nine months of garrison duty in Maryland. "Arms were to be drawn, stores turned in and the regiment forced to the front in a moment." This was all done in the pouring rain, with horses and men sinking up to their knees in mud. "I went out to the front," Adams continued, "and selected a camp and the morning after I landed, sent out one battalion [2/5]." The rain stopped the afternoon of Friday, 31 March. "Meanwhile confusion in affairs regimental had become worse confounded and it needed all the head I had to keep things straight at all; but keeping cool and the assistance of first rate officers brought things round and Friday evening, having got ten companies sent forward, I broke up the receiving camp [near Deep Bottom] and moved out to the front." Ned Bartlett described the march of the 2nd Battalion (Companies E, F, G, and H), under Major Zabdiel B. Adams, in a letter to his sister Martha written 31 March "Before Richmond": "We lay at our old camp in the mud and rain; at last the order came to saddle up." The battalion moved out in the early afternoon, with a hard rain still falling, "passing by camp on camp and through a number of lines of works, now disused . . . thrown up by our forces as they advanced."

The country was one vast trench, Bartlett noted. Here had been the front line, two lines of works; "near together and in front of each were the rifle pits of the skirmishers, which looked very much like shallow graves."

The 2/5 Mass. Cavalry went into camp at the abandoned bivouac of the 1st New York Mounted Rifles, "one of the finest camps I ever saw," wrote Bartlett. Situated in a pine grove, the 1st New York had had the winter to improve their living arrangements. The barracks and stables were built of stockade fencing. "The officers quarters are gay and are furnished from the houses of the neighborhood." Bartlett noted that his new quarters had a glazed window, a painted door, and a four-poster bed—more comfortable than Point Lookout! Their new camp was six or seven miles from Richmond, "as near Richmond as any troops . . . but our picket line is three miles nearer," wrote Bartlett. A detachment of a captain, a lieutenant, and sixty-six privates was immediately sent out as videttes, as mounted pickets were called. Colonel Adams continued in his letter: "Here, in the deserted camp of the First New York, I found myself very comfortable on Saturday night [1 April], and the next evening the balance of the regiment arrived, and once more we were all together."

The 5th Massachusetts Cavalry was officially designated Cavalry Escort, Headquarters, Army of the James, but the reality was different. On Sunday, 2 April, Colonel Adams found himself "in command of all the cavalry detachments North of the James—some two-thousand men in all, of whom about 1,000 were mounted." Adams now commanded his own black troopers, three companies (I, L, and M) of the 4th Massachusetts Cavalry, and the 1st New York Mounted Rifles.

Union arms saw great success on 2 April 1865. Sheridan had decisively defeated the Confederates the day before at Five Forks. Now came the beginning of the end. General Lee's line was broken; he telegraphed Confederate president Davis that he must move his army out of the trenches. The Petersburg–Richmond front was doomed, and with it the Confederate capital. The Petersburg defenses fell by 8:00 a.m. on 2 April; a message from Lee urging abandonment of Richmond found Davis attending services at St. Paul's Church. White-faced and tight-lipped, President Davis read the note, got up quietly, and walked out in silence. He had already sent Mrs. Davis and his children south. Now he and most of his cabinet members, along with $500,000 in gold from the Confederate Treasury, boarded a special train for Danville, Virginia. By midnight, 2 April, Richmond was in chaos. The streets were filled with Confederate deserters, desperate refugees, and criminals who had broken out of the state prison. Fires had been deliberately set in tobacco and cotton warehouses to deny those goods to the federals; fanned by a high wind, the fires spread and ordnance stores began exploding. The Confederate gunboats in the James River were blown up, further shaking the city. Looters—black, white, of both sexes, many drunk—were lit up by the flames like demons from hell. Confederate government records lay scattered in the gutters or whirled about by the wind, fueling the fire. "All Sunday," Colonel Adams wrote, "reports of Grant's successes were coming in and we were anxious and expectant." He went to bed that night "anxious merely and disgusted enough," for the "miscellaneous Brigade of which I had charge was the hardest body to handle of which I had any experience, being made up of all sorts of detachments and being without any staff or organization." Colonel Adams took his mounted troops toward Richmond at dawn the next day, 3 April 1865:

> I had about one thousand mounted men and a battery. I got out to the Darby-town road, and by this time heavy explosions were heard towards Richmond, like the sound of heavy, distant fighting. Finding the enemy's lines deserted and no orders coming I concluded something was up and it was best to push ahead; so we went through the lines and took the Richmond road. Then came an exciting march, not without vexations; but nine o'clock found me in the suburbs of Richmond.

Colonel Adams impressions of the capture of Richmond were sent to Governor Andrew on 5 April. His report is worth quoting entire:

> Your Excellency:
>
> Deeming the entry of the regiment which I have the honor to command, into the City of Richmond, as a part of the column which took possession of that city on the 3rd inst., an incident in the closing events of this war of sufficient moment to justify especial mention, I have the honor to submit to you the following report. I do so for the additional reason that I believe this regiment was the only one from Mass. in that column and as it is the only mounted Regt. of colored cavalry east of the Alleghenies.
>
> The last detachment of the Regt. arrived before Richmond from Point Lookout Md. where the whole Regt. had been stationed during the nine months previous, late in the day on Sunday, April 2nd. At the same moment that it arrived, orders were received to be in readiness for instant movement. Early in

the morning of Monday the 3rd orders came for the provisional brigade of which it was a part, to move out on the Darbytown road to Richmond and there to await further orders. Capt. Newell's Co. (A) being there upon picket, the Regiment numbered, when formed as part of the column, some 700 sabres. It entered the city at about 9 a.m., was marched through it, halting for orders in front of the Capitol, and was there put upon the duty of guarding all the roads leading from the city on which duty it is now engaged.

As the Regiment marched through the city the scene was one of the wildest confusion and enthusiasm. Nearly one half of the city was in flames—the dense smoke hid the sun and the explosions in the burning buildings were incessant. The professed and latent Union feeling of the white inhabitants was largely evinced by the waving of the national flag, but the real enthusiasm of the black population was unbounded. This sentiment was peculiarly called forth by the appearance of this Regiment. Strong in numbers, admirably mounted and thoroughly equipped, so fine a body of black Cavalry was something of which these people had no previous conception, and our line of march soon became one long continued ovation. Black faces—men, women and children—poured out of the houses and seemed to spring up from the pavement evincing astonishment and delight in every conceivable way. When the Regiment halted they could no longer be kept back, but rushed through the ranks, embracing the knees of officers and forcing upon the men everything they had to give. The whole formed a curious coincidence of war, a Regiment of black cavalry from the State of Massachusetts marching amid the wildest enthusiasm into the capital of the State of Virginia.

I am happy to be able to state that the conduct of the mounted portion of the Regiment on this occasion was most exemplary, not only were they guilty of no disorder or act of pillage, but not one man left his rank and not a single case of intoxication, even, came under my notice. Both in its appearance and conduct the Regiment did credit to itself and the Commonwealth.

Second Lieutenant Ned Bartlett wrote his sister from Richmond on 3 April: "Today, is the most glorious in the history both of the country and our regiment. We entered Richmond at 10 o'clock this morning just on the heels of the retreating [Confederate] army." Bartlett described the advance of the 5th Massachusetts. The regiment advanced dismounted, in a skirmish line across the road, until Colonel Adams determined that the Confederate trenches were deserted. Mounted once more, the regiment galloped down the road in column of companies, four abreast. "When we came out of the woods I saw right ahead the line of rebel works and very strong they were, surrounded by a cheveaux de frieze of pointed stakes." Passing through this first line of deserted trenches, Bartlett noticed that the rebel cook fires were still burning. The sound of explosions came clearer, and heavy smoke hung over Richmond. The 5th Massachusetts moved from the Darbytown road to the right, northeast to the Charles City road, which lead straight into the city, now about four miles away. "We expected a fight every moment but as we passed fort on fort deserted—we then came to the conclusion that they had retired into their inner line of fortifications." This line was reached a little over two miles from the city, but the works were empty and the cannon silent. Bartlett found it difficult to describe their entry into Richmond, "but I never saw so much enthusiasm in my life." The 5th Massachusetts marched at the head of a division of African American infantry. Preceded only by a squadron of the 4th Massachusetts Cavalry who provided General Weitzel's escort, Bartlett wrote, "It will be an event in history that colored troops were the first into the city." Bands played the "Battle Hymn of the Republic" and "The Girl I Left Behind Me." The business and warehouse part of town, about seventeen city blocks near the James River, was fully engulfed in flames. "We were greeted on all sides by the colored people, who were frantic with joy," Bartlett recounted.

Under the headline "From the Regiments," the 22 April 1865 edition of the *Anglo-African* had this letter:

Extract From a Letter Received By Rev. Amos G. Beman From His Son
Richmond, Va., April 5th, 1865.
DEAR FATHER: I am happy beyond measure to write you from the Rebel Capital *that was*, but is no longer in the power of Jeff. Davis and Co.

We entered the city about 9 o'clock a.m., Monday April 3d. I wrote you a letter on Friday from Chapin's Farm. We left there on Monday morning, about 6 o'clock, and proceeded toward Richmond for about four miles, when we dismounted to fight on foot. We waited about half an hour, and as heavy cannonading was going on in front, and skirmishing on our right, we again mounted, and the balance of the distance to Richmond we went on a gallop. We passed several forts and breastworks, which had heavy guns on them, and other guns which I heard were made of wood to frighten Uncle Sam's boys with. We passed infantry, artillery and some cavalry, and entered Richmond, the first mounted men in the city, which was almost entirely evacuated by the Confederate army. We were informed by a great many citizens that Jeff. Davis had gone to North Carolina; but no matter where he has gone, the Confederate States of America have fallen. Going through the city we passed thousands of citizens, colored and white, who cheered and cheered us as we rode in triumph along the streets.

Libby prison was fired as were several other buildings containing shells and other munitions of war, which, as they exploded from time to time, sounded as if there was an engagement going on in the city.

The rebels set fire to some boats and wharfs and to a magazine of powder, before they left.

The magazine exploded and killed a number of persons, some a quarter of a mile distant. I have not heard of any cases of poisoning yet, or of any accidents from torpedoes, several of which were buried by the "Johnnies," but they were watched by the "contrabands," who informed us where they were hidden.

Yesterday I visited the 29th Connecticut Volunteers, and saw Sergt. Maj. Thos. J. Griffin, William Hancock, Joseph Cassell, Daniel Lathrop, John Cowes, George Livingston, Lewis Van Dine, and many others of New Haven—all well, but much fatigued in marching "on to Richmond."

This is certainly a city of hills, for it is going up and coming down all the time. There are many fine building and nice-looking colored people here. They shouted, "God bless you! We have been waiting for you and looking for you a long time," and with many other expressions they showed their joy at our appearance in the old rebel capital.

* * * * * * * * * * * * * * * * * * *

Affectionately, your son,

CHAS. T. BEMAN, 5th Mass. Cavalry.

Burke Davis's *To Appomattox: Nine April Days, 1865* makes extensive use of archival and published primary sources to describe the last days of the war in Virginia. The troopers of the 5th Massachusetts were unusual enough to be commented on in a few accounts. Fannie Walker was a Confederate War Department copying clerk who, standing on her front steps shortly before dawn on 3 April, was knocked off her feet by the explosions of the gunboats in the river. Miss Walker left her house with her aunt and made her way to the Valentine House on Clay Street, behind the Virginia Capitol building. From the Valentine House, now the site of the Confederate War Museum,

Walker saw her first victorious Union soldier: "I looked down the street and to my horror beheld a Negro cavalryman yelling: 'Richmond at last!'"

John Beauchamp Jones, the "Rebel War Clerk," noted that Capitol Square was filled with African American cavalry and infantry surrounded by a jubilant crowd of their race. The square was scattered with furniture and household goods dragged from houses threatened by fire. Jones recorded that a passing Union officer said to him, "We'll picket the city with a white brigade tonight." The officer spoke to the women around him: "I assure you there won't be a bit of molestation, ladies. Not a particle." A young woman named Sallie Brock Putnam recorded the scene as well: "Long lines of Negro cavalry swept by the Exchange Hotel [on Franklin and Fourteenth Streets, across from the post office], brandishing their swords and uttering savage cheers, replied to by the shouts of those of their own color, who were trundling along under loads of plunder.... Some colored troops passed, singing 'John Brown's Body.'" Putnam noted that Capitol Square was crowded with refugees intermingled with Union troops and was "almost as hot as a furnace" because of the fires. Colonel George A. Bruce had been a captain in the 13th New Hampshire Infantry a year before when he disembarked at Bermuda Hundred with the XVIII Army Corps. Now he was a colonel on the staff of Major General Charles Devens, commanding the 3rd Division of the XXIV Army Corps. Bruce described the scene as Union troops neared Richmond on the morning of 3 April:

> On a hill just by the line of inner defense we gained our first sight of Richmond—a sight that none will ever forget. The city was wrapped in a cloud of densest smoke, through which great tongues of flame leaped in madness to the skies. A few houses on the higher hills, a spire here and there half smothered in smoke, and the hospitals to the east, were the only buildings that could be seen. Added to the wild tumult of the flames, ten thousand shells bursting every minute in the Confederate arsenals and laboratories were making an uproar such as might arise from the field when the world's artillery joins in battle.

Colonel Bruce also recorded the scene in Capitol Square, an "indescribable confusion" of "men, women and children, white and black," the sick and infirm on pallets crowded about whatever could be saved from the flames. "Bureaus, sofas, carpets, beds and bedding, in a word, every conceivable article of household furniture, from baby-toys to the most costly mirrors, were scattered promiscuously on the green." All around the wind was blowing like a hurricane, "hurling cinders and pieces of burning wood with long trails of flame over the houses to distant quarters of the city." Situated amid a grove of trees in the center of the square, "amid this carnival of ruin, stood the great statue of Washington, against which firebrands thumped and rattled, little respecting the majestic form of the Father of his Country."

Colonel Charles Francis Adams Jr. expressed his eminent satisfaction with the events in a letter to his father: "To have led my regiment into Richmond at the moment of its capture is the one event which I should most have desired as the culmination of my life in the Army. That honor has been mine and now I feel as if my record in this war was rounded and completely filled out." The 5th Massachusetts remained near Richmond for three days, picketing the approaches to the city. Ned Bartlett wrote home on 4 April. He had spent most of the night before "on a high hill on the outskirts of the city watching Richmond burn. Can you conceive any greater satisfaction to a soldier?" Bartlett mentioned that the regiment was stretched around the city, patrolling and picketing the roads. "The object is to keep all citizens out or in and to arrest deserters and rebel soldiers."

On Thursday afternoon, 6 April, Colonel Adams received orders to move the regiment to Petersburg and report to Major General George L. Hartsuff, commanding the newly created District of Nottaway, headquartered in Petersburg. Adams wrote his father, "The regiment marched through Richmond at ten o'clock [p.m.] and found that conquered city quiet and silent as a graveyard." The behavior of Union troops in occupied Richmond had been "wonderful," reported Adams. "I have not seen or heard of any riot, blood-shed or violence." There had been a great deal of drunkenness, however, as the inhabitants of Richmond, "with an insane idea of propitiating our soldiers," had "actually forced liquor on them in the streets," but this had been stopped not long after the arrival of the troops on 3 April. "We found the slaves and the poor whites pillaging freely, but that was put a stop to and the soldiers, so far as I could see, behaved admirably." The regiment arrived at Petersburg the morning of 7 April and was sent out the next day to Sutherland Station, Virginia, to cover the South Side Railroad. The regiment's line, Adams wrote, ran through both former camps of the two armies. It was a "curious region of desolation." It seemed to Adams like a great broom of destruction had swept over the landscape:

All landmarks are defaced, not only trees and fences, but even the houses and roads. It is one broad tract, far as the eye can reach, dotted here and there with clumps of trees which mark the spot where some Headquarters stood, and for the rest covered with a thick stubble of stumps of the pine. You ride through mile after mile of deserted huts, marking the encampments of armies, and over roads now leading from nowhere, nowhither. Large houses are gone so that even their foundations can no longer be discovered. Forts, rifle-pits and abattis spring up in every direction, and in front of Petersburg the whole soil is actually burrowed and furrowed beyond the power of words to describe.

The Army of Northern Virginia under General Robert E. Lee surrendered on Palm Sunday, 9 April 1865. The troopers of the 5th Massachusetts Cavalry continued to picket the South Side Railroad until the end of April. A week after the surrender of Lee and his men came the assassination of President Lincoln, on 14 April. Lieutenant Bartlett wrote his sister on 16 April to vent his rage at the act. "I feel blood-thirsty tonight for we have just received the news that Lincoln has been assassinated in the streets of Washington." Bartlett described both officers and men as "wild." He had never seen so much excitement: "It goes ahead of Richmond." The young lieutenant expressed the wish that XXV Army Corps might be given "a strong commission to go through Virginia to burn, kill and destroy and I tell you the 'niggers' would raise him [Lincoln] a monument of dead rebels." Bartlett felt that the life of the martyred chief executive was worth more than the whole state.

Colonel Adams was not in camp to share the rage of his officers and men because he was under arrest. Adams received an order on 16 April from Major General E. O. C. Ord, commanding the Army of the James, placing him "in arrest for neglect of duty in allowing his command to straggle and maraud, and will report to the Commanding Officer, Fort Monroe where he will be tried." Colonel Adams duly reported himself at the fort, and there he seems to have been forgotten ("buried alive," as he put it) for ten days. "The whole difficulty seemed to arise," he wrote to his father on 2 May, "from certain horse-stealing propensities of my men." Sufficient horses had not been furnished at Point Lookout to mount the entire regiment, and apparently while stationed near Richmond some of the troopers "commandeered" some citizens' horses.

The whole affair was resolved on 26 April when General Ord came down to Fort Monroe to visit his family. Colonel Adams requested and obtained an interview with Ord. "General Ord treated me with marked attention and civility. . . . He at once gave me an order exonerating me from all blame and directing me to resume command of my regiment." This Adams refused to do because the cloud still hung over the 5th Massachusetts Cavalry. "My course was, not to defend my regiment, but, allowing all they said, simply to demand facts on which to punish officers and men." This could not be done because headquarters had "gone off at half-cock on a parcel of verbal complaints of citizens against my regiment, and now they only had blind wrath to show, and lots of it, but neither facts nor evidence."

During Adams's absence at Fort Monroe, an investigation of the regiment, "with a view to smashing it and me generally," had taken place. Adams sent a report of this investigation to General Ord, who sent it back requesting Adams's recommendations. Adams endorsed and sent back the report once more, recommending that in future all complaints be sent to him in writing and that he would investigate and settle any problems arising from the 5th Massachusetts Cavalry. "The deliciously ludicrous result was thus arrived at, that, after being under arrest a fortnight, the inspector's report on the very facts on which I was to stand trial was referred to me, and finally the facts themselves sent back to me to do what I saw fit about them." This whole contretemps had done little to endear his men to Colonel Adams, despite his glowing report to Governor Andrew. He considered his troopers "as hard a pack to manage as any I ever had to handle and a most inveterate set of stragglers and pilferers."

On 26 April 1865, the second major army of the Confederate States of America, some thirty thousand men under General Joseph E. Johnston, surrendered to Union forces under General William T. Sherman. Confederate president Davis remained at large, and two small Confederate forces, one under General E. Kirby Smith in the Trans-Mississippi Department and the other commanded by General Richard Taylor in Alabama and Mississippi, had yet to surrender. For the officers and men of the 5th Massachusetts Cavalry, however, the war had ended. Ned Bartlett wrote on 1 May that the regiment, now stationed at Coggins Point on the James River, was "doing

nothing but drill, in fact that is all there is to do now for there is no picketing or guard duty to do for the war is over and there are no more rebels
left to fight." Bartlett found the regiment's new camp a pleasant one, situated on a high bluff overlooking the James in a grove of cedars. He could
look down the river from the back of his tent and observe the river traffic.
The breeze from the river relieved some of the Virginia heat. Most of the
officers had gone swimming in the morning. "Now this afternoon the men
are enjoying the same luxury and they are shouting and having a great
time—they look like great black toads from here." With the war substantially over, speculation was rife as to what was to happen to the regiment.
Rumors flew "thick as bees." One rumor was that the XXV Corps was to be
sent to Texas; Bartlett believed this "an idle story." Another, more wishful
rumor was that the regiment would be paid off and mustered out immediately. Bartlett did not believe that rumor either. He was willing to wait
and see and to continue "to play soldier." He was "happy enough to stay
here—never felt better in my life and am in no hurry to get out of it except
I don't think much of serving in peace times."

Several other officers, however, wanted to go home. Second Lieutenant
George Farnsworth resigned on 3 May. A few days later, the regiment
received orders that probably prompted others to send in their resignations:
There would be no immediate muster out. Instead, XXV Corps was brought
together and encamped at Light House Pointe, Virginia, a place designated
"Camp Lincoln" on 7 May. "This corps having been ordered to this point
for drill and instruction, the most thorough discipline of troops in garrison
will be exacted in all its details," read General Weitzel's order. All noncommissioned officers were required to wear their chevrons. No boots were to
be worn by infantry soldiers. "All on duty except fatigue men will wear their
dress coats." Clothes were to be brushed, boots blacked, brass polished, hair
and beards neatly trimmed. Except on Saturdays and Sundays, there were to
be three drills a day: squad drill from 7:00 to 8:00 a.m., company drill from
9:00 to 10:00 a.m., and battalion drill from 3:30 to 5:15 p.m. Two company
drills out of every six were designated as skirmish drills, and at least three
out of ten battalion drills were to be brigade or division drills.

Though days must have passed rather slowly at Camp Lincoln, and
despite the end of the war, it was not enough for an officer to simply want to
go home. Second Lieutenant Henry R. Hinckley of Company A (William

Lloyd Garrison's friend, it will be remembered) tendered his resignation on 15 May. "Affairs of the highest personal importance require my presence in England at an early date; and hostilities having now ceased, I do not consider my position of sufficient importance to the service to make it my duty to remain longer in the army to the detriment of my future prospects," Hinckley wrote. Furthermore, he pointed out that the captain and first lieutenant of his company were present with it, and "I can very well be spared."

Lieutenant Hinckley's resignation was not approved, so he wrote again on 20 May: "At the request of Colonel Adams commanding this regiment I have the honor again to submit my resignation on the same grounds on which it was tendered in my communication of the fifteenth instant which was not favorably considered." This time Colonel Adams added the following endorsement: "This officer is very anxious to leave the service, and, on various grounds, is entitled clearly to an early discharge. If his resignation is accepted now, it is in my power to more than replace him at once, which will not be the case after the regiment is transferred to a more remote department." General Weitzel took Adams's point, and Hinckley was discharged.

As Colonel Adams intimated in his endorsement of Lieutenant Hinckley's resignation, the rumor of the transfer of XXV Corps "to a more remote department" persisted. In Washington, DC, a grand review of the Army of the Potomac took place on 23 May 1865. By regiment, by brigade, by division, and by army corps, the long lines of blue-clad infantry paraded through Washington, reviewed by the president and Mrs. Johnson, his cabinet, General Grant and wife, and a host of dignitaries and citizens. The cavalry in its thousands trotted by, the artillery, the engineers and pontoniers with their boats, and the ambulances and quartermasters' wagons by the thousands. The next day, Sherman's western veterans repeated the spectacle. There was no grand review for the Army of the James.

The troops of the white XXIV Army Corps were rapidly mustered out, but the African American soldiers of XXV Army Corps were on their way to Texas. Although General Weitzel received orders to break up Camp Lincoln and march his corps to City Point on 25 May, it took a full two weeks before enough transports could be assembled for the 5th Massachusetts. Second Lieutenant Ned Bartlett wrote from City Point on 3 June. The regiment was playing the old game of "hurry up and wait." Bartlett expected to embark the next day, "or rather we are likely to as we have been in readiness to do [so] for the last three days." The regiment had broken camp on 31 May, "expecting to embark at once but instead of going aboard we squatted down into this field near City Point and here we have been ever since." The 5th Massachusetts Cavalry was joined with two other African American cavalry units, the 1st and 2nd Regiments, U.S. Colored Cavalry, on 30 May, forming the Cavalry Brigade of XXV Army Corps. There were, however, no brigade drills. It was so hot and humid that drill was dispensed with. The officers and men simply sat in their tents and sweltered. "Active exercise of all kind is utterly impossible. Our poor horses suffer more than the men—standing all the day in the hot sun without any shelter." Jackets and vests were discarded, the troopers took off their undershirts, "and many of the men even dispense with their pantaloons and go about in drawers, and often even without drawers," Bartlett noted.

Several officers declined to make the trip to Texas. Colonel Charles Francis Adams Jr. went home on sick leave on 1 June. In his autobiography, Adams described his health: "I was then a mere wreck—pitiably reduced and weak. Eaten up with malarial poison, I weighed scarcely one hundred and thirty pounds, while my knees would at night so ache from mere weakness that sleep was out of the question. Intestinally corroded, I was never free from the influence of opium, which acting on my nerves drove me almost to insanity."

Adams had to face reality. He put in his resignation on 21 July 1865, based on "surgeon's certificates of disability." That resignation was accepted by the War Department on 1 August, and after three years, eleven months, and twelve days, Charles Adams was a civilian once more. Major Henry P. Bowditch resigned on 3 June and Captains C. Chauncy Parsons and James L. Wheat on 16 June. First Lieutenant J. Davenport Fisher went home the first week of June as well, discharged for disability on account of increasing deafness. Assistant Surgeon Isaac S. Cushman had resigned on 26 May at the request of Colonel Adams. "The value of my services to the Government have been of late greatly impaired by mental anxiety on account of domestic and pecuniary troubles," wrote Cushman in his letter of resignation.

Many of the enlisted men of XXV Army Corps could have claimed "mental anxiety" if they had been allowed to resign. A particularly ugly situation arose in the 1st and 2nd Regiments of U.S. Colored Cavalry, brigaded with the 5th Massachusetts Cavalry. The 1st and 2nd U.S. Colored

Cavalry were raised in the tidewater region of Virginia. Consequently, many of the men saw their wives and children just before the regiments were to leave for Texas.

As long as the war lasted and their brothers, husbands and fathers were in uniform, the federal government issued rations to the families of these men. With the war over and the men about to be sent to Texas, the commander of the District of Eastern Virginia, Brigadier General George H. Gordon, decided to stop these rations. This was the same General George H. Gordon who had raised and commanded the 2nd Massachusetts Infantry, the regiment that first cousins Henry Sturgis Russell and Robert Gould Shaw had joined in May 1861. Now the tide of war had washed Gordon up in Virginia. Regular army to the core, General Gordon was determined to correct any irregularity in his department. Gordon wrote to Captain O. Brown, assistant commissioner of the Virginia Freedmen's Bureau, on 6 June 1865: "Sir: I understand that you are feeding with government rations, from fifteen hundred to two thousand colored persons, families of colored soldiers, many, if not all of these persons being able to gain a livelihood by work. . . . I do not consider the United States Government, through its agent, Major General Butler, bound by the contract of December 5, 1863, since the pay of the colored soldier was raised; the reasons for the contract failing, and the necessity no longer existing, you will at once discontinue an issue so pernicious in its effects to the colored persons, so unwarranted by precedent, and so exhaustive upon the public treasury."

General Gordon's order was to go into effect on 10 June, which was the day the transports arrived to take the Cavalry Brigade to Texas. Brevet Brigadier General George W. Cole, commanding the brigade, sent a letter to XXV Army Corps headquarters when he arrived in Texas. The two U.S. Colored Cavalry regiments had not been paid for almost a year, their families' rations were about to be cut off, and there was an ugly rumor circulating that the troops were to be "colonized" in Texas. The trouble began in the 2nd U.S. Colored Cavalry. General Cole wrote, "The majority of the First and Second Regiments United States Colored Cavalry are residents of Portsmouth and Norfolk and vicinity, and the 2d United States Colored Cavalry having met their families and children (nearly 1,000 as I am informed) they were unwilling to leave them unprovided with money or rations. . . . Consequently they became excited and decidedly insubordinate." The 2nd U.S. Colored

Cavalry was under the command of a Major Dollard, who instead of taking charge of the situation took refuge on the transport in the river "and sometime after called the Line Officers away from their commands, probably for consultation thus leaving the men on shore unrestrained by their presence." Cole estimated that about twenty troopers deserted during the excitement, but order was restored in a few hours, with the leaders of the mutiny arrested and put in irons. The men were "contented before seeing their families," and some even assisted in arresting their fellow soldiers, "but were enraged at the threat of using white troops to coerce them, as was offered by Major Dollard, Second United States Colored Cavalry."

The mutiny soon spread to the 1st U.S. Colored Cavalry, and for the same reasons. Like Dollard, a Major Brown in command of the 1st U.S. Colored Cavalry absented himself during the crisis. Brown's "subordinate officers . . . found it necessary to shoot (not fatally) one man and turn over to me six more whom I ironed," wrote the brevet brigadier general. General Cole would have liked to arrest Majors Brown and Dollard but thought it would encourage the insubordination of the enlisted men. "With the exception of Major Brown, First United States Colored Cavalry and Major Dollard, Second United States Colored Cavalry the officers of the Brigade both Staff and Regimental were all prompt and dutiful, and for their close attention to duty, and sober, earnest labor in the prompt and thorough embarkation of this command, (no boat being detained an hour) they merit my warmest thanks, not one being behind time or neglecting an order[,] a course of conduct which if pursued by their superiors would, I am convinced, have prevented any disturbance whatever, for every man left camp as cheerfully as ever before."

The Cavalry Brigade, XXV Army Corps, took transport on 10, 11, and 12 June in five vessels, the steamers *General McClellan*, *Meteor*, *Ashland*, *H. S. Hagar*, and *Dudley Buck*. They arrived at Fort Monroe on 13 June, taking on coal, water, forage, rations, and 250,000 rounds of ammunition, and sailed on 16 June. The fleet reached Fort Morgan, Mobile, Alabama, on 23 June. There orders were waiting for General Cole to take the brigade to Brazos Santiago, at the mouth of the Rio Grande River. At South West Pass, Mississippi River, the vessels took on coal and water on 25 June and sailed for Texas on the 28th. Most of the trip was like a pleasure cruise. Lieutenant Ned Bartlett wrote his sister Martha from the steamer *George B. McClellan* on 21 June.

They were five days at sea and had just rounded the Florida Keys. Bartlett had been seasick the first two days but was enjoying himself immensely when he wrote. "We have so far had a very peaceful trip, beautiful as it can be. The sea is now as calm as Walden [Pond] ever was."

The *McClellan* was the headquarters transport and so held General Cole, who was accompanied by his wife and children, Cole's staff, Lieutenant Colonel Weld now commanding the 5th Massachusetts, and the regimental staff officers. The 2nd Battalion of the 5th Massachusetts was also aboard, which explains Bartlett's presence. "Last night we had a gay sing on deck, we kept it up till midnight." The officers also organized a rowboat race between those on different vessels. "Major Adams has picked his crew of three others of which I am one and has challenged any other four officers to row," Bartlett wrote. The enlisted men took their ease in the sun on the forward deck and were also enjoying themselves, "now they have got over being sea sick." The fleet transporting Cole's brigade arrived at Brazos Santiago, Texas, on 30 June. Bartlett wrote Martha on 2 July, "We have at last arrived at our land of promise and of all the God forsaken holes this is the worst one I ever saw." The seas had turned rough after they left the Mississippi, and Bartlett was soon feeling that "unpleasant sensation" again. He lay on deck in misery for forty-eight hours as the *McClellan* pitched and rolled through a heavy fog. His first glimpse of Texas was a low beach on which the breakers crashed, "ten times as high as you ever saw them at Pigeon Cove [near Gloucester, Massachusetts]."

Brazos Santiago was a barrier island at the mouth of the Rio Grande River. Entirely devoid of trees, Brazos Santiago lay to the southwest of Padre Island and to the southeast of Point Isabel, across Laguna Madre. A wooden bridge connected Brazos Island with the town of Boca Chica on a peninsula formed by Laguna Madre on the north and the Rio Grande on the south. A road ran from Boca Chica about twenty-five miles northwest to Brownsville and Fort Brown. Across from Boca Chica was the town of Bagdad, Mexico, which had sprung up during the war. Up the river, across from Brownsville, was Matamoras. It was largely on account of those two towns, which had been smuggling depots for the Confederacy, and the river that lay between them that XXV Army Corps had been sent to Texas. General Grant wanted any still-active Confederate troops to be disarmed and blocked from crossing the Texas-Mexico border to join Mexican emperor Maximilian and his French troops. After Confederate general Kirby Smith surrendered to Union general Edward R. S. Canby on 26 May 1865, Confederate general Joseph O. Shelby and some 1,800 men of his "Iron Brigade" refused to surrender and crossed into Mexico. Several thousand Confederate army and navy officers, government officials, and large plantation owners—some with their families and their slaves—fled to Mexico after the war. The further prevention of such escapes was one reason for Union troops along the Rio Grande. The federal government also knew that Maximilian had met with high-ranking Confederates near Brownsville and had permitted supplies to be smuggled to the Confederacy through Bagdad and Matamoras. Secretary of State Seward agreed with General Grant's plans, wanting the French out of Mexico, while avoiding another war.

France's 1861 Mexican intervention, which England and Spain joined initially as a debt-collection scheme, was based on a miscalculation: Napoleon III gambled that the Confederacy would win the war, establishing a regime allied to imperial Mexico and developing strong commercial links with France. President Jefferson Davis and his then secretary of state, Judah P. Benjamin, also miscalculated. They expected that Maximilian would recognize the Confederacy, thus leading to French (and British) recognition. Maximilian, however, while collaborating with the shipment of goods to Texas under the (neutral) Mexican flag, would not risk formal recognition. Maximilian truly saw himself as a reformer, saving Catholic Mexico from the vicious, anticlerical republicanism of Benito Juarez. So, with his regime already propped up on French bayonets, Maximilian was reluctant to accept the aid of slaveholding "gringos." Those French bayonets, for a time, were victorious. Until the American Civil War, Napoleon III had the largest professional and most technically advanced army of the 1850s and 1860s. Victorious in Italy, North Africa, the Crimea, and Indochina, it established world military standards. By 1865, under General François Achille Bazaine, victor at Sebastopol and Solferino, France had virtually conquered Mexico. Bazaine's French force of forty thousand included the Foreign Legion, which still holds bright the memory of Camerone, where sixty-two legionnaires fought to the death against some 3,400 Juaristas. Augmenting the French were Belgian, Austrian, Hungarian, and North African (Senegalese) volunteers. The French drove Juarez over the border at El Paso Del Norte (now Ciudad Juárez) and captured, killed, or imprisoned most of the leading Juaristas, including their best general, Porfirio Díaz. The French held the major seaports and the cities. Then came the end of the Civil War. The Lincoln administration had recognized the Juarez government, and now Secretary Seward began "to grow bolder in extending to France a courteous and friendly, but persuading, invitation to exit from Mexico, couched in pressing and admonishing language which the Emperor was finally induced to accept," wrote James M. Callahan in *American Foreign Policy in Mexican Relations*. The threat of armed intervention into Mexico was always underneath Seward's careful diplomatic notes. By July 1865, there were some forty-six thousand Union troops in Texas. The XIII Army Corps had marched overland from Alabama, and two divisions of cavalry, under Generals George A. Custer and Wesley Merritt, rode six hundred miles from Louisiana to Austin and San Antonio.

The XXV Army Corps was stationed at various points and in various units: at Brazos Santiago to Boca Chica to Clarksville, and thence to Brownsville and Roma up the Rio Grande. Also, brigades were sent to Corpus Christi and Indianola. As Bartlett had noted to his sister, the mouth of the Rio Grande in 1865 was not particularly pleasing to the eye. When not dry as a bone, it was waterlogged. Brevet Major General Giles A. Smith, 1st Division commander, sent a report of a march from Brazos Santiago to Brownsville to XXV Army Corps Headquarters in Corpus Christi on 29 June 1865. "The roads are horrible," Smith wrote. Wagons had been lightly loaded but were still unable to get through. "Some of the way we were obliged to have the men carry the loads and then twelve mules stalled with empty wagons." General Smith advised that no more wagons be sent "until the water goes down." Smith found Brownsville "not much of a town." He noted that the houses were "shingled with straw." Smith sent two Brownsville newspapers to Corps Headquarters. As for the women of the region, they "all have black hair and eyes. Some hair straight, some curly. They sit in their Ranches in the middle of the floor, chairs being an article of too civilized luxury to be known in this country."

Brevet Brigadier General Cole also reported in. His second report to Corps Headquarters, dated 4 July 1865 from Clarksville, Texas, dealt with matters more serious than a relatively pleasant sea voyage. The brigade was without ambulances and hospital tents. "The Senior Medical Officer of my command informs me that several of the officers are quite sick and the enlisted men are many of them taken sick—a portion of them having fallen out by the road to this place unable to travel," Cole wrote. General Cole requested three hospital tents until a post hospital could be built.

Besides dysentery and typhus, many of the ill enlisted men were suffering from scurvy. It is hard to believe that men not confined on a months-long sea voyage could lack vitamin C until it is remembered that these troops had been in the trenches for nine months or on garrison duty at Point Lookout. The winter diet of coffee, salt pork, beans, and cornbread might not have been modified by fresh vegetables and fruits before the brigade left Virginia. A brigade inspection report on 25 July confirmed this. Under the heading "Health," the inspector wrote, "Diarrhea with a tendency to scurvy." The 2nd U.S. Colored Cavalry in particular was suffering from "General Debility." The acting assistant inspector general, 3rd Cavalry Brigade, 3rd Division, a Captain Smith of the 2nd U.S. Colored Cavalry, left us a glimpse of the Cavalry Brigade in the "Remarks" section of his report. The 1st U.S. Colored Cavalry, 730 effectives, was "doing duty as a stevedore gang at Brazos Santiago therefore have not the same opportunity of drills and inspection as they would were they in Camp of Instruction." The 2nd U.S. Colored Cavalry, 709 effectives, was "divided in small detachments along the line of Railroad about being built from Brazos to Brownsville thus depriving them of their usual amounts of drills and Inspections." The 5th Massachusetts Volunteer Cavalry's aggregate strength was put at 1,133, but its effectives numbered 640. The other two regiments had the same broad discrepancy. This can be explained by the fact that several companies had been detached to guard various points. We know from the Bartlett Letters, for instance, that he guarded the bridge from Brazos Santiago to Boca Chica with two platoons. General Cole's troop returns for the various steamers that brought his command to Texas enumerated 910 men for the 1st U.S. Colored Cavalry, 900 for the 2nd U.S. Colored Cavalry, and 950 for the 5th Massachusetts. It just doesn't seem possible that almost seven hundred men of the Cavalry Brigade were sick. In any case, Captain Smith wrote that the 5th Massachusetts Cavalry was "encamped near the mouth of the Rio Grande and are drilling two hours a day and under the persevering energy of Lieutenant Colonel Weld, its present Commander it is rapidly being brought to proper standard of discipline."

As Captain Smith's report mentioned, a railroad was being constructed from Boca Chica to Brownsville. Special Order No. 40, issued by 3rd Division commander Brevet Brigadier General Alonzo Draper on 18 July, detailed 650 enlisted men from the 3rd Brigade to be furnished daily as a fatigue party to construct the railroad. Another special order, dated 26 July 1865 from 3rd Brigade Headquarters, detailed a further one hundred men from the 5th Massachusetts Cavalry, "with proper non-commissioned and commissioned officers," to help construct this railroad.

Major General Weitzel came up with a unique plan to alleviate the scurvy apparently prevalent not only in the 3rd Brigade, 3rd Division, but also throughout XXV Army Corps. Weitzel sent out a "circular" on 25 July explaining his ideas: "Nature has made a provision here for the lack of vegetables, and the tendency to scurvy among the residents. The juice of the 'Algave A Mexicana' or American Aloe, which is found in groves of greater or less sizes, will cure scurvy or prevent it, in those systems that are inclined in that way."

Weitzel ordered that aloe trees be cut down, pressed, and the juice collected for patients suffering from scurvy. The major general commanding noted that the juice did ferment in a few days and gave off a disagreeable smell and tasted foul when fermenting. "In the open air the fermentation lasts only a few days, and after this it again has a more pleasant but acid taste." Weitzel urged his command to drink the juice before it fermented, as it always tasted better. Detachments were ordered out from "each post or brigade, with two or three wagons, to collect this tree and make this drink which is called by the common people 'Pulque.'" Detachments were allowed to "combine pleasure with duty" and to hunt as much as they wanted, "the country being full of deer and other game."

Of course, for some, Texas was not all fatigue duty and illness. Lieutenant Bartlett liked having his own independent command away from the drills and discipline of the regiment at Clarksville. "It's pleasant to be the biggest toad in the puddle even if it is a very small puddle," he wrote on 16 July. He was not lonely, however, as he had a "prime cook" and many visiting officers down from the regiment. He did his own "marketing every morning from the boats that supply us from Bagdad." He ate the "most delicious red fish," fresh beef occasionally, and bananas and pineapples for dessert. He drew the "chief stand-bys" from the commissary: bread, potatoes, and hominy. Bartlett had been detailed to repair the regiment's ordnance, which kept him busy enough along with his other duties to stave off boredom. Bartlett wrote home again on 23 July 1865 to describe a visit across the river to the town of Bagdad. Accompanied by his friends Lieutenants Abner Mallory and Charles Wheeler, he had spent the afternoon "wandering about the dirty streets, going into every store but making very few purchases." They sat under a tree in the market and had a "feast" of fresh fruit: oranges, bananas, pineapples, prickly pears, and pomegranates. They had an amusing time trying to communicate with "the old cock of a market man" who insisted on silver for payment, as neither U.S. "greenbacks" nor Confederate currency were accepted in Mexico. Bartlett explained to his sister that Bagdad had grown from a "little fisherman's colony" into a large town during the war. "Goods were shipped there from New York and England and run across the Rio Grande into Texas to supply the southern states." Every building in the place was a store or warehouse, but now the occupation had come across the river and "every day the place is dwindling down." There was still a great quantity of goods in Bagdad and an international flavor to the place, with "English, French, a good many southerners and a few Yankeys [*sic*], Spanish and the native Mexicans." With the exception of the Mexicans, who were the "rightful possessors" of Bagdad, the rest were "sharpers, smugglers and blockade runners." The last named were "leaving every day for New Orleans with their pockets lined with gold."

Bartlett reported that Brazos was growing as fast as Bagdad was shrinking; stores and houses were being built, sutlers had arrived in a swarm, and the construction of the railroad would make Brazos Santiago "quite a town." Bartlett was not homesick, but he found the Texas landscape monotonous. "Oh I would give a good deal to see a tree!" He had not "seen anything green (growing) since we left Virginia." Several of the 5th Massachusetts officers were attempting to resign, but Bartlett thought resignation an "impossibility . . . for those high in authority will not approve any resignations from this corps." The young lieutenant was willing to "wait the action of the government," as the regiment had only another year and a half before its term of enlistment expired. There was also the question of the officers' duty to remain with their men. "They cannot go home and we ought to see the thing out with them. Don't you think so?" Service in Texas was not particularly pleasant, especially with no prospect of leaving soon. But Bartlett was determined to do the best he could and to enjoy himself. Besides, he wrote, "I want to see the country, and I like army life."

Ned Bartlett was correct in his assumption that the regiment would be in Texas some time longer. He duly wrote home every week, describing hunting and fishing parties, a small boat he had built on Padre Island, visits to Bagdad, and visits from friends for dinner. The regiment continued to work on the railroad, to drill and picket, and to make a show of force along the border, although there is no record that the 5th Massachusetts ever prevented any Confederates from crossing into Mexico. The enlisted men performed their fatigue duty in turn, sweated through the mounted and dismounted drills, and sometimes managed to slip across the river for some illegal amusement. One trooper, Private William Mitchell, Company G, was drowned on 22 July at Clarksville. Regimental records note that Mitchell was "swept out to sea while bathing at the mouth of the Rio Grande River." All speculated on when they would go home.

Occasionally an incident served to break the routine. Ned Bartlett wrote of a "little excitement" on 20 August "in shape of a fight between the provost guard (colored) and a crew of navy seamen (white)." The sailors were drunk and looking for a fight, and the provost guard obliged them. The African American provosts fired on the sailors, "and then there was a free fight and there was a few broken heads on both sides until the guard arrested them and sent the sailors off to their gunboat." There were several wounded, but no one was killed. Bartlett's tent was still a "regular hotel" for officers of the regiment and brigade. He could "hardly write," the place was so full of conversation and tobacco smoke. "Many of them are good fellows and I enjoy their society."

One officer of whom Bartlett and his fellow officers distinctly did not approve of was Second Lieutenant John V. Apthorp. Apthorp was commissioned on 25 July and mustered with the regiment as second lieutenant, Company B, on 22 August 1865. "Governor Andrews has sent us out another white livered boy for a Second Lieutenant," Bartlett wrote. "Davidson was bad enough but Apthorp is worst." Bartlett may have been hasty in his judgment of Second Lieutenant Francis S. Davidson, Company C (commissioned 20 May 1865), for he had subsequent service with the black 9th U.S. Cavalry. As for Apthorp, Bartlett had absolutely no respect for him. The young officer had been "for the last two years fitting for the war at a military school and now as the danger is over, he goes into the army for the first time." Bartlett had "spotted him when he came off the boat and called him into my tent." The tent was crowded with officers, "and we roughed him not a little." That treatment was gentle compared with what Apthorp experienced that night when he reported to the regiment. "A report was circulated that Captain Allen had the smallpox and they brought Allen in and laid him in Apthorp's blankets and then reported in his hearing that Allen was bad with the smallpox." The young lieutenant tore his blankets off the bunk and rushed out of the tent. The officers told Apthorp "horrid stories" about snakes and the Texas climate. While he was eating his first meal with the regiment, "Captain Kaler got a carbine and commenced shooting over and around his tent, rather unpleasantly near." Apthorp was so frightened that he put his blankets over his head and hid under his bunk. "You may think that this is rather a rough reception to give a brother officer but every one was so disgusted that he should have the cheek to come out just as the war was over when there were so many old soldiers who want and should have the position."

One old soldier that Bartlett did not welcome the sight of was Brevet Brigadier General Samuel E. Chamberlain, who reported in and took command of the 5th Massachusetts on 19 September 1865. Bartlett felt that promotion should have gone to Lieutenant Colonel Horace Weld, "for he has been with the regiment ever since its organization and has commanded it more than half of the time." Bartlett had some hard words for the governor of the Bay State: "Governor Andrew never does the square thing on promotions so I don't think we could have expected anything else."

By September, with the long, hot Texas summer over, the health of the men improved. Antiscorbutic measures had been effective by the middle of August. Work continued on the railroad, with a further detail of one hundred men added to the first hundred. Their work was hampered by the arrival of a long period of rain, which began toward the end of August and continued off and on for several weeks. As rumors grew rife of a possible muster out, some enlisted men of the regiment began to lose their discipline and military bearing. Several troopers were put in the guardhouse in September for stealing, absence without leave, neglect of duty, disobedience of orders, and drunkenness. The regiment was by no means going to pieces, as there were never more than six men in the guardhouse at one time during the month.

There was certainly a rising level of impatience at "playing soldier" when the war had been over for five months. One trooper, Private William Boyd of Company L, was killed on 29 September. Regimental records list Boyd as having died at "Brazos, Texas of wounds not received in action." If a fellow soldier had killed Boyd, that soldier would have been arrested and tried; there is no such record. More likely Boyd got in a fight while absent without leave in Bagdad and was killed, but we will never know.

At long last the expected order came. Dated 28 September 1865, General Order No. 65, Headquarters XXV Army Corps, read, "In accordance with Special Order Number 29 Headquarters Department of Texas dated Galveston, Texas, September 16th, 1865 the Twenty-Second United States Colored Troops, 29 Conn Vols. (col'd) Forty-Third, Eighth, Twenty-Ninth, Thirty-First, Forty-First, Forty-Fifth, Twenty-Eighth, One-Hundred and Twenty-Seventh United States Colored Troops and the Fifth Massachusetts Cavalry (Colored) will be mustered out as soon as possible in accordance with General Orders Number 94 War Department. AGO Washington, D.C. May 15, 1865."

Ned Bartlett wrote happily to his cousin Ripley on 6 October. He expected to be a "citizen" again before two weeks' time, for "by order from the War Department mustering out all colored regiments raised in the free states the Fifth Cavalry leaves the service." Officers were preparing the muster out rolls, turning in government property, and packing to go home. "Now I am going to take time by the fore lock and request that you will come home to Concord and spend Thanksgiving, for I have no doubt that I shall be at home on that day and I wish very much that the whole family might be got together."

General Weitzel wished to leave some parting words with the African American soldiers now going home:

The Commanding General desires to express to the many good regiments that are about to be mustered out his regret at their departure, and to congratulate them on the pleasure they will experience in returning to their friends and relatives at home. Although none of them have as many battlefields to be proud of as the regiments that were raised in the beginning of the war, still they have an equally brilliant record, because they have always accomplished well, everything that was required of them. Olustee, Petersburg, the Mine, Deep Bottom, New Market Heights, Fussell's Mills and Nine Mile Road are among those fields where they proved their valor, and settled the question as to the capacity of the colored man to make a good soldier. The Commanding General has no doubt, that in their future conduct as citizens at home, they will, by their good behavior preserve untarnished the brilliant record they have made in the Army.

The last paragraph of the description of the regiment's service in *Massachusetts Soldiers, Sailors, and Marines in the Civil War* reads, "The prospect of trouble in Mexico having ended, the regiment was mustered out of the federal service at Clarksville, Texas, October 31, 1865, and immediately started for Massachusetts, making most of the trip by steamer. On arriving in Boston Harbor the regiment was landed at Galloup's Island where it remained until the latter part of November when it was paid off and discharged."

Some men, of course, could not make the trip. Private Morris Herman was one such. Herman enlisted in Holyoke, Massachusetts, on 29 June 1864. He stated that he was thirty-six years old, had been born in Virginia, and was a farmer by occupation. Herman was described as five feet, nine inches tall with black eyes, black hair, and black complexion. He made his mark and joined Company I at Point Lookout. The records of the Corps D'Afrique Hospital, New Orleans, Louisiana, note that Herman died of "Diarrhea Chronic" on 10 August 1865. On a form headed "Inventory," a clerk wrote, "He had no effects."

The 5th Massachusetts Volunteer Cavalry lost seven men killed and a hundred and sixteen men to disease during its service. We can only hope that on Thanksgiving Day 1865, someone raised a glass or said a prayer in memory of these faithful men.

Point Lookout, Maryland: Guarding Confederate Prisoners, Training as Cavalry

Point Lookout, Maryland—view of Hammond General Hospital

Brigadier General Barnes and staff, Point Lookout

The 2nd Squadron (Companies C and D) of the 1st Massachusetts Volunteer Cavalry was the Cavalry Escort for Headquarters, Army of the Potomac, from mid-1864 to the end of the war. Seated in the center is Captain Charles F. Adams Jr. Adams joined the 5th Massachusetts Cavalry as lieutenant colonel in September 1864. On Adams's right is Captain George H. Teague, who also joined the 5th Massachusetts Cavalry in September 1864. Several troopers of Companies C and D of the 1st Massachusetts Cavalry accepted promotion into the 5th Massachusetts Cavalry, including Sergeant Major George L. Bradbury, Sergeant John H. George, Sergeant Cornelius Kaler, Sergeant George D. Odell, and Private George F. Scott. (CREDIT: PHCW)

Lieutenant Colonel Charles F. Adams Jr.
(CREDIT: MHS)

Lieutenant Edward J. Bartlett
(CREDIT: MHS)

5th Massachusetts Cavalry officers' housing, Point Lookout, Maryland (CREDIT: AHEC)

5th Massachusetts Cavalry officers (CREDIT: AHEC)

Sergeant Gustavus Booth, Company D (CREDIT: LIBRARY OF CONGRESS, ACCESSED 6 MARCH 2019 FROM HTTP://USCTWILLCOTN.BLOGSPOT.COM)

Sidney Lanier (CREDIT: PHCW)

Confederates swearing oath of allegiance at Point Lookout POW camp (CREDIT: PHCW)

Confederate prisoners take oath before Brigadier General Barnes (CREDIT: PHCW)

Virginia and Texas: "In the Field"

Cavalry horses in ruined Richmond (CREDIT: PHCW)

President Lincoln in Richmond, 4 April 1865 (CREDIT: PHCW)

Richmond ruins (CREDIT: PHCW)

Ruins of Richmond, April 1865 (CREDIT: PHCW)

Tredegar Iron Works, April 1865 (CREDIT: PHCW)

Mourning women in the Richmond ruins (CREDIT: PHCW)

CHAPTER EIGHT

Losing the Peace

A double purpose induced me and most others to enlist, to assist in abolishing slavery and to save the country from ruin. Something in furtherance of both objects we have certainly done, and now it strikes me that now more could be done for our welfare in the pursuit of civil life. I think that a camp life would be a decided injury to our people. No matter how well and faithfully they may perform their duties they will shortly be considered as "lazy nigger sojers"—as drones in the great hive.

—SERGEANT MAJOR CHRISTIAN A. FLEETWOOD,
4TH U.S. COLORED TROOPS, JUNE 1865

THERE IS NO DEFINITIVE END DATE FOR THE AMERICAN CIVIL WAR, NO eleventh hour of the eleventh day of the eleventh month, no VE- or VJ-day. Few whites on either side seemed to have felt like celebrating. No strangers hugged or shared champagne, taking to the streets with joy. While true that African Americans celebrated the entry of Union troops into Richmond and the subsequent tour of President Lincoln, there was awe, a religious fervor, to those celebrations. The Year of Jubilee had arrived: blacks were finally free, just like in the book of Exodus. But what did "freedom" mean? And Father Abraham, a week after Lee's surrender, was murdered at Ford's Theatre.

No, the Civil War ended not with joy and triumph but with anxiety, exhaustion, anger, and assassination. Lee's bitter veterans stacked their weapons and shredded their flags, weeping for their lost cause. The cause that had brought them so much death and destruction left them in rags, shoeless and starving. They had the rest of their lives to dwell on what might have been—if only the North had had fewer men, factories, and ships, less organization, money, and will.

The United States had defeated the section that was in rebellion against it, but with the death of Lincoln there was no strong leader to bring the country together again and move it forward. Without Lincoln, there were competing theories on how to repair the relationships between the federal government and the states and on whether African Americans were entitled to full citizenship.

As far as African American troops went, their place in a *post bellum* America seemed to be as far as possible from any recognition or gratitude from the white politicians or their Union brothers-in-arms. The black units present at the surrender of Lee's army at Appomattox were quickly moved to isolated garrison duty preparatory to embarking for Texas. White regiments prepared for the Grand Review in Washington and got ready to muster out. Remember that the entire XXV Army Corps—thirty-two infantry, three cavalry regiments, and artillery units comprising fifty-six guns—were shipped to Texas in May and June 1865. William F. Fox, in his *Regimental Losses in the American Civil War (1861–1865)*, writing about XXV Corps, noted, "In May, 1865 the corps accompanied General Weitzel to Texas, where it joined the Army of Occupation, and remained until January 8, 1866, when the corps was discontinued, it being the last corps mustered out."

There is a well-known, two-volume compendium of information about the Union army published by Frederick H. Dyer in 1908. The first volume contains information such as the vital statistics for each state that furnished troops for the Union army, the structural changes of the Union armies over time, and a state-by-state listing of every battle fought by that state's troops and the troops engaged. The second volume contains the organization of every Union regiment formed during the war, along with its service record, listing all the events in which the regiment took part during its existence. A glance through the section for the U.S. Colored Troops shows service entries such as "Post duty at Springfield, Tenn. and in the District of Middle Tennessee until April 1866; Duty at Brownesville and on the Rio Grande, Texas until January 1867; Garrison at Charleston and Mt Pleasant, S.C. until August 1865 and at various points in South Carolina and Georgia until October 1869; Duty at Ghent, Paducah, LaGrange, Crab Orchard and Camp Nelson [Kentucky] until August 1865, and the Department of Arkansas until March 1866."

Dyer's entry for the 5th Massachusetts Cavalry is equally dry: "Duty at City Point, Va. as infantry until June 16, 1864. Before Petersburg June 16–19. Moved to Point Lookout, Md., June 30 and duty there guarding prisoners until March 1865. Ordered to the field and duty near Richmond, March, near Petersburg, April, near City Point, May, and at Camp Lincoln until June 16. Ordered to Texas and duty at Clarksville until October. Mustered out October 31, 1865."

In these few lines are the triumph and frustration, the suffering and the satisfaction of almost three years together as a regiment. The 5th Massachusetts Cavalry spent a couple of weeks together on one of the Boston Harbor islands, in November no less, and then the 5th was paid off and broken up, the men scattering to the four winds. Troopers and officers mustered out in Texas or Virginia, or New York City, wherever the troopships touched on the long journey back. And there were the men left in hospitals from Boston to the Gulf Coast, left to recover or die and be buried next to their brothers. Sometimes the cemeteries were segregated, or the stones had "Col'd" after the name to preclude doubt. Other times, a simple wooden board was left to fade, or a stone reading "unknown Union soldier."

The regiment was mustered out, and the men, now Union veterans, had to figure out what to do next in their lives. Dyer's Compendium shows that the federal government, once it had enlisted, clothed, armed, and trained the black regiments, was reluctant to let them go. Most African American units remained on duty for months after the shooting stopped. The Union army had employed schoolteachers to teach African American troops (and their families, if nearby) reading, writing, and arithmetic; the army was seen as a positive influence on the lives of former slaves. Legislation was filed in Congress to have black regiments stationed permanently on the frontier. But the four African American regiments eventually authorized (two of infantry, two of cavalry) were miniscule compared to the over 180,000 black men who in 1865 manned the seven cavalry regiments (including the 5th Massachusetts), the 140 numbered infantry regiments (including two from Massachusetts), and the twenty-three artillery units.

In June 1865, Sergeant Major Christian A. Fleetwood, who had won the Medal of Honor with the 4th U.S. Colored Infantry regiment at Chaffin's (or Chapin's) Farm in Virginia in September 1864, wrote to his friend Dr. James Hall, who had evidently urged the sergeant major to remain in the army. Readers will remember it was Fleetwood who engaged "Africano" in the pages of the *Weekly Anglo-African* about the events at Baylor's Farm in June 1864. Fleetwood's letter is worth quoting at length because he was an articulate observer who took his letter to Dr. Hall as an opportunity to explain his frustration at the treatment of black troops. Accordingly, Fleetwood wrote, "I have trespassed upon your time to a much greater extent than I intended but I wished you correctly to appreciate my motives for leaving the service." Fleetwood regretted that Dr. Hall did not understand that he was "actuated by the same motives" that led him to enlist in the first place, "some personal ambition to be sure but mainly from a desire to benefit my race." At one time the sergeant major may have considered making a career in the army, and at one point every officer in his regiment signed a letter to Secretary Stanton urging Fleetwood's commissioning. "From representations made by Col. [William] Birney and from the position assumed by our friends in Congress, you remember we were induced to believe or hope that on evidence of merit and ability to do our duty we should receive promotion, at least to the rank of company & regimental officers." As testimony to their ability to do their duty, Fleetwood outlined the "active, arduous, dangerous service" of the 4th U.S. Colored Infantry and modestly mentioned his award of "a medal conferred for some special acts as a soldier." In four paragraphs, the sergeant major discusses his regiment's testing to destruction, from the assault on Petersburg of 15 June 1865 to the Dutch Gap Canal, New Market Heights, Fort Harrison, and the two assaults on Fort Fisher, North Carolina. "Upon all our record there is not a single blot and yet no member of this regiment is considered deserving of a commission or if so cannot receive one." Christian Fleetwood wanted to make sure that Dr. Hall understood it was not individual disappointment that prompted him to leave the army. "But I see no good that will result to our people by continuing to serve, on the contrary it seems to me that our continuing to act in a subordinate capacity, with no hope of advancement or promotion is an absolute injury to our cause." If African Americans continued on in the army with no possibility for promotion, it seemed to Fleetwood a "tacit but telling acknowledgement on our part . . . that we are satisfied to remain in a state of marked and acknowledged subserviency." The army as an educational institution was not enough for Christian Fleetwood. Black soldiers had done their part to save the republic; they had more than held up their end of the bargain: "A double purpose induced me and most others to enlist," he wrote, "to assist in abolishing slavery and to save the country from ruin. Something in furtherance of both objects we have certainly done, and now it strikes me that more could be done for our welfare in the pursuits of civil life." Fleetwood thought "a camp life would be decidedly an injury to our people. No matter how well and faithfully they may perform their duties they will shortly be considered as 'lazy nigger sojers'—as drones in the great hive."

As Fleetwood's letter shows, he was a thoughtful man. He did achieve promotion, but that was long after the Civil War. After his discharge in 1866, Fleetwood moved to Columbus, Ohio, where he worked as a bookkeeper. He moved to Washington, DC, in 1867 and lived out his life there, holding positions in the Freedmen's Bank and the War Department. Fleetwood rose to major in a District of Columbia National Guard unit.

The 5th Massachusetts Cavalry was made up of men from all over the United States. Because of its interracial character, there were no reunions of officers and men, and until now, no one saw fit to write a regimental history. Like Sergeant Major Fleetwood, the troopers embarked on the pursuit of civil life. Any consideration of the fates of the troopers and officers after the war is thus limited by the sources available. If one wants to track down what happened after the war to a relative who served with the 5th Massachusetts, pension records are a great place to start. Pension records state where the veteran lived and what he did for a living after the war. An enormous pension department was organized in the War Department. At one point in the nineteenth century, the War Department was by far the largest bureau in the federal government because of the pension process.

Most of the men worked, owned or rented property, got married, had children, and joined churches and social organizations—living out their lives as peaceful, productive citizens. Consider the case of Sergeant Joshua Dunbar of Company F, 5th Massachusetts Cavalry. Dunbar escaped from slavery in Kentucky and made his way to Troy, Ohio. He was recruited there for the 55th Massachusetts Volunteer Infantry. Dunbar was forty-one years old when he enlisted in the 55th; he became ill and was discharged from that regiment on 28 October 1863. Joshua Dunbar still wanted to serve his country, however. He enlisted in the 5th Massachusetts

Cavalry in January 1864, making sergeant the following May. He mustered out in Texas and made his way back to Ohio, to Dayton, becoming a plasterer by trade and marrying another former slave. Together they had a son. Sergeant Dunbar learned to read and write and instilled a love of history and literature in his child. Later, the son, although earning his living as an elevator operator to support his widowed mother, became the poet Paul Laurence Dunbar, called by William Dean Howells "the only man of pure African blood and American civilization to feel the negro life aesthetically and express it lyrically." Howells, whom the *Dictionary of American Biography* called the "leader of American letters for the quarter-century ending in 1920," wrote the introduction to Paul Dunbar's 1896 poetry anthology, *Lyrics from a Lowly Life*.

Howells felt that Dunbar's "brilliant and unique achievement was to have studied the American negro objectively, and to have represented him as he found him to be, with humor, with sympathy, and yet with what the reader must instinctively feel to be entire truthfulness." Dunbar's poetry might be judged harshly today because he wrote in dialect, considered now frightfully politically incorrect. In describing these dialect poems, Howells wrote, "In nothing is his essentially refined and delicate art so well shown as in these pieces . . . which describe the range between appetite and emotion, with certain lifts far beyond and above it, which is the range of the race." Howells wrote that Dunbar showed in his dialect poems "a finely ironical perception of the negro's limitations, with a tenderness for them which I think so very rare as to be almost quite new." Lest we stray too far from the story of Sergeant Joshua Dunbar and his comrades in the 5th Massachusetts Cavalry, none of the dialect poems are included here.

There is a Dunbar poem, however, "The Colored Soldiers," that deals with African Americans' service during the Civil War. There is nothing of the personal in the poem, nor is there a particularly strong political message. Remember that Paul Dunbar wrote primarily for a white audience. We are left without really knowing what the poet felt about his father's service, or about Reconstruction or race relations at the end of the nineteenth century. Instead, the poem has a sentimental tone. Dunbar argues respectfully in the poem that the service of African American troops seemed to have been forgotten. The stanza that comes closest to being critical ends with a whimper, not a bang:

They were comrades then and brothers,
Are they more or less to-day?
They were good to stop a bullet
And to front the fearful fray.
They were citizens and soldiers,
When Rebellion raised its head;
And the traits that made them worthy,
Ah! Those virtues are not dead.

This poem is printed in its entirety in appendix 2. Paul Dunbar, like his father, died young. He is remembered as "one of the first African-American" or an "important nineteenth century black" poet. It is important to look beyond his body of work and see him as the son of former slaves, the son of an honorably discharged veteran who worked a menial job in an environment barely tolerant of African Americans but who so felt the power of language that it burst out of him. We hope that Sergeant Joshua Dunbar understood and respected his son's art and was proud of him.

What separated black veterans from white was the fact that most African Americans had left slavery to join the army. After their discharge, they had to choose whether to go back to their old homes or to start a new life somewhere else. Sometimes home could be a dangerous place indeed.

There is a chilling account of three murders that took place in October 1865. In a source sent to the author because of an unrelated article about genealogy, the spring 2004 edition of the *South Carolina Magazine of Ancestral Research* has exact transcriptions of "Laurens [County, South Carolina] District Coroner's Inquisitions." When someone died, the district coroner called a "lawful jury of inquests." On 10 October 1865, Coroner John Nabers called fourteen men "for said district upon view of the body of Ben formerly the property of Abner Putnam." The jury, "who being charged and sworn on the part of the state of South Carolina [to determine] by what means the said death upon their oaths do say that the boy Ben came to his death from a gunshot wound in the head and the cutting of his throat with some sharp instrument by persons unknown to the jurors on the night of the 9th inst."

The next step after the jury of inquest and the coroner had determined the cause of death was to collect sworn statements from witnesses. The first two statements in the case of "The State vs. the dead body of Ben a freedman" were from Chesley and Charles Hughes. Chesley was illiterate; he made his mark on the sworn statement that "he was returning from hunting opossums last night sometime after 12 o'clock in company with Chas Hughes & a negro boy named Sam and one named Jim, that he discovered something in the corn field of Mr. J. H. Shell and told one of the negro boys to see what it was, and when he saw it was some body they all went to where he was and saw that it was a dead negro boy but they did not know him." Charles Hughes, who was also illiterate, concurred with Chesley's account that they did not know the "dead negro boy." Mr. R. Thomas was the next witness. Thomas testified that "this morning the boy Sam called him" and told him about finding the "dead negro in Mr. Shell's field" on his way home from opossum hunting. Thomas continued that "after breakfast he came up to S. Barksdales & there found J. W. Shell and H. Hill & one or two other persons and they all went to the place indicated and found a dead body which was said to be (by George Motes) named Ben and he had a gun shot wound in the right arm and also in the right side of the head and his throat was cut, that he thinks either the wound in the head or throat would have cosed [*sic*] his death." Mr. J. H. Shell concurred with the statement of R. Thomas. He added that "the boy was lying about 3 to six steps from the fence on the side of his plantation next to Abner Putnam." R. Thomas and J. H. Shell were able to sign their names. The next witness was not sworn in, nor did he sign his name or make his mark.

Negro man Wilson states that some time last night seven men came to his house on the plantation of Abner Putnam and called him by name & said they were Yankees & inquired how they were getting along at home and wanted to know where the other negro men were and carried himself and the deceased (illegible) to a grove of trees 2 or 3 yards from Mr. Shell's field and tied him and whipped him severily [sic] and before they got Ben tied he made his escape that 3 men ran after him and he heard as many as three shots, that one of the men was called Lieut. & one a Sergeant that they were armed.

The three men who murdered Ben came back before the other four were finished whipping Wilson. He testified that he did not know "any of the men unless it was the Lieut. who (illegible) him if he was not the boy Wilson that was with the Yankees below Columbia & he Wilson thinks he saw this man when below Columbia."

The next case, "The State vs. the dead bodies of Squire & [blank]," occurred less than two weeks later, on 23 October 1865. Samuel Austin appeared before Acting Coroner Thomas J. Sullivan to report, "There has been the bodies of two negro men found dead in the old field near where Alexander Culbertson formerly lived." The jury found "that these two negroes came to their deaths by being shot by some person or persons unknown to us from the evidence we think one of them is the boy Squire."

There were a total of five witnesses called to this inquest. The first, D. Y. Pope, testified, "He pas'd on yesterday morning [the morning of 22 October] in company with Mr. Witty a path between his house & Mrs. Neely [ink spot] two negroes lying within 15 or 20 paces of the path[,] supposed they were asleep[,] thought of rousing them up but Mr. Witty said let them alone & they went on heard report of three guns about half hour before day light."

Nancy Neely made her mark on a statement that she "saw two negroes yesterday evening near the path as she went to Mrs. Pope's was most alarm'd & went back and got her mother & Mrs. Knight & on their return saw the same negroes—did not go near enough to see whether they were dead or not." Elizabeth Neely and Elizabeth Knight both made their marks concurring with Nancy Neely's statement. Then Samuel Austin testified that "he was present when the bodies of these two negroes was removed from the above described place one was dead and the other had some signs of life but died this morning—one of them supposed to be squire formerly the property of James Epps—the other not known who he is."

Let's review: Messrs. Pope and Witty passed by the prostrate men "yesterday morning" and heard gunshots "about half hour before daylight." Nancy Neely was on the same path "yesterday evening" and got her mother and Mrs. Knight but didn't go close enough to determine whether the men were dead or alive. Finally, Samuel Austin was present when the two men were removed, some time during the night or early morning, as one died "this morning." What this testimony shows is that the two black men lay wounded and dying beside a path for approximately twenty-four hours. The war may have freed African Americans, but in many places it did not make them safer.

The 5th Massachusetts Cavalry was full of contrasts. White regiments were usually raised in a geographic region and officered by men who grew up with those they commanded. In the early months of the war, officers were even elected. When the war ended, the men who survived went home and kept the memory of the sacrifices of their youth alive in veterans' organizations. In the North, the Military Order of the Loyal Legion was for officers only; enlisted men joined the Grand Army of the Republic. The 5th Massachusetts was not homogenous; compounding the diversity of geography and race was the vast gulf of class. Consider the differences in wealth and education among the white officers. Lieutenant Edward Jarvis Bartlett went back to Concord, was active in the Unitarian Church, married, raised a family, and worked as a clerk, as he had done before the war. To honor their ancestor, Bartlett's letters, retained after his death in 1914, came to the Massachusetts Historical Society in 1962 and 1963, gifts of Ruth J. Bartlett and Mrs. William B. Bartlett. Through their generosity we have some insight into the life of a junior line officer in a regiment of black cavalry, a young man who liked army life, who believed that "the Negro is going to be the saving of the country," and who was willing to travel to a windswept point in Maryland, a burning city in Virginia, and the barren flats of Texas to prove it.

Major Henry Bowditch became a doctor, a physiologist, graduating from Harvard Medical School in 1868. After studying in Paris and Leipzig in 1871, Bowditch accepted a professorship in physiology at Harvard Medical School. He taught at Harvard for thirty-five years, serving as dean of the medical school faculty from 1883 to 1893. He was a founder of the American Physiological Society in 1887 and the society's president in 1888. Bowditch was the recipient of honorary doctoral degrees from the Universities of Cambridge (1898), Edinburgh (1898), Pennsylvania (1904), and Harvard (1906). From 1872 to 1891, apart from his physiological study, Bowditch studied the rate of growth of school-age children (juvenile anthropometry), data which was used to plan school nutrition programs. Dr. Bowditch spoke out against public drunkenness as a member of "blue ribbon" committees in 1872, 1894, and 1903. In his spare time, Henry made and repaired furniture, blew glass, and was an inventor. His wife, two sons, five daughters, and ten grandchildren survived him.

Charles Bowditch was an archaeologist who received his AM from Harvard in 1866. He became a member of the faculty of the Peabody Museum at Harvard and one of the greatest benefactors the museum ever had, filling two large exhibit halls in the museum with artifacts collected in Mexico and

Central America. He gave to the museum over fifty thousand pages of photographic reproductions of manuscripts dealing with and in the languages of Mexico and Central America. He was the greatest scholar of Mayan hieroglyphic writing in nineteenth- and early twentieth-century America and wrote a book, *The Numeration, Calendar Systems and Astronomical Knowledge of the Mayas* (1910), which began the modern study of that people. Bowditch was treasurer of the American Academy of Arts and Sciences from 1905 to 1915 and president from 1917 to 1919. "His benefactions included the founding of fellowships and instructorships in Central American archaeology. There is perhaps no other instance in American anthropology where an effort was so long sustained, so intense, and so productive of result," wrote his biographer in the *Dictionary of American Biography*. The Bowditches, in turn, would have been familiar with two of the regiment's three colonels, Charles Francis Adams Jr. and Henry Sturgis Russell.

After the war, Charles Francis Adams Jr. became a writer, a historian, among other things. Time did not mellow the 5th's second colonel. When he wrote his "autobiographical sketch" in 1912, which was published after his death in 1915 as *Charles Francis Adams, 1835–1915: An Autobiography*, he was still bitter about his decision to continue with the black regiment. Adams considered this decision, "though not vital," a matter "for life-time regret." Adams did himself "the justice to say" that he had acted "largely under a sense of obligation and duty," but those good intentions were misdirected. "From every point of view I decided wrong; for I did the regiment no good and myself much harm."

Adams explained that his mistakes in staying with the regiment were twofold: "In the first place, by an ingenious move through my influential friends at the Headquarters of the Army of the Potomac, I got the regiment mounted." That was his first error, because the 5th Massachusetts was "doing very good service" at Point Lookout dismounted. Adams, who conveniently forgot his successful plan to use broken-down horses, wrote that mounting the 5th "meant only the waste of twelve-hundred much-needed horses." His second mistake was to "work the regiment into active service" using the same contacts at headquarters. Adams wrote that "the only result of so doing was to afford myself convincing proof that the negro was wholly unfit for cavalry service, lacking absolutely the essential qualities of alertness, individuality, reliability and self-reliance."

We can only wonder what convincing proof Adams had; he mentions only the "horse-stealing propensities" of his men in his April 1865 letters. Adams was not finished, however. He went on to condemn African Americans for an inability to scout and to take care of themselves in unfamiliar situations. The colonel felt he should have left the regiment at Point Lookout; instead he "took the negro out of it, and put him where he was of no possible use." Adams's regret and bitterness seem to have grown out of his missing the Confederate surrender at Appomattox, compounded with a hefty dose of bigotry: "As for myself, I sacrificed the whole ripe reward and happy culmination of my three years of service. True, I had the satisfaction of leading my regiment into burning Richmond, the day after Lee abandoned it. I did have that satisfaction; and it was a great one. But it was purchased at a great cost. . . . Then came a few weeks of wretched breaking down, until I became a confirmed invalid, and had to crawl ignominiously home, leaving my regiment ordered to Texas and almost in a state of mutiny. It was a bitter and humiliating termination of nearly four years of faithful effort. And all from a sense of duty! And I might have been in at the death with Humphreys and the Second Corps!"

Near the end of his autobiography, Adams gave his assessment of his life. He had been, he wrote, "a remarkably, an exceptionally, fortunate man." He was healthy in 1912, and so was his family—or, as Adams put it in his inimitable way, he had an "absence of death, of dissipation and worthlessness in my family." He had been given infinite opportunity. Only his own limitations, he felt, had held him back. "It was so in the army; it was so in railroads, in politics and in business; it was so in literature and history." However, he had also possessed "considerable . . . more than respectable" ability. Adams claimed to have enjoyed himself in life, particularly when compared to his father, grandfather, and great-grandfather: "In other directions also I have perhaps accomplished nothing considerable, compared with what my three immediate ancestors accomplished; but, on the other hand, I have done some things better than they ever did; and, what is more and most of all, I have had a much better time in life—got more enjoyment out of it. In this respect I would not change with any of them."

The rancor that Adams held against his black troopers is even more extraordinary given these statements of satisfaction, especially as Adams held on to that anger and disappointment for some fifty years. It should be further noted that Colonel Adams, like his predecessor Colonel Henry Sturgis Russell and successor Samuel Emery Chamberlain, was made a brevet brigadier general of volunteers as a reward and honor for a job well done.

Colonel Harry Russell, despite his rather abrupt departure from the 5th, was promoted to brevet brigadier general on 13 March 1865. This was the date of the omnibus promotions in the Union army, recognizing and rewarding the volunteer soldiers who had served so gallantly and endured so much. Russell's deserved promotion was for "action outside of Petersburg, June 15, 1864." Lieutenant Edward J. Bartlett had speculated, when he heard of Russell's resignation, that perhaps the colonel's wife had not wanted him to go into combat once again. Credence is lent to that speculation by a study of the Russell family's records at the New England Historic Genealogical Society. Russell's second child, Ellen Forbes Russell, was born on 30 October 1865. Mary Forbes Russell would thus have been pregnant, newly so, when Russell decided to resign. So, whether because of another baby on the way or, as he claimed at the time, an illness in the family, Russell found himself a civilian in the spring of 1865. Russell joined his father-in-law, John Murray Forbes, in business, where he worked for some three years. However, as his biographical sketch in *Sons of the Puritans* relates, Russell "developed little taste for business and gladly escaped to more congenial pursuits." He was fortunate to be a wealthy man, for except for during two periods on appointive political commissions, Harry Russell lived the rest of his life as a country gentleman. He lived first at the "Home Farm" in West Roxbury, and then from 1870 on at his "handsome estate midway between Milton Hill and the Blue Hills," not far from Camp Meigs, where the 5th Massachusetts had formed.

Russell "indulged his passion for horses, built fine stables, laid out broad pastures, and kept some of the most famous trotting stallions in the country," notably "Fearnaught," "Smuggler," and "Edgemark." He later turned his hand to the raising of Jersey cattle. In 1878, Russell accepted the position of chairman of the Board of Police Commissioners for the city of Boston. A board of aldermen, a holdover from colonial times, had run the police up until the appointment of Russell as head of a three-man commission. As Russell's biographer John T. Morse Jr. wrote, the city police force "had of course sank into a pitiable condition," largely, it may be inferred, from the influence of Irish Catholic, Democratic politicians, and Russell's "great faculty for organization and his extraordinary capacity for the control of men" was needed to set matters straight. Russell worked as chairman of the police commissioners, "vigilant by night and laborious by day," for two years, whereupon he resigned, leaving the force in "fine shape." Morse explained that Russell was "altogether too much of a man" to sit for long on a committee, even of three: "He was not meant to be a fraction, or to contribute to averages and compromises."

His next call came in 1895, when another Protestant, Republican mayor, Edwin Upton Curtis, like Mayor Henry Lillie Pierce in 1878, needed Russell's organizational talent, this time as fire commissioner of the city of Boston. There were supposed to be three commissioners, but Russell never got around to requesting that two other men share the burden. Russell served as fire commissioner until his death on 16 February 1905. According to Morse, "It was long and arduous work to bring the department up to his ideal, but he left it undoubtedly the best organized, and the most efficient fire department in the country."

The same pattern as on the police commission, with Russell as the Protestant dike to stem the Irish Catholic flood, can be inferred here, for Morse wrote, "At the beginning the politicians came with their usual demands for 'influence,' but quickly learned that they had none! Shocked and angry at so 'un-American' a condition, they would fain have ejected the Colonel; but they found him evenly indifferent to threats, gallantly backed by the powerful insurance interests, and attending to business as if such cattle as politicians did not exist."

The same qualities that had made Russell an effective Civil War officer now stood him in good stead at the fire department. He was popular with both officers and rank-and-file firemen, "for though very rigid and a strict disciplinarian, he was not a martinet." His men respected him and found a growing pride in their organization, so much so that the "disquieting agitations concerning hours and pay which meddlesome politicians sought to stir" were quelled without protest. Morse drew an accurate portrait of Russell, "whose friends knew that his qualities surpassed his achievements." He was a man of character rather than intellectual genius. "His mind worked in a simple, straightforward way, and he reached his conclusions by direct processes, without subtlety." Russell held strong convictions and followed those convictions with action, "resolutely, decisively, without compromise."

Russell was forceful and not to be trifled with, but he was also modest and reserved. He commanded, but he did not scream or bully. "Without being imperious, he was always the master of his soldiers, his policemen, his firemen, and his employees." He was "strict, but just, and as generous as the circumstances would permit," Morse wrote. Russell also retained that dry New England humor that kept his spirits up and buoyed those around him. "At times taciturn, and indisposed to sustained conversation; he yet had a terse, original, and lively wit, which never failed him even in the latest days of weakness and suffering." Russell was never impulsive or demonstrative, but he was not cold: "His moral courage was equal to his physical, and fear of any sort was utterly absent in his make-up; but with his masculine strength he combined a very affectionate nature; loyal and kindly, he gave and received warm affection; domestic in his tastes, he knew nothing else so pleasant as to live always at home; the family circle, his own house, his own fields gave him complete and sufficient happiness."

When Harry Russell died in 1905, his widow received letters of condolence from friends, male and female, from all over the world. These letters are preserved as typescript copies in a slim volume bound in blue leather, now in the archives of the Massachusetts Historical Society. Charles Pickering Bowditch sent one, so did Charles Adams, from Washington, DC. The letter that had perhaps the longest distance to travel was from Egypt, sent by Russell's adjutant in the 5th Massachusetts Cavalry.

First Lieutenant Daniel Henry Chamberlain had had an interesting life since leaving his regiment. He had indeed come far since he was born into poverty on a farm in West Brookfield, Massachusetts, the ninth child of Eli and Achsah Chamberlain. As a young man, Chamberlain had struggled to gain an education. He attended various secondary schools—Amherst Academy, 1849–1850, and Phillips Academy, Andover, 1854—while his money held out. He finally graduated from Worcester High School in 1857. He spent the next year teaching school, which he had done since 1852, and working on the family farm, scraping up enough money to enter Yale in 1858. Despite having to work his way through Yale and endure a rather hand-to-mouth existence, Chamberlain achieved distinction in English composition and oratory when he was graduated in 1862. His desire to serve his country had cut short his studies at the "Cambridge Law School," later Harvard Law. After the war, in the spring of 1866, as Chamberlain's biographer noted in his sketch in the *Dictionary of American Biography*, Chamberlain was in South Carolina, where, sent "to settle the affairs of a dead classmate, he thought he saw opportunity to earn money to repay what he had borrowed for his education."

In short, Lieutenant Chamberlain became what was commonly called a "carpetbagger." Chamberlain first tried his hand at cotton planting, which proved unprofitable, and then went into politics. He was chosen in 1867 as a representative from Berkeley County to the South Carolina constitutional convention, which met in January 1868. This convention was the first in South Carolina's history to seat blacks alongside whites as lawmakers. This convention, like the other Southern constitutional conventions of 1867–1869, was heterogeneous—"motley," according to Chamberlain's sketch in the *Dictionary of American Biography*. Eric Foner, in his masterful *Reconstruction: America's Unfinished Revolution, 1863–1877*, described the composition of these conventions as "the first large group of elected Southern Republicans" that "epitomized the party's social composition."

Foner identified white Southern Republicans as one group, usually "upcountry farmers and small town merchants, artisans, and professionals, few of whom had ever held political office." These men had almost all opposed secession; some had been imprisoned for their support of the Union, and some had served in the Union army. Southern Democrats and conservatives, who continued to defend slavery and the Dred Scott decision and to bitterly assail political equality as miscegenation, dubbed white Southern Republicans "scalawags." At the South Carolina constitutional convention, African Americans were a majority of the delegates. Some of these men were freeborn; many had served in the Union army. A few, like William J. Whipper, were Northern blacks who moved south in search of opportunity. "Nearly half the black delegates [of all the constitutional conventions], and a majority of those born free, served in South Carolina and Louisiana," Foner writes, "where political organizing, led by the free urban elite, had the longest history. . . . The educated, confidently articulate, and politically experienced freeborn delegates of South Carolina and Louisiana played major roles in their conventions, dominating debate and often outmaneuvering white participants."

The third group identified by Foner was the carpetbaggers, who numbered about one-sixth by his count. "Generally veterans of the Union Army, carpetbaggers were the best-educated Republican delegates, numbering many lawyers, physicians, and other professionals. Talented, ambitious and youthful (their average age was thirty-six); carpetbaggers usually chaired the key committees and drafted the most important provisions of the new constitutions." Chamberlain served on the judiciary committee of the 1868 constitutional convention and gained the approval of party leaders, one of whom, H. H. Kimpton (who became state fiscal agent in 1868), had been Chamberlain's roommate at Yale.

In April 1868, the Republican Party came to power in South Carolina, and Chamberlain was elected attorney general of the state. The *Dictionary of American Biography* drily observed of his tenure as attorney general, "Nothing of his record in this office was notable, but in the most corrupt quadrennium of South Carolina history, though an *ex officio* member of several thieving boards, he was never charged with personal dishonesty." Chamberlain practiced law in Columbia, South Carolina, for two years before winning the governorship himself in 1874, running as a reform candidate, promising to reduce public expenditure, revise taxation and assessment, and curb corruption. Such reform, although strengthening white rule in the Republican Party and appealing to Democrats, was much needed, for, as Foner noted, "the first Republican governor, Robert K. Scott, who served from 1868 to 1872, had compiled an unenviable record of malfeasance in office," and his successor, scalawag Franklin J. Moses Jr., proved to be even worse.

In courting white voters of both parties, Chamberlain alienated African Americans, who were solidly Republican. Black disgust with Chamberlain came to a head at the end of 1875, when he barred Franklin Moses Jr. and William J. Whipper from the judgeships to which the black-controlled legislature had elected them. Moses was white and, as his inept administration as governor had shown, probably unqualified to be a judge. But Chamberlain "played the race card" by refusing to seat Whipper, who was a bit of a rogue and a gambler but also a trained lawyer. Apparently, only the color of Whipper's skin kept him from the bench. Governor Chamberlain asserted in a public speech that Whipper's judgeship would be "a horrible disaster" and a crime against "the civilization of the Puritan and the Huguenot."

Chamberlain's attempt to forge a centrist, mostly white coalition in South Carolina between the two parties foundered on the issue of race. Democratic white supremacists, now calling themselves "Redeemers," returned to the open racism and violence of early Reconstruction. Chamberlain's support among centrist Democrats—"fusionists," they were called—gradually slipped away, weakened by interracial violence.

The savage race riot in Hamburg, South Carolina, in July 1876, which saw a white mob led by former Confederate general Matthew C. Butler confront a black militia company, particularly poisoned the political atmosphere. Hamburg's black marshal was killed, and five black men among the twenty-five who surrendered to overwhelming force were murdered in cold blood. Black shops and homes were ransacked and destroyed. According to Dock Adams, Union army veteran, skilled carpenter, and the African American militia's commander, whites kept screaming, "This is the beginning of the redemption of South Carolina," as they looted and killed.

In August 1876, the Democratic Party in South Carolina nominated former Confederate general Wade Hampton for governor, and the fusion of Republicans and Democrats under Chamberlain was over. Blacks may not have liked Chamberlain's appeal to moderate whites, but they had little choice when the Democratic ticket was composed to a man of former Confederate officers. The 1876 contest in South Carolina was a bitter one, marked by violence on both sides. As Eric Foner noted, "with so much at stake, the 1876 campaign became the most tumultuous in South Carolina's history, and the one significant exception to the Reconstruction pattern that cast blacks as the victims of political violence and whites as the sole aggressors." African Americans fought back, it is true, but their resistance was sporadic and disorganized compared to the systematic intimidation practiced by Hampton's supporters. Murder, whippings, burnings, and beatings were dispensed to both black and white Republicans, but particular attention was paid to keeping blacks from the polls.

When the dust settled, Governor Daniel Chamberlain had received the largest Republican vote in South Carolina's history and believed he had won reelection. Wade Hampton also felt he had won, based on the massive white majorities in several counties in which African Americans, previously a majority, were prevented from voting. Both governors were formally inaugurated, and the South Carolina capitol was the scene of rival legislatures, armed to the teeth, glaring at each other in high tension. Governor Chamberlain should have seen how the wind was blowing when President Grant refused to recognize his administration.

Daniel Chamberlain's second term as Republican governor of South Carolina was a casualty to what became known as the "Compromise of 1877" and what was, in fact, the abandonment of Reconstruction by the Republican Party—indeed, the abandonment of the policy of protecting African Americans in the South. Eric Foner wrote, "Among other things, 1877 marked a decisive retreat from the idea, born during the Civil War, of a powerful national state protecting the fundamental rights of American citizens." One of the prices paid by Rutherford Hayes for the presidency in 1877 was the withdrawal of federal troops in South Carolina and the recognition of Wade Hampton as governor.

Daniel Chamberlain was not driven from South Carolina; he visited the state many times after 1877 and was welcomed, at least by some. He was, after all, a moderate and a reformer who had not been overawed by the power of the black vote. After his ouster, Chamberlain went north and pursued a successful career as an attorney in New York City. He was honored with the appointment by Cornell University in 1883 as nonresident professor of constitutional law. Chamberlain returned to the family farm in 1897, but West Brookfield was made unhappy by the death of a son in 1902. He spent the remaining five years of his life as a restless wanderer. Chamberlain spent a few months in South Carolina, a year in Europe, twenty months in Egypt, and finally settled in Charlottesville, Virginia, in 1906. Toward the end of his life, Chamberlain apparently felt that his youthful abolitionist ideals, his service with a black Massachusetts regiment, and Reconstruction in South Carolina had all been a terrible mistake. Reconstruction had been "a frightful experience" that tried to "lift a backward or inferior race" to equality; this attempt had produced "shocking and unbearable misgovernment."

There is something rather pathetic in Chamberlain's apparently complete surrender to the "redemption" of South Carolina. It is no defense, but Chamberlain was not alone in expressing embarrassment and regret at the "excesses" of the Southern Republican Party during Reconstruction. However, writing from the twenty-first century, Chamberlain seems to have become an apologist for white supremacy.

Another officer named Chamberlain in the 5th Massachusetts Cavalry, Colonel Samuel Emery Chamberlain, made the most of his experiences as a soldier. Brevetted brigadier general of volunteers for gallantry in action at the Battle of St. Mary's Church, Virginia, on 25 June 1864, Chamberlain never missed an opportunity to wear his uniform, attend and address veterans' meetings, and show off the magnificent scar on his cheek.

In 1866, Governor Alexander Bullock appointed Chamberlain assistant quartermaster general of Massachusetts with the rank of colonel. He was reappointed by Bullock's successor, Governor William Claflin, and continued to wear the uniform until 1871. Chamberlain became warden of the Massachusetts State Penitentiary at Charlestown that year. He was a warden in Massachusetts from 1871 to 1881, first at Charlestown and then at the Middlesex County Jail in Concord. Chamberlain apparently made a name for himself in correction circles. He became warden of the Connecticut State Prison in Wethersfield in 1885, serving eight years, until 1893.

Chamberlain's tenure at Wethersfield was marked by controversy. He was accused of abusing prisoners, and his administration was investigated. Chamberlain was exonerated, but there was no doubt he could be tough when he needed to be. The *Hartford Courant* of 18 February 1889 related an instance of that force: a convict named Burke, who had a knife and declared "he would cut the bowels out of the first man who laid hands on him," confronted Chamberlain. Chamberlain told him calmly, "Drop that knife." Burke refused, and Chamberlain, who evidently carried a pistol at all times, drew his revolver and said, "'I will wing you this time, but the next time you draw a knife on me you are a dead man.' Thereupon he fired, inflicting a flesh wound just above the elbow of the right arm. The knife dropped instantly from Burke's fingers and he was secured."

Not long after he left the warden job in Wethersfield, Samuel Chamberlain retired to a rambling hilltop home, Maple-Hill, in Barre, Massachusetts. He regularly attended meetings of the Grand Army of the Republic and cultivated his image as a soldier-hero of the Mexican and Civil Wars. When Chamberlain died of heart failure in 1908, "from the effects of a general breaking down due to old age," read one obituary, he was lauded as "the 'veteran of veterans' of Massachusetts . . . known throughout the circles of the Grand Army of the Republic."

It is doubtful that for all his "veteraneering" Sam Chamberlain spent much time with his former comrades in arms from the 5th Massachusetts Cavalry. He had only been with the regiment when it was stationed in Texas, and his rank as colonel did not lend itself to fraternization with the enlisted men, but the simpler reason is that most of the Grand Army of the Republic was segregated. If any officers attended the "Reunion of Colored Veterans" on 1 and 2 August 1887 in Boston, their presence was not remarked upon. Speeches were made, stories told, toasts drunk, and meals eaten, but apparently only by African Americans. The "colored veterans," it turned out, were all from the 5th Massachusetts Cavalry, or at least all those whose names appeared on the broadside announcing the reunion, seven in all.

Sergeant Amos Webber of Company D topped the list. It will be recalled that Webber had enlisted in Worcester on New Year's Eve 1863 and was quartermaster sergeant of Company D when he mustered out. Webber remained in Massachusetts, for the veterans gave their home cities after their names. Webber lived in Worcester. Sergeant Gustavus Booth's name was next, with "Hartford, Connecticut," as his home. On his enlistment papers, Booth noted that he had been a carpenter in Springfield, Massachusetts, before the war. He also was in Company D. Former private George T. Fisher of New Bedford also attended. He had been a butcher in Mansfield, Massachusetts, before joining Company C in January 1864. Two other troopers from Company C were at the reunion. Joseph H. Bates was discharged for disability on 29 January 1865 from Point Lookout. Almost twenty-two years later, Private Bates traveled from Wilkes-Barre, Pennsylvania, to attend. Private Samuel J. Patterson had been an eighteen-year-old laborer when he enlisted in Boston. Patterson lived in Wilkes-Barre. It seems likely that Patterson and Bates traveled together. John Davis, a corporal in Company E, also came from Pennsylvania, from Carlisle. Davis was thirty-five years old, a waiter, credited to Boston, when he answered his country's call. Corporal Davis had been mustered out from the hospital at Fort Monroe on 3 June 1865. The last name on the list was spelled differently in regimental records. Benjamin W. Phenix (spelled "Phoenix" in the announcement) was eighteen and a laborer, credited to Lynn when he joined Company G in February 1864. In 1887, Phenix lived in Boston. All we have are the names, home cities, and what information these men gave when they signed up, gleaned from a printed broadside and the regimental records. We do know that these men thought enough of each other and their old regiment to come together some twenty-two years after their muster out.

There was an African American Grand Army Post in Boston, of which Benjamin W. Phenix was at one time post commander. It is probable that the above-listed seven names were in fact sponsors of a reunion that included a gathering of enlisted men of the regiment, at least of those who remained in the Northeast after the war. Robert A. Bell Post, No. 134, Department of Massachusetts, Grand Army of the Republic, was headquartered in the building known as the Smith Schoolhouse, on the corner of Smith Court and Joy Street, not far from the State House in Boston.

Now the Museum of African American History, the Smith Schoolhouse had been given to the city of Boston in the 1820s as a school for African American children, who at that time were not allowed to attend school with whites. At the rear of the school is a building housing the Independent Baptist Church, the oldest African American church in New England. The Robert A. Bell Post was founded in June 1870 and was one of the first African American posts in the Grand Army of the Republic. Robert A. Bell was a black sailor killed in action during the combined army, navy, and marine corps assault on Fort Fisher, North Carolina, on 15 January 1865. Together with black U.S. Navy sailors and members of the U.S. Colored Troop regiments, membership in the post was composed of Massachusetts's three black regiments, the 54th and 55th Massachusetts Infantry Volunteers and the 5th Massachusetts Volunteer Cavalry.

The members of the Robert A. Bell Post provided the catalyst for the commissioning of the memorial to Robert Gould Shaw and the 54th Massachusetts Infantry. The black veterans conducted a letter-writing campaign and collected small sums for many years before sculptor Augustus St. Gaudens was retained to create the bronze monument that sits across from the State House in Boston. The St. Gaudens Memorial was unveiled in 1897, over thirty years after Shaw's death.

The last surviving member of the Robert A. Bell Post was a 5th Massachusetts Cavalry noncommissioned officer. Corporal Amos F. Jackson gave his occupation as farmer and his residence as West Brookfield, Massachusetts, when he enlisted. It is probable that he knew Daniel Chamberlain's family. Jackson joined Company I in February 1864 at the age of twenty-four. It may be recalled that in Baltimore on the way south, it was at the drunken then-sergeant Jackson that Captain Erik Wulff fired the shot that killed Private Albert White in May 1864.

Born in 1840, Amos Jackson lived to be ninety-nine, dying in Boston in 1940. Jackson lived through remarkable industrial and technological changes. He saw America fight against Spain at the end of the nineteenth century and then join one world war and prepare to enter a second. Born during the administration of Martin Van Buren, he lived to see Franklin Roosevelt campaign for a third term. He saw all those changes and more, but he left no memoir, no letters, and no interviews to let us know what he thought. When Jackson died, the Bell Post was disbanded and its records sent to Room 27, the Grand Army of the Republic Archives, in the basement of the State House.

There were indeed great contrasts within the regiment and in the postwar careers of those who served in it. Consider the postwar careers of the Douglasses, Charles, Lewis, and Frederick Jr. Frederick Douglass's sons found their postwar world much like the army; they could rise only so far because of the color of their skin. They had talent, education, and will, but persistent prejudice kept them below men with lesser gifts. Lewis, who had been sergeant major of the 54th Massachusetts Infantry, and Frederick, who had been a recruiter of African Americans in the Deep South during the war, went west in 1866, to Colorado. Together they published a newspaper, but their hopes and borrowed money sank amid a lack of opportunity, indifference, or outright hostility, and they returned east in 1870. They were trained printers and typesetters, sons of the most famous black publisher in America, but the typesetters' union refused them membership. A newspaper venture with their father, *The New National Era*, failed after three years, unable to show a profit because of too few subscriptions.

Frederick Douglass was able to get a clerkship for his son Charles at the Freedmen's Bureau in 1866. At one point, Charles was one of only two African American clerks in the entire federal government, but he was fired in 1869, a victim of government cutbacks. Charles sought work in the State Department and was sent to a remote station in Santo Domingo in 1875. He wrote to his father in 1876 in deep despair, "Under the circumstances of my many failures in life, I have felt my letters were not desired. I wrote again, however, risking the result. It seems that under any circumstances I am to fail in my undertakings, and my life is to be one series of blunders. I have been here nearly a year and I don't know how I have lived." More than ten years after crushing the Confederacy and helping to free his people, former first sergeant Charles Remond Douglass was still seeking his father's help, still searching for his father's approval, still searching for his place in the world.

What did Frederick Douglass think about a world without slavery? It's an interesting question because Douglass tailored his response to his audience. When he addressed whites, he was accusatory, such as when he addressed the Republican National Convention in 1876: "You say you have emancipated us. You have; and I thank you for it. But what is your emancipation?" Douglass compared the experiences of other freed peoples with that of African Americans. "When the Israelites were emancipated they were told to go and borrow of their neighbors—borrow their coin, borrow their jewels, load themselves down with the means of subsistence; after, they should go free in the land the Lord God gave them. When the Russian serfs had their chains broken and given their liberty, the government of Russia—aye, the despotic government of Russia—gave to those poor emancipated serfs a few acres of land on which they could live and earn their bread." In the next sentence, Douglass ignores the contribution black soldiers made during the Civil War and the efforts of the federal government during Reconstruction: "But when you turned us loose, you gave us no acres. You turned us loose to the sky, to the storm, to the whirlwind, and, worst of all, you turned us loose to the wrath of our infuriated masters."

Contrast those remarks with those he made to another audience. On 1 October 1880, Frederick Douglass addressed the Second Annual Exposition of the Colored People of North Carolina. This was an agricultural fair held in Raleigh. The governor of North Carolina spoke, as well as other dignitaries. Douglass was the marshal of the District of Columbia at the time, and certainly the most famous black man in America. The transcript of this speech, as printed in an African American–owned newspaper, the *Journal of Industry*, runs eighteen pages. About halfway through his talk, Douglass addressed "The Wants of Our Race." Douglass said, "Poverty is the colored man's greatest social enemy." Freedom had been won, and "freedom is a great blessing and we have at last got that; but what is freedom without the respect and friendship of the people among whom we live?" Douglass noted that the "sentiment that greeted the colored people nearly all over the South, when they were liberated from slavery, was naturally enough an unfriendly sentiment." Expanding on this idea, Douglass said, "Perhaps there never was a people emancipated under circumstances less favorable than the colored people of this country." He used familiar language when talking about the plight of other peoples: "When the Hebrews were emancipated they were told to spoil the Egyptians. When the Russian serfs were emancipated the heads of families were given three acres of land. But in the case of the colored people no provision was made for their protection and preservation." Blacks were freed "in an hour of angry passion," not for moral reasons, but because of "military necessity, not from love of the slave but from love of the Union." Astutely Douglass noted that the "master class" blamed their defeat, at least in part, on emancipation. "The Southern people always did love the Negro as a slave, but hated him as a free Negro." Then Douglass had a message for the black people gathered before him, men, women, and children who had dressed in their best clothes to show off their efforts, the fruits of the vine and the work of their hands, some who doubtless had risen before dawn to come and hear the great man speak. This "concourse of newly emancipated people," as Douglass described them, was "at the starting point in the race of mental, moral and social progress." He continued: "I have sometimes wondered in view of the manner in which freedom came that so many colored people are found in the census. Though turned loose, to the open sky, old and young, sick and well, with neither money nor friends, with neither houses to live in, nor land to live upon. We seem to have held our own pretty well. I doubt if any other emancipated people could have done as well."

The history of the 5th Massachusetts Volunteer Cavalry is not one of terrible combat, great gallantry, desperate charges, and heavy casualties. But because of their endurance, their perseverance, their commitment to duty and country, the officers and troopers of the 5th Massachusetts were heroic. The African American troopers of the 5th Massachusetts traveled great distances to enlist in the regiment. Some came out of the South and slavery; for others the journey was one of self-discovery: into self-respect, discipline, and pride. There were many impediments along the way, not least the persistent, ubiquitous racism that pervaded American society. That racism held back the men's bounties, was at least partially responsible for dismounting the regiment, and then punished the men for doing the best they could under extremely difficult circumstances at Baylor's Farm. This book was meant to show these men, officers and troopers alike, as deserving of our respect. They were neither passive victims nor heroes in the mythic-poetic sense, but rather men who served with honor.

In these collective lives, some broad themes can be perceived. What the black troopers of the 5th wanted was to be given a chance to serve their country, to prove their manhood, to free their race, to crush the rebellion. And they wanted to do it as cavalry. They wanted to make a difference as volunteer troopers from the state that had led the way in putting African American men in the uniform of the United States. In April 1865, they got their chance to do just that. Did the entrance into burning Richmond alleviate the humiliations of being dismounted, of having to beg for their bounty, of Point Lookout and Texas? We can never really know. It seems doubtful, however, that the abandonment of the South to the "Redeemers" in 1877, the active hostility of one political party, and the indifference of the other toward black Americans, for that matter, could ever be justified with the vision African Americans had of a world without slavery.

It is only now, four generations and 150 years later, that the contributions of the 5th Massachusetts Cavalry, and all the other black regiments, are beginning to be recognized. Across the years, we offer our gratitude for the men who persevered, who served with courage and fidelity.

Recruiting for the 5th Massachusetts Cavalry

THE FOLLOWING MASSACHUSETTS JOINT COMMITTEE REPORT DETAILS AN investigation into recruiting and bounty payments in Boston's Ward Nine during 1863 and 1864. The illiterate African American recruits who "made their mark" and signed away about a third of their bounty money for "transportation expenses" all served in the 5th Massachusetts Cavalry. What is interesting about this report, inter alia, is that the majority party at the time was the Democrats, and the minority member of the committee, Mr. William Bingham, was a Republican vigorously seeking to refute statements made by a Republican adjutant general (William Schouler) appointed by a Republican governor, John Andrew. Perhaps in Schouler's case, conscience trumped politics.

Judge for yourself whether the "mass of evidence from the highest sources," as Bingham put it, absolves the gentlemen of the Ward Nine Committee of some rather sharp dealing.

HOUSE .... No. 389

Commonwealth of Massachusetts

Boston, April 30, 1866.

The Joint Standing Committee on Military Claims who were directed "to investigate the charges against the citizens of Ward 9 in the city of Boston, made by the Adjutant-General of the Commonwealth in his last Report, and to report what legislative action is necessary or expedient in reference thereto," has the honor to submit the following:

REPORT:

In order to understand the case correctly, it is proper to quote the language used by the Adjutant-General, to which exceptions have been taken. On pp. 31 and 32, in speaking of certain bounties paid to men in the Fifth Regiment Massachusetts Cavalry, the report says:—

"While upon the subject, I cannot refrain from calling your excellency's attention to the case of one hundred and twelve men who enlisted in the same regiment to the credit of Ward 9 of the city of Boston, from whom orders were taken to draw portions of their State bounty. These orders were chiefly for $125; one was for $150, sixteen were for $130, &c. The whole amount represented by these orders and paid was upwards of $10,000. It is claimed by the gentlemen of the ward that the men were given to understand what they were signing, and that each one put his mark to the paper with a full knowledge of its effect.

The ward gentlemen claim that the money was thus taken from the men to pay their transportation to Massachusetts. That the men knew the whole effect the signing the paper would have, I very much doubt. A number of the men whose bounties were thus razeed, came to this office after the regiment came home and was discharged, claiming the remainder of their bounty, and stating that they did not know when they put their mark on the orders that they were signing away a third part of their bounty. The orders having been paid, the men thus claiming it had no redress. The State had paid what the law allowed, and unless the ward to which the men were credited should make up to them what it had taken from them, they must be contented as they are. At the time these men enlisted, most of the towns in the Commonwealth would gladly have paid them local bounties if passed to their credit; but these men received no local bounty from the ward to which they were credited, but, on the contrary, they were made to turn over to the ward a third of the State bounty, which the law provided they should receive. Thus the ward was saved from recruiting expenses while it filled its quota. Probably it was thought a smart thing to draw this money from the State treasury and deny it to the soldiers, as it saved the ward of its own substance and only 'unragged the poor.' The whole transaction suggests to my mind 'Nathan's parable of the ewe lamb, 12th chapter, 2d Samuel.'"

The simple question which the Committee had to consider was, "Were the charges true or false which the Adjutant-General had made?"

Ex-Alderman Standish, D. N. Spooner, Treasurer of the Ward Recruiting committee, George V. Leicester and F. H. Sprague, recruiting agents employed by the ward committee, and a number of other citizens of the ward, appeared before the Committee and gave their testimony.

It appeared by the several witnesses that there was raised in the ward for recruiting purposes, by individual subscriptions, about $17,000, which money was used to pay the expenses of recruiting, and paying local bounties to white men who enlisted to the credit of the ward. It also appeared that recruiting in the ward was not very successful. It was then arranged to send out agents to Canada, West Virginia and other places South to enlist colored men for the ward; and Messrs. Leicester and Sprague were appointed on that duty. They were instructed to arrange with the colored men, and to state to them that the State offered a bounty of $325 a man; but they were to sign orders not to exceed $125, by which the ward was to draw that sum, from the bounty which was due them from the State. These orders were given, and the money was drawn from the State treasury, and used to pay the expense of recruiting the men and bringing them to Boston.

After the men were mustered in and placed in camp, a number of them repudiated the orders they had given and demanded the whole bounty. The matter was referred to the judge-advocate-general of the Commonwealth, who investigated the matter, and decided that the orders were properly given and should be paid by the State from the men's bounties; and they were paid. About 112 colored men were put in to fill the quota of the ward, and from each of them orders were taken and the money paid upon them, amounting to over twelve thousand dollars. It did not appear to the committee that white men were asked to give such orders upon their State bounty.

It appeared, further, that among the recruits obtained in West Virginia was a colored preacher, who was put in uniform and sent back with the agents of the ward to West Virginia and Kentucky to help enlist men. His part was to address colored meetings and induce men to enlist for the ward. The recruits thus obtained were brought to Ward 9 and were induced to contribute of their bounty as the other recruits had before them.

It appeared, further, by the testimony of the treasurer of the ward committee, that after paying all expenses of recruiting, including the colored men, the fees of the agents, and the other incidental expenses, that the ward had a surplus, derived from the negroes' certificates, of about five thousand dollars, which was placed in bank. When the regiment came home, the committee of the ward thought it would be right and liberal to pay each of the men who had given certificates for a portion of their State bounty the sum of twenty-five dollars, and accordingly arrangements were made to pay it to the men at Gallop's Island. But some of them never came back—some of them had been killed, some had died of disease in Virginia, Maryland and Texas. But those who came back got their twenty-five dollars. The balance, some fourteen hundred dollars, remains on deposit at the bank to this day.

Such is the case as exhibited by the parties interested, and which, as far as the committee are able to comprehend facts, fully corroborate the statements made by the Adjutant-General.

When the ward had finished its testimony, the Adjutant-General was asked if he had any witnesses to produce. He said he had none. He thought that his statements remained not only unshaken, but strengthened. He would, however, put in attested copies of rolls bearing the names of the recruits, showing the sum which each man had been asked to give the ward upon his certificate, and also the sworn statements made by Leicester and Sprague, the recruiting agents, and by Mr. Spooner, the treasurer, when the case was heard in June, 1864, by the judge-advocate-general. These papers did not vary materially from the testimony just given, though he would call the attention of the Committee to the reason just given by Mr. Spooner for making black men pay the expenses of their own recruitment, and the privilege of filling the quota of Ward 9. Mr. Spooner's words are as follows:

"As soon as we ascertained the probable expense of recruiting these men, it was thought but right by our Committee that they (contrabands and fugitives as they were) should bear some part of the expense of rescuing them from at least a humble and doubtful position, and introducing them to the service of the United States. We accordingly instructed Messrs. Sprague and Leicester to make such arrangements with the recruits when engaging them; and these arrangements were finally verified in the enlistment of the recruits here, by taking from them the orders herein referred to, and varying in amounts from eight to one hundred and twenty-five, and, in a few cases, to one hundred and thirty dollars each.

"I myself have seen and conversed with a very large number of these recruits as they have arrived at our office, and been present when Mr. Standish has inquired particularly of them if they understood the orders which they were sign-ing, and the amount of bounty they were to receive, and there is not a shadow of doubt that each and every man who has signed an order left for collection by any member of the recruiting committee of Ward 9, as distinctly understood his agreement as ever a contract was understood between one man and another."

The Adjutant-General does not question the statement made by Alderman Standish, or Mr. Spooner, that the effect of signing the certificates was fully explained to the colored men, and that they believed the colored men under-stood its effects; but he does not believe the colored men fully understood their rights in the case. He also contends that the money thus drawn from the State treasury belonged to the whole people of the Commonwealth. It was to be used for paying bounties to men for filling its quota, and was not to be used by a city, town or ward, to defray its expenses for filling its local contingent. He thought the ward should repay the money to the State, to be by it paid to the men, or their heirs, and if they could not be found it should remain in the State treasury where it belonged.

It was attempted to be shown by the ward committee, in a subsequent hearing, that the practice complained of was sanctioned by Governor Andrew, and that other towns and recruiting committees had done the same thing that Ward 9 had done. The evidence was, that some towns and committees had taken orders from recruits for a portion of their bounties, but it did not appear, save in one instance, that the money thus obtained was used to pay the expenses of any city or town for filling its own contingent; but on the contrary, it was put into a general fund to defray the expenses of raising the regiment. But admitting the facts to be as claimed by Ward 9, your Committee are unable to see how they justify the acts complained of, or invalidate the statements of the Adjutant-General.

These are substantially the facts as they appeared in evidence before the Committee, and the undersigned, while purposely refraining from expressing any opinion as to the plan adopted by the ward, are clearly of the opinion that the statements of the Adjutant-General, relative to the action of the 9th ward of the city of Boston, in taking from the colored men who enlisted and were accredited to the ward as a part of its quota, a portion of their bounty, for the purpose of defraying the expenses of filling its own contingent, are true.

ALDEN LELAND,
Of the Senate.
EDGAR J. SHERMAN
JAS. A. CUNNINGHAM
GEO. P. CARTER
BENJ. F. PRATT
T. E. Hall
Of the House.

MINORITY REPORT

The undersigned, dissenting from the majority of the Committee on Military Claims, and being unable to concur in their Report concerning the charges against the citizens of Ward 9 in the city of Boston made by the Adjutant-General, and which the Committee was directed to investigate, respectfully submits the following

REPORT:

The question before the Committee arises upon the fact that orders for portions of their State bounty were given by certain recruits at various dates in the winter of 1863–4 and the following spring, which orders the Adjutant-General, in his last Annual Report, expresses his belief never should have been given, and when given, never should have been paid. The precise language used by him in this expression of opinion, is quoted in full in the Report of the majority of your Committee, and therefore needs not to be repeated.

This question is one which must be regarded in two different and distinct relations. In the first and inferior relation, it is a question between the Adjutant-General, on the one hand, and on the other hand, a respectable committee of citizens of Boston, who feel aggrieved at the aspersions made by him, which in the hearings before the Committee, he reiterated in even stronger terms. In the second and more important relation, it is a question whether the executive government of the Commonwealth did its full duty during the war in respect to guarding military recruits against imposition and extortion, and also whether it attached a correct construction to the military bounty statutes.

In the first place, as the whole issue rests upon the matter of fact as to what was done with and concerning the bounty orders in question, and as the understanding of the facts by the undersigned differs materially from the recital in the majority Report, the undersigned begs to state them as they appeared to him in the evidence.

By the Act of March 17, 1863 (Sect. 2,) it was made unlawful "for any person within the territory or jurisdiction of this Commonwealth to recruit for or enlist in military service, except under the authority of the governor thereof or of the President of the United States." Under that Act the governor organized a corps of recruiting officers by conferring such authority, in the various towns upon the selectmen, and in the cities upon the mayors and aldermen. The recruiting districts in the city of Boston being the various wards, the alderman of each ward became its official recruiting officer. The alderman of Ward 9, in 1863–4, was L. Miles Standish, Esq. To co-operate with him, an informal committee of twenty citizens was organized at a public meeting held in the ward; but this committee, like similar organizations which sprang into existence at that time all over the State, was purely voluntary, and had no official representative character. Its members comprised many of the most public-spirited, liberal, and patriotic citizens of the ward, and were as follows: 1, Thacher Bea; 2, Gilbert G. Brown; 3, C. Allen Browne; 4, William Carpenter; 5, Charles R. Codman; 6, George A. Curtis; 7, Joseph S. Drew; 8, Jonas Fitch; 9, Richard C. Greenleaf; 10, John C. Haynes; 11, Horace Jenkins; 12, R. B. Lincoln; 13, Dennis O'Brien; 14, O. W. Peabody; 15, Francis Richards; 16, M. D. Ross; 17, Daniel N. Spooner; 18, J. H. Stephenson; 19, S. A. Stetson; 20, Newell A. Thompson. A fund of more than $17,000 in all was collected by this committee at various times, by voluntary subscriptions of citizens of the ward, and was applied to aid the ward recruiting officer. For most of the period covering the transactions in issue before your Committee, such voluntary subscriptions, in this ward and elsewhere in the State, constituted the sole recruiting funds, except the State fund authorized by the Act of March 17, 1863, for the Act authorizing towns and cities to raise and apply money for recruiting and expenses did not become a law until March 18, 1864.

It was during this period that first Mr. George V. Leicester, and afterwards, also, Mr. F. H. Sprague, were sent by this committee to Western Virginia, Kentucky, and Tennessee as recruiting agents. In the technical, legal sense of the word "agents," a relation of agency cannot perhaps be said to have been created between the committee and Messrs. Sprague and Leicester; but they went out under the auspices of the committee, and with the understanding between them and the committee that they should put to the credit of the ward all the recruits they should procure, and that the committee should reimburse all their expenses, and should pay them such a sum per man as should be a liberal compensation for their risk and labor.

The Fifth Regiment of Massachusetts Cavalry was at this time being raised at the camp at Readville, and a large number of colored recruits were collected by Messrs. Sprague and Leicester in the distant localities named, and were transported by them here, and here enlisted into that regiment to the credit of Ward 9, the orders of the War Department not then permitting musters to the credit of any State to take place elsewhere than within the boundary of such State. With most, if not all of the recruits thus collected and transported hither from Kentucky and Tennessee and elsewhere, Messrs. Sprague and Leicester made bargains by which, in consideration of their advancing the funds for the collection, transportation, subsistence and other expenses necessary to enable the men to reach Massachusetts where they could enlist, those men agreed to execute orders after enlistment, assigning to Messrs. Sprague and Leicester sums varying in separate cases from $80 to $125 of their $325 State bounty, in re-imbursement of such expenses, Messrs. Sprague and Leicester assuming all risk of refusals to enlist and of refusals to fulfil the bargain after enlistment by executing such orders. Such men thus brought here for recruits, as on surgical examination were rejected, were in all instances kindly cared for by the committee at its own expense, and were either provided with remunerative civil employment here, or were transported back to the places from which they came, according as they expressed their wishes.

The 112 men mentioned in the Adjutant-General's Report were men thus obtained and enlisted, who after enlistment fulfilled their bargain by executing such orders. A few of these orders, not more than half a dozen in all, were executed, payable to the treasurer or other officers of the citizens' committee. The remainder were executed payable to either Mr. Sprague or Mr. Leicester. And all of them were cashed by the treasurer of the citizens' committee, just as any promissory notes or other negotiable securities might be discounted, and the amount of them was paid by him to Messrs. Sprague and Leicester, together with an additional sum per man. These orders passing thus into the hands of that committee, were by it filed with the State paymaster, and presented by the pay-table on bounty pay-day, according to the usual system established by the State authorities concerning bounty orders, which system is fully explained in the testimony of ex-Governor Andrew, which is hereto annexed, marked A. An opportunity was thereby afforded to each man to repudiate his order, if he should desire. In some instances this repudiation occurred, and in all such cases, the order was at once referred to the judge-advocate-general for investigation and report to the governor whether the order should or should not justly be paid. The judge-advocate-general appeared as a witness before your Committee and testified that after a full examination, he was satisfied that all the orders in question were just, and should be paid, and that they were in accordance with the recruiting system then generally pursued throughout the State, and that he so reported to the governor, who thereupon ordered their payment, which was accordingly made.

The report of the majority of your Committee states that the amount of the orders thus paid, exceeded by $5,000 the amount of the expenses for which the orders were given. The understanding of the testimony by the undersigned was directly the reverse of this, and was to the effect that those expenses exceeded the amount of the orders. The testimony of Messrs. Sprague and Leicester, also of Mr. Standish, the recruiting officer of the ward, and of Mr. Spooner, the treasurer of the committee, was clear upon this point. And it was corroborated by the evidence of the judge-advocate-general, who testified that he withheld for several months his report upon the repudiated orders, until he could clearly determine, by the items, what was the relative proportion of the amount of the orders to the amount of expenses in re-imbursement of which they were given, and that no order referred to him for investigation was reported upon until the fact appeared clearly that those expenses exceeded the amount of the orders, and that such expenses were reasonable in character and amount.

With high deference to the majority of your Committee, the undersigned infers that they have fallen into this error from the fact which appeared in evidence, that at the end of the war a balance of between $3,000 and $4,000 remained in the treasury of the Ward 9 committee, from the $17,000 raised by private subscription, which balance, instead of distributing among the subscribers, the committee have generously applied to relieving cases of need among the discharged soldiers who enlisted on the quota of the ward.

There was no evidence that in any case any deception or misrepresentation was practised upon any recruit. Messrs. Sprague and Leicester testified that each recruit, before starting from the place where he was collected, fully understood his bargain. Dr. Jeffries, the examining surgeon, and Captain Quincy, at whose office the men were sworn in and the orders given, testified in the same effect, that the bargain was, at the time of examination and muster, fully understood. Moses Briggs, an intelligent lieutenant of police, detailed for duty by authority of the mayor of Boston, in connection with these recruits, testified also to the same effect, his opportunities for observation and inquiry having been ample, not only at Boston, at the time of the examination and muster of the recruits, but also in Kentucky, where he at one time accompanied Mr. Sprague, and further on the long transit of the recruits from there to Boston. Alderman Standish testified that before witnessing any order, he in each case fully satisfied himself, by interrogating the recruit, that the bargain was clearly understood. Colonel Henry S. Russell, then in command of the regiment, (now aide-de-camp on the staff of His Excellency Governor Bullock,) testified that in his capacity of colonel of the regiment, he deemed it his especial duty to protect the men from imposition, and that he was satisfied that these orders were made "with perfect understanding and good faith." A copy of Colonel Russell's evidence is hereto annexed, marked (B.) And Messrs. Richard C. Greenleaf, William Carpenter, J. H. Stephenson and Daniel W. Spooner testified that one or more of them was present when the men were enlisted and the orders executed, and that in all cases, when present, they satisfied themselves that such a "perfect understanding" existed. The result of the investigation of the judge-advocate-general, confirmed by the action of the governor upon his report, in directing the orders to be paid, is conclusive to the same effect; and the language of the judge-advocate-general's testimony was that "in no case was any order so approved by him and directed by the governor to be paid, in which the evidence would not have been sufficient to sustain in any court in the State an action for the amount in favor of the party holding the order, allowing to the soldier disputing it the full benefit of his statement."

Opposed to this mass of evidence from the highest sources, there was presented to your committee only the expression of the Adjutant-General's individual doubt whether the men who signed the orders knew what they were doing, and his statement that several of the men had assured him that they did not; but no man whatever appeared or was produced before your Committee to testify to that effect, although by the evidence of Mr. Leicester it appeared that a large number of those recruits are at the present time in and about the city of Boston.

The conclusion, therefore, at which the undersigned arrives is, that in the whole transaction the gentlemen of the Ward 9 committee acted in the strictest integrity and good faith, and that there is no cause whatsoever for any reflection injurious to their conduct or their motives. They all voluntarily appeared before your Committee, and expressed a warm desire to exhibit all their transactions, in the full consciousness that no act was done or contemplated by any of them deserving of reproach. And the testimony of ex-Governor Andrew, of Colonel Russell, of Paymaster-General Marshall, Paymasters Bond and Braman, and Judge-Advocate-General Burt, was in the highest degree complimentary to their patriotic efficiency and zeal, and to the effect that they were distinguished above almost every other recruiting committee in the State, by the exactness of all their business transactions and the aid they thereby rendered to the executive officers of the State.

The offence, if any, then of the Ward 9 committee, consists in their agents, Messrs. Sprague and Leicester, having bargained with recruits collected in places remote from the State, to come here to Massachusetts and enlist, and after enlistment to assign to those agents a portion of their State bounty in re-imbursement of the expenses of collecting and subsisting them and bringing them here; and in the committee having cashed these orders, and presented them for collection.

Of this offence, if it be deemed one, the committee frankly admit that they are guilty; but they deny that is an offence, and affirm that on the contrary it was a general practice in the recruiting system of the State, and that it was sanctioned by the co-operation of the whole executive government of the State, including the Adjutant-General himself.

It is in this second and more important relation,—involving the whole recruiting policy of the State government—that the question before your committee assumes a higher importance than merely the issue between the Adjutant-General on the one hand, and the gentlemen of Ward 9 on the other hand, who feel aggrieved at the Adjutant-General's language. In this second relation, the question involves the propriety of the whole system of such bounty orders, and although the majority of your Committee at the conclusion of their report state that they "purposely refrain from expressing an opinion" as to that system, yet by indorsing the language of the Adjutant-General's report upon the Ward 9 case, it is evident that an opinion strongly condemnatory of the system is implied.

But your Committee, in their report made to the House of Representatives on April 16, upon the petition of Jacques Vrancx and others, had already passed upon the propriety of this system, and in the case of a precisely similar bargain between gentlemen advancing funds to bring recruits hither from abroad, on condition that such recruits should assign portions of their bounty in re-imbursement, had reported that they "regard it as in a very high degree creditable to the character of the immigrants that in so few instances does refusal or avoidance appear to have occurred." (See House, Document 321, page 7.) And in Appendix H to that report (see same document, page 17,) appears a copy of a special order over the signature of the Adjutant-General, wherein after reciting that such a bargain is "reasonable, fair, and clear in its terms," it is ordered that "it is approved." (See Appendix, [C.] to this Report.)

Having fully concurred in the report of your Committee in the case of Vrancx, the undersigned is unable to apply to this case any different standard than was applied by your Committee to that case; nor is the undersigned, after careful study of the facts in both cases, able to perceive on what reasonable theory the report of the majority of your Committee now, can be reconciled with the unanimous report of your Committee then.

It was fully in evidence before your Committee at the hearing in the present case, that the whole of the Fifth Cavalry Regiment was recruited under such a system of bounty orders. With inconsiderable exceptions, all the men of that regiment were recruited in other States. Between one hundred and two hundred of its recruits were furnished through the Ward 9 committee, and most of the remainder were furnished through a committee of one hundred gentlemen, appointed by Governor Andrew, and representing all parts of the State, of which committee John M. Forbes, Esq., of Milton, was chairman, and Richard P. Hallowell, Esq., of Boston, was treasurer. The following is a list of the members of that committee:

J. M. Forbes	G. S. Hale	C. W. Loring
A. A. Lawrence	Martin Brimmer	J. B. Congdon
R. P. Hallowell	S. H. Phillips	John Gardner
Le Baron Russell	Richard P. Waters	John G. Palfrey
C. W. Slack	Geo. Putnam, Jr.	J. Amory Davis
C. G. Loring	Isaac Livermore	Alpheus Hardy
J. H. Wolcott	F. W. Bird	Wm. Dwight
S. G. Ward	E. R. Hoar	Henry B. Rogers
J. M. Barnard	Edward Whitney	S. C. Thwing
W. F. Weld	Charles Hale	Osborn Howes
J. Wiley Edmunds	R. W. Emerson	Charles Beck
W. Endicott, Jr.	Edw. Atkinson	O. Ellsworth
O. Ames	Charles D. Head	R. W. Hooper
James L. Little	T. P. Chandler	Sam'l N. Payson
Geo. Higginson	Henry Sayles	J. H. Stephenson
Thos. Russell	Geo. R. Russell	B. H. Silsbee
E. S. Philbrick	Thomas Sherwin	Geo. W. Bond
Russell Sturgis, Jr.	J. Z. Goodrich	Josiah Quincy, Jr.
W. A. Wellman	S. M. Weld	B. F. Butler
W. B. Rogers	C. W. Spooner	O. W. Holmes
Marshall S. Scudder	J. P. Putnam	M. D. Ross
Ginery Twichell	Thomas Howe	Avery Plummer, Jr.
J. W. Brooks	J. Sturgis	Emory Washburn
S. Cabot, Jr.	J. S. Tyler	B. A. Gould
John Lowell	Wm. Brigham	A. B. Alcott
Jas T. Fields	F. W. G. May	J. Vincent Browne
F. L. Lee	H. N. Hooper	Henry Wilson
Henry Lee, Jr.	T. D. Eliot	Thomas T. Bouve

Henry James	J. C. Delano	Henry I. Bowditch
Henry W. Kingsley	Geo. Winslow	John C. Tyler
Frank B. Fay	Estes Howe	John Quincy Adams
Franklin King	Gardner Colby	Sam'l M. Worcester

Mr. Forbes, its chairman, and Mr. Hallowell, its treasurer, and also Captain Quincy, its chief recruiting agent, appeared as witnesses before your Committee, and their testimony showed that the system pursued by it in relation to the recruits it furnished for the Fifth Cavalry Regiment, was precisely similar to the system pursued by the Ward 9 committee in relation briefly as follows: Recruiting agents were sent out into the Southern States and elsewhere by this committee, under written agreements, by which such agents were guaranteed their expenses and a certain sum per man for each recruit obtained and brought to Massachusetts, and were instructed to make bargains with the recruits, by which, in re-imbursement of the committee's expenses in collecting, subsisting and transporting them hither, the recruits agreed to execute orders after enlistment, assigning to the committee certain portions of their State bounty, varying in amount, in the different contracts put in evidence, from $25 to $125 per man. Various towns and cities throughout the State made bargains with the committee, by which its recruits thus obtained under that system were enlisted to the credit of such towns and cities, precisely in the same manner as the recruits obtained by Messrs. Sprague and Leicester were enlisted to the credit of Ward 9. A list of some twenty or thirty towns and cities to which these recruits were thus credited, was furnished by Captain Quincy, and the books of the committee, showing letter-press copies of the original instructions and agreements between the committee and its agents, were also put in evidence.

And it further appeared from the testimony of Paymaster-General Marshall, Paymasters Bond and Braman, and Judge-Advocate General Burt, that this system was universal, and that similar orders in favor sometimes of town officers officially, but generally in favor of town officers individually, were of common occurrence.

In the instance of the town of Newton, the intelligent and patriotic representative from that town to the present general court was called as a witness, and his testimony, given with much detail, showed that the system there pursued was in all respects similar to that in the case of Ward 9.

The full co-operation of the State government in the system was shown by the testimony of ex-Governor Andrew, as well as by that of the judge-advocate-general and the officers of the pay department, and as the testimony of the governor lays down briefly but completely the policy of the State government on the question, the undersigned begs to quote here two of the interrogatories addressed to him, with his answers, thereto, although the same are hereinafter also recited in Appendix, [A.]

"*Question.* Did you know anything of the system of orders on the State Paymaster, taken by the said Citizens' Committee of one hundred and the said Ward 9 Committee, in the recruiting of colored troops?

"*Answer.* The subject of orders was made matter of personal conference between myself and Mr. Forbes, the chairman of the Citizens' Committee. I applied to those orders a principle which I regarded as of general application to the whole recruiting system, to wit: that if any recruit from any other State than Massachusetts chose to come here and enlist, and not having the means to do so himself, entered into a bargain with another person to bring him here, the expenses fairly attendant upon bringing him here were a legitimate subject to be covered by an assignment by the recruit, to such person, of a part of his bounty, sufficient for that purpose,—always supposing a reasonable bargain as to amount was understandingly made. The Commonwealth was not, after recruitment of the 54th and 55th infantry volunteers, and prior to the Act of July, 1864, engaged in recruiting out of the State. I assumed every volunteer offered here to belong to Massachusetts, and if a man wanted to come here, in order to be eligible to enlist here, I did not regard it with disfavor. What was to be considered reasonable was to be determined by the circumstances of each case, and their interpretation in the light of natural equity, and good faith. Being well aware that my decision was final, I endeavored to have a system rigid enough to give all the advantages to the volunteer, and make every one feel that he must take the orders at his own risk.

"*Question.* Did any bounty orders, after being repudiated by the men, come to you for consideration on reports of the judge-advocate-general?

"*Answer.* Yes, and in each case my decision was based upon the principle above stated. If the order appeared to have been the result of an intelligent bargain between the recruit and another person, and to have been given in re-imbursement of such proper expense, at his request, incurred in his behalf for the purpose of enabling him to reach Massachusetts, or for any other just and lawful purpose, which the recruit might fairly consider valuable to him and free from oppressiveness or inequity, I allowed it. Until the law of March 18th, 1864, no town or city could legally appropriate money *for recruiting purposes.* From the time of the passage of the State bounty act, in November, 1863, until March 18th, 1864, the only public funds applicable for recruiting purposes were therefore *the State bounty* provided by the law of November, 1863, and the State recruiting allowance of twenty-five dollars per man, provided by the law of March 17th, 1863."

In view of the facts thus presented in evidence, the general conclusions at which the undersigned arrives upon the questions submitted to your Committee by the joint order of the two houses of the legislature, are as follows:

1. That no injustice appears to have been done by the alderman of Ward 9, in the city of Boston, or by the citizens' recruiting committee of that ward, in the case of the recruits furnished by the ward to the Fifth Massachusetts Cavalry.

2. That the orders taken from these recruits in re-imbursement of the expenses of bringing them to Massachusetts to enlist, were reasonable, and were in conformity to the recruiting system sanctioned by the State government, and generally practised throughout the State.

3. That any aspersions upon the character and conduct of the alderman and the citizens' recruiting committee of Ward 9, in reference to those orders, are not warranted by the facts, and must be attributed to an imperfect knowledge of the facts, or a decided opinion adverse to the system.

4. That the patriotic character and conduct of the alderman and citizens' recruiting committee of Ward 9, is fully attested by the highest testimony.

5. That no legislation is "necessary or expedient" "in reference to the charges against the citizens of Ward 9 in the city of Boston, made by the Adjutant-General of the Commonwealth in his last annual report."

6. That by the evidence before your Committee, it appeared that the subject of those charges was a matter pertaining to the departments of the Paymaster-General, the Judge-Advocate-General, and the Governor, and not to that of the Adjutant-General.

WM. BRIGHAM

APPENDIX

[A]

Boston, 19th of April, 1866.

To Col. Albert G. Browne, Jr., *Boston, Mass.*

My Dear Colonel,—Below you will find your interrogatories, to each of which I have appended my replies, to wit:—

Q. Please to state the origin of the system of bounty-orders on the State paymaster, giving a general description of the System?

A. The system originated simultaneously with the payment of the bounties at all. When the State bounty law, passed at the extra session of 1863, went into operation, and bounties came to be paid by the State paymasters, who were agents of the governor, (for the Act provided that *the governor* should pay the bounties,) orders given by the recruits for portions of their bounties were continually presented to the paymaster with a request for their allowance. Such orders were presented by persons of every description—in numerous cases by town officers. Immediately, therefore, the organization of some system became necessary. Two views of the governor's relation to the soldiers' State bounty were then presented to me; one, that he had no supervision over it whatsoever beyond its mere payment, and that if the recruit chose to assign it, no matter to whom or for what cause, it was the governor's duty to give effect to such assignments; the second, that the governor's relation to the recruit was in a certain degree fiduciary, and that it was his duty to place certain checks and safeguards against fraud on such bounty assignments or orders.

I held to this second view, and accordingly organized this system.

All orders by the recruit for portions of his bounty were received at the paymaster's office and filed, until bounty pay-day. They were then taken by the paymaster to the pay-table, and when it came the turn of the recruit to be paid, they were presented to him, and he was given an opportunity to repudiate any of them whatsoever, if he should desire. It was the paymaster's duty to explain this fully to each recruit. That if the recruit did not repudiate the orders, the amount of bounty assigned by him on the orders were transferred by the paymaster to the State treasurer, to be by him paid to the parties in whose favor the orders were given. But if, in any instance, from any cause whatsoever, the recruit should repudiate an order, the order and the whole case was immediately transferred by the paymaster to the judge-advocate-general for thorough investigation into all the circumstances of the order, the cause for which the order was given, whether, in the giving or taking of it, any unfair advantage was taken of the recruit, &c, &c; and it was the judge-advocate-general's duty to consider all *equitable* considerations that would make in favor of the recruit,—not merely the *legal rights* of the recruit, *but all equitable considerations also.* Having thus investigated the case, the judge-advocate-general reported on it to me, and upon the basis of his report, as revised by myself, final action on the order was taken.

If on this basis it seemed proper that the order should be allowed, I ordered its allowance and payment; if otherwise, I disallowed it, and that was the end of it. Of course I trusted largely to the intelligence, legal ability and impartiality of the judge-advocate-general, who was an officer appointed by myself, in whom I had confidence, and whose position and duties, being absolutely disconnected from the raising of recruits, insured his impartiality. But the ultimate responsibility, under the law, of course rested with the governor. I think I ought to say, however, that the industry, integrity and ability of General Burt, in discharging his onerous duties, deserved the warmest approval.

Q. Were such cases ever referred for investigation to the adjutant-general?

A. The adjutant-general being an officer connected directly with the raising and organizing of troops and the preparation of pay-rolls, and it being my object to have them referred to an officer absolutely disconnected therefrom, who could hear and decide judicially on what might be alleged by all officers and all persons impartially, I assigned this duty to the judge-advocate-general.

Q. Did you have any knowledge of the raising of colored troops by the citizens' committee of which J. M. Forbes was chairman and R. P. Hallowell treasurer?

A. That committee was appointed by myself, and its operations were matters of frequent conference between myself and the officers and those gentlemen.

Q. Did you have any knowledge of the recruiting of colored troops by the committee of ward nine of the city of Boston, of which Alderman Standish was chairman, and R. C. Greenleaf, Daniel N. Spooner and others were members?

A. The alderman was the appointed recruiting officer. He reported directly to the adjutant-general, or to the superintendent of recruiting, when we had one. Among all the recruiting committees of the State, I know of no one composed of gentlemen who commanded my confidence more than the ward nine committee. Some of them I had personally known for a long time, and were, I believe, most public-spirited citizens and honorable men. They did not, however, report directly to me, and I do not remember that any one complained at any time of their acts or omissions.

Q. Did you know anything of the system of orders on the State pay-master, taken by the said citizens' committee of one hundred, and the said ward nine committee, in the recruiting of color troops?

A. The Subject of orders was made matter of personal conference between myself and Mr. Forbes, the chairman of the citizens' committee. I applied to those orders a principle which I regarded as of general application to the whole recruiting system, to wit: That if any recruit from any other State than Massachusetts chose to come here and enlist, and not having the means to do so himself, entered into a bargain with another person to bring him here,— the expenses fairly attendant upon bringing him here were a legitimate subject to be covered by an assignment by the recruit to such person, of a part of his bounty, sufficient for that purpose,—always supposing a reasonable bargain as to amount was understandingly made. The Commonwealth was not, after the recruitment of the 54th and 55th infantry volunteers, and prior to the Act of July, 1864, engaged in recruiting out of the State. I assumed every volunteer offered here to belong to Massachusetts, and if a man wanted to come here, in order to be eligible to enlist here, I did not regard it with disfavor. What was to be considered reasonable was to be determined by the circumstances of each case, and their interpretation in the light of natural equity, and good faith. Being well aware that my decision was final, I endeavored to have a system rigid enough to give all the advantages to the volunteer, and make every one feel that he must take the orders at his own risk.

Q. Did any bounty-orders, after being repudiated by the men, come to you for consideration on report of the judge-advocate-general?

A. Yes; and in each case my decision was based upon the principles above stated. If the order appeared to have been the result of an intelligent bargain between the recruit and another person, and to have been given in reimbursement of such proper expenses, at his request, incurred in his behalf, for the purpose of enabling him to reach Massachusetts, or for any other just and lawful purpose, which the recruit might fairly consider valuable to him, and free from oppressiveness or inequity—I allowed it. Until the law of March 18, 1864, no town or city could legally appropriate money for recruiting expenses. From the time of the passage of the State bounty act, in November, 1863, until March 18, 1864, the only public funds applicable for recruiting purposes were therefore the State bounty, provided by the law of November, 1863, and the State recruiting allowance of twenty-five dollars per man, provided by the law of March 17, 1863.

Q. When was the whole system of bounty-orders abolished, and why?

A. On May 31st, 1864. I abolished it by a general order, because at that time it had become so complicated that it was impossible to investigate fully and adjudicate cases of repudiated orders;—and on the representation of General Pierce, commandant of camps, that gross frauds were committed under them, and a like representation of General Burt. The chief opposition to my abolishing the system was made by town officers. Some town officers circulated printed memorials addressed to me, remonstrating against its abolition. But notwithstanding the convenience to some recruits, and the strong desire of nearly every town and city officer charged with recruiting duty, who wrote to or conferred with me, I felt that it had become impossible to guard the service against fraud and injustice under any system not more inconvenient by its machinery and its delay, than the utmost inconvenience of abandoning orders entirely.

I however did not preclude myself form the power of relaxing the general rule in clear cases, exceptional in their nature, and where the orders could be inquired into and cleared up in advance. But the system, as a system, was abandoned,—though I well knew that my conduct in doing so was at the time unpopular and unsatisfactory. I may be allowed to add, that in making these answers I have done so without reading the criticisms said to have been made on Adjutant-General Schouler's report on the conduct of the committee of ward nine. I speak simply from my own best recollection, without consultation with him or the officers of my former staff.

Yours faithfully,
JOHN A. ANDREW.

[B]

Boston, April 18, 1866

I was colonel of Fifth Massachusetts Cavalry from the time of its first organization till February 15, 1865, and acted at one time in connection with the committee for recruiting colored troops, for the purpose of getting recruits for my regiment from the West and South. Orders were taken from the men by the agents we employed for different sums of their State bounty, but never without the matter being first explained to the recruit. In many cases where I have seen the men sign orders with perfect willingness, I have known them to repudiate when the time for payment came, without the least reason for doing so. Of course it was my duty to protect the man; and sometimes, at my request, the paymaster refused to pay orders against them; but, excepting in a few instances, the error seems to have been in the man's memory rather than in any neglect on the part of the holder to explain the case fully before receiving the order. In this connection I beg leave to state that the gentlemen representing Ward Nine were among the most earnest in behalf of the soldiers, and I do not believe they held any orders which were not made with perfect understanding and good faith. These gentlemen especially showed how they felt when they divided among the men recruited for the ward $2,000 and more, left on their hands at the end of the war.

The sums of money received by the committee for recruiting colored troops from the various towns to which the men recruited by that committee were accredited, went towards making a fund which has always been spent for comforts to the enlisted men, and necessities for keeping the regiment on a proper footing, such as band uniform, band leader, veterinary surgeon, (for a time till he was paid by the government,) stoves for barracks, and a thousand things that go to keeping up the standard in health and appearance. When the regiment was mustered out, about $1,500, the same being the remainder of the fund, was placed in the hands J. I. Bowditch, Esq., Major N. P. Bowditch, and myself, to be expended in relieving any destitute cases connected with the members of the regiment, and we now have $500 on hand, daily growing less from the charity administered. The fund has been a godsend, both while the regiment was in the field and since it has been at home, and very few of the men would to-day complain of its having existed. As colonel of the regiment and well-wisher of the men, the only feeling I have ever had towards the gentlemen of Ward Nine is that of gratitude for the services which they have rendered to us.

HENRY S. RUSSELL

State of Massachusetts

County of Suffolk, SS.

Subscribed and sworn to this eighteenth day of April, A. D. eighteen hundred and sixty-six.

Before me,

A. W. Adams, Justice of the Peace.

[C]

COMMONWEALTH OF MASSACHUSETTS

HEAD-QUARTERS, BOSTON
September 1, 1864

[Special Order, No. 1065.]

Whereas, M. D. Ross, of Boston, has entered into a written contract with certain persons who have enlisted or are about to enlist in the military service of the United States as part of the contingent of Massachusetts; and whereas said contract has been submitted by said Ross to the examination of a board appointed by his excellence the governor for that purpose, from whose report it appears that the contract is reasonable, fair and clear in its terms, it is approved; and whereas Mr. Ross has in fulfilment of his part of the contract incurred large expense of transportation and otherwise for such persons: It is ordered that M. D. Ross be authorized to sign all State elective and pay rolls in behalf of any volunteers who may have or shall authorize him, by virtue of the above mentioned contract, to receive the State bounties due them as enlisted volunteers on the quota of Massachusetts, pursuant to such contract, and the orders given by the aforesaid men so enlisting.

By order of the Commander-in-Chief

WILLIAM SCHOULER,
Adjutant-General

The Colored Soldiers

If the muse were mine to tempt it
And my feeble voice were strong,
If my tongue were trained to measures,
I would sing a stirring song.
I would sing a song heroic
Of those noble sons of Ham,
Of the gallant colored soldiers
Who fought for Uncle Sam!
In the early days you scorned them,
And with many a flip and flout
Said "These battles are the white man's,
And the whites will fight them out.'
Up the hills you fought and faltered,
In the vales you strove and bled,
While your ears still heard the thunder
Of the foes' advancing tread.
Then distress fell on the nation,
And the flag was drooping low;
Should the dust pollute your banner?
No! the nation shouted, No!
So when War, in savage triumph,
Spread abroad his funeral pall—
Then you called the colored soldiers,
And they answered to your call.
And like hounds unleashed and eager

For the life blood of the prey,
Spring they forth and bore them bravely
In the thickest of the fray.
And where'er the fight was hottest,
Where the bullets fastest fell,
There they pressed unblanched and fearless
At the very mouth of hell.
Ah, they rallied to the standard
To uphold it by their might;
None were stronger in the labors,
None were braver in the fight.
From the blazing breach of Wagner
To the plains of Olustee,
They were foremost in the fight
Of the battles of the free.
And at Pillow! God have mercy
On the deeds committed there,
And the souls of those poor victims
Sent to Thee without a prayer.
Let the fullness of Thy pity
O'er the hot wrought spirits sway
Of the gallant colored soldiers
Who fell fighting on that day!
Yes, the Blacks enjoy their freedom,
And they won it dearly, too;
For the life blood of their thousands
Did the southern fields bedew.
In the darkness of their bondage,
In the depths of slaver's night,
Their muskets flashed the dawning,
And they fought their way to light.
They were comrades then and brothers.
Are they more or less to-day?
They were good to stop a bullet
And to front the fearful fray.
They were citizens and soldiers,
When rebellion raised its head;
And the traits that made them worthy,—

Ah! Those virtues are not dead.
They have shared your nightly vigils,
They have shared your daily toil;
And their blood with yours commingling
Has enriched the Southern soil.
They have slept and marched and suffered
'Neath the same dark skies as you,
They have met as fierce a foeman,
And have been as brave and true.
And their deeds shall find a record
In the registry of Fame;
For their blood has cleansed completely
Every blot of slavery's shame.
So all honor and all glory
To those noble sons of Ham—
The gallant colored soldiers
Who fought for Uncle Sam!

—Paul Laurence Dunbar, 1872–1906

ACKNOWLEDGMENTS

I WOULD LIKE TO TAKE THIS OPPORTUNITY TO THANK THE MANY PEOPLE who helped make *Riders in the Storm* a reality. First, I want to express my appreciation for the late, great Thomas H. O'Connor, PhD, my dissertation advisor at Boston College. Tom was always gracious and generous with his time and one of the foremost subject-matter experts on nineteenth-century American history. Having Tom agree to supervise my dissertation was like hitting the lottery for me. Tom told me, "Find a story that has a beginning, middle, and an end." He also insisted on the accurate reporting of authentic voices. "Bring people up out of the dust and let them speak for themselves," he used to say.

I want to thank my son, John Fitzpatrick Warner, for his efforts and support in crafting a successful book proposal. His encouragement and technical skill made this book possible. I appreciate the opportunity that David Reisch and Stephanie Otto of Stackpole Books have given me. Thank you, Dave and Stephanie. It's been great to work with you. I owe thanks to my parents, John Dwight and Sheila McKenzie Warner, who instilled in me a love of history and the written word. I want to express my love and respect for my wife, Ann, who was always there for me. All three of my children, Margaret, John, and Owen, grew up with this project. I am grateful that they share in its success.

I want to thank Mike Quinn and my brother Chris Warner for their cogent criticism. Your different editorial takes on an academic work made it more lively, readable, and better. Kudos and sincere gratitude to Robert Kidd of EditFast. You are the prince of editors—many thanks. Thanks to James Spencer, a direct descendent of Private John Harvey of the 5th Massachusetts Volunteer Cavalry. Thank you, Jim, for your encouragement and friendship. I want to commend David and Maureen Horn for their mentorship and guidance on this project. Thank you all for your friendship and confidence in me.

Of course, any errors or infelicities in *Riders in the Storm* are my own.

NOTES

NOTES TO CHAPTER 1

1 "Organize a colored regiment of Massachusetts volunteers": Frank P. Stearns, *Life and Public Services of George Luther Stearns* (Philadelphia: J. P. Lippincott, 1907), 266.

2 "On this point 'I am inflexible'": Allan Nevins, *Ordeal of the Union*, 4 vols. (New York: Scribner, 1971), II, pt. 2, 397–98.

2 "Model of compromise and common sense": James D. Richardson, ed., *A Compilation of the Messages and Papers of the Presidents*, 8 vols. (New York: Johnson Reprint, 1968), VI, 6–12.

3 "Inadequate for putting down the rebellion": U.S. Army strength in 1861 from U.S. Census, quoted in Mary Berry, *Military Necessity and Civil Rights Policy* (Port Washington, NY: Kennikat Press, 1977), 34–35.

3 "As its meaning sank in": Nevins, *Ordeal of the Union*, III, pt. 1, 223.

3 "Earned the right to citizenship in the United States": Benjamin Quarles, *The Negro in the Civil War* (Boston: Little, Brown, 1953), 26–30, 184, 253. These famous remarks by Douglass were first made in a speech in New York in July 1863 and reported in *The Liberator* newspaper on 24 July 1863.

4 "Chief heroes of that ever memorable battle": Joseph T. Wilson, *The Black Phalanx* (reprint; New York: Arno Press, 1968), 33–35.

4 "Nor any stroller, negro, or vagabond": Quoted in Philip S. Foner, *Blacks in the American Revolution* (Westport, CT: Greenwood, 1976), 44.

5 "'Impossible to recruit our battalions in any other way' than by accepting slaves": Foner, *Blacks in the Revolution*, 57.

6 "Blacks as messmates among the crew": Quoted in Wilson, *Black Phalanx*, 78, 81–82.

6 "General Jackson had issued a proclamation": Quoted in Robert Vincent Remini, *The Battle of New Orleans* (New York: Viking, 1999), 47–49.

6 "A rumored slave uprising": *The War of the Rebellion: A Compilation of the Official Records of the Union and Confederate Armies*, 128 vols. (Washington, DC: U.S. War Department, 1880–1901), ser. 3, II, 43 (hereafter *O.R.*).

7 "Suppress servile insurrections": *O.R.*, ser. 3, II, 29, 30; *O.R.*, ser. 1, II, 662.

7 "New term for fugitive slaves: 'contraband'": Dudley Cornish, *The Sable Arm: Black Troops in the Union Army, 1861–1865* (Lawrence: University Press of Kansas, 1956), 17; Benjamin Quarles, *Lincoln and the Negro* (New York: Oxford University Press, 1972), 68–69.

7 "Future action by Congress or the courts": *O.R.*, ser. 3, V, 654–56; Berry, *Military Necessity*, 36; Cornish, *Sable Arm*, 12–13; Quarles, *Lincoln and the Negro*, 71.

8   "Are hereby declared free men": Nevins, *Ordeal of the Union*, III, pt. 1, 332.

8   "Fraternal reunion of North and South after the war": Nevins, *Ordeal of the Union*, III, pt. 1, 334, 339.

8   "The executive initiative and its radical contemporary significance": Lawanda Cox, *Lincoln and Black Freedom: A Study in Presidential Leadership* (Columbia: University of South Carolina Press, 1981), 151.

9   "Ending the struggle, must and will come": Roy Basler, *The Collected Works of Abraham Lincoln* (New Brunswick, NJ: Rutgers University Press, 1953), IV, 144–45.

10   "So far as respects such declaration": Basler, *Works of Lincoln*, V, 222–26.

10   "Limits of their several commands": O.R., ser. 3, II, 31.

10   "Should never see again": O.R., ser. 3, II, 57.

11   "Every kind of opinion, conviction and reaction": Cornish, *Sable Arm*, 40.

11   "Wholly lost in any other event": Basler, *Works of Lincoln*, V, 317–19.

12   "Shall then, thenceforward, and forever, be free": Basler, *Works of Lincoln*, V, 336–37.

12   "Concurred with Seward on the importance of timing": Benjamin P. Thomas and Harold M. Hyman, *Stanton: The Life and Times of Lincoln's Secretary of War* (New York: Knopf, 1962), 239; Howard K. Beale, ed., *Diary of Gideon Welles*, 2 vols. (New York: Norton, 1960), I, 70–71.

12   "Equally liable to loss of their estates": Nevins, *Ordeal of the Union*, III, pt. 2, 146; *Congressional Globe*, 37th Cong., 2nd Sess. 3197–207, 3266–68 (1862).

13   "Difficulty would at once vanish": Basler, *Works of Lincoln*, V, 328–31.

13   "Monthly pay may be in clothing": O.R., ser. 3, V, 654–55.

14   "Deepened peril to the Union": Quoted in Henry Greenleaf Pearson, *Life of John A. Andrew*, 2 vols. (Boston: Houghton Mifflin, 1904), II, 44.

14   "All men everywhere could be free": Basler, *Works of Lincoln*, V, 388.

14   "Should be then, thenceforth, and forever free": The text of the Preliminary Emancipation Proclamation can be found in O.R., ser. 3, V, 656.

15   "Vessels of all sorts in said service": The Emancipation Proclamation issued on 1 January 1863 has this language in it. Basler, *Works of Lincoln*, VI, 30.

15   "Appeared to me to be a military necessity": Basler, *Works of Lincoln*, VI, 48–49.

15   "But died without the sight": Pearson, *Life of Andrew*, I, 100–101; II, 50–51.

15   "Because I sympathize with and believe in the eternal right": John A. Andrew, *Speeches of John A. Andrew at Hingham and Boston: Together with his testimony before the Harper's Ferry Committee of the Senate, in relation to John Brown; Also, the Republican platform and other matters*, published by order of the Republican State Committee (Boston, MA, 1860), 8.

16   "To injure him, [and] out of it to harm Lincoln": *Springfield Republican*, 30 August 1860.

16   "Lurked always in our national system": Pearson, *Life of Andrew*, I, 248, 249.

16   "But all understood an attack on the Union": Sarah Forbes Hughes, ed., *Letters and Recollections of John Murray Forbes*, 2 vols. (Boston: Houghton Mifflin, 1899), I, 202.

17   "Speakers of the tribe are utterly unbridled in their speech": The newspaper editorials quoted here are from the *Springfield Republican*, 6 June and 15 July 1861, and *The Pilot*, 25 January 1862.

17   "Asked no favor and gave no quarter": William Schouler, *History of Massachusetts in the Civil War*, 2 vols. (Boston: E. P. Dutton, 1868), I, 44.

18 "Attacked by Democrats and Conservatives": Edith E. Ware, *Political Opinion in Massachusetts during the Civil War and Reconstruction* (New York: AMS Press, 1916), 90.

18 "Embarrass the civil ends which the war is meant to secure": *Boston Daily Advertiser*, 21 September 1861.

18 "Seemed to meet so admirably the exigency of the case": Quotes in the *Springfield Republican* are from 17 and 21 September 1861.

18 "Now we are divided": Sarah Forbes Hughes, ed., *Letters (Supplementary) of John Murray Forbes*, 3 vols. (Boston: Houghton Mifflin, 1905), I, 292.

19 "To write leading articles to enforce his views": Hughes, *Recollections of Forbes*, I, 10–11.

19 "Between taking it up and absolute submission": *Recollections of Forbes*, I, 235.

19 "The elevating of our national character": Amos A. Lawrence to Sumner, 10 December 1861, Sumner MS, Houghton Library, Harvard, quoted in Ware, *Political Opinion*, 94.

19 "It would help us to weaken the enemy": John Murray Forbes to Major General Hunter, 7 July 1862, Hughes, *Letters (Supplementary) of Forbes*, II, 9–10.

20 "Should be exploded in South Carolina": Quoted in Pearson, *Life of Andrew*, II, 9.

20 "Described as a 'colossal blunder' by his biographer": Thomas and Hyman, *Stanton*, 201–2; *O.R.*, ser. 3, II, 2.

20 "Pour out to obey your call": Pearson, *Life of Andrew*, II, 10–13.

21 "Break up the Army in twenty-four hours": *Boston Post*, 23 June 1862, quoted in a note by Ware, *Political Opinion in Massachusetts*, 99.

21 "With all the rest of us, hates slavery in all its aspects": *Springfield Republican*, 30 May 1862.

21 "Weren't sure what to think": Schouler, *Massachusetts in the Civil War*, 333–34; Pearson, *Life of Andrew*, II, 12–20; Thomas and Hyman, *Stanton*, 195–200.

22 "Watching the wind for evidence": Andrew to Sumner, June 1862, quoted in Pearson, *Life of Andrew*, II, 23.

22 "Before throwing away more valuable lives": Hughes, *Recollections of Forbes*, I, 314, 317–18.

23 "They are in great measure prepared for it": *Boston Daily Advertiser*, 20 August 1862.

23 "An intolerable effluvia exudes from their persons": *The Pilot*, February 1862.

23 "Everything will soon be reversed": *The Pilot*, 4 October 1862.

24 "Persons of African descent, organized into separate corps": Schouler, *Massachusetts in the Civil War*, I, 337.

24 "The greatest interest in this experiment": John A. Andrew to Francis G. Shaw, 30 January 1863, John A. Andrew Papers, Massachusetts Historical Society (hereafter MHS).

24 "Governor Andrew personally desired to appoint": Emilio's quote is found in Luis F. Emilio, *A Brave Black Regiment: History of the Fifty-Fourth Regiment of Massachusetts Volunteer Infantry, 1863–1865*, 2nd ed. (Cambridge, MA: Harvard University Press, 1868), 6–7.

25 "A most heinous crime in the South": *O.R.*, ser. 3, III, 20.

26 "Penetrated beyond the Mississippi": Emilio is quoted in Cornish, *Sable Arm*, 130; *O.R.*, ser. 3, III, 215, 216.

26 "They will be designated '_____ Regiment of U.S. Colored Troops'": *O.R.*, ser. 3, III, 215. General Order No. 143 establishing the Bureau of U.S. Colored Troops was issued on 22 May 1863.

26 "Under central control from Washington": Cornish, *Sable Arm*, 107–10.

27 "He would have an obvious and important advantage": Theophilus Parsons to Andrew, 3 September 1863, Governor John A. Andrew Papers, Massachusetts State Archives (hereafter MSA), Letters Official, vol. 36, 90.

28 "Selected for the 54th and 55th (infantry) volunteers'": J. A. Andrew to E. M. Stanton, 5 September 1863, Andrew Papers, MSA, Letters Official, vol. 36, 87.

28 "But would get back to Andrew 'speedily'": For Stanton's reply to Andrew, see E. M. Stanton to J. A. Andrew, 10 September 1863, Andrew Papers, MSA, Letters Official, vol. 36, 358.

28 "This present [1863] quota of 15,120 men": J. A. Andrew to J. M. Forbes, 20 November 1863, 21 November 1863, Andrew Papers, MSA, Letters Official, vol. 39, 321–25, 443–46.

29 "Put it into shape & I to help him": J. M. Forbes to J. A. Andrew, 21 November 1863, Andrew Papers, MSA, Letters Official, vol. 39, 363.

29 "To these troops no bounties will be paid": *O.R.*, ser. 3, III, 1090.

30 "This we must never submit to": J. A. Andrew to J. M. Forbes, 30 November 1863, Andrew Papers, MSA, Letters Official, vol. 39, 381.

30 "Please give me similar order to former one": *O.R.*, ser. 3, III, 1095.

30 "The officers of said regiment may be appointed by you": *O.R.*, ser. 3, III, 11.

NOTES TO CHAPTER 2

32 "As you did when that regiment was formed": MSA, 5th Mass. Cav. File, box 10, vol. 80, 11.

32 "Go far on myself if you will send transportation": MSA, 5th Mass. Cav. File, 10 1/2.

33 "Col'd man to reconnoitre in his vicinity": MSA, 5th Mass. Cav. File, 12.

33 "Honor of rendering some assistance": MSA, 5th Mass. Cav. File, 12.

34 "Conducting our war to a successful issue": MSA, 5th Mass. Cav. File, 16.

34 "Propose to go South after contrabands for your cavalry": MSA, 5th Mass. Cav. File, 35.

35 "Willing to fight and if need be to die for them": MSA, 5th Mass. Cav. File, 34.

35 "Giving his residence as Somerville, Massachusetts, not Watkins, New York": Entry for John D. Berry, Massachusetts Adjutant General's Office, *Massachusetts Soldiers, Sailors and Marines in the Civil War*, 8 vols. and index (Norwood, MA: Norwood Press, 1933), VI, 502 (hereafter *MA Soldiers and Sailors*).

35 "Very few, however, were paid more than two hundred dollars each": Schouler, *Massachusetts in the Civil War*, 475.

39 "Helped create it or to save it": Quoted in Schouler, *Massachusetts in the Civil War*, 509. The letterpress copy appears in Andrew to Hayden, 19 November 1863, Andrew Papers, MSA, Letters Official, vol. 39, 420.

40 "Common estimation towards their own level": Parsons to Andrew, MSA, 5th Mass. Cav. File, 22.

41 "I can always have a good regiment": Andrew to Stanton, 22 August 1863, MSA, Letters Official, vol. 35, 478.

42 "The best man to head the regiment": Forbes to Andrew, 23 November 1863, Andrew Papers, MSA, Letters Official, vol. 39, 440; Andrew to Forbes, 26 November 1863, MSA, Letters Official, vol. 39, 443.

42   "A little discouraging for a colored man to enlist": MSA, 5th Mass. Cav. File, 16.

42   "Complete with arson, murder, pillage and rapine": Dudley Cornish, *Sable Arm*, 158.

43   "At such time and place as the President shall order": *O.R*, ser. 1, XIV, 599.

43   "On the proper and usual parole": *O.R.*, ser. 2, V, 807–8, 12 January 1863.

43   "According to the present or future law of such State or States": Luis Emilio, *Brave Black Regiment*, 6; Cornish, *Sable Arm*, 160.

44   "Treatment due a prisoner of war": Emilio, *Brave Black Regiment*, 96–97; *O.R.*, ser. 2, VI, 163. The president's order was published as War Department General Order No. 252, 31 July 1863.

44   "With a brutal equality": For instances of African American soldiers murdering Confederates after they had surrendered and "finishing off" wounded rebels, see Wilbur Fisk, *Anti-Rebel: The Civil War Letters of Wilbur Fisk* (Croton-on-Hudson, NY: E. Rosenblatt, 1983), 321; Harry F. Jackson and Thomas F. O'Donnell, eds., *Back Home in Oneida: Hermon Clarke and His Letters* (Syracuse, NY: Syracuse University Press, 1965),141–43; Thomas L. Livermore, *Days and Events* (Boston: Houghton Mifflin, 1920), 355–58.

45   "We quietly refused, and continued to do our duty": Unnamed African American soldier, purportedly in the 54th Massachusetts Infantry, quoted by Theodore Tilton, *Boston Evening Journal*, 16 December 1863.

46   "Justice of Congress at the next session": *O.R.*, ser. 3, III, 420. See also Pearson, *Life of Andrew*, II, 99–117; Berry, *Military Necessity*, 63–66; Cornish, *Sable Arm*, 184–85.

46   "Pay and bounty as white troops receive, is recommended": House Executive Documents No. 1, 38th Cong., 1st Sess. 8 (1864), quoted in Cornish, *Sable Arm*, 189.

46   "Of the highest merit and influence": Andrew to Stanton, 3 February 1863, quoted in Schouler, *Massachusetts in the Civil War*, 407–8.

47   "Being killed a little for the benefit of our pockets?": Unsigned editorial, *Boston Traveller*, 18 January 1864.

47   "Until it mustered out in November 1865": *MA Soldiers and Sailors*, VI, 497.

47   "All points of the compass": The roster of Company A is found in *MA Soldiers and Sailors*, VI, 494–98.

48   "Left the plow to go into the army": James M. McPherson, *Battle Cry of Freedom: The Civil War Era* (New York: Oxford University Press, 1988), 607–8.

50   "Your freedom will be secure": Frank P. Stearns, *Life and Public Services of George Luther Stearns* (reprint; New York: Arno Press, 1969), 286–87.

50   "If I can be of any service to you at any time please inform me": Ibid., 290.

50   "Twenty-five dollars bounty at the volunteer's election": Stearns to Wilkerson, 5 December 1863, MSA, Letters Official, vol. 40, 325.

50   "To act as our Recruiting Agent": Lewis Hayden's meeting with federal recruiting agent Robert Corson is described in Hayden to Andrew, 2 December 1863, MSA, 5th Mass. Cav. File, 24 1/2.

51   "Objections in a letter written the next day": Andrew to Hayden, 3 December 1863, MSA, Letters Official, vol. 41, 296.

52   "194 Broadway in New York City": Andrew to Howe, 7 December 1863, MSA, 5th Mass. Cav. File, 14.

53   "Who had been colonel of the 55th Massachusetts Infantry": Andrew to Hallowell, 7 December 1863, MSA, Letters Official, vol. 41, 111.

53 "Anxious to join your cavalry": For Lewis Hayden's answer to Governor Andrew's letter of 3 December, see Hayden to Andrew, 12 December 1863, MSA, 5th Mass. Cav. File, 23.

54 "Your cavalry reg't. at Readville": Foster to Andrew (telegram), 17 December 1863, MSA, 5th Mass. Cav. File, 26 1/2.

54 "Prudent or of usefulness": C. L. Remond to J. A. Andrew, 18 December 1863, MSA, 5th Mass. Cav. File, 26.

55 "Test the matter without committing you": Howe to Andrew, 21 December 1863, MSA, 5th Mass. Cav. File, 30.

55 "Provost marshals turned them back": The story about recruiters leading African Americans out of Washington to "chop wood" is in Pearson, *Life of Andrew*, II, 92–93.

55 "To volunteer and fight in New England regiments": Quoted in *Boston Commonwealth*, 29 January 1864.

56 "Willing to do and die in the service of their country?": Drew to Andrew, 6 February 1864, MSA, 5th Mass. Cav. File, 77.

56 "Are forbidden to come?": *Pearson*, Life of Andrew, II, 92–93. See also Basler, *Works of Lincoln*, VII, 190–91, 204.

57 "Recruiters in and around Washington, DC": Pearson, *Life of Andrew*, 93; Basler, *Works of Lincoln*, VII, 204.

57 "Until remedy is provided": Forbes to Andrew, 2 January 1864, MSA, 5th Mass. Cav. File, 42.

57 "Especially as the 54th wants no more men": Russell to Andrew, 6 January 1864, MSA, 5th Mass. Cav. File, 47.

58 "Will be your crack regiment": Parsons to Andrew, 20 January 1864, MSA, 5th Mass. Cav. File, 58.

59 "Camp Meigs was a busy place": Description of Camp Meigs is from James Roland Corthell, "The Story of Camp Meigs," *New England Magazine* 32, no. 4 (June 1905): 385–87.

59 "2,270 men were at the camp": Schouler, *Massachusetts in the Civil War*, 507.

Notes to Chapter 3

64 "Wasted heroism at the end, and perhaps not even that": Colonel Higginson's opinions were set forth in Thomas W. Higginson, "Regular and Volunteer Officers," *Atlantic Monthly* 14 (September 1864): 349, 351.

64 "A gentleman 'of the highest tone and honor'": Governor John A. Andrew to Major M. Vincent, AAG, 18 December 1863, MSA, Executive Department Files, Letters Official, vol. 41, 409.

64 "Disappearance of slavery as a happy result": John T. Morse Jr., *Sons of the Puritans* (Boston: Beacon, 1908), 158.

65 "And thus simply settled the matter": Morse, *Sons of Puritans*, 158.

66 "In the war of the Slaveholders' Rebellion": Norwood P. Hallowell, "The Negro as a Soldier in the War of the Rebellion," *Papers of the Military Historical Society of Massachusetts*, vol. XIII, *Civil and Mexican Wars* (Boston, 1913), 301–2.

68 "Which I should accept with pleasure": Henry S. Russell to John A. Andrew, 27 November 1863, MSA, 5th Mass. Cav. File, box 10, vol. 80, 3.

69   "Taken much interest in the Black Movement": Colonel Lowell's recommendations are included in Charles R. Lowell Jr. to Albert G. Browne Jr., 30 November 1863, MSA, 5th Mass. Cav. File, 3 1/2. For information on individuals mentioned and Massachusetts units, see also James L. Bowen, *Massachusetts in the War, 1861–1865* (Springfield, MA: C. W. Bryan, 1899), 755–66, and Thomas W. Higginson, ed., *Massachusetts in the Army and Navy*, 2 vols. (Boston: Wright and Potter, 1895), I, 199.

71   "Respectfully referred to Col. Russell for a report": On the matter of the Reverend George B. Farnsworth, see MSA, 5th Mass. Cav. File, 10.

72   "Send for him to call": MSA, 5th Mass. Cav. File, 13.

72   "Commissioning him colonel only on 2 March 1864": Colonel Henry S. Russell to John A. Andrew, MSA, 5th Mass. Cav. File, 55.

74   "By reason of disability incurred in the line of duty": For the "California Hundred" and "California Battalion," see Samuel W. Backus, "Californians in the Field: A Historical Sketch of the Organization and Services of the California 'Hundred' and 'Battalion'; 2nd Massachusetts Cavalry," *War Paper No. 4, California Commandery of the Military Order of the Loyal Legion of the United States*, 1889.

75   "Whom Lowell valued among his best Captains": Hughes, *Letters (Supplementary) of Forbes*, II, 147–48.

76   "Remained on duty for a week": Bowen, *Massachusetts in the War*, 630, 633.

77   "Abner Mallory was F Company's first lieutenant": For officers promoted from the 44th Massachusetts Volunteer Militia, see *MA Soldiers and Sailors*; Howe, Newell, and Whittemore appear in vol. VI, pp. 496, 497, and 518, respectively.

77   "Wd. be pleased to have Lt. Parsons in our Movement": MSA, 5th Mass. Cav. File, 18.

77   "See Captain Bowditch as soon as possible": MSA, 5th Mass. Cav. File, 22, 22 1/2.

79   "Prizes Lieutenant Weld highly as an officer": Major Henry L. Higginson to Brigadier General R. A. Pierce, 14 December 1863, MSA, 5th Mass. Cav. File, 23.

79   "Render me & the battalion any service": Brigadier General R. A. Pierce to Governor Andrew, 14 December 1863, MSA, Executive Department Files, Letters Official, vol. 41, 391.

81   "Whenever they could be spared": Governor John A. Andrew to Major M. Vincent, AAG, 18 December 1863, MSA, Executive Department Files, Letters Official, vol. 41, 409–10.

82   "Duly prepared to pass a good examination": Colonel S. M. Bowman, USA, to Governor Andrew, 18 December 1863, MSA, 5th Mass. Cav. File, 26.

82   "Carefully examined by a skillful and experienced cavalry officer": Governor Andrew to Colonel S. M. Bowman, 22 December 1863, MSA, Executive Department Files, Letters Official, vol. 42, 82.

83   "These officers will be mustered": Russell to Andrew 20 December 1863, MSA, 5th Mass. Cav. File, 28; Andrew to Stanton 21 December 1863, MSA, Letters Official, vol. 42, 31.

84   "Fit for a 2nd Lieutenancy": "Case of Geo F. Wilson," MSA, 5th Mass. Cav. File, 61.

85   "Keeping accurate accounts is certainly necessary": Governor Andrew to W. L. Garrison, 23 December 1863, Andrew Papers, MSA, Executive Department Files, Letters Official, vol. 42, 155; H. S. Russell to John A. Andrew, 24 December 1863, Andrew Papers, MSA, Executive Department Files, Letters Official, vol. 80, 36.

86 "Swain was G Company's first lieutenant": For the commissioning and subsequent careers of Abram O. Swain, Francis L. Gilman, George A. Fisher, and Jacob B. Cook, see MSA, 5th Mass. Cav. File, 39; *MA Soldiers and Sailors*, VI, 507, 512, 536.

86 "Recommendation of Private McNeill for the position he asks": MSA, 5th Mass. Cav. File, 8.

86 "Citizens of this place whom you may choose to mention": MSA, 5th Mass. Cav. File, 31.

88 "Whittier's pen to write the poem here enclosed": MSA, 5th Mass. Cav. File, 44.

90 "Increase of pay of a cavalry officer would be no privilege to him": MSA, 5th Mass. Cav. File, 45.

90 "Before embarking on board the transport": "War Letters of Charles P. Bowditch," *Proceedings of the Massachusetts Historical Society* 57 (1923–1924): 422 (hereafter Bowditch, "War Letters").

90 "Walking was not easy in my weakened condition": Bowditch "War Letters," 438–39.

91 "Slight enough for him to enjoy his Christmas": Bowditch, "War Letters," 450–51, 453–54.

92 "Not wonderful that I should have to wait a little while": Bowditch, "War Letters," 456, 459, 466–67.

93 "Too good a one to be lost": Bowditch, "War Letters," 471–72.

93 "The First Michigan Cavalry is at home on furlough": MSA, 5th Mass. Cav. File, 68.

93 "Issued the commission and informed Congressman Baxter": MSA, 5th Mass. Cav. File, 83.

95 "Rec. by General McClellan for Massachusetts Commission": MSA, 5th Mass. Cav. File, 59.

96 "And will I am sure do credit to the service": MSA, 5th Mass. Cav. File, 62.

97 "By sending their affidavit": For information on the eleven soldiers who signed the letter to Governor Andrew, see MSA, 5th Mass. Cav. File, 54; *MA Soldiers and Sailors*, VI, 494, 495, 497, 498, 500, 501, 502, 503, 505.

98 "The left hand hangs by the side of the sabre": Philip S. Cooke, *Cavalry Tactics, or Regulations for the Instruction, Formations, and Movements of the Cavalry of the Army and Volunteers of the United States* (Washington, DC: U.S. War Department, 1862), 33–34.

Notes to Chapter 4

100 "1st. Guards. 2nd. Working-parties or fatigue. 3rd. Daily Duty": August V. Kautz, *Customs of Service for Non-Commissioned Officers* (Philadelphia: J. B. Lippincott, 1864), 27.

100 "Examined by an officer or non-commissioned officer of the guard": Kautz, *Customs of Service*, 28–29.

100 "To carry orders, messages &c": Kautz, *Customs of Service*, 42–43.

101 "And be presented at headquarters by a Sergeant": National Archives, Record Group (hereafter NA, RG) 94, Regimental Order Books.

103 "Sunday inspection as far as practicable": NA, RG 94, Regimental Order Books.

104 "Our desire to put 'the right man in the right place'": Correspondence regarding Daniel H. Chamberlain, MSA, 5th Mass. Cav. File, 128.

105 "Also joined the 5th Massachusetts Cavalry on 30 January": On the Higginsons in the 5th Massachusetts Cavalry, see Mary C. Crawford, *Famous Families of Massachu-*

setts, 2 vols. (Boston: Little, Brown, 1930), I, 254–55, 271; author's research, Higginson Papers, New England Historic Genealogical Society.

105 "Thirty-three had been named by the middle of February": MSA, 5th Mass. Cav. File, 68. The officers on Russell's roster were (in the order written) Captains C. Chauncy Parsons, Charles P. Bowditch, Horace B. Welch, Cyrus C. Emery, Albert R. Howe, and Francis L. Higginson. First lieutenants were James S. Newell, Windsor Hatch II, Charles E. Allan, John Anderson, Andrew Chapman, Jacob B. Cook, James L. Wheat, Edgar M. Blanche, Abner F. Mallory, and Peter J. Rooney. The following were second lieutenants in February: George B. Farnsworth, J. Davenport Fisher, Abram O. Swain, George A. Fisher, Francis L. Gilman, Rienzi Loud, Curtis H. Whittemore, Charles P. Wheeler, Curt Gersdorff, Daniel H. Chamberlain, and Robert M. Higginson.

106 "For men to be out of camp after retreat": NA, RG 94, Regimental Order Books.

106 "From the cavalry regiments now in the field": MSA, 5th Mass. Cav. File, 85.

107 "Extra trouble which this requirement may occasion you": MSA, 5th Mass. Cav. File, 100.

108 "Promoted to quartermaster sergeant of the 1st Massachusetts": For men accessioned from the 1st Massachusetts Cavalry in March and April of 1864, see Benjamin Crowninshield, *A History of the First Regiment of Massachusetts Cavalry Volunteers* (Boston: Houghton Mifflin, 1891), P. T. Jackson Jr., 187, 200, 329; G. Odell, 364; C. Kaler, 330; E. H. Adams, 341; cf. *MA Soldiers and Sailors.*

109 "And yet others did not report for service": Bowen, *Massachusetts in the War*, 673.

110 "Became 'I' Company's first sergeant": NA, RG 94, Company Muster in and Descriptive Roll of Charles R. Douglas; see also *MA Soldiers and Sailors*, VI, 528, 531.

111 "Martin Becker, Commissary Sergeant, 55th Regiment of Massachusetts Volunteers": C. R. Douglass to F. Douglass, 6 July 1863, Frederick Douglass Papers, Manuscript Division, Library of Congress (hereafter Douglass Papers).

113 "Would have turned them against me": C. R. Douglass to F. Douglass, 8 September 1863; C. R. Douglass to F. Douglass, 18 September 1863; C. R. Douglass to F. Douglass, 20 December 1863; Douglass Papers.

113 "Same class in many cases as those of my old regiment": Bowditch, "War Letters," 472–73.

114 "Lies with the officers and not with me": John A. Andrew to Rev. Isaac S. Cushman, 23 December 1863, MSA, 5th Mass. Cav. File, 154.

115 "Not so great as if the whole were received": MSA, 5th Mass. Cav. File, 93.

115 "178,975 black men enlisted in the army, beginning in late 1863": *O.R.*, ser. 3, V, 661.

116 "Men who can choose the $50 and $20 per month": Colonel H. S. Russell to John A. Andrew, 16 March 1864; J. F. B. Marshall to Governor Andrew, 17 March 1864; H. S. Russell to J. A. Andrew, 17 March 1864, MSA, 5th Mass. Cav. File, 100.

117 "Let 'those who chose to prefer Mass.' know what to expect": MSA, 5th Mass. Cav. File, 103.

118 "Records do not reveal what became of his wife": For Private William Vance, see *MA Soldiers and Sailors*, VI, 506.

119 "To the amount of several thousands of dollars": A. G. Browne Jr., Lt. Col.[,] Mil. Sec'y to John S. Rock Esq., 21 March 1864, MSA, Executive Department Files, Letters Official, vol. 45, 448–51.

120 "'Untiring & patriotic efforts for the nation' and for Massachusetts": MSA, 5th Mass. Cav. File, 109.

122 "But this does not look so to me": Lewis Hayden to John Andrew, 12 April 1864, MSA, 5th Mass. Cav. File, 110.

123 "This instance of yours is one illustration": MSA, 5th Mass. Cav. File, 134.

123 "Fifty-four days after the 2nd Battalion was complete": For the dates of muster in of the three battalions of the 5th Massachusetts Volunteer Cavalry, see *MA Soldiers and Sailors*, VI, 492.

123 "The 5th Massachusetts Cavalry had substantially fewer desertions": For the rate of desertion in the 5th Massachusetts Cavalry, see Report of Provost Marshal General, 17 March 1866, House Executive Documents, 39th Cong., 1st Sess., doc. 1, pt. 1, 76 (1864).

124 "Not yet been turned in by the contractors, but are expected daily": MSA, 5th Mass. Cav. File, 99, 101.

125 "Same retreating Confederate soldier at seven hundred yards": On "whittled sights," see C. A. Stevens, *Berdan's United States Sharpshooters in the Army of the Potomac* (St. Paul, MN: Price-McGill, 1896), 7. The Kelly's Ford incident is found in Robert V. Bruce, *Lincoln and the Tools of War* (Indianapolis: Bobbs-Merrill, 1956), 284–85.

125 "Samuel Colt's factory in Hartford, Connecticut, during the war": Arcadie Gluckman, *United States Martial Pistols and Revolvers* (Buffalo, NY: Otto Ulbrich, 1944), 153–60.

125 "Required to keep all the federal cavalry mounted": *O.R.*, ser. 3, III, 884–86; "Cavalry Bureau Report," *O.R.*, ser. 1, vol. XXIX, pt. 2, 398–99, 405.

126 "Discourage the organization of any new volunteer organizations": John V. Barton, "The Procurement of Horses," *Civil War Times Illustrated* 6 (1967): 20–23.

126 "Major Weld to act as inspector of horses for the regiment": Regimental Special Order No. 36, dated 18 April, detailed Major Weld to act as inspector of horses for the regiment. This is the first official mention of the arrival of horses for the 5th Massachusetts. NA, RG 94, Regimental Order Books, Special Order No. 36.

126 "In answer to a dispatch from General Devens": MSA, 5th Mass. Cav. File, 111.

126 "General Devens was not fully informed": MSA, 5th Mass. Cav. File, 138.

127 "Horses being furnished promptly. Urge McKim": MSA, 5th Mass. Cav. File, 138.

128 "Whether the Adjutant General will issue marching orders today": MSA, 5th Mass. Cav. File, 115.

129 "Nothing but absolute necessity can excuse it": MSA, 5th Mass. Cav. File, 116.

129 "When will the regiment arrive here[?]": MSA, 5th Mass. Cav. File, 117.

129 "May be here with the least possible delay": MSA, 5th Mass. Cav. File, 118.

130 "Death after muster before the payment of the volunteer": MSA, 5th Mass. Cav. File, 120.

130 "Wish to obtain maximum for each company": MSA, 5th Mass. Cav. File, 138.

132 "The last line: 'accede to my request for justice'": Samuel Hooper to John Andrew, 2 May 1864; Charles Sumner and Henry Wilson to John Andrew, 2 May 1864; Brigadier General E. R. S. Canby to John Andrew, 2 May 1864, MSA, 5th Mass. Cav. File, 122–24.

132 "But since it can be tortured into a requisition I treat it as such": MSA, 5th Mass. Cav. File, 138.

NOTES TO CHAPTER 5

133 "They shouted, 'Fort Pillow,' and the rebs were shown no mercy": Trooper Charles T. Beman's letter was quoted in the *Weekly Anglo-African*, vol. III, no. 49, whole no. 153, 9 July 1864.

134 "Reassembling across the Potomac from Washington": *MA Soldiers and Sailors*, Griffin and Hodge, 504; Monroe, 522; Smith, 530, Miller, 537; Murray, 497; and NA, RG 94, A Company, Order and Record Books. The men who deserted immediately after the arrival of their respective battalions in Washington were Privates William Johnson, Company D in Alexandria, 13 May; William H. Rogers, Company D in Washington, 13 May; James A. Hall and Joshua Hunt, both Company M and both in Alexandria, 13 May. See *MA Soldiers and Sailors*, VI, 508, 509, 540.

134 "Which was part of the defenses of Washington": George B. Davis, Joseph W. Kirkley, and Leslie J. Perry, *The Official Military Atlas of the Civil War* (reprint; Avenel, NJ: Outlook Book Co., 1983), plate LXXXIX, "Defenses of Washington."

135 "Railroad accident between New York and here": Colonel H. S. Russell to Governor Andrew, 10 May 1864, MSA, 5th Mass. Cav. File, box 10, vol. 80, 144.

136 "They are great institutions, very refreshing indeed": For the description of the 2nd Battalion of the 5th Massachusetts Cavalry's trip south, see Bowditch, "War Letters," 473–75.

136 "Fed at the refreshment saloon during the war": Quoted in Francis A. Lord, *They Fought for the Union* (Harrisburg, PA: Stackpole, 1960), 131.

137 "No more at present": C. R. Douglass to Frederick Douglass, 31 May 1864, Douglass Papers.

137 "Died May 12, 1864, of disease, at Baltimore, Maryland": *MA Soldiers and Sailors*, VI, 531.

138 "A true copy: attest [signed] J. S. Newell 1st Lt. & Adjt 5th Mass. Cav": NA, RG 94, 5th Mass. Cav., Regimental Order and Record Books.

139 "Send their horses to General Meade": *O.R.*, ser. 1, vol. XXXVI, pt. II, 328.

139 "Less than their forage on horseback": Halleck to Grant, *O.R.*, ser. 1, XXXIII, 966; Grant to Halleck, *O.R.*, ser. 1, vol. XXXVI, pt. II, 329.

139 "Lost their horses and were made to serve as infantry": Halleck's report is found in *O.R.*, ser. 1, vol. XXXVI, pt. III, 569. Stephen Z. Starr, *The Union Cavalry in the Civil War*, 3 vols. (Baton Rouge: Louisiana State University, 1981), III, 117.

140 "The officers are almost as bad": Bowditch, "War Letters," 474.

141 "Was in the same division as the 5th Massachusetts": For deserters claimed by U.S. Colored Troops regiments, see *MA Soldiers and Sailors*, VI: Murphy, 541; Moore, Price, and Smith, 537, 538; Henly and Marshall, 532, 533; Johnson and Johnston, 521. Table of Organization for IX Army Corps, 1 June 1864, Robert U. Johnson and Clarence C. Buel, eds., *Battles and Leaders of the Civil War*, 4 vols. (reprint; New York: T. Yoseloff, 1956), IV, 186; *O.R.*, ser. 1, vol. XXXVI, pt. III, 430.

141 "With an army of approximately thirty-six thousand men": Andrew A. Humphreys, *The Virginia Campaign of '64 and '65: The Army of the Potomac and the Army of the James* (New York: Scribner, 1883), 137. Humphreys enumerated 35,916 infantry and artillery and 4,701 cavalry, for a total of 40,617 officers and enlisted of all arms.

141 "Three days after the lieutenant-general gives the order": B. F. Butler, *Autobiography and Personal Reminiscences of Major-General Benjamin F. Butler: Butler's Book* (Boston:

A. M. Thayer, 1892), appendixes 25–26 (hereafter *Butler's Book*). Butler's telegram to Stanton also appears in *O.R.*, ser. 1, vol. XXXVI, pt. II.

141 "Such as may have been provided in your programme with him": Stanton to Butler, 8 May 1864, *Butler's Book*, appendix 26.

142 "A green outfit, 1,200 strong": William Glenn Robertson, *Back Door to Richmond: The Bermuda Hundred Campaign, April–June 1864* (Baton Rouge: Louisiana State University, 1987), 121. Grant to Halleck, *O.R.*, ser. 1, vol. XXXVI, pt. II, 561, 586.

142 "Order them to be detached for special service": *O.R.*, ser. 1, vol. XXXVI, pt. II, 688.

142 "Received 24,700 men during the same period": *O.R.*, ser. 1, vol. XXXVI, pt. II, 696–97.

143 "Point Lookout, Maryland, where he served for two months": Ezra J. Warner, *Generals in Blue* (Baton Rouge: Louisiana State University Press, 1964), 229–30.

143 "Today we should be better prepared for an emergency": Colonel Henry S. Russell to Governor John A. Andrew, 17 May 1864, MSA, 5th Mass. Cav. File, 146.

144 "Practiced the ancient art of field fortification": On Grant's strategy for the spring 1864 campaign, see Herman Hattaway and Archer Jones, *How the North Won* (Chicago: University of Chicago, 1983); Archer Jones, *Civil War Command and Strategy* (New York: Free Press, 1992), 187, 192–95.

144 "Such men as Banks, Butler [and] McClernand": Halleck to Sherman, 29 April 1864, *O.R.*, ser. 1, vol. XXXIV, pt. III, 33.

145 "Displayed in Richmond shop windows": *Butler's Book*, 269–70; E. B. Long and Barbara Long, *The Civil War Day by Day* (Garden City, NY: Doubleday, 1971), 84.

145 "Woman of the town plying her avocation": *O.R.*, ser. 1, XV, 424. Also quoted in Richard S. West Jr., *Lincoln's Scapegoat General: A Life of Ben Butler, 1818–1893* (Boston: Houghton Mifflin, 1965), 139–40.

146 "Those of his family and friends seems equally evident": Warner, *Generals in Blue*, 230.

146 "By means of transports the two armies would become a unit": *O.R.*, ser. 1, vol. XXXIII, 794–95.

147 "In General Grant's and General Halleck's dispatches": *Butler's Book*, 638.

148 "Against Richmond as Grant's plan specified": Robertson, *Back Door to Richmond*, 250.

148 "That city as either a primary or a secondary goal": Ulysses S. Grant, *Personal Memoirs*, 2 vols. (New York: Charles L. Webster, 1886), II, 141; Horace Porter, *Campaigning with Grant* (New York: Century Company, 1906), 36.

148 "Police commissioner more than a combat commander": Robertson, *Back Door to Richmond*, 20.

148 "Was known in the army as 'Baldy'": For William Farrar "Baldy" Smith, see Warner, *Generals in Blue*, 462–63.

149 "Department of Virginia and North Carolina, some sixteen thousand men": William Farrar Smith, *From Chattanooga to Petersburg under Generals Grant and Butler* (Boston: Houghton Mifflin, 1893), 16.

149 "Came about as a result of successful engineering work": Warner, *Generals in Blue*, 176–77.

150 "Commanding large units in a campaign of maneuver": Robertson, *Back Door to Richmond*, 250–51.

150 "A different way from what he was told": Opinions on Major General William F. Smith: Adam Badeau, *Military History of Ulysses S. Grant, from April, 1861, to April, 1865*, 3 vols. (New York: D. Appleton, 1885), 2, 43–44, 259; Porter, *Campaigning with Grant*, 246; *Butler's Book*, 687. The Wilson quote appears in Robertson, *Back Door to Richmond*, 27.

150 "Most highly politicized fighting force in American history": Edward G. Longacre, "Black Troops in the Army of the James, 1863–65," *Military Affairs* 45 (February 1981): 1–2.

151 "Dependents of troops enlisted in the Army of the James": Ibid., 3.

151 "Stormed ashore to find empty emplacements": *O.R.*, ser. 1, vol. XXXVI, pt. II, 21, 165.

152 "So there was no danger of a surrender": *Butler's Book*, 670.

152 "Did not see it until our attention was called to it": For Captain Livermore's description of the capture of City Point, Virginia, see Livermore, *Days and Events*, 334–36.

154 "Which proved a formidable obstacle to his advance": This quote from Livermore's *Days and Events*, 337, is reproduced as punctuated by the author.

154 "I thought it was my duty not to go": *Butler's Book*, 641–42. See also Bruce Catton, *Never Call Retreat* (Garden City, NY: Doubleday, 1965), 346–47, and Allan Nevins, *The War for the Union: The Organized War to Victory, 1864–65* (New York: Scribner, 1971), 47.

154 "Two guns (a section) of Battery L, 4th U.S. Artillery": *O.R.*, ser. 1, vol. XXXVI, pt. II, 146, 153–54.

155 "Into line of battle and preparing to advance": Ibid., 251, 255–56.

156 "Giving my reasons for making the request": *O.R.*, ser. 1, vol. XXXVI, pt. II, 153–55, 475, 518; *Butler's Book*, 642–43.

156 "Several telegraph lines broken": Robertson, *Back Door to Richmond*, 89.

157 "Come back to your starting point every night?": S. Millet Thompson, *Thirteenth Regiment of New Hampshire Volunteer Infantry in the War of the Rebellion, 1861–1865* (Boston: Houghton Mifflin, 1888), 259–60. See also *Butler's Book*, 645.

159 "Disgusted with the result of our first advance": Livermore, *Days and Events*, 340–42.

159 "The time of writing was 7:00 p.m.": *Butler's Book*, 645, appendixes 28–29; *O.R.*, ser. 1, vol. XXXVI, pt. II, 35, 36, 590, 593, 624; Johnson and Buel, *Battles and Leaders*, IV, 208; Smith, *From Chattanooga to Petersburg*, 117–18.

160 "A bridge for West Point men to retreat over": Johnson and Buel, *Battles and Leaders*, IV, 208, 206.

161 "Up the James from the right of our position [at Bermuda Hundred]": *Butler's Book*, appendixes, 28–29.

161 "Another dispatch from him is being translated": *Butler's Book*, 645–46; *O.R.*, ser.1, vol. XXXVI, pt. II, 587.

161 "Making ready to move by daylight on the 12th": *Butler's Book*, 649–50.

162 "The Army of the James passed to the defensive": Robertson, *Back Door to Richmond*, 170.

162 "Without any attack or interference by the enemy": *Butler's Book*, 664.

162 "Carefully corked by a Confederate earth-work": Johnson and Buel, *Battles and Leaders*, IV, 211.

163 "Lightly held by Confederate forces": Robertson, *Back Door to Richmond*, 247.

163 "All this news was very discouraging": Grant, *Personal Memoirs*, II, 238.

163 "And what in his judgment it is advisable to do": Lieutenant General U. S. Grant to Major General Henry Halleck, 21 May 1864, *O.R.*, ser. 1, vol. XXXVI, pt. III, 43.

164 "Send Smith in command": The Butler quote is from Jesse Ames Marshall, ed., *Private and Official Correspondence of General Benjamin F. Butler during the Period of the Civil War*, 5 vols. (Norwood, MA: Plimpton Press, 1917), IV, 263. Grant to Halleck, 23 May 1864, *O.R.*, ser. 1, vol. XXXVI, pt. III, 77.

164 "The numbers which might be drawn from here": *O.R.*, ser. 1, vol. XXXVI, pt. III, 140–41.

165 "Has shown such rare and great ability": *O.R.*, ser. 1, vol. XXXVI, pt. III, 177–78.

165 "When Butler and the Army of the James were 'bottled up'": It was Brigadier General Barnard, by the way, who in his verbal report to Grant compared Butler's position to being in a bottle. Grant first used the image in his official report to Secretary Stanton immediately after the war, without attribution. Grant, *Personal Memoirs*, II, 568; Bruce Catton, *Never Call Retreat*, 351; Nevins, *War for the Union*, 34; James M. McPherson, *Ordeal by Fire: The Civil War and Reconstruction* (New York: Knopf, 1982), 413; Hattaway and Jones, *How the North Won*, 563.

166 "Much experience and the ability to take advantage of it": Smith, *Battles and Leaders*, IV, 208; Robertson, *Back Door to Richmond*, 230.

166 "To chat or make merry with us": For Captain Thomas Livermore's description of life on General Hincks's staff at City Point, see Livermore, *Days and Events*, 342–43.

167 "Wounds received from a sentinel under his charge": For the mortal wounding of Corporal Gambol and the guard routine, see *MA Soldiers and Sailors*, VI, 516; Bowditch, "War Letters," 475.

168 "Which he sent to his friend the first sergeant": Charles R. Douglass to "Dear Father," 31 May 1864, Douglass Papers.

169 "The attack Charles Douglass referred to in his letter": For the affair at Wilson's Wharf, see *O.R.*, ser. 1, vol. XXXVI, pt. II, 24, 31, 193, 269–72; pt. III, 180–82; *Butler's Book* 669–70; Livermore, *Days and Events*, 346.

169 "More like a New York 'Blood-tub' or a 'Plug-ugly' than anything else": Bowditch, "War Letters," 476.

171 "Advanced four or five miles on his way without a shot": Bowditch, "War Letters," 476–77. The quotes about General Hincks and Dr. Eppes and Lieutenant Curtis Whittemore's foraging are both from the same 25 May 1864 letter.

171 "Positive orders that they should at once go to Grant": *Butler's Book*, 671; Smith, *From Chattanooga to Petersburg*, 121.

173 "When they have freedom and Fort Pillow to nerve them": Bowditch, "War Letters," 478.

174 "Duty as Assistant Provost Marshall for the division": NA, RG 94, 5th Mass. Cav., Regimental Order Books.

174 "Never seen service, except in the 5th Cav": MSA, 5th Mass. Cav. File, box 10, vol. 80, 148.

175 "Lee isn't a man to give up easily": Bowditch, "War Letters," 478–79; Grant, *Personal Memoirs*, II, 279–80.

175 "Crossing to the south side of the James River": *O.R.*, ser. 1, vol. XXXVI, pt. III, 662.

177 "It would be by an army corps": Livermore, *Days and Events*, 345–55; *Butler's Book*, 683–84.

177 "The operation was a fiasco from the beginning": Robertson, *Back Door to Richmond*, 240.

177 "Taken hold of the new arm with praiseworthy energy": MSA, 5th Mass. Cav. File, 118.

177 "They will be splendidly mounted by and by": MSA, 5th Mass. Cav. File, 118.

178 "Arriving there on the night of the 14th of June": *Butler's Book*, 685.

179 "Seven miles to get to the trenches outside Petersburg": The plan of attack for 15 June 1864 is outlined in Smith, *From Chattanooga to Petersburg*, 21; Humphreys, *The Virginia Campaign*, 206.

179 "Protect what they considered the key to the Confederacy": Smith, *From Chattanooga to Petersburg*, 23–25.

180 "The infantry force defending Petersburg was very small": Humphreys, *The Virginia Campaign*, 208.

182 "Three hundred men out of thirty-five hundred became casualties": For Captain Thomas Livermore's account of the Battle of Baylor's Farm, see Livermore, *Days and Events*, 355–58.

183 "With another regiment breaking through them": For Captain Charles P. Bowditch's description of the Battle of Baylor's Farm, see Bowditch, "War Letters," 479–81.

184 "Carter and Johnson were in Company I": Troopers of the 5th Massachusetts Volunteer Cavalry killed in action are described in *MA Soldiers and Sailors*, VI, 510, 520, 527, 529.

Notes to Chapter 6

185 "Who dodged in time, and passing through his company": Bowditch, "War Letters," 481.

187 "Heard some very heavy firing in that direction": Bowditch, "War Letters," 481–82.

187 "One of the long-standing controversies of the war": See, in particular, *Papers of the Military Historical Society of Massachusetts*, vol. V, *Petersburg, Chancellorsville, Gettysburg*, published in 1906, containing articles titled "The Failure to Take Petersburg, June 15, 1864," by Colonel Thomas L. Livermore; "The Movement against Petersburg, June, 1864," by Major General William F. Smith; "Letter of General Beauregard to General C. M. Wilcox," which gives Confederate numbers in the Petersburg defenses on 15 June; "Crossing the James and First Assault upon Petersburg," by Frank E. Peabody, Esq.; and "Some Observations concerning the Opposing Forces at Petersburg on June 15, 1864," also by Peabody. In vol. XIV (1918) of *The Papers of the Military Historical Society of Massachusetts*, John C. Ropes, Esq. continued the argument with "The Failure to Take Petersburg on June 16–18, 1864." Colonel George Bruce in his article "Petersburg, June 15—Fort Harrison, September 29: A Comparison" in the same volume also took opportunity to condemn General William F. Smith.

187 "Petersburg, which lay not over a mile ahead of us": Livermore, *Days and Events*, 361–62.

187 "Hope that Hancock might join his left in the charge": Understandably, the time of the arrival of the 2nd Corps became a part of this controversy. See Livermore,

Days and Events, 360–62; *Papers of the Military Historical Society of Massachusetts*, vol. V, *Petersburg, Chancellorsville, Gettysburg* (Boston, 1906), 58–59; and *Butler's Book*, 689–703.

188   "Capture of Petersburg and possession of the north bank of the Appomattox": Humphreys, *The Virginia Campaign*, 210.

188   "In the captured works, which was done before midnight": Ulysses S. Grant, "Report of Lieutenant-General U.S. Grant, of United States Armies 1864–1865," in *Personal Memoirs*, II, 575.

188   "By the time I arrived the next morning the enemy was in force": Ibid., 575.

188   "And taking part in various expeditions": Bowen, *Massachusetts in the War*, 782.

189   "Though picket work and night alarms kept us busy": Livermore, *Days and Events*, 363–65.

190   "But it has to be done and can't be helped": Bowditch, "War Letters," 482–83.

190   "In XVIII Army Corps hospital at Fort Monroe, Virginia": *MA Soldiers and Sailors*, VI, 536.

190   "Around the enemy's works at Jordan's house about 1:30p.m.": *O.R.*, ser. 1, vol. XL, pt. I, 705.

191   "They have displayed all the qualities of good soldiers": For Major General Smith's circular to XVIII Army Corps, 17 June 1864, see *O.R.*, ser. 1, vol. XL, pt. I, 706.

193   "So active part in the operations before Petersburg as I desired to": General Hincks's report to Major General Butler, *O.R.*, ser. 1, vol. XL, pt. I, 720–21.

193–200   "Hoping it may not inconvenience you to give this an insertion, I remain, very respectfully, yours": *Weekly Anglo-African*, vol. III, no. 47, whole no. 151, editions of 25 June 1864, 2 July 1864, 23 July 1864.

201   "Volunteers from the heavy artillery in this corps": Major General Smith to General Rawlins, 26 June 1864, *O.R.*, ser. 1, vol. XL, pt. II, 202–3.

202   "And without drill and proper discipline": Brigadier General Hincks to Major General Smith, Major Russell, A.A.G., XVIII Army Corps, *O.R.*, ser. 1, vol. XL, pt. II, 459–60.

203   "Such communications without an interchange of views": *O.R.*, ser. 1, vol. XL, pt. II, 458–59.

205   "Arm they are now required to serve with": Brigadier General Hincks to Major General Butler, 27 June 1864, *O.R.*, ser. 1, vol. XL, pt. II, 489–91.

206   "That Grant 'judged it best for the interest of the service'": General Smith to General Rawlins, 28 June 1864, *O.R.*, ser. 1, vol. XL, pt. II, 488–89.

207   "Our men had been discharging their duties very well": Bowditch, "War Letters," 484–85.

208   "And send the former regiment to General Butler": *O.R.*, ser. 1, vol. XL, pt. II, 582.

209   "The water gets polluted with the surface water I suppose": Bowditch, "War Letters," 485–87.

212   "Whose hellish propensities shock nature itself": *Weekly Anglo-African*, vol. III, no. 47, whole no. 151, 16 July 1864.

214   "Mustered out with the regiment on 31 October 1865": *MA Soldiers and Sailors*, VI, 538, 539.

215   "Show ourselves one of the best cavalry regiments in the service": *Weekly Anglo-African*, vol. III, no. 52, whole no. 156, 30 July 1864.

215 "From July 1864 until June 1865 when the camp was closed down": Warner, *Generals in Blue*, 20–21.

217 "Such as could find comfort in that substitute for nourishment": Anthony M. Keiley, "In Vinculis: A Prisoner of War," *Civil War Times, Illustrated* 23, no. 8 (December 1984).

217 "17,000 gallons of fresh water daily": Surgeon Thompson's report of conditions at Point Lookout, 23 June 1864, *O.R.*, ser. 2, VII, 399–400.

218 "Cowardice in the presence of the enemy": Keiley, "In Vinculis," 28.

219 "Scurvy and the tendency thereto now existing": The report of Surgeon C. T. Alexander, USA, is found in *O.R.*, ser. 2, VII, 449–50.

219 "The death rate was heavy": Keiley, "In Vinculis," 28; N. F. Harman, "Prison Experiences at Point Lookout, M.D.," *Confederate Veteran*, no. 9 (September 1907): 400.

219 "Some service, with information of the enemy's movement": Sidney Lanier to Milton H. Northrop, 11 June 1866, quoted in the 1969 (University of North Carolina Press) edition of *Tiger-Lilies*.

222 "A hundred different applicants for the situation": Lanier's description of life in the Point Lookout Prison Camp for Confederates is found in Sidney Lanier, *Tiger-Lilies* (reprint; Chapel Hill: University of North Carolina Press, 1969), 198–206. See also Edwin Mims, *Sidney Lanier* (Boston, 1905), 42–62.

223 "The letters requesting them have been lost": Captain Edward R. Merrill's name does not appear in the roster of the regiment; he was apparently never formally mustered in. Captain Wulff's descriptive list is in *MA Soldiers and Sailors*, VI, 531. Their requests for furlough are found in NA, RG 393, Department of St. Mary's, 22nd Army Corps.

224 "And the receipt of marching orders for the regiment": NA, RG 393, pt. II, District of St. Mary's, Whiskey Orders Received.

225 "As the enemy had received notice of it in some way": Jubal A. Early, "Early's March to Washington in 1864," in *Battles and Leaders of the Civil War*, ed. Robert U. Johnson and Clarence C. Buel (New York, 1887), IV, 492, 495, 498.

226 "Port wine, three bottles of which I have already disposed of": Bowditch, "War Letters," 487.

226 "Officers of the First are delighted to have him come here": Bowditch, "War Letters," 487–88.

227 "Published in 1956 as *My Confession: The Recollections of a Rogue*": For Chamberlain's highly colored account of his experiences up to 1850, see Samuel E. Chamberlain, *My Confession: Recollections of a Rogue* (New York: Harper, 1956). His career up to the Civil War is briefly outlined on pages 299–300 of the above book. Chamberlain's Civil War career is contained in Bowen, *Massachusetts in the War*, 898–99; Higginson, *Massachusetts in the Army and Navy*, II, 172; Benjamin W. Crowninshield, *History of the First Regiment*, 317.

228 "Get along well with Lieutenant Colonel Chamberlain": Theophilus Parsons to Governor John A. Andrew, 10 December 1863, MSA, 5th Mass. Cav. File, box 10, vol. 80, 19.

230 "Cannot be spared from his duties at the present time": The exchange between Governor Andrew, Theophilus Parsons, and the War Department concerning Major Samuel E. Chamberlain of the 1st Massachusetts Cavalry is found in MSA, 5th Mass. Cav. File, 27 1/2, 58, 69, 75, 78, 104.

231 "As soon as in the First and he may be ready in time": Colonel Henry S. Russell's letter to Governor Andrew concerning Major Henry L. Higginson is in the same file, page 113.

231 "If I can have you in the end": Bliss Perry, *Life and Letters of Henry Lee Higginson* (Boston: Atlantic Monthly Press, 1921), 219.

231 "For then there would be no hesitation": MSA, 5th Mass. Cav. File, 140; Perry, *Letters of Higginson*, 220.

232 "There is no one whom I should prefer to him": MSA, 5th Mass. Cav. File, 150.

233 "And six members of the regimental band": The following signatures appear on the petition to Governor Andrew of 30 July 1864: Sergeant Major Alfred Froward; Ordnance Sergeant John Malone; Quartermaster Sergeant John Grayson; Commissary Sergeant William Jacobs; Hospital Steward George Whitzel; Sergeant Amos Webber, Company D; Sergeant Gustavus Booth, Company D; Sergeant Bazzel C. Barker, Company M; Sergeant Prince Romerson, Company M; First Sergeant Isaac A. Watson, Company E; Commissary Sergeant Warwick Reed, Company E; Quartermaster Sergeant Joseph T. Cook, Company I; Sergeant Thomas J. Laurel, Company G; Sergeant William Michaels, Company G; Sergeant Robert H. Morris, Company G; Sergeant Antonio F. Olivadoes, Company G; Sergeant George L. Malson, Company G; Sergeant William Holmes, Company G; First Sergeant George W. M. Ward, Company G; Corporal James Kelley, Company G; Sergeant William L. Hanley, Company G; Sergeant John H. Townson, Company M; Sergeant Benjamin F. Coke, Company M; Regimental Clerk A. D. W. DeLeon; Sergeant William Harris, Company I.

"God save the Commonwealth of Massachusetts is the heartfelt wish of the above named soldiers."

Below that are the following signatures: Sergeant Henry H. Wood, Company M; Sergeant Andrew Wilson, Company M; First Sergeant William Smith, Company K; Sergeant Lewis H. Thompson, Company K; Sergeant James Camrel, Company K; Sergeant John A. Mitchell, Company K; Sergeant Charles Lewis, Company K; Sergeant William R. Rogers, Company K; First Sergeant Harrison Taylor, Company L; Sergeant Levi J. Lewis, Company L; Commissary Sergeant Francis Boyd, Company L; Sergeant William Randolph, Company L; First Sergeant Benjamin F. Parker, Company H; Sergeant George D. Rex, Company H; Quartermaster Sergeant James Martin, Company H; Sergeant B. F. Jones, Company H; Sergeant George W. Brown, Company H; Sergeant John Boggs, Company H; and members of the regimental band, all privates: Elijah Reeves, John Chadwick, David C. Fisher. It should be noted that the regimental band was not a formally recognized official body; the men messed, marched, fought, and were mustered out of their respective companies.

234 "This has induced me to resign": Bowditch, "War Letters," 489–90.

235 "Respectfully returned to Brigade General Barnes. Disapproved": NA, RG 94. See also *MA Soldiers and Sailors*, Descriptive List of First Lieutenant Andrew F. Chapman, Company A.

235 "Back with the regiment by the end of September": NA, RG 393, pt. II, vol. 252, District of St. Mary's, Endorsements to Letters Sent.

237 "The course proposed by Lieutenant Colonel Adams": Charles F. Adams Jr. to John A. Andrew and endorsement, 5 August 1864, MHS, "Adams All Generations" File.

238 "Killing him instantly for no provocation whatever": Bowditch, "War Letters," 491; B. Y. Malone, *Whipt 'Em Everytime: The Diary of Bartlett Yancey Malone*, ed. William W. Pierson Jr. (Jackson, TN: McCowat-Mercer, 1960), 101; Charles W. Hutt, *The Diary of Charles Warren Hutt*, quoted in Edwin Beitzell, *Point Lookout Prison Camp for Confederates* (Abell, MD: St. Mary's County Historical Society, 1972), 79.

238 "Wounded him very badly it is thought that he will die": Malone, *Diary*, 104.

238 "Fully instructed in all their duties, and in this respect particularly": For General Barnes's order on shooting of prisoners of war, see *O.R.*, ser. 2, VII, 698.

239 "And dat quick, or I'll blow half dat nail-kag off!": William Wells Brown, *The Negro in the American Rebellion: His Heroism and His Fidelity* (Boston, 1880; New York: Books for Libraries, 1969), 274–75.

240 "For the murder of two men who were asleep when shot": N. F. Harman, "Prison Experiences at Point Lookout, MD," *Confederate Veteran*, no. 9 (September 1907): 400.

241 "Such petty malice and cowardly vengeance could originate only in ignoble minds": Robert E. Park, "Diary of Captain Robert E. Park, Twelfth Alabama Regiment," *Southern Historical Society Papers* 2 (July–December 1876): 232–33.

241 "Grovel in the pine cuttings of the great man's tent": C. F. Adams Jr. to Theodore Lyman, August 1864, Theodore Lyman Papers, MHS.

242 "Officers who are unable to do any duty in this camp": Bowditch, "War Letters," 492–93.

243 "For old Halleck's capacity in this respect I can vouch": C. F. Adams Jr. to his mother, 27 August 1864, Worthington C. Ford, ed., *A Cycle of Adams Letters, 1861–1865*, 2 vols. (Boston: Houghton Mifflin, 1920), II, 184, 186–87.

243 "Quartermaster's stores, necessary to remount the Fifth Massachusetts Cavalry": NA, RG 393, vol. 251, District of St. Mary's, Order Book.

NOTES TO CHAPTER 7

246 "He was honorably discharged on 15 September": NA, RG 94, 5th Mass. Cav. File, Charles R. Douglass Descriptive List.

247 "In their eternal contact with a race like ours": Ford, *Cycle of Adams Letters*, II, 194–95.

248 "Brooks was exempt from all other duties": For Regimental Special Orders 160 and 161, see NA, RG 94, 5th Mass. Cav. File, Order Books.

249 "Perhaps better than mine, but still another and unfortunate change": Ford, *Cycle of Adams Letters*, II, 198–99.

249 "Robert S. Oliver, who was only seventeen": For the accession of officers to the 5th Massachusetts, see *MA Soldiers and Sailors*, VI: Cushman, 493; George, 508; Hatch, 524; Oliver, 522.

250 "Are required to leave this district without delay": NA, RG 393, District of St. Mary's, Order Books.

250 "Which can here be procured is strongly recommended to aid officers": NA, RG 94, 5th Mass. Cav. File, Order Books.

252 "But then a little light reading would be acceptable": EJB to Mother, 15 October 1864, MHS, Civil War Correspondence, Diaries and Journals, Edward J. Bartlett Letters (hereafter Bartlett Letters).

254 "If some other of the officers would follow his example": EJB to Martha, 23 October 1864, MHS, Bartlett Letters.

254 "He married her in 1867": *Charles Francis Adams, 1835–1915: An Autobiography* (Boston: Houghton Mifflin, 1966), 156, 163.

257 "More than fulfill every expectation which I entertained": CFA II to Charles Francis Adams, 2 November 1864, Ford, *Cycle of Adams Letters*, II, 212–19.

259 "Lincoln and Johnson for liberty and the union": "Are Colored Soldiers to Vote?" *Weekly Anglo-African* IV, no. 10, 166, 8 October 1864.

259 "Disagreeableness of being here on that day": EJB to Dear Martha, 13 November 1864, MHS, Bartlett Letters.

261 "All of which he was sadly deficient in": EJB to Edward Emerson, 26 November 1864, MHS, Bartlett Letters.

262 "I wish I could always do it": EJB to Martha, 30 November 1864, MHS, Bartlett Letters.

263 "To have it conveyed safely to Cambridge, Mass": A. W.'s (possibly Amos Webber) letter to the *Weekly Anglo-African* is in vol. IV, no. 18, whole no. 174, 3 December 1864.

264 "Their mother having recently died": EJB to Martha, 4 and 23 December 1864, MHS, Bartlett Letters; NA RG 393, pt. II, vol. 252, District of St. Mary's, Endorsements to Letters Sent.

265 "That he is not indebted to the Government": *MA Soldiers and Sailors*, VI, 519; NA, RG 393, District of St. Mary's, Order Books; NA, RG 94, 5th Mass. Cav. Order Books.

265 "Old fracture of left arm, result of a gunshot wound": For troopers discharged for disability in October, November, and December of 1864, see NA, RG 393, II, District of St. Mary's, Endorsements to Letters Sent.

266 "Cakes and ale in quantity also in the future": Ford, *Cycle of Adams Letters*, II, 239–40.

267 "Take steps to get myself put on some detached duty": Ford, *Cycle of Adams Letters*, II, 246–47.

267 "Catechizing us as if we were a parcel of school boys": 5 January 1865, 22 January 1865, 25 January 1865, MHS, Bartlett Letters.

268 "A new and more influential life nearer Headquarters": Ford, *Cycle of Adams Letters*, II, 251–52.

268 "Must be determined by the Major General Commanding": NA, RG 393, District of St. Mary's, Endorsements to Letters Sent.

269 "It's good practice and great fun": EJB to Martha, 5 February 1865, MHS, Bartlett Letters.

269 "The position I might have held in the Second Corps staff": Ford, *Cycle of Adams Letters*, II, 256.

270 "One of the pleasantest episodes of man's life": CFA II to JA Andrew, 9 March 1865, MHS, Adams All Generations File.

270 "John G. S. White was promoted to first lieutenant for Newell": Officer promotions are in MSA, 5th Mass. Cav. File, box 10, vol. 80, 130. CFA II to JAA, 3 March 1865, MHS, Adams All Generations File.

270 "His excellency wishes to have the reason specifically stated": MSA, 5th Mass. Cav. File, box 10, vol. 80, 131.

271 "I cannot recommend him for promotion": Colonel Adams's endorsement to 6 March 1865 letter of Major William Rogers, Mass. AAG, MSA, 5th Mass. Cav. File, box 10, vol. 80, 133.

271 "Adjutant Chamberlain being judge advocate": EJB to Martha, 19 March 1865, MHS, Bartlett Letters.

274 "Than by his confinement at hard labor": NA, RG 393, pt. II, vol. 252, District of St. Mary's, General and Special Orders.

274–277 "Amounted to very little and nobody thought of it two days after": EJB to Martha, 19 March 1865, MHS, Bartlett Letters. The incident is described in NA, RG 393, pt. II, vol. 252, District of St. Mary's, General and Special Orders. See also *MA Soldiers and Sailors*, VI, 525, entry for Private Albert Jones.

278 "Camp and garrison equipage, and six wagons": *O.R.*, ser. 1, vol. XLVI, pt. III, 58, 70, 71.

278 "Inactive life and this hard guard duty and muskets": EJB to Ripley, 23 March 1865, MHS Bartlett Letters.

279 "And gave to the land of their [birth] Peace, Union and Glory": NA, RG 393, pt. II, vol. 9, Records of 25th Army Corps.

281 "Two-thousand men in all, of whom about 1,000 were mounted": EJB to Martha, 31 March 1865, MHS, Bartlett Letters; Ford, *Cycle of Adams Letters*, II, 259–61.

282 "But nine o'clock found me in the suburbs of Richmond": Ford, *Cycle of Adams Letters*, II, 259–61.

283 "The Regiment did credit to itself and the Commonwealth": Ford, *Cycle of Adams Letters*, II, 259–61. The letter is also in MSA, 5th Mass. Cav. File, box 10, vol. 80, 154.

284 "By the colored people, who were frantic with joy": EJB to Martha, 3 April 1865, MHS, Bartlett Letters.

285 "Our appearance in the old rebel capital": *Weekly Anglo-African* IV, no. 38, whole no. 194, 22 April 1865. (Note: This was the edition of the *Anglo-African* published with the columns bordered in black after the assassination of President Lincoln. Headline reads, "Extract from a Letter Received by Rev. Amos G. Beman from His Son Richmond, Va., April 5th, 1865 /s/ Chas. T. Beman, 5th Mass. Cavalry.")

286 "Beheld a Negro cavalryman yelling: 'Richmond at last!'": Burke Davis, *To Appomattox: Nine April Days, 1865* (New York: Rinehart, 1959), Fannie Walker quoted at 132, J. B. Jones at 136–37, Sallie Brock Putnam at 137.

286 "From the field when the world's artillery joins in battle": Colonel George A. Bruce, "The Capture and Occupation of Richmond," in *Papers of the Military Historical Society of Massachusetts*, vol. 14, *Civil War and Miscellaneous Papers* (Boston, 1918), 131.

287 "The majestic form of the Father of his Country": Ibid., 135.

287 "My record in this war was rounded and completely filled out": Ford, *Cycle of Adams Letters*, II, 262–64.

287 "To arrest deserters and rebel soldiers": EJB to Martha, 4 April 1865, MHS Bartlett Letters.

288 "Furrowed beyond the power of words to describe": Ford, *Cycle of Adams Letters*, II, 262–64.

288 "Would raise him [Lincoln] a monument of dead rebels": EJB to Martha, 16 April 1865, MHS Bartlett Letters.

289 "A most inveterate set of stragglers and pilferers": Ford, *Cycle of Adams Letters*, II, 267–69.

290 "I don't think much of serving in peace times": EJB to Martha, 1 May 1865, MHS, Bartlett Letters.

290 "All on duty except fatigue men will wear their dress coats": NA, RG 393, pt. II, vol. 9, Headquarters 25th Army Corps, General Order No. 34.

291 "Of the fifteenth instant which was not favorably considered": NA, RG 94, 5th Mass. Cav. File, Letterbooks.

292 "And go about in drawers, and often even without drawers": EJB to Martha, 3 June 1865, MHS Bartlett Letters.

292 "Charles Adams was a civilian once more": See Adams, *Autobiography*, 166–67; Ford, *Cycle of Adams Letters*, II, 270; and regimental records for Adams's resignation letter and the War Department Order.

292 "On account of domestic and pecuniary troubles": NA, RG 94, 5th Mass. Cav. File, Letterbooks.

293 "And so exhaustive upon the public treasury": NA, RG 393, pt. II, vol. 72, Letters Sent, District of Eastern Virginia.

294 "For every man left camp as cheerfully as ever before": NA, RG 393, pt. II, vol. 9, Headquarters 25th Army Corps, Letters Received.

295 "Of all the God forsaken holes this is the worst one I ever saw": EJB to Martha, 21 June and 2 July 1865, MHS, Bartlett Letters.

296 "It established world military standards": For troop deployment along the Texas-Mexico border in 1865, see William L. Richter, *The Army in Texas during Reconstruction: 1865–1870* (College Station: University of Texas Press, 1987), 12–14, 17, 23–27, and Leslie Bethell, ed., *The Cambridge History of Latin America*, 5 vols. (Cambridge: Cambridge University Press, 1985), III, 464–70.

297 "Language which the Emperor was finally induced to accept": Bethell, *Cambridge History of Latin America*, III, 469; James Martin Callahan, *American Foreign Policy in Mexican Relations* (New York: Macmillan, 1932), 314.

297 "Rode six hundred miles from Louisiana to Austin and San Antonio": Richter, *Army in Texas*, 14, 16–18.

297 "Too civilized luxury to be known in this country": NA, RG 393, Headquarters 25th Army Corps, Letters Received.

298 "Fallen out by the road to this place unable to travel": NA, RG 393, Headquarters 25th Army Corps, Letters Received.

298 "Rapidly being brought to proper standard of discipline": NA, RG 393, Headquarters 25th Army Corps, Letters Received.

299 "The country being full of deer and other game": NA, RG 393, pt. II, vol. 9, Orderbooks of 25th Army Corps.

301 "I want to see the country, and I like army life": EJB to Martha, 16 and 23 July 1865, MHS, Bartlett Letters.

301 "While bathing at the mouth of the Rio Grande River": NA, RG 94, 5th Mass. Cav. File, Company Records.

302 "So many old soldiers who want and should have the position": EJB to Martha, 20 and 27 August 1865, MHS, Bartlett Letters; *MA Soldiers and Sailors*, VI: Apthorp, 498; Davidson, 503.

303 "Brazos, Texas of wounds not received in action": *MA Soldiers and Sailors*, VI, 535.

303 "War Department. AGO Washington, D.C. May 15, 1865": NA, RG 393, pt. II, vol. 9, General Orders, 25th Army Corps.

303 "Wish very much that the whole family may be got together": EJB to Ripley, 6 October 1865, MHS Bartlett Letters.

304 "Preserve untarnished the brilliant record they have made in the Army": NA, RG 393, pt. II, vol. 9, General Orders, 25th Army Corps.

304 "On a form headed 'Inventory,' a clerk wrote, 'He had no effects'": NA, RG 94, 5th Mass. Cav. File, Descriptive List and Inventory of Effects of Private Morris Herman.

NOTES TO CHAPTER 8

306 "It being the last corps mustered out": William F. Fox, *Regimental Losses in the American Civil War (1861–1865)* (Albany, NY: Albany Publishing Co., 1889), 287.

307 "Mustered out October 31, 1865": Frederick H. Dyer, *Compendium of the War of the Rebellion Compiled and Arranged from Official Records of the Federal and Confederate Armies, Reports of the Adjutant Generals of the Several States, the Army Registers and Other Reliable Sources*, 2 vols. (Des Moines, IA: Dyer, 1908). The U.S. Colored Troops are in II, 1720–1742; for the 5th Massachusetts Cavalry, see II, 1240.

309 "As drones in the great hive": Christian A. Fleetwood to Dr. James Hall, Carter G. Woodson Manuscript Collection, Library of Congress.

311 "Understood and respected his son's art and was proud of him": For Sergeant Joshua Dunbar, see *MA Soldiers and Sailors*, VI, 516; Paul Laurence Dunbar's writings can be found at several sites, including the University of Dayton and Cornell University. Wright State University maintains the Dunbar Digital Text Collection.

313 "Property of James Epps—the other not known who he is": Brent Holcomb, ed., "Laurens District Coroner's Inquisitions, 1802–1865," *South Carolina Magazine of Ancestral Research* 32, no. 2 (Spring 2004).

315 "So long sustained, so intense, and so productive of result": Allen Johnson, *Dictionary of American Biography*, 22 vols. (New York: Scribner, 1929), Charles Pickering Bowditch, I, 492; Henry Pickering Bowditch, I, 494–96.

316 "At the death with Humphreys and the Second Corps": Adams, *Autobiography*, 165–67, 208–9, 210–11.

316 "In this respect I would not change with any of them": Adams, *Autobiography*, 220.

319 "Sent by Russell's adjutant in the 5th Massachusetts Cavalry": On Henry S. Russell, see Morse, *Sons of the Puritans*, 159–62.

320 "To repay what he had borrowed for his education": For biographical data on Daniel Henry Chamberlain, see Allen Johnson, ed., *Dictionary of American Biography*, 22 vols. (New York, 1929), III, 595, and prefatory note to Daniel H. Chamberlain, "Some Conclusions of a Free-Thinker," North American Review, October 1907.

321 "Had been Chamberlain's roommate at Yale": On the makeup of the South Carolina Constitutional Convention of 1868, see Eric Foner, *Reconstruction: America's Unfinished Revolution, 1863–1877* (New York: Harper, 1988), 316–19.

321 "He was never charged with personal dishonesty": Allen Johnson, ed., *Dictionary of American Biography*, 22 vols. (New York, 1929), III, 595.

321 "Crime against 'the civilization of the Puritan and the Huguenot'": Walter Allen, *Governor Chamberlain's Administration in South Carolina* (New York: Putnam, 1888), 92–201, 237–40.

322 "As they looted and killed": Joel Williamson, *After Slavery: The Negro in South Carolina during Reconstruction* (Chapel Hill: University of North Carolina Press, 1965), 267–69; Thomas Holt, *Black over White: Negro Political Leadership in South Carolina during Reconstruction* (Urbana: University of Illinois Press, 1977), 201.

323 "Protecting the fundamental rights of American citizens": Foner, *Reconstruction*, 582.

323 "Had produced 'shocking and unbearable misgovernment'": Daniel H. Chamberlain, "Reconstruction in South Carolina," *Atlantic Monthly* 87 (April 1901), 476–78.

324 "Known throughout the circles of the Grand Army of the Republic": Bowen, *Massachusetts in the War*, 898–99; Major General William A. Bancroft, M.V.M (Ret.), Brigadier General U.S. Vol., "Brevet Brigadier General S. E. Chamberlain," in *The Chamberlain Association of America* (Boston, 1909), 38; *Hartford Courant*, 22 June 1893; *Boston Daily Advertiser*, 10 November 1908.

325 "Some twenty-two years after their muster out": Broadside, Archives of the Grand Army of the Republic, Room 27, State House, Boston (hereafter Archives of the G.A.R.); *MA Soldiers and Sailors*, VI: Webber, 510; Booth, 506; Fisher, 503; Bates, 523; Davis, 512; Patterson, 505; Phenix, 522.

326 "Not far from the State House in Boston": *G.A.R. Scrapbook, February 1898–May 1901*, Archives of the G.A.R.; records of Amos F. Jackson, Archives of the G.A.R.; *MA Soldiers and Sailors*, VI, 528.

327 "I have been here nearly a year and I don't know how I have lived": Charles R. Douglass to Douglass, Puerto Plata, Santo Domingo, 5 August 1876, Douglass Papers.

328 "Turned us loose to the wrath of our infuriated masters": Excerpt from the speech "Why Reconstruction Failed," given 1 August 1880 in Elmira, New York, *Life and Times of Frederick Douglass* (Boston, 1892).

329 "I doubt if any other emancipated people could have done as well": "Oration by the Hon. Frederick Douglass on the Occasion of the Second Annual Exposition of the Colored People of North Carolina, Delivered on Friday October 1st, 1880," *Journal of Industry* 2, no. 27 (9 October 1880).

Sources

Sources for Illustrations, Maps, and Photographs

AHEC: Military Order of the Loyal Legion (MOLLUS) Massachusetts Civil War Photograph Collection, American Heritage & Education Center, Carlisle, Pennsylvania, formerly U.S. Army Military History Institute

BA: Boston Athenaeum, Harriet Hayden Albums

CoA: Collection of the author

FLIH: Frank Leslie's *Illustrated History of the Civil War*

LoC: Library of Congress

MHS: 5th Massachusetts Cavalry Regiment Carte de Visite Photo Album, Photo. Coll. 228, Massachusetts Historical Society

PHCW: *Photographic History of the Civil War*

SCUA-UMD: John J. Omenhausser Civil War Sketchbook, Special Collections and University Archives, University of Maryland Libraries

SLM: State Library of Massachusetts

Manuscripts

Boston Public Library

Newspapers: *The Liberator, Boston Evening Journal, Worcester Spy, Springfield Republican, National Anti Slavery Reporter*

Periodicals: *Army and Navy Journal, United Services Magazine, Harper's, Atlantic*

Papers of the New England Loyal Publication Society

Countway Medical School Library

Letters and diary of Major Henry Pickering Bowditch

Library of Congress

Frederick Douglass Collection

Charles G. Goodson Collection

Massachusetts Archives

Office of the Governor:

Executive Department Letters

Letters Official

Journal of the Massachusetts House of Representatives, April 30, 1866

Executive Office of Public Safety, Adjutant General:
Annual Reports
Clothing Accounts, 1861–1865
Consolidated Morning Reports
List of Soldiers Receiving Municipal Bounties, 1862–1865
Lists of Recruits Enrolled at Washington, DC, 1863–1865
Muster Rolls of Massachusetts Volunteers

Massachusetts Commandery, Grand Army of the Republic
Papers of the Robert A. Bell Post

Massachusetts Historical Society
Adams Family Collection
Edward J. Bartlett letters
Personal papers of Governor John A. Andrew
Papers of Amos A. Lawrence
Papers of John Murray Forbes
Henry Sturgis Russell letters
Papers of William J. Schouler
Weekly Anglo-African newspaper

National Archives and Records Administration
Record Group 94: Records of the Adjutant General's Office
Address Books, 1860–1894
Adjutant General's Office Miscellaneous File ("Colored Troops")
Compiled Military Service Records
Index to Letters Received, Adjutant General's Office
Letters Received, Division of Colored Troops, 1863–1868
Letters Received Relating to Recruiting, 1863–1868
Letters Regarding Recruiting, Division of Colored Troops
The Negro in the Military Service of the United States, 1607–1889
Records of Surgeons in Charge of Civil War Posts and General Hospitals, compiled
    1861–1865
Regimental Descriptive Books
Regimental Order Books
Regimental Letter Books
Regimental Unbound Papers

Record Group 153: Records of the Office of the Judge Advocate General (Army)
Index to Proceedings of General Courts Martial
Proceedings of General Courts Martial

Record Group 159: Records of the Office of the Inspector General (Army)
Inspection Reports, 1865
Inspection Reports, Arranged by States
Letters Received, Inspector General's Office, 1864

Record Group 393: Records of U.S. Army Continental Commands
Letters Received, Department of Virginia and North Carolina
Reports of Examinations of Officers, Department of Virginia and North Carolina

New England Historical Genealogical Society
Forbes Family
Howland Family
Russell Family
Shaw Family
Sturgis Family

PUBLISHED PRIMARY SOURCES

Adams, Charles Francis, Jr. *Charles Francis Adams, 1835–1915: An Autobiography.* Boston: Houghton Mifflin, 1916.
Agassiz, George R., ed. *Meade's Headquarters, 1863–1865: Letters of Colonel Theodore Lyman from the Wilderness to Appomattox.* Boston: Massachusetts Historical Society, 1922.
Andrew, John A. *Speeches of John A. Andrew at Hingham and Boston: Together with his testimony before the Harper's Ferry Committee of the Senate, in relation to John Brown; Also, the Republican platform and other matters.* Published by order of the Republican State Committee. Boston, MA, 1860.
Backus, Samuel W. "Californians in the Field: A Historical Sketch of the Organization and Services of the California 'Hundred' and 'Battalion'; 2nd Massachusetts Cavalry." *War Paper No. 4, California Commandery of the Military Order of the Loyal Legion of the United States.* 1889.
Basler, Roy, ed. *The Collected Works of Abraham Lincoln.* 9 vols. New Brunswick, NJ: Rutgers University Press, 1953.
Beale, Howard, ed. *Diary of Gideon Welles.* 2 vols. New York: Norton, 1960.
Beauregard, P. G. T. "Defense of Drewry's Bluff." *Battles and Leaders* 4 (March 1887): 195–206.
———. "Four Days of Battle at Petersburg." *Battles and Leaders* 4 (December 1887): 540–45.
———. "Drury's Bluff and Petersburg." *North American Review* 144, no. 364 (March 1887).
Berlin, Ira, Joseph P. Reidy, and Leslie S. Rowlandet, eds. *Freedom: A Documentary History of Emancipation, 1861–1867,* ser. 2, vol. 1, *The Black Military Experience.* New York: Cambridge University Press, 1982.
Bowditch, Charles P. "War Letters of Charles P. Bowditch." *Massachusetts Historical Society Proceedings* 57 (October 1923–June 1924).
Bowen, James L. *History of the Thirty-Seventh Regiment Massachusetts Volunteers in the War of 1861–1865.* Holyoke, MA: C. W. Bryan, 1884.

Bruce, George A. "General Butler's Bermuda Campaign." *Military Historical Society of Massachusetts Papers*, vol. IX. Boston, 1912.
———. "Petersburg, June 15–Fort Harrison, September 29: A Comparison," *Military Historical Society of Massachusetts Papers*, vol. XIV. Boston, 1912.
———. *The Twentieth Regiment of Massachusetts Volunteer Infantry, 1861–1865*. Boston, 1906.
Butler, Benjamin F. *Autobiography and Personal Reminiscences of Major-General Benjamin F. Butler: Butler's Book*. Boston: A. M. Thayer, 1892.
Chamberlain, Daniel H. "Reconstruction in South Carolina." *Atlantic Monthly* 87 (April 1901).
———. "Some Conclusions of a Free Thinker." *North American Review* 186, no. 623 (October 1907).
Chamberlain, Samuel E. *My Confession: Recollections of a Rogue*. Edited by Roger Butterfield. New York: Harper, 1956.
Congressional Globe. Various issues.
Cooke, Philip St. G. *Cavalry Tactics, or Regulations for the Instruction, Formation and Movements of the Cavalry*. Washington, DC: U.S. War Department, 1862.
Crowninshield, Benjamin W. *A History of the First Regiment of Massachusetts Cavalry Volunteers*. Boston: Houghton Mifflin, 1891.
Dennett, Tyler, ed. *Lincoln and the Civil War in the Diaries of John Hay*. New York: Dodd, Mead, 1939.
Emilio, Louis F. *A Brave Black Regiment: History of the Fifty-Fourth Regiment of Massachusetts Volunteer Infantry*. Cambridge, MA: Harvard University Press, 1868.
Ford, Worthington C., ed. *A Cycle of Adams Letters, 1861–1865*. 2 vols. Boston: Houghton Mifflin, 1920.
Fox, Charles B. *Record of Services of the Fifty-Fifth Regiment of Massachusetts Volunteer Infantry*. Cambridge, MA: John Wilson, 1868.
Gordon, George H. *Brook Farm to Cedar Mountain in the War of the Rebellion, 1861–1862*. Boston: J. R. Osgood, 1883.
Grant, Ulysses S. *Personal Memoirs*, 2 vols. New York: Charles L. Webster, 1885.
Hallowell, Norwood P. "The Negro as a Soldier in the War of the Rebellion," *Military Historical Society of Massachusetts Papers*, vol. XIII. Boston, 1913.
Harman, N. F. "Prison Experiences at Point Lookout, MD." *Confederate Veteran*, no. 9 (September 1907).
Higginson, Thomas W. *Army Life in a Black Regiment*. Boston: Riverside Press, 1900.
———. *Letters and Journals*. Boston: Houghton Mifflin, 1921.
———. "Regular and Volunteer Officers." *Atlantic Monthly* 14 (1864).
Holcomb, Brent, ed. "Laurens District Coroner's Inquisitions, 1802–1865" *South Carolina Magazine of Ancestral Research* 32, no. 2 (Spring 2004).
Hughes, Sarah Forbes, ed. *Letters and Recollections of John Murray Forbes*. 2 vols. Boston: Houghton Mifflin, 1900.
———. *Letters of John Murray Forbes*. Supp. ed. 3 vols. Boston: Houghton Mifflin, 1905.
———. *Reminiscences of John Murray Forbes*. 3 vols. Boston: George H. Ellis, 1902.
Hutt, Warren, B. "An Interesting Human Document." *Confederate Veteran*, no. 36 (1928).
Johnson, Robert U., and Clarence C. Buel, eds. *Battles and Leaders of the Civil War*. 4 vols. New York: Century Co., 1887.

Kautz, August V. *Customs of Service of Non-Commissioned Officers and Soldiers*. Philadelphia: J. B. Lippincott, 1865.

Keiley, Anthony M. "In Vinculis: A Prisoner of War." *Civil War Times Illustrated* 23, no. 8 (December 1984).

Kimmel, Ross M., and Michael P. Musick. *I Am Busy Drawing Pictures: The Civil War Art & Letters of Private John Jacob Omenhausser, CSA*. Annapolis, MD: Friends of the Maryland Historical Society, 2014.

Lanier, Sidney. *Tiger-Lilies*. Reprint. Chapel Hill: University of North Carolina Press, 1969.

Livermore, Thomas L. *Days and Events*. Boston: Houghton Mifflin, 1920.

———. "The Failure to Take Petersburg June 15, 1864." *Military Historical Society of Massachusetts Papers*, vol. V. Boston, 1906.

———. "Grant's Campaign against Lee." *Military Historical Society of Massachusetts Papers*, vol. IV. Boston, 1906.

Lyman, Theodore. "Crossing of the James and Advance on Petersburg." *Military Historical Society of Massachusetts Papers*, vol. V. Boston, 1906.

———. "Operations of the Army of the Potomac, June 5–June 15, 1864." *Military Historical Society of Massachusetts Papers*, vol. V. Boston, 1906.

Mahan, Dennis H. *An Elementary Treatise on Advanced-Guard, Out-Post, and Detached Service of Troops*. New York: Wiley, 1862.

Malone, Bartlett Yancey. *Whipt 'Em Everytime: The Diary of Bartlett Yancey Malone*. Edited by William W. Pierson Jr. Jackson, TN: McCowat-Mercer, 1960.

Marshall, Jesse Ames, ed. *Private and Official Correspondence of General Benjamin F. Butler during the Period of the Civil War*. 5 vols. Norwood, MA: Plimpton Press, 1917.

Massachusetts Adjutant General. *Massachusetts Soldiers, Sailors and Marines in the Civil War*. 7 vols. Norwood, MA: Norwood Press, 1933.

———. *Reports: 1863, 1864, 1865*. Boston, 1866.

McCabe, W. Gordon. "Defense of Petersburg." *Southern Historical Society Papers*, vol. II, no. 6 (December 1876).

Park, Robert E. "Diary of Robert E. Park." *Southern Historical Society Papers*, vol. I (1876), II (1876), III (1877).

Perry, Bliss, ed. *Life and Letters of Henry Lee Higginson*. Boston: Atlantic Monthly Press, 1921.

Porter, Horace. *Campaigning with Grant*. New York: Century Co., 1898.

Richardson, James D. *A Compilation of the Messages and Papers of the Presidents, 1789–1897*. 8 vols. New York: Johnson Reprint, 1968.

Smith, William Farrar. *From Chattanooga to Petersburg under Generals Grant and Butler: A Contribution to the History of the War and a Personal Vindication*. Boston: Houghton Mifflin, 1893.

Thompson, S. Millet. *Thirteenth Regiment of New Hampshire Volunteer Infantry in the War of the Rebellion, 1861–1865*. Boston: Houghton Mifflin, 1888.

The War of the Rebellion: A Compilation of the Official Records of the Union and Confederate Armies. 128 parts in 70 vols. Washington, DC: U.S. War Department, 1880–1901.

Yacovone, Donald, ed. *A Voice of Thunder: The Civil War Letters of George E. Stephens*. Urbana: University of Illinois Press, 1997.

SECONDARY SOURCES

Abbott, Richard H. "Massachusetts and the Recruiting of Southern Negroes." *Civil War History* 14 (1975).

Allen, Walter. *Governor Chamberlain's Administration in South Carolina.* New York: Putnam, 1888.

Amann, William F., ed. *Personnel of the Union Army.* 2 vols. Reprint. New York: T. Yoseloff, 1961.

Antrim, Earl. *Civil War Prisons.* New York: Collectors Club, 1930.

Badeau, Adam. *Military History of Ulysses S. Grant, from April, 1861, to April, 1865.* 3 vols. New York: D. Appleton, 1885.

Barton, John. "The Procurement of Horses." *Civil War Times Illustrated* 6 (1967).

Beath, Robert B. *History of the Grand Army of the Republic.* New York: Bryan, Taylor, 1889.

Beitzell, Edwin W. *Point Lookout Prison Camp for Confederates.* Abell, MD: St. Mary's County Historical Society, 1972.

Belz, Herman. "Law, Politics and Race in the Struggle for Equal Pay during the Civil War." *Civil War History* 22 (1984).

———. *Reconstructing the Union: Theory and Policy during the Civil War.* Ithaca, NY: Cornell University Press, 1969.

Berry, Mary F. *Military Necessity and Civil Rights Policy.* Port Washington, NY: Kennikat Press, 1977.

Bethell, Leslie, ed. *The Cambridge History of Latin America.* 5 vols. Cambridge: Cambridge University Press, 1985.

Blassingame, John W. "The Recruitment of Colored Troops in Kentucky, Maryland and Missouri, 1863–1865." *Historian* 24, no. 4 (August 1967).

———. "The Selection of Officers and Non-commissioned Officers of Negro Troops in the Union Army, 1863–1865." *Negro History Bulletin* 30, no. 1 (January 1967).

———. "The Union Army as an Educational Institution for Negroes, 1861–1865." *Journal of Negro Education* 34, no. 2 (Spring 1965).

Blight, David W. *Frederick Douglass' Civil War: Keeping Faith in Jubilee.* Baton Rouge: Louisiana University Press, 1988.

Bowen, James L. *Massachusetts in the War, 1861–1865.* Springfield, MA: C. W. Bryan, 1889.

Brown, Francis H. *Harvard University in the War of 1861–1865.* Boston: Cupples, Upham, 1886.

Brown, William Wells. *The Negro in the American Rebellion: His Heroism and His Fidelity.* Reprint; New York: Books for Libraries, 1969.

Bruce, Robert V. *Lincoln and the Tools of War.* Indianapolis, IN: Bobbs-Merrill, 1956.

Burchard, Peter. *One Gallant Rush: Robert Gould Shaw and His Brave Black Regiment.* New York: St. Martin's, 1965.

Callahan, James Martin. *American Foreign Policy in Mexican Relations.* New York: Macmillan, 1932.

Catton, Bruce. *Mr. Lincoln's Army.* Garden City, NY: Doubleday, 1962.

———. *Never Call Retreat.* Garden City, NY: Doubleday, 1965.

———. *Terrible Swift Sword.* Garden City, NY: Doubleday, 1963.

Cole, Garold L. *Civil War Eyewitnesses: An Annotated Bibliography of Books and Articles, 1955–1986.* Columbia: University of South Carolina Press, 1988.

———. *Civil War Eyewitnesses: An Annotated Bibliography of Books and Articles, 1986–1996*. Columbia: University of South Carolina Press, 2000.

Cornish, Dudley. *The Sable Arm: Black Troops in the Union Army, 1861–1865*. Lawrence: University Press of Kansas, 1956.

Corthell, James R. "The Story of Camp Meigs." *New England Magazine* 32, no. 4 (June 1905).

Cox, Lawanda. *Lincoln and Black Freedom: A Study in Presidential Leadership*. Columbia: University of South Carolina Press, 1981.

Craven, Avery. *Reconstruction: The Ending of the Civil War*. New York: Holt, Rinehart and Wilson, 1969.

Crawford, Mary C. *Famous Families of Massachusetts*. 2 vols. Boston: Little, Brown, 1930.

Current, Richard N. *Those Terrible Carpetbaggers*. New York: Oxford University Press, 1988.

Daniels, John. *In Freedom's Birthplace: A Study of the Boston Negroes*. Boston: Houghton, Mifflin, 1914.

Davis, Burke. *To Appomattox: Nine April Days, 1865*. New York: Rinehart, 1959.

Davis, George B., Joseph W. Kirkly, and Leslie J. Perry. *The Official Military Atlas of the Civil War*. Reprint. Avenel, NJ: Outlook Book Co., 1983.

Dearing, Mary R. *Veterans in Politics: The Story of the G.A.R.* Baton Rouge: Louisiana State University Press, 1952.

Dyer, Frederick A. *A Compendium of the War of the Rebellion*. 3 vols. Des Moines, IA: Dyer, 1908.

Edelstein, Tilden G. *Strange Enthusiasm: A Life of Thomas Wentworth Higginson*. New Haven, CT: Yale University Press, 1968.

Fisk, Wilbur. *Anti-Rebel: The Civil War Letters of Wilbur Fisk*. Croton-on-Hudson, NY: E. Rosenblatt, 1983.

Foner, Eric. *Reconstruction: America's Unfinished Revolution*. New York: Harper, 1988.

Foner, Philip S. *Blacks in the American Revolution*. Westport, CT: Greenwood, 1976.

Foote, Shelby. *The Civil War: A Narrative*. 3 vols. New York: Random House, 1958–1974.

Fox, William F. *Regimental Losses in the Civil War*. Albany, NY: Albany Publishing Co., 1898.

Gerteis, Louis. *From Contraband to Freedman: Federal Policy toward Southern Blacks, 1861–1865*. Westport, CT: Greenwood, 1973.

Glatthaar, Joseph T. *Forged in Battle: The Civil War Alliance of Black Soldiers and White Officers*. New York: Free Press, 1980.

Gluckman, Arcadi. *United States Martial Pistols and Revolvers*. Buffalo, NY: Otto Ulbrich, 1944.

Gould, B. A. *Investigations in the Military and Anthropological Statistics of American Soldiers*. New York: Hurd and Houghton, 1869.

Gray, Alonzo. *Cavalry Tactics as Illustrated by the War of the Rebellion*. Ft. Leavenworth, KS: U.S. Cavalry Association, 1911.

Griffith, Paddy. *Battle Tactics of the Civil War*. New Haven, CT: Yale University Press, 1989.

Hammerlein, Richard F. *Prisons and Prisoners of the Civil War*. Boston: Christopher Publishing House, 1934.

Hatcher, Edward W. *The Last Four Weeks of the War*. Columbus, OH: E. N. Hatcher, 1892.

Hattaway, Herman, and Archer Jones. *How the North Won*. Chicago: University of Chicago Press, 1983.

Hesseltine, William B. *Civil War Prisons*. Kent, OH: Kent State University Press, 1962.

Higginson, Thomas W, ed. *Harvard Memorial Biographies*. 2 vols. Cambridge, MA: Harvard University Press, 1866.

———. *Massachusetts in the Army and Navy*. 2 vols. Boston: Wright and Potter, 1896.

Hollis, John P. *The Early Period of Reconstruction in South Carolina*. Baltimore, MD: Johns Hopkins University Press, 1905.

Holt, Thomas. *Black over White: Negro Political Leadership in South Carolina during Reconstruction*. Urbana: University of Illinois Press, 1977.

Humphreys, Andrew A. *The Virginia Campaign of '64 and '65: The Army of the Potomac and the Army of the James*. New York: Scribner, 1883.

Jackson, Harry F., and Thomas F. O'Donnell, eds. *Back Home in Oneida: Hermon Clarke and His Letters*. Syracuse, NY: Syracuse University Press, 1965.

Johnson, Allen. *Dictionary of American Biography*. 22 vols. (New York: Scribner, 1929).

Jones, Archer. *Civil War Command and Strategy*. New York: Free Press, 1992.

Linderman, Gerald F. *Embattled Courage: The Experience of Combat in the American Civil War*. New York: Free Press, 1987.

Litwack, Leon. *North of Slavery: The Negro in the Free States, 1790–1860*. Chicago: University of Chicago Press, 1961.

Litwack, Leon, and August Meier, eds. *Black Leaders in the Nineteenth Century*. Urbana: University of Illinois Press, 1988.

Livermore, Thomas L. *Numbers and Losses in the Civil War in America*. Boston: Houghton Mifflin, 1900.

Logan, Rayford W., and Michael R. Winston. *Dictionary of American Negro Biography*. New York: Norton, 1982.

Long, E. B., and Barbara Long. *The Civil War Day by Day*. Garden City, NY: Doubleday, 1971.

Longacre, James E. "Black Troops in the Army of the James." *Military Affairs* 45, no. 1 (February 1981).

Lord, Francis A. *They Fought for the Union*. Harrisburg, PA: Stackpole, 1960.

McFeely, William S. *Frederick Douglass*. New York: Simon and Schuster, 1991.

McPherson, James M. *Battle Cry of Freedom: The Civil War Era*. New York: Oxford University Press, 1988.

———. *Drawn with the Sword: Reflections on the American Civil War*. New York: Oxford University Press, 1996.

———. *The Negro's Civil War: How American Negroes Felt and Acted during the War for the Union*. New York: Vintage, 1967.

———. *Ordeal by Fire: The Civil War and Reconstruction*. New York: Knopf, 1982.

———. *The Struggle for Equality: Abolitionists and the Negro in the Civil War and Reconstruction*. Princeton, NJ: Princeton University Press, 1964.

Miller, Edward A. *The Black Civil War Soldiers of Illinois: The Story of the Twenty-Ninth U.S. Colored Infantry*. Columbia: University of South Carolina Press, 1998.

Mims, Edwin. *Sidney Lanier*. Boston: Houghton Mifflin, 1905.

Morse, John T., Jr. *Sons of the Puritans: A Group of Brief Biographies*. Boston: Beacon, 1908.

Nevins, Allan. *The Ordeal of the Union*. 4 vols. New York: Scribner, 1971.

———. *The War for the Union: The Organized War to Victory, 1864–65.* New York: Scribner, 1971.

Paradis, James M. *Strike the Blow for Freedom: The 6th United States Colored Infantry in the Civil War.* Shippensburg, PA: White Mane, 1998.

Patrick, Rembert. *The Fall of Richmond.* Baton Rouge: Louisiana State University Press, 1960.

Pearson, Henry G. *The Life of John A. Andrew.* 2 vols. Boston: Houghton Mifflin, 1904.

Quarles, Benjamin. *Black Abolitionists.* New York: Oxford University Press, 1969.

———. *Frederick Douglass.* New York: Athenaeum, 1970.

———. *Lincoln and the Negro.* New York: Oxford University Press, 1962.

———. *The Negro in the American Revolution.* Chapel Hill: University of North Carolina Press, 1961.

———. *The Negro in the Civil War.* Boston: Little, Brown, 1953.

Reid, Richard M. *Freedom for Themselves: North Carolina's Black Soldiers in the Civil War Era.* Chapel Hill: University of North Carolina Press, 2008.

Remini, Robert Vincent. *The Battle of New Orleans.* New York: Viking, 1999.

Reynolds, John S. *Reconstruction in South Carolina.* Columbia, SC: State Company Publishers, 1905.

Richter, William L. *The Army in Texas during Reconstruction: 1865–1870.* College Station: University of Texas Press, 1987.

Ripley, Edward H. *The Capture and Occupation of Richmond, April 3, 1865.* New York: Putnam, 1907.

Robertson, William G. *Back Door to Richmond: The Bermuda Hundred Campaign, April–June, 1864.* Baton Rouge: Louisiana State University, 1987.

Ropes, John C. *Campaigns of the Civil War.* Vol. 4, *The Army under Pope.* New York: Scribner, 1905.

Schouler, William. *History of Massachusetts in the Civil War.* Boston: E. P. Dutton, 1868.

Sefton, James E. *The United States Army and Reconstruction, 1865–1877.* Baton Rouge: Louisiana State University Press, 1967.

Shannon, Fred A. "The Federal Government and the Negro Soldier, 1861–1865." *Journal of Negro History* 11, no. 4 (October 1926).

———. *Organization and Administration of the Union Army.* 2 vols. Cleveland: Arthur H. Clark, 1928.

Singletary, Otis. *Negro Militia and Reconstruction.* Austin: University of Texas Press, 1957.

Smith, John D. *Black Soldiers in Blue: African American Troops in the Civil War Era.* Chapel Hill: University of North Carolina Press, 2005.

Starr, Stephen Z. *The Union Cavalry in the Civil War.* 3 vols. Baton Rouge: Louisiana State University Press, 1979–1986.

Stearns, Frank P. *Life and Public Services of George Luther Stearns.* Philadelphia: J. P. Lippincott, 1907.

Stevens, C. A. *Berdan's United States Sharpshooters in the Army of the Potomac.* St. Paul, MN: Price-McGill, 1896.

Swart, Stanley L. "The Military Examining Board in the Civil War: A Case Study." *Civil War History* 16 (1976).

Thiele, T. F. "The Evolution of Cavalry in the American Civil War, 1861–1863." PhD diss., University of Michigan, 1951.

Thomas, Benjamin P., and Harold Hyman. *Stanton: The Life and Times of Lincoln's Secretary of War*. New York: Knopf, 1962.

Thompson, Henry T. *Ousting the Carpetbagger*. Chapel Hill: University of North Carolina Press, 1926.

Trudeau, Noah. *The Last Citadel: Petersburg, Virginia, June 1864–1865*. Boston: Little, Brown, 1991.

———. *Like Men of War: Black Troops in the Civil War*. Boston: Little, Brown, 1988.

Ware, Edith E. *Political Opinion in Massachusetts during the Civil War and Reconstruction*. Reprint. New York: AMS Press, 1968.

Warner, Ezra J. *Generals in Blue*. Baton Rouge: Louisiana State University Press, 1964.

Webb, Alexander S. *Campaigns of the Civil War*. Vol. 3, *The Peninsula*. New York: Scribner, 1907.

West, Richard S. Jr. *Lincoln's Scapegoat General: A Life of Ben Butler, 1818–1893*. Boston: Houghton Mifflin, 1965.

Wiley, Bell I. *The Life of Billy Yank: The Common Soldier of the Union*. Indianapolis, IN: Bobbs-Merrill, 1951.

Williams, George W. *History of the Negro Race in America, 1619–1880*. Reprint. New York: Putnam, 1985.

Williamson, Joel. *After Slavery: The Negro in South Carolina during Reconstruction*. Chapel Hill: University of North Carolina Press, 1965.

Wilson, Joseph T. *The Black Phalanx*. Reprint. New York: Arno Press, 1968.

Wilson, Keith. *Campfires of Freedom: The Camp Life of Black Soldiers during the Civil War*. Kent, OH: Kent State University Press, 2002.

Index